W9-BTL-182

SharePoint 2003
User's Guide

SETH BATES AND TONY SMITH

SharePoint 2003 User's Guide

Copyright © 2005 by Seth Bates and Tony Smith

All rights reserved. No part of this work may be reproduced or transmitted in any form or by any means, electronic or mechanical, including photocopying, recording, or by any information storage or retrieval system, without the prior written permission of the copyright owner and the publisher.

ISBN (pbk): 1-59059-514-9

Printed and bound in the United States of America 9 8 7 6 5 4 3 2 1

Trademarked names may appear in this book. Rather than use a trademark symbol with every occurrence of a trademarked name, we use the names only in an editorial fashion and to the benefit of the trademark owner, with no intention of infringement of the trademark.

Lead Editor: Jim Sumser
Technical Reviewers: Martin Reid, Cherry Tun-Smith
Editorial Board: Steve Anglin, Dan Appleman, Ewan Buckingham, Gary Cornell, Tony Davis,
    Jason Gilmore, Jonathan Hassell, Chris Mills, Dominic Shakeshaft, Jim Sumser
Associate Publisher: Grace Wong
Project Manager: Beth Christmas
Copy Edit Manager: Nicole LeClerc
Copy Editor: Ami Knox
Production Manager: Kari Brooks-Copony
Production Editor: Katie Stence
Compositor and Artist: Diana Van Winkle, Van Winkle Design Group
Proofreader: Liz Welch
Indexer: Michael Brinkman
Interior Designer: Diana Van Winkle, Van Winkle Design Group
Cover Designer: Kurt Krames
Manufacturing Manager: Tom Debolski

Distributed to the book trade in the United States by Springer-Verlag New York, Inc., 233 Spring Street, 6th Floor, New York, NY 10013, and outside the United States by Springer-Verlag GmbH & Co. KG, Tiergartenstr. 17, 69112 Heidelberg, Germany.

In the United States: phone 1-800-SPRINGER, fax 201-348-4505, e-mail orders@springer-ny.com, or visit http://www.springer-ny.com. Outside the United States: fax +49 6221 345229, e-mail orders@springer.de, or visit http://www.springer.de.

For information on translations, please contact Apress directly at 2560 Ninth Street, Suite 219, Berkeley, CA 94710. Phone 510-549-5930, fax 510-549-5939, e-mail info@apress.com, or visit http://www.apress.com.

The information in this book is distributed on an "as is" basis, without warranty. Although every precaution has been taken in the preparation of this work, neither the author(s) nor Apress shall have any liability to any person or entity with respect to any loss or damage caused or alleged to be caused directly or indirectly by the information contained in this work.

Contents at a Glance

Foreword. xi

About the Authors xv

About the Technical Reviewers xvii

Acknowledgments xix

Introduction. xxi

CHAPTER 1 Introduction to SharePoint Technologies. 1

CHAPTER 2 Using the Portal 5

CHAPTER 3 Using Windows SharePoint Services Sites. 45

CHAPTER 4 Custom Lists and Data. 91

CHAPTER 5 Template Lists. 129

CHAPTER 6 Libraries 163

CHAPTER 7 Pages, Web Parts, and Alerts 211

CHAPTER 8 SharePoint Document Collaboration Solutions 243

CHAPTER 9 SharePoint Project Collaboration Solutions 269

CHAPTER 10 SharePoint Meeting Management Solutions 287

CHAPTER 11 SharePoint Information Center Solutions 307

INDEX 327

Contents

Foreword xi

About the Authors xv

About the Technical Reviewers xvii

Acknowledgments xix

Introduction xxi

CHAPTER 1   Introduction to SharePoint Technologies 1

What Is Microsoft SharePoint? 2
Why Is It Valuable? 2
What Are the Building Blocks? 4

CHAPTER 2   Using the Portal 5

Portal Areas 6
Navigating Through Areas 9
Portal Site Groups 9
Managing Areas 12
Portal Listings 17
Adding Listings 18
Adding a Person Listing 20
Editing Listings 21
Editing a Person Listing 23
Deleting Listings 24
Managing Grouping and Ordering of Listings 24
Special Areas 27
Home Area 27
Topics Area 28
News Area 29
Sites Area 33
Portal Search 38
Performing a Simple Search 38
Performing an Advanced Search 38
Working with Search Results 40
My Site 41
Private View 42
Public View 44

■**CHAPTER 3** **Using Windows SharePoint Services Sites** 45

    Sites 46

        Site Layouts 48

        Navigating Through WSS Sites 60

        Creating Sites 63

        Managing Site Security 69

        Changing General Site Details 78

    Site Templates 80

        Creating Site Templates 80

        Editing Site Templates 82

        Deleting Site Templates 82

    WSS Site Search 83

    Site Statistics 83

        Site Usage Statistics 84

        Site Collection Usage Statistics 86

        Site Hierarchy 87

        Storage Space Allocation 88

■**CHAPTER 4** **Custom Lists and Data** 91

    Creating Custom Lists 91

    Working with Custom Lists 92

        Adding, Editing, and Deleting Items 92

        Filtering and Sorting the List 94

        Using Views 96

        Faster Data Manipulation Using the Datasheet 96

    Managing Custom Lists 97

        Settings 98

        Content Approval 98

        Security 100

        Managing Columns 102

        Managing Views 113

        Creating a List Template 119

        Deleting the List 120

        Adding a Listing to the Portal 121

        Differences Between Portal Lists and Site Lists 122

    Advanced Office 2003 Integration 123

        Exporting SharePoint Lists to Excel 123

        Creating Custom Lists Using Excel 125

        Advanced Datasheet Features 127

■CHAPTER 5   Template Lists... 129

Standard Lists 129

    Links.. 130

    Announcements.. 131

    Contacts 132

    Events 136

    Tasks 143

    Issues... 145

Meeting Workspace Lists.. 148

    Agenda.. 149

    Decisions.. 150

    Objectives 151

    Text Box 151

    Things to Bring.. 152

    Attendees 153

Special Lists.. 155

    Discussion Boards.. 155

    Surveys 157

Advanced Office 2003 Integration 159

    Exporting SharePoint Lists to Excel 160

    Advanced Datasheet Features................................... 161

■CHAPTER 6   Libraries... 163

Document Library 163

    Creating Document Libraries................................... 164

    Working with Document Libraries............................... 165

    Managing Document Libraries 175

Form Library.. 182

    Creating Form Libraries 182

    Working with Form Libraries................................... 183

    Managing Form Libraries 186

Picture Library 189

    Creating Picture Libraries.................................... 189

    Working with Picture Libraries................................ 190

    Managing Picture Libraries 200

Advanced Office 2003 Integration 202

    Open and Save As Integration 202

    Shared Workspace Task Pane 204

    Creating Form Libraries Through InfoPath Form Publishing...... 207

    Exporting Library Metadata to Excel.......................... 208

    Advanced Datasheet Features.................................. 209

■CHAPTER 7 **Pages, Web Parts, and Alerts**............................. 211

Pages.. 211
    Basic Pages 212
    Web Part Pages 214
Web Parts 218
    Adding Web Parts to Pages 219
    Managing the Web Part Page................................... 220
    Exporting and Importing Web Parts 225
    Standard Galleries and Web Parts.............................. 227
    Further Customization... 230
Alerts 232
    Alerts in the Portal 232
    Alerts in Sites 237

■CHAPTER 8 **SharePoint Document Collaboration Solutions** 243

Document Collaboration Overview................................... 243
    Collaboration Teams 244
    Collaboration Resources...................................... 244
Challenges of Document Collaboration 245
Needs for Document Collaboration................................. 246
SharePoint Document Collaboration Solutions....................... 247
    RFP Response Requirements................................... 248
    SharePoint Solution Components 248
    RFP Response Process Definition 249
    SharePoint Environment Layout 250
    RFP Response Process Walk-Through........................... 260
Benefits of SharePoint Document Collaboration Solutions............ 266
Tips for Creating Effective Document Collaboration Solutions 267

■CHAPTER 9 **SharePoint Project Collaboration Solutions** 269

Project Collaboration Overview.................................... 269
Challenges of Project Collaboration 270
Needs for Project Collaboration................................... 271
SharePoint Project Collaboration Solutions......................... 272
    Service Plan Project Requirements............................. 272
    Service Plan Project Process Definition 273
    SharePoint Environment Layout 274
    Service Plan Project Process Walk-Through.................... 280
Benefits of SharePoint Project Collaboration Solutions.............. 284
Tips for Creating Effective Project Collaboration Solutions 286

CHAPTER 10 SharePoint Meeting Management Solutions 287

Meeting Management Overview. 287

Challenges of Meeting Management 288

Needs for Meeting Management 290

SharePoint Meeting Management Solutions. 290

    Quarterly Business Review Meeting Requirements. 291

    Quarterly Business Review Meeting Process Definition 291

    SharePoint Environment Layout 292

    Quarterly Business Review Meeting Walk-Through. 299

Benefits of SharePoint Meeting Management Solutions. 305

Tips for Creating Effective Meeting Management Solutions 305

CHAPTER 11 SharePoint Information Center Solutions 307

Information Center Overview. 307

Challenges of Information Centers 308

Needs for Information Centers 309

SharePoint Information Center Solutions. 310

    HR Information Center Requirements. 310

    HR Information Center Environment Layout 310

    HR Information Center Walk-Through. 323

Benefits of SharePoint Information Centers 325

Tips for Creating Information Centers 325

INDEX 327

Foreword

At DataLan Corporation, we spend a significant amount of time discussing a select group of people that we refer to as *Professional Information Workers*. We define this group as people who spend most of their working day creating documents and sending e-mail. Personally, I use a simple litmus test to identify Professional Information Workers; if you start your day checking mail in Microsoft Outlook, then you are probably a Professional Information Worker. I certainly fall squarely into this category.

As Professional Information Workers, we are unique because we deal with data in many different forms such as documents, e-mails, transactional information, schedules, contacts, and task lists. We are often expected to retrieve information from these various sources and synthesize it together so that decisions can be made in a business process. What's more, this usually involves coordinating the efforts of other Professional Information Workers. The challenges of coordinating information, people, and processes within an organization are significant and frustrating.

In the vast majority of organizations, information is stored and retrieved by type as opposed to business context. In other words, documents are stored on a file server simply because they are in document form. Similarly, e-mail is stored on Exchange regardless of the business information the messages contain. The same is true for transactional information, which is all stored in databases. The situation resulting from this seemingly logical decision to store information by type is chaos for the Professional Information Worker.

Imagine for a moment that you are a Professional Information Worker asked to assemble all available information pertaining to your top ten customers. How many different data stores would you have to visit in order to complete a profile for these customers? You might start by searching the file system for all known documents concerning these important customers. Then, you might search your e-mail inbox for related messages. You'd also ask other people to search their inboxes for messages and forward them to you. While everyone is searching for messages, you might ask them to make a list of pertinent contacts they have in Microsoft Outlook and forward them to you as well. Finally, you might request the IT department run a series of reports to assemble financial information about the customers. Profiling your top ten customers turns out to be a significant project that can take days or weeks to complete.

Now imagine that you are a Professional Information Worker responsible for publishing the quarterly financial report internally to executive management. This report is a Microsoft Word document that pulls together information from several different lines of business and includes analysis by key sales and operations managers. Clearly, you have many of the same information issues as I discussed previously, but you now have the additional burden of coordinating several contributors to the same document. In most organizations, this coordination is accomplished by sending countless e-mails with attachments as you attempt to get content reviewed and approved. In all likelihood, you will also need several meetings to coordinate efforts and manage the process. Once again, this turns out to be a significant project that will require days or weeks to complete.

The scenarios I describe are significant because they reveal a wide gap between the needs of Professional Information Workers and the information systems that support them. Consequently, most Professional Information Workers spend the bulk of their day compensating for the weaknesses of these systems. In fact, many Professional Information Workers have simply become part of the overall information system and spend their entire day augmenting, organizing, and managing information. This strikes me as an incredibly poor use of highly talented people.

How did we arrive at this place where people are spending their day bridging data stores together through spreadsheets and e-mail? Well, I suppose it was inevitable. After all, software vendors—including Microsoft—have historically been more concerned with selling discreet applications as opposed to creating an environment that supports Professional Information Workers. All of these discreet applications have found their way onto our desktops, laptops, and servers to create the current mess. This is where SharePoint technology comes into the picture.

SharePoint invites Professional Information Workers to organize and retrieve information differently. Instead of storing data by type, SharePoint provides an infrastructure that allows information to be stored by business context. This means that you can have a single destination, which contains all relevant information for a business topic. Instead of assembling a customer profile manually, for example, you could navigate to a single SharePoint site dedicated to providing a complete customer profile. Similarly, you can have a single SharePoint site dedicated to the creation of a document like the quarterly report in my scenario. While not without some flaws, SharePoint does have the power to transform the way Professional Information Workers access and use information.

While I believe that SharePoint can have significant positive benefits for an organization, it is impossible to overstate the level of change required to bring it to fruition. I have witnessed many organizations install a SharePoint "pilot" project only to see it fail because the end users did not understand how to use the system or embrace the required changes. Ultimately, the success of any SharePoint implementation is in the hands of the Professional Information Workers who use it. Users like you must commit to mastering the SharePoint system, and the *SharePoint 2003 User's Guide* has been written to help you accomplish that goal.

Seth Bates and Tony Smith have been working with Professional Information Workers and helping them embrace SharePoint solutions since the product was released. They are in a unique position to understand the difficulties faced by individuals and organizations when transitioning from a traditional work environment to a SharePoint solution. They have used this knowledge to construct a logical learning path for Professional Information Workers and encapsulate it in a book.

Because a SharePoint solution is a dynamic system driven by the needs of its users, Professional Information Workers must become familiar with the basic building blocks of the system. Seth and Tony have provided this information in the first part of the book, which is essential reading for everyone. The second part of the book focuses on specific business scenarios where SharePoint can be helpful. These scenarios are excellent starting points and will undoubtedly help you visualize new ways to use SharePoint technology. I'd recommend that you review all of the scenarios even if they do not apply directly to your daily work.

In all my years of architecting and building solutions, I have found that projects rarely fail because of the underlying technology. The primary threat to any business solution is that the end users will not accept the system and refuse to change their work habits. This is why the *SharePoint 2003 User's Guide* is so important to the industry. SharePoint is one of the fastest-growing products in Microsoft history and promises to be as widespread as Microsoft Office itself. Without a strong effort to educate Professional Information Workers, many of these systems will not be successful. I wish you all the best in leading the transformation of your organization.

Scot Hillier
Author of *Microsoft SharePoint: Building Office 2003*
Solutions and *Advanced SharePoint Services Solutions*

About the Authors

 **SETH BATES** is a software architect and practice manager for DataLan Corporation, the 2004 NY/NJ Microsoft Platform Partner of the Year located in White Plains, New York. Seth performed the technical editing for *Microsoft SharePoint: Building Office 2003 Solutions* and *Advanced SharePoint Services Solutions*. He has also been published in *Dr. Dobb's Journal* (his article, titled "SharePoint Web Part Development," appears in the April 2005 edition). Seth has over 7 years of experience engineering business solutions, primarily using Microsoft technologies. With experience in all phases of the software engineering life cycle, he brings a broad mix of analysis, design, and implementation expertise to his work.

 **TONY SMITH** is a product manager for DataLan Corporation, the 2004 NY/NJ Microsoft Platform Partner of the Year located in White Plains, New York. With a background that includes business analysis, network engineering, and application development, Tony has over 10 years of experience engineering business solutions, and regularly presents to engineers, analysts, and business decision makers. Tony has been working with a wide range of organizations, including Fortune 500 and Fortune 50 companies, to design and deploy Microsoft SharePoint 2003 and Office System solutions since these products were made available. You can find additional information about Tony and topics discussed in this book at `http://www.sharepointextras.com`.

About the Technical Reviewers

MARTIN REID is an analyst at Queen's University Belfast. He has coauthored two books, *SQL: Access to SQL Server*, published by Apress, and *Beginning Access 2002 VBA*, published by Wrox, and has been a technical editor for many others. Martin has written several articles including some published by Microsoft on MSDN. Martin's primary interest is in database technology, .NET, and SharePoint Services to provide easy access to individual and corporate data to end users. He is married to Patricia, and together they have six children (Aine, Liam, Maeve, Emer, Roisin, and Eoin).

CHERRY TUN-SMITH is a project manager for DataLan Corporation, a consulting company based in White Plains, NY. Cherry has over 7 years of experience in managing commercial software development projects for organizations ranging from nonprofits to Fortune 100 firms. Implementing portal solutions and custom enterprise applications over the years has given her valuable insight into creating successful solutions for team collaboration and information sharing. During leisure time, Cherry enjoys spending time with her family and friends, scuba diving, snowboarding, and exploring new cultures.

Acknowledgments

Our experience writing this book has been a very positive one. The people at Apress have been great to work with, and we would like to specifically thank several of them. We would like to thank Jim Sumser for managing the partnership between authors and publisher, being the initial sounding board for our ideas, and handling any questions we had along the way. We would also like to thank Beth Christmas, the project manager, for coordinating the many efforts that went into creating this book on an increasingly tight schedule. Also, thanks to Ami Knox for copy editing and Katie Stence for production editing. Both of them were instrumental in the quality of this book. We are also appreciative to everyone else at Apress whom we were not fortunate enough to work with directly.

Along with the coordination and help provided by Apress, we would also like to thank the technical editors, Cherry Tun-Smith and Martin Reid, who did a great job reviewing this book. Their constant vigilance and content ideas helped to ensure that this book would be accurate and beneficial for the readers. We also would like to thank our colleagues at DataLan who work to successfully market, sell, and deliver Information Worker Solutions. Our real-world experiences there have contributed to our ability to organize and create this book.

I would like to thank Tony. It seems like an eternity has passed since we first began having grand ideas about publishing a SharePoint book, and finally we have succeeded.

Lastly, I would like to convey my love and appreciation for my wife Jennifer and son Dylan. You have provided support and guidance when I needed it, and I am now looking forward to being able to spend more time with you both.

— Seth Bates

I would like to thank Seth. Working with you on this book has been a positive and enjoyable experience.

Finally, I would like to thank my wife Lynn. I could not have done this without your love and support. You have encouraged and supported me through this entire process.

— Tony Smith

Introduction

SharePoint 2003 is quickly becoming more prevalent in the workplace, and all types of business professionals are becoming involved in using and managing SharePoint-based resources. We have seen many situations where, after SharePoint is introduced, individuals struggle to leverage these resources without a good enough understanding of the capabilities to gain the most value possible. *SharePoint 2003 User's Guide* was an outcome of this need, and our book can serve as a reference for people working within a SharePoint environment.

The goal of this book is to deliver a tool to all levels of SharePoint users. Beginners will be supplied with the information they need to most effectively use SharePoint's capabilities. Intermediate users will be given the information they need to manage their SharePoint resources. Advanced users will be provided the foundation needed for building business solutions using SharePoint's capabilities. We have spent a great deal of effort putting our experiences working with a variety of organizations and knowledge of the product into an easily understood format for learning about SharePoint 2003, which we hope will enable you to gain the in-depth knowledge you need to effectively use and manage these tools.

Further reading about the topics provided in this book can be found at http://www.sharepointextras.com where we provide additional information about SharePoint including references to other resources.

Who This Book Is For

The goal of this book is to provide the knowledge necessary for people to effectively use SharePoint. Whether you have not yet used SharePoint, just started using the basic features, or have been using it for a long of time, this book provides the skills you need to work efficiently with the capabilities SharePoint gives you.

If you want to learn about these capabilities in a detailed yet understandable approach, this book is for you. Being a user guide, this book does not require you to have any programming knowledge. It does assume you have a basic understanding of navigating web sites. Some of the more advanced topics require prior working knowledge of Microsoft Office products like Word and Excel.

How This Book Is Organized

The chapters in this book are organized into two groups. Chapters 1 to 7 provide the fundamental knowledge of SharePoint that users need in order to successfully utilize the capabilities supplied by the technology. This group can be used as a reference guide, allowing you to easily look up specific SharePoint topics, and includes step-by-step instructions, figures, tables, and examples. The capabilities described in these chapters are important and act as the building blocks for the second group of chapters.

The second group consists of Chapters 8 to 11. These four chapters present business solutions commonly deployed through SharePoint. Each of these chapters contains an example scenario that will help you understand the challenges faced along with the benefits that SharePoint provides to the situation. The scenarios also include the necessary steps for creating these solutions within a SharePoint environment.

Chapter 1: Introduction to SharePoint Technologies

This chapter introduces you to the world of Microsoft SharePoint. It contains an explanation of the technology, its uses, and related terminology.

Chapter 2: Using the Portal

This chapter provides an understanding of portals and areas making up Microsoft SharePoint Portal Server 2003. We cover security, content, structure, personalization, and search capabilities using detailed examples.

Chapter 3: Using Windows SharePoint Services Sites

This chapter focuses on the use of sites and workspaces created from Windows SharePoint Services. It contains the details you need to understand how to customize and use sites including the available templates, security features, and usage analysis.

Chapter 4: Custom Lists and Data

This chapter provides the knowledge needed to work with lists within SharePoint. We describe the use and management of custom lists in detail. You also learn about the advanced integration with Office that SharePoint's custom lists provide.

Chapter 5: Template Lists

This chapter contains a detailed look at the lists that are provided by SharePoint for you to use as templates when creating your own lists. We discuss the use and management of each list in detail along with any advanced integration with Office that they provide.

Chapter 6: Libraries

This chapter teaches the use and management of libraries within SharePoint. Used to manage a variety of files from Office documents to images, these SharePoint libraries encompass many collaborative features, which we cover in this chapter. Advanced integration between these libraries and Office products, which can enhance your experience with SharePoint, is also covered.

Chapter 7: Pages, Web Parts, and Alerts

Pages and web parts allow for the customization of portals and sites. This chapter uses detailed steps to show you how to customize SharePoint using the various types of pages and the functional components known as web parts. Additionally, we discuss the concept of alerts, which give you a powerful way to notify SharePoint users of changes to information within SharePoint.

Chapter 8: SharePoint Document Collaboration Solutions

One of the most common ways SharePoint is used is to create document collaboration solutions. This chapter describes the challenges SharePoint document collaboration solutions can address, the benefits you can receive by creating these solutions, and tips to be mindful of when creating these solutions. We construct a sample document collaboration solution and describe how the solution would be used.

Chapter 9: SharePoint Project Collaboration Solutions

Project collaboration is another common use for SharePoint. In this chapter, we describe how to create project collaboration solutions through SharePoint. We construct a sample solution and describe the benefits that can be received by creating these solutions.

Chapter 10: SharePoint Meeting Management Solutions

SharePoint provides strong meeting management capabilities. We discuss meeting management and how a SharePoint environment can be configured to support meeting management processes. We also build a sample meeting management solution and describe the benefits that can be received by creating these solutions.

Chapter 11: SharePoint Information Center Solutions

SharePoint is commonly used to create intranet or extranet solutions. We refer to these solutions as information centers. We describe the value of creating SharePoint-based information centers and discuss the capabilities to include and create a sample information center solution.

CHAPTER 1

■■■

Introduction to SharePoint Technologies

Microsoft SharePoint technologies are the foundation of the Microsoft Office System. The Office System is a new term Microsoft has coined to describe a collection of applications, servers, and services that work together to improve user and team productivity. These products are tightly integrated and can be combined to address a wide range of business needs. The Office System contains Office 2003 (including new applications like InfoPath and OneNote), Windows SharePoint Services, SharePoint Portal Server 2003, Project Server, and Live Communications Server. The goals behind the Office System are to

- Provide business users better access to information. This includes not only making more information available, but also providing capabilities to locate the information most relevant to a business user's needs.

- Enable groups of individuals within a company and between different companies to work together effectively and more easily share information.

- Improve individual and team productivity by making it easier to create information and provide this information to the appropriate people, allowing them to make informed business decisions.

The Office System products and services are brought together to create Information Worker solutions. An information worker is anyone who contributes knowledge to a business process or uses that knowledge to make decisions. This includes anyone who enters data into systems, discusses that information with others, or takes action based on the information. Information Worker solutions are business solutions, which include applications and processes, that allow information workers to improve their productivity, enhance collaboration with others, make information available to others, and reduce the time it takes to make accurate, informed business decisions.

Microsoft SharePoint technologies are an integral part of the Office System framework. SharePoint is the next generation of Microsoft's information management and collaboration platform and provides the foundation on which Information Worker solutions are built.

What Is Microsoft SharePoint?

Microsoft SharePoint is made up of two main products, Windows SharePoint Services and SharePoint Portal Server 2003. Windows SharePoint Services (WSS) is an add-on service for Windows Server 2003. Through WSS Microsoft provides the platform and services necessary to build information sharing and collaboration solutions. WSS is an individual and team productivity platform and a key component in the development of Information Worker solutions. WSS provides web-based team collaboration services needed to enable information workers to effectively create, manage, and share documents and other information. In addition to the creation of collaborative web sites, WSS can be used as the foundation for the development of business applications and to provide the information management capabilities needed by these applications.

Microsoft SharePoint Portal Server 2003 (SPS) is a set of technologies designed to unify systems and information from different sources into enterprise solutions to effectively bring together people, information, and processes. SPS includes navigational capabilities that help guide business users through enterprise resources including WSS sites, documents, applications, processes, and data. SPS contains powerful searching and indexing capabilities, which allow for relevant, high-quality information to be easily located and accessed regardless of where this information is located in the enterprise and in what system this information resides. Targeting particular information to groups of users and allowing users to create their own customized spaces within the portal are also features of SharePoint Portal Server. SPS expands on the development capabilities of WSS, allowing application developers to use virtually all of the capabilities of SPS and WSS within their custom applications.

Why Is It Valuable?

Together Windows SharePoint Services and SharePoint Portal Server provide the next step in the evolution of the Microsoft information management and collaboration platform. They provide an application solutions foundation, a document management and collaboration platform, and the building blocks necessary to create Information Worker solutions. Through the use of these products intelligent portal-based solutions can be created to connect teams of business users with the applications, processes, and information they need to perform their jobs.

In the current work environment individuals often find it difficult to identify and locate information they need in a timely manner. When they do find needed information, it is often outdated and no longer relevant. As multiple workers collaborate on content, multiple versions are created, and confusion occurs when workers become unaware which version is current. Also, when more than one worker is responsible for editing information, there is a high risk of this information being lost in the transition. These different versions of the information get copied to numerous locations and are often e-mailed to large groups of people unnecessarily, wasting disk space and resulting in confusion about which version is the latest copy. Conversely, managers and other workers needing these materials are not notified that the information is available or when the information is updated after it has been distributed. All of these issues result in time being lost to searching for information and verifying the accuracy of the information.

In the first part of this book, Chapters 2 through 7, we will discuss the components that make up a SharePoint environment and give you the information you need to effectively work with these components. Then in the second part of this book, Chapters 8 through 11, we will discuss some of the most common situations in which SharePoint solutions are used to solve a variety of business challenges. The solutions that we will focus our discussions around include the following:

- *Document collaboration*: Often the goal of a group of information workers is to create materials based on enterprise information. Often these individuals are geographically dispersed, with each individual needing the same level of access to the materials being created and the enterprise information the materials are based on. The group must know where the most recent copies of documents are located and be able to gain the appropriate level of access to these items. In addition, the ability to effectively communicate between team members is crucial to the efficiency of the collaboration process. The management of responsibilities and deadlines around the creation of the materials is also important to the document collaboration process.

- *Project collaboration*: When teams of people are brought together to work on a project, how well the project is managed will significantly impact its success. All aspects of the project, including the process, communications, deliverables, timelines, and tasks, need to be properly managed to ensure the success of the project. All interested parties, including team members, stakeholders, and managers, need visibility into the progress of the project and all associated resources. These individuals need to be kept aware of project status, timelines, issues, and any other pertinent information.

- *Meeting management*: Individuals spend a significant amount of time preparing for and participating in meetings. Organizations often try to find ways to reduce the quantity and duration of meetings in order to reduce the impact meetings have on people's time. To increase the effectiveness of a meeting, all aspects of the meeting must be properly managed. This includes preparation tasks, meeting facilitation, and post-meeting follow-up. Prior to a meeting, objectives and agendas must be defined and meeting materials must be created. These items must then be communicated to attendees so that they can adequately prepare for the meeting. During a meeting, facilitators need to keep the meeting on topic, decisions must be recorded, and action items must be tracked. Finally, after the meeting, follow-up materials must be distributed and the progress of the identified action items must be managed. Managing these aspects must also take into account remote meeting attendance so that remote attendees can effectively participate in the meeting.

- *Information centers*: Organizations often need to provide groups of individuals the ability to distribute items for use throughout the organization. Information owners will create and then need to publish materials for use by others. The information owners need to be able to effectively manage these materials, keeping them current and verifying that they are accurate. These materials also must to be organized in such a way that they are easy to find when they are needed.

What Are the Building Blocks?

Windows SharePoint Services and SharePoint Portal Server 2003 include many tools that can be combined to create a wide range of business solutions. Sites and workspaces provide a central place to consolidate a wide variety of information in a secure manner. Lists and libraries allow users to create and edit documents and other information. Alerts give users the ability to receive notifications when content has been added or changed. Pages and web parts allow for the customization of sites so that data and documents are presented in ways that make it easier for workers to find the information they need. Portal area navigation and searching capabilities provide the tools necessary to find relevant information when it is needed regardless of its location. My Site allows you to create your own customized site in SharePoint Portal Server to store your documents, tasks, and other information, and then make any of this information available to others.

In this book we will further define what these tools are, how they are used, and how to combine them into useful Information Worker solutions.

■ ■ ■

CHAPTER 2

Using the Portal

A SharePoint Portal Server 2003 (SPS) portal is the entry point into a SharePoint environment. A portal acts as the centralized access point for locating, working with, and managing an organization's information. The portal allows you to do the following:

- Search for information, such as people, sites, and documents, regardless of the information's location or format. This enables you to retrieve all relevant information you have access to on a topic or containing specific references.

- Organize information into meaningful structures using areas so that portal users can easily browse through this information.

- Maintain personal sites that enable you to create personal views of portal information for your use and public views of your information to share with others.

- Create alerts that are personal notifications you can configure to be notified when relevant information is added or changed in SharePoint areas or sites.

- Target specific content to groups of individuals for whom the information is particularly relevant.

In this chapter we will familiarize you with the general layout and structure of SPS. We will describe the elements that make up a SharePoint portal, including areas, listings, portal search, and My Site. We will review the layout of these elements and discuss how they are used.

Portal Areas

Areas are the primary organizational units of a SharePoint portal. They are used to group and structure content so that information can be easily located through browsing. A defined area structure acts as a portal blueprint or site map enabling the creation of an information hierarchy that maps to the way people need to work with the information. Figure 2-1 shows the typical layout of an area.

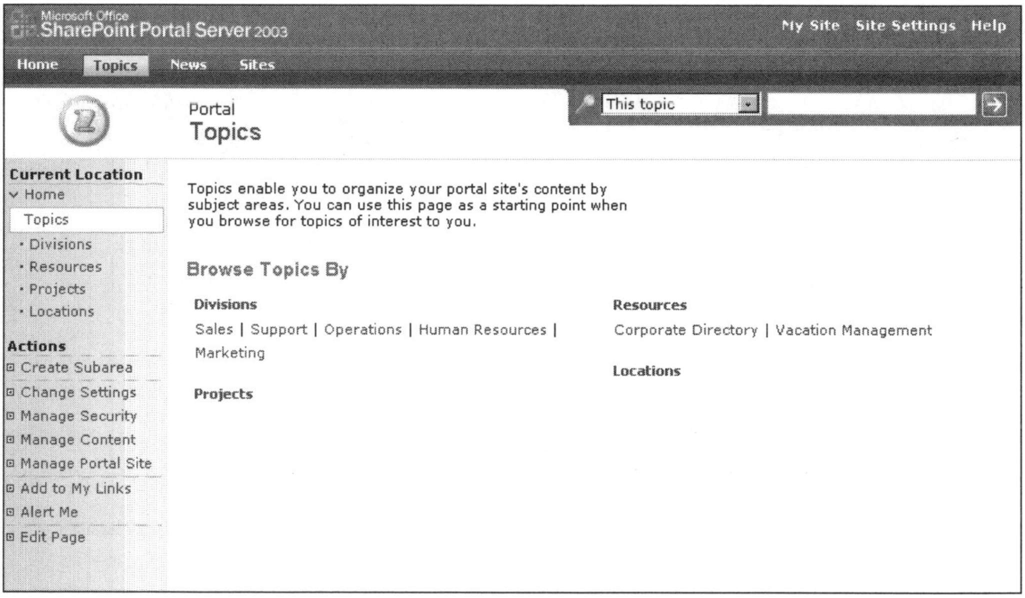

Figure 2-1. *Topics area*

Figure 2-1 shows the default layout of the Topics area. The Topics area is one of the default areas created as part of a new SharePoint portal. An area is organized so that navigation and management options are grouped within the banner and in the left-hand bar, leaving the remainder of the area for the presentation of content, applications, listings, or any other type of information an area manager chooses to make available. We can break an area down into the following groupings of options:

- *Area Listings Bar*: Located across the top of the portal page, the Area Listings Bar presents the list of top-level areas, which includes the home page and any areas directly under the home page. When a portal is initially created, this list will include Home, Topics, News, and Sites. However, this list may differ in your environment as it will reflect the top-level area structure of your SharePoint portal environment.

- *Portal Toolbar*: Located in the top right of the portal, the Portal Toolbar contains portal management and help links. The list of links in this area can include the following:

  - *My Site*: My Site is listed for portal users that have been granted the right to have a personal site. The My Site link gives you access to your personal site. We will discuss My Site in more detail later in this chapter.

- *Site Settings*: The Site Settings link is available for users having some level of management capabilities within the portal, which is typically someone who is at least a Content Manager for the portal. The Site Settings link gives you access to the Site Settings page containing the portal management tools. From this Site Settings page you will only have access to the management capabilities that have been made available to you based on your role in the portal. Other management capabilities beyond those you have access to may be listed; however, you will not be able to make changes to these other items.

- *Help*: The Help link is available to all portal users and provides online context-sensitive assistance for SharePoint capabilities.

- *Search Tools*: Located in the upper right just below the Area Listings Bar, the Search Tools allow you to perform basic and advanced searches for information available through SharePoint and crawled by the SharePoint index services. The information available for searching usually includes all content stored in SharePoint Portal Server and Windows SharePoint Services and may also include content stored in other sources, such as Exchange Public Folders, network file shares, or other internal or external web sites.

- *Current Area Navigation*: Located in the left-hand section just below the Area Listing Bar, the Current Area Navigation shows context-centric navigation. This includes the hierarchy of areas above the current location as well as any subareas within the current location. For example, if you are currently in the Divisions area, which is located under the Topics area, and this area has two children called Domestic and International, the area navigation will show the hierarchy of areas above Divisions, which includes Home and Topics, and the list of subareas contained within Divisions, which includes Domestic and International.

- *Actions*: Located in the left-hand section just below the Current Area Navigation, the Actions section provides the list of area management and area content management tasks that are available to you for the currently displayed area. This list only contains those options that are available to you based on your security rights within the area. Table 2-1 shows the options that are available based on a user's site group assignment. Assigning users to site groups defines the rights that those users will have within the portal. We will discuss site groups in more detail in the "Portal Site Groups" section later in this chapter. The following are the options that can be made available in the Action section:

  - *Add Listings*: Allows you to add new portal listings to an area in the portal. Portal listings are references to materials, web sites, etc. We will discuss listings in more detail in the "Portal Listings" section later in this chapter.

  - *Add Person*: Allows you to add a listing to a portal user with an area. We will discuss people listings in more detail in the "Portal Listings" section later in this chapter.

  - *Create Subarea*: Used to create a new portal area under the area currently being displayed. We will discuss creating and managing areas in the "Managing Areas" section later in this chapter.

- *Upload Document*: Takes you to the document upload screen for the default document library created within the area. We will discuss managing documents in Chapter 6.

- *Change Settings*: Used to change the configuration settings for the currently displayed portal area.

- *Manage Security*: Used to manage the security settings for the area currently being displayed.

- *Manage Content*: Provides access to the area's Documents and Lists page where all of the content items available in the area including all listings, libraries, and lists can be accessed and managed.

- *Manage Portal Site*: Presents a graphical view of the portal area structure, allowing for drag-and-drop management of the area hierarchy. It also provides access to some of the more common area management features including editing area properties, managing area security, creating listings, and creating subareas.

- *Add to My Links*: Allows you to create a link to the currently displayed area that will be available within the My Links list in your My Site. We will discuss My Site in more detail in the "My Site" section toward the end of this chapter.

- *Alert Me*: Allows you to create an alert that will notify you of changes made to materials within the currently displayed area. We will discuss alerts in more detail in Chapter 7.

- *Edit Page*: Gives you access to the area editing options including the Modify Page capabilities and the page content management options. We will discuss page management in more detail in Chapter 7.

Table 2-1. *Actions Available by Security Site Group*

	Reader	Member	Contributor	Content Manager	Web Designer	Administrator
Add Listing	✓	✓	✓	✓	✓	✓
Add Person	✓	✓	✓	✓	✓	✓
Create Subarea			✓	✓	✓	✓
Upload Document	✓	✓	✓	✓	✓	✓
Change Settings				✓	✓	✓
Manage Security						✓
Manage Content			✓	✓	✓	✓
Manage Portal Site				✓	✓	✓
Add to My Link	✓	✓	✓	✓	✓	✓
Alert Me	✓	✓	✓	✓	✓	✓
Edit Page			✓	✓	✓	✓

- *Content*: Located to the right of the Current Area Navigation and Actions sections and below the Search Tools, the Content section is the main body of the portal page. This is the part of the page that contains the elements for display within the area. This may include documents, lists, portal-based applications, and references to sites or other content.

■**Note** Portal areas can be customized by administrators through the use of available third-party add-ins and tools like Microsoft FrontPage. If changes are made to the overall structure of an area or to an area template, the location or presentation of the preceding groupings of options may vary.

Navigating Through Areas

Navigation through the portal can be a little confusing. Portals can bring together a wide variety of information located in many sources. Areas can provide access into Windows SharePoint Services sites, web sites (internal or external), applications, and content stored on network file shares or in Exchange. It is important for the portal's area structure to provide a path that is logical and easy for portal users to follow.

To navigate through available portal areas, you click the area to access either from the Area Listings Bar or the Current Area Navigation section. This will bring you to the selected area. When you navigate to an area, the content contained within the area is displayed and the name of the area is listed for easy reference at the top of the Content section. Also, the Current Area Navigation section will be updated to list the area hierarchy information for the currently displayed area.

Once you have navigated to the area, any available area management options will be listed in the Actions list. The options in this list will vary based on your rights within the area. Table 2-1 presents the complete list of actions and the security levels, or site groups, for which the options are available. When you select one of these available actions, the options listed under the action will sometimes be further restricted based on your security rights. In the following sections we will discuss the capabilities provided by the options available under the Actions section.

■**Note** There are several third-party navigation solutions that can be added to SharePoint to extend and enhance the existing portal navigation capabilities. These options can allow you to provide alternative navigation methods as well as ways to extend the default navigation capabilities if they do not completely meet your organization's needs.

Portal Site Groups

As we mentioned, many options that are available to users within the portal are dependent on the user's security rights. Security rights are assigned through roles called site groups. Users can be assigned to site groups individually or based on their membership in Active Directory groups. Role assignments determine who can view areas, manage content in areas, edit areas, create areas, etc. A standard set of site groups is available by default with a portal. However, it is possible to create additional site groups in order to provide customized permission levels. It is also possible to change the permissions associated with existing site groups. However, this should be done sparingly and only when creating a new site group will not meet the security requirements. The following are the standard site groups defined in an SPS portal:

- *Readers*: Can view SPS areas and area content. Readers cannot add or edit content or perform any management functions on areas. By default, Readers cannot use personal features of the portal, such as creating alerts or maintaining a personal My Site.

- *Members*: Have all the rights of a Reader as well as the ability to view and personalize areas and area content. Members can use the personal features of the portal, like alerts and My Site.

- *Contributors*: Have all rights of a Member as well as the ability to add, edit, and delete content items within an SPS area. Contributors can also browse directories and create and manage personal views of areas. Contributors cannot create new libraries and lists or manage shared views of areas.

- *Content Managers*: Have all rights of a Contributor as well as the ability to create and manage areas and listings and create WSS sites.

- *Web Designers*: Have all rights of a Content Manager as well as the ability to apply style sheets to areas.

- *Administrators*: Have full user and administrative rights to all portal areas and content.

Adding Users to Site Groups

To add a user or Active Directory group to a site group:

1. From the portal home page, click the Manage Users link under Actions.

2. On the Manage Users page, click the Add Users option.

3. On the Add Users page:

   a. Select users to add in one of two ways. The first way is to enter the Active Directory user ID (in the form domain\user), user e-mail address, or Active Directory group name (in the form domain\group) that you wish to add.

   The second way is to click the Select Users and Groups option. This option allows you to search for the desired users or groups. To use this searching capability, you would select a Find By value, which allows you to choose what attribute to search for; you then enter the search criteria and click Find. The list of accounts meeting the entered criteria will be listed. You can then add the desired users and groups to the Selected Accounts list. Once all needed accounts are in the Selected Accounts list, click OK to return to the Add Users page.

   b. Check the site groups membership that you wish to assign to the user or group.

   c. Click the Next button.

4. If the user or group information was not found in the Active Directory, an error screen will be displayed. If this screen is presented, click the browser Back button to return to the Add Users page, update the information so that it refers to a valid active directory user or group, and click the Next button.

5. If the user or group was found in Active Directory, the Add Users page containing step 3 and step 4 is presented. On this page, verify the account information and determine whether an e-mail should be sent to the user notifying that user of the change in rights by checking or unchecking the send e-mail option. This option will be disabled if a group account was selected. If a user was selected and you wish to send a notification e-mail to the user, you enter the text to be sent in the Subject and Body fields. Once the send e-mail option information has been appropriately set, click the Finish button.

■**Note** The Confirm Users information in step 3 of the Add Users page should never need to be updated. This information is pulled from the Active Directory as part of the user profile. If this information is not accurate, it should be appropriately updated in the Active Directory by a network administrator instead of being changed in the SharePoint portal.

The user or group is added to the selected site group. The Manage Users page is displayed and the newly added site group assignment is listed.

Changing Existing Site Group Assignments

To change an existing site group assignment:

1. From the portal home page, click the Manage Users link under Actions.

2. On the Manage Users page, check the boxes in front of the site group assignments that you will be updating and click the Edit Site Groups of Selected Users option. If you are updating a single site group assignment, you can simply click the name of the assigned user or group.

3. On the Edit Site Group Membership page, update the site group assignment by checking and unchecking the site group options and then clicking the OK button to save the changes.

The updates to site group assignments are saved. The Manage Users page is displayed and the updates made are reflected in the site group assignment list.

Deleting Existing Site Group Assignments

To remove an existing site group assignment:

1. From the portal home page, click the Manage Users link under Actions.

2. On the Manage Users page, check the boxes in front of the site group assignment(s) that you will be removing and click the Remove Selected Users option.

3. Confirm the deletion of the site group assignment by clicking the OK button on the displayed message box.

The selected site group assignments are deleted. The Manage Users page is refreshed to reflect the changes made.

Managing Areas

One of the most significant benefits of a SharePoint portal is that the business owners of content can be responsible for the management of the areas and sites in which their content resides. Content owners do not need to rely on IT departments to manage portal areas, post content, or organize materials. This allows the content owners to have control over the entire information management process and allows the IT group to focus on the management of the overall portal without needing to get involved in the management of business team resources.

When SharePoint is introduced into an organization, a decision must be made concerning the level of ownership business teams will have around the management of SharePoint sites and areas. In many cases, the responsibility of maintaining the areas and the information contained in areas is given to the information owners. That said, it is often also true that the organization will want to maintain some level of consistency with navigation and layout of the overall SharePoint environment. To meet this goal, the organization will incorporate certain restrictions or policies involving area management. In this section, we will discuss the structure of areas and how they are managed. This information can then be applied to your organization in the way that best meets your desired balance between business owner control and navigation and layout consistency.

As we discussed earlier in this chapter, SPS areas are the primary tools used to organize enterprise resources being made available through a SharePoint portal. A portal area structure is made up of areas created by portal managers as well as some default specialty areas available automatically that are used to manage specific portal services. These specialty areas include the following:

- *Home*: Portal home page designed to be the gateway or entry point into the overall SharePoint environment.

- *Topics*: Default area that includes a sample area hierarchy. The Topics area is provided to allow for information to be organized by subject area.

- *News*: Area designed to contain corporate news postings.

- *Sites*: Area that organizes portal site listings. The Sites area provides a complete list of WSS and web sites and allows users to sort, filter, and group these sites based on need. The management of site listings is also handled through this area.

We will review the capabilities provided by these specialty areas later in this chapter. First we will discuss the capabilities around creating and working with basic areas.

Creating an Area

Areas can be organized to provide a navigation structure that makes it easy for workers to browse through enterprise resources when looking for resources. Areas can be nested within each other to create any hierarchy necessary. A nested area, or subarea, is created by doing the following:

1. Navigate to the area under which you wish to create the new subarea.

2. From the Actions list of the area, click the Create Subarea link.

3. On the Create Area page:

   a. Enter the name for the subarea. This is the name that will appear in the area listings. You can also enter an optional description that is displayed at the top of the subarea when it is accessed.

   b. Enter the publication date information that is used to determine when the subarea should be available for users. By default, the start date is set to today's date and the expiration date is blank, which will make the site available immediately and for an unlimited duration. You can update these two dates to limit the availability of the subarea to within a specific timeframe.

   c. Choose the location where the area will be listed. By default, the subarea will be placed under the area in which you clicked the Create Subarea link. If you wish to change this, you can click the Change Location link and select a different **area** under which to place the new subarea.

4. Once all of the options have been appropriately set on the Create Area page, click the OK button.

The subarea is created, and you are returned to the area in which you clicked the Create Subarea link. The new subarea is listed in the Current Area Navigation.

■**Note** Areas can also be created through the Portal Site Map. We will discuss this in more detail in the "Managing Areas Through the Portal Site Map" section later in this chapter.

Editing Properties of an Area

Areas that have been created in SPS can be updated to address changing needs. These needs may come in the form of restructuring the site, requiring that areas be placed in different locations; or in the form of an adjustment in the purpose of an area, requiring that some attributes about the area, like title or description, be updated. To make any of these changes to an area:

1. Navigate to the area that needs to be updated.

2. From the Actions list in the area, click the Change Settings link.

3. On the Change Settings page, make the necessary updates to the area. The Change Settings page is divided into five tabs organizing the area attributes. The information that can be changed about an area includes the following:

   a. On the General tab, the title, description, and location information entered when the area was created can be updated. This tab also lets you specify a contact for the area. You can either select a contact from the list of users or enter the contact's information. The contact information can be presented in the portal area using the Area Details web part.

   b. On the Publishing tab, you can update the publishing start and expiration dates that were entered when the area was created. This tab also lets you set listing approval options. You can specify whether listings must be approved before they are made available to users and whether listings added by area managers should be automatically approved. Listings are references to any type of information located in the enterprise and referenced through a portal area. We will discuss listings in the "Portal Listings" section later in this chapter.

   c. On the Page tab, page template information is updated. You can specify the templates that are available for use on subareas created within this area, and you can change the template that this area is using. Page templates provide look-and-feel parameters for the portal area. This includes information layout parameters and color schemes in use.

   d. On the Display tab, you can specify whether the area should be excluded from the portal navigation bars and whether listings should be sorted alphabetically or manually within the area. You can also update image information for the area and specify an icon image. The image appears at the top of the content section of the area, and the icon image is displayed next to links pointing to this area.

   e. On the Search tab, you can specify whether the area and its content are included in search results and whether the area is included in Topic Assistance. Topic Assistance suggests content for the area when content is automatically categorized. Topic Assistance can be used to automatically populate areas with listings based on SharePoint "learning" what types of information should be listed in the area. An administrator must activate and configure Topic Assistance to make this capability available.

4. Once all changes have been made on the Change Settings page, click the OK button.

The area is updated based on the changes made to the area settings, and you are returned to the area.

Manage Area Security

By default, an area inherits the security from its parent area, and the Home area security is based on the overall portal site group assignments, which we discussed earlier in this chapter. If an area requires permissions different from its parent, the area security must be updated to reflect this change. Setting permissions on an area works slightly different from setting the overall site group assignments. Since the assignment of the users into site groups was done at the portal level, to change the permissions that the users who have been assigned to the site groups have in a specific area, the permissions of the site groups within that area must be altered. For example, if the portal users that have been assigned to the Contributor site group should not be allowed to update content within the Topics area, the rights of the Contributor site group must be changed in the Topics area to reflect the needed permission restrictions.

If additional permissions must be added beyond the existing site group assignments, these permissions can be explicitly defined within the area. For example, if an individual is a member of the Reader site group who requires Contributor-level rights to a specific area, that person can be explicitly defined in the area security as having the ability to edit content.

Editing Existing Area Security

To edit existing security information within an area:

1. Navigate to the area in which security needs to be updated.

2. From the Actions list of the area, click the Manage Security link.

3. On the Manage Security Settings page, check the box in front of the site group, user, or group that must be updated, and click the Edit option.

4. If you selected a site group, the Advanced Edit Rights on Area page is presented. If you selected a user or group, the Simple Edit Rights on Area page is presented. You have the ability to toggle between the Advanced and Simple views.

5. You then select the appropriate rights and click the OK button.

The area security is updated based on the changes made, and you are returned to the area.

Adding New Area Security

To add permissions for a new user or group within an area:

1. Navigate to the area in which the user or group needs to be added.

2. From the Actions list of the area, click the Manage Security link.

3. On the Manage Security Settings page, click the New User option.

4. On the Add New User to Area page, enter the user or group to add and select the security the user or group should have in the area. You have the ability to toggle between the Advanced and Simple views in order to set the appropriate level of security. Once the user information and security level have been entered, click the OK button.

The area security is updated based on the additions made, and you are returned to the area.

Deleting Existing Security

To delete existing security permissions within an area:

1. Navigate to the area in which the security information needs to be deleted.

2. From the Actions list of the area, click the Manage Security link.

3. On the Manage Security Settings page, check the box in front of the site group, user, or group to remove, and click the Remove Permissions option.

4. Confirm the deletion of the permissions by clicking the OK button on the displayed message box.

The area security is updated based on the changes made, and you are returned to the area.

Managing Areas Through the Portal Site Map

The Portal Site Map provides a pictorial view of the portal's area hierarchy. This page allows you to perform area management tasks from this central hierarchy without having to navigate to the individual areas. Many of the area management tasks we have been discussing can be performed on the Portal Site Map page. You access the Portal Site Map page by clicking the Manage Portal Site link in the Actions list from any area. Figure 2-2 shows the Portal Site Map page.

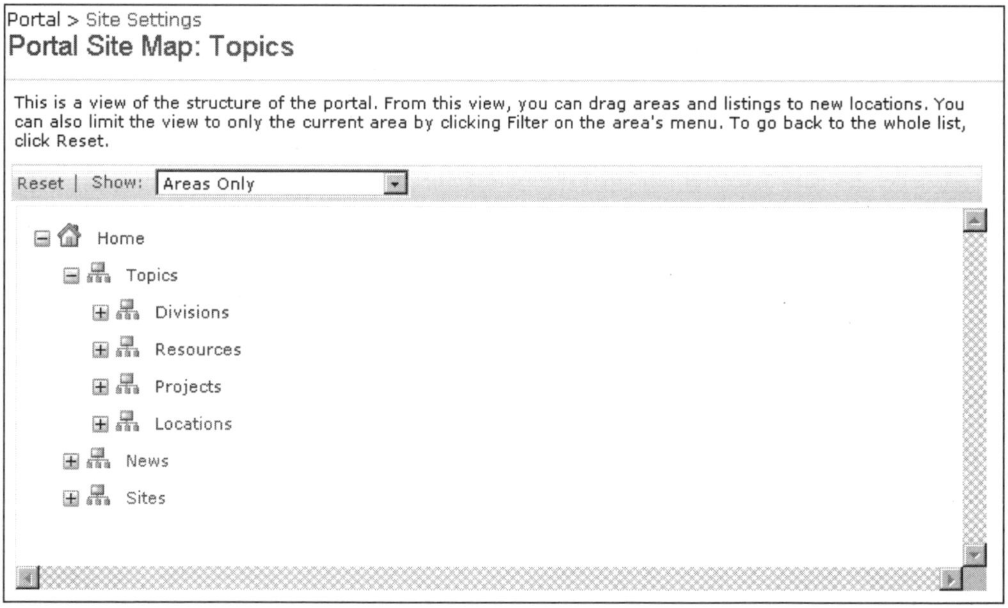

Figure 2-2. *Portal Site Map*

You can expand and collapse the area structure in order to view as little or as much of the area hierarchy as necessary. You can then hover over an area in the tree to make the drop-down list for that area visible, as shown in Figure 2-3.

Figure 2-3. *Portal Site Map drop-down options*

From this drop-down list, you can perform any of the following functions:

- *Create an area* by clicking the Create Subarea option from the drop-down list or by clicking the Create Area option in the Actions section. This will take you to the Create Area page discussed earlier in this chapter.

- *Edit properties of an area* by clicking the Edit option from the drop-down list. This will take you to the Change Settings page for the selected area that we discussed earlier in this chapter.

- *Manage area security* by clicking the Manage Security option from the drop-down list. This will take you to the Manage Security Settings page for the selected area that we discussed earlier in this chapter.

- *Delete an existing area* by clicking the Delete option from the drop-down list. This will present the deletion confirmation prompt. Clicking the OK button on this prompt will delete the area and refresh the Portal Site Map.

- *Move an area* by dragging an existing area to a new location in the Portal Site Map. As you drag the area, you will notice reference bars that are presented as you move. These bars are provided as a guide to where the area will be placed if you release the mouse button.

Portal Listings

Listings are references or links that get placed in a portal area to point to content. Listings can reference WSS sites, internal or external web sites, network directories, files, or applications. Listings can also reference HTML information created through SPS for the sole purpose of being referenced by the listing. Listings are what allow SharePoint areas to organize enterprise resources into a logical hierarchy.

Listings are displayed in the content section of areas through the use of the Listings web part. This web part is available on areas by default when they are created. Figure 2-4 depicts a standard area containing listings.

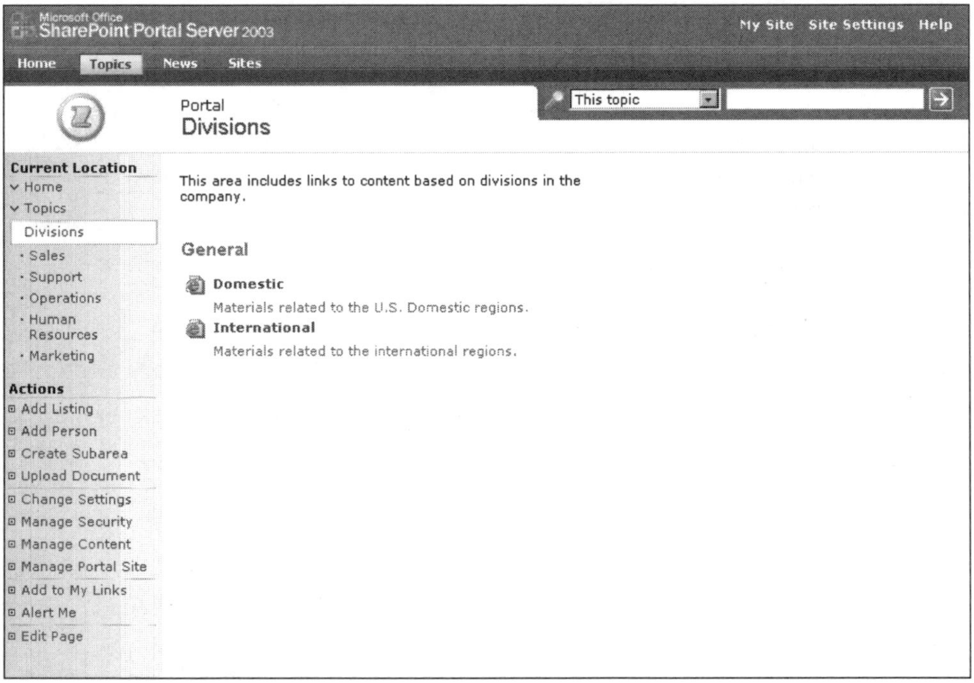

Figure 2-4. *Divisions area*

Adding Listings

Listings can reside in any area. To add a listing to an area:

1. Navigate to the area where you wish to create the listing.

2. From the Actions list in the area, click the Add Listing link.

3. On the Add Listings page:

   a. Enter the title of the listing. This is the name by which the listing will be displayed in the portal area. You can also add a listing description, which if entered is displayed directly beneath the listing title in the portal area.

   b. Enter the content for the listing. Listing content is either in the form of a web or file path address or is text entered for use as the listing content. To reference existing WSS sites, web content, network directories, files, or applications, select the Existing Listing option and enter the full web address or UNC path to the desired content. To create a listing by entering text to be displayed, select the Add a Listing by Entering Text option and click the Open Text Editor button. The text editor is presented in which you can enter the content for the listing. Once the information is entered, click the OK button to return to the Add Listings page.

c. Select a group for the listing from the group drop-down list. Groups are used to organize listings in the area.

d. Optionally, you can enter the path to an image file. This image is used for listings where the Add Listing by Entering Text option was selected. For these types of listings, the image will appear at the top of the listing when it is viewed.

e. Select the location for the listing. By default, the listing location will be set to the area in which you click the Add Listing link. However, this information can be changed, and listings can be configured to appear in multiple areas. Listing locations are updated by clicking the Change Location link and then selecting all of the areas in which the listing should appear. Once all of the locations have been selected, click the OK button on the Change Location window to save the changes and return to the Add Listing page.

f. Optionally, you can select audiences for the listing. Audiences are used to identify groups of individuals for which the listing is important. By selecting audiences, you can target listings to a specific group of people. While audiences do not determine what users have the right to access the listing (access is determined by the area security), they do identify the individuals for which the listing is important. When audiences are selected, the listing will appear in the targeted web parts and in the Targeted links section of My Site for users that are members of the audience. Defining audiences and targeting content is a way to highlight or emphasize information for select portal users.

■Note Audiences must be created by a technical SharePoint administrator. By default, only one audience is available, called All Portal Users, which is used when content should be targeted to all SharePoint users.

---

4. Once all the necessary listing information has been entered on the Add Listings page, click the OK button.

The listing is saved, and you are returned to the area from which you clicked the Add Listing link. The listing will be displayed in the area's Listing web part. By default, this web part is located in the Content section of an area. If site managers have removed the web part from the page, it would need to be readded for the listing to be visible. We will describe working with web parts in Chapter 7.

Listings can also be added from the Portal Site Map page. To add a listing through the Portal Site Map page:

1. From the Actions section of any area, click the Manage Portal Site link.

2. On the Portal Site Map page, highlight the area in which to add the listing, and select the Add Listing option from the drop-down menu.

3. Enter the information for the new listing into the Add Listings page as described previously, and click the OK button.

The listing is saved, and you are returned to the Portal Site Map page.

We discussed earlier in this chapter that areas can be configured so that listings require approval before they are made available to portal users. When an area is configured so that listings must be approved, any listings added to an area by a nonarea manager will not appear until an area manager approves them. Those that are added by an area manager will also not appear until they are approved if the area was configured to require approval for listings posted by managers. Approving or rejecting a listing is done by editing the listing. We will discuss setting the listing approval status in the upcoming "Editing Listings" section.

Adding a Person Listing

There is a second type of listing you can add: a person listing, which provides a reference to a portal user's My Site. Person listings are grouped with all other listings once they have been created. To create a person listing:

1. Navigate to the area in which you wish to add the listing.

2. From the Actions list in the area, click the Add Person link.

3. On the Add Person page:

    a. Select the account name to be listed by clicking the Select Person link and then entering the search options for the person you wish to locate. Then add the name to the Selected Account Name list by clicking the Add button. Only one account name can be listed in the Selected Account Name list. Once the needed name is in the Selected Account Name list, click the OK button to return to the Add Person page. You can also add a listing description, which if entered is displayed directly beneath the listing title in the portal area.

    b. Select a group for the listing from the group drop-down list. Groups are used to categorize listings when you access the area.

    c. Select the location for the listing. By default, the listing location will be set to the area in which you click the Add Listing link. However, this information can be changed, and listings can be configured to appear in multiple areas. Listing locations are updated by clicking the Change Location link and then selecting all of the areas in which the listing should appear. Once all of the locations have been selected, click the OK button on the Change Location window to save the changes and return to the Add Listing page.

    d. Optionally, you can select audiences for the listing. Audiences are used to group individuals for whom the content will be targeted. While audiences do not determine what users have the right to access the listing (access is determined by the area security), they do identify the individuals for whom the listing is important. When audiences are selected, the listing will appear in targeted web parts and in the Targeted Links section of My Site for users who are members of the audience. Defining audiences and targeting content is a way to highlight or emphasize information for select portal users.

4. Once all the necessary listing information has been entered on the Add Listings page, click the OK button.

The person listing is saved, and you are returned to the area from which you clicked the Add Person link.

Editing Listings

Assuming that the Listings web part is included in the Content section of the area containing a listing that you want to edit, follow these steps to edit the listing:

1. Navigate to the area containing the listing that needs to be updated.

2. From the Actions list, click the Edit Page link. The Edit Page link activates the management options for the content area and any content elements available in the content area.

3. Hover over the listing you want to update, and click the down arrow to display the Listing Management options as shown in Figure 2-5.

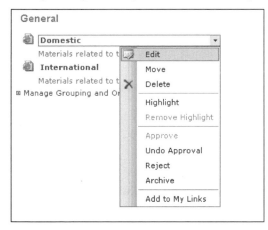

Figure 2-5. *Listing Management options*

4. Click the Edit option from the Listing Management options drop-down list.

5. On the Change Settings page, make the necessary updates to the listing. The Change Settings page is divided into four tabs organizing the listing attributes. The information that can be changed about a listing includes the following:

   a. On the General tab, you can update general listing information. The title, description, content, and location information that were entered during the creation of the listing can be updated. When the listing references external content, a list of related items is also presented. This is a list of other listings that exist in the portal that reference the same document. This related-items list can be used to easily locate other listings that may need to be updated as well.

   b. On the Publishing tab, you can update publishing start and expiration dates and approval status information. Publishing dates are used to determine when the listing should be available to users. By default, the start date is set to the date the listing is created and the expiration date is left blank. This makes the listing available from the time it was created for an unlimited duration. These dates can be updated to limit the availability of the listing. The approval status is used to identify whether the listing is approved for use. Listings will not be available for portal users if they are not in an approved status. When areas are configured so that approvals to listing elements are not required, all listings default to an approved status. If areas are configured so that listing approvals are required, the listings will be given a pending status when they are created and must be approved before available for use. Listing statuses can be Pending (waiting for approval), Approved (available for access), Rejected (not to be displayed), and Archive (flagged for later archival).

    c. On the Display tab, you can change the group information and audiences that were selected when the listing was created. You can also update the image reference that was set when the area was created and specify an icon image. The icon image is displayed next to links for the listing in the area.

    d. On the Search tab, you can specify whether the listing should appear in search results. By default, when a listing is created, this option is set to yes.

  6. Once all changes have been made to the listing, click the OK button.

The changes to the listing are saved, and you are returned to the area that contained the listing.

Changing the approval status information and the ability to move the listing to another area are options that are also made available directly through the Listing Management options drop-down list presented in Figure 2-5. To move a listing to a different location:

  1. Navigate to the area containing the listing that needs to be updated.

  2. From the Actions list in the area, click the Edit Page link.

  3. Hover over the listing you want to move and click the down arrow to display the Listing Management options drop-down list as shown in Figure 2-5.

  4. Click the Move option from the Listing Management options drop-down list.

  5. On the Move Listing page, click the Change Location option and select the new location for the listing. Then click the OK button to save the changes.

The listing is moved to the new location, and you are returned to the area originally containing the listing.

To change the approval status of a listing from the Listing Management options drop-down list:

  1. Navigate to the area containing the listing that needs to be updated.

  2. From the Actions list, click the Edit Page link.

  3. Hover over the listing you want to change the status of and click the down arrow to display the Listing Management options drop-down list as shown in Figure 2-5.

  4. Click the approval status to which the listing should be changed. The options that are available include Approved, Undo Approval, Reject, and Archive. The option representing the current approval status of the listing will be disabled in the drop-down list.

The listing approval status is updated, and the area is refreshed to reflect the change.

■**Note** Listings in anything other than an approved status are not visible in the list when viewing the page. In order to make these listings visible, you must click the Edit Page link in the Actions section. This will make unapproved listings available for management.

Editing a Person Listing

To edit a person listing:

1. Navigate to the area containing the person listing that needs to be updated.

2. From the Actions list, click the Edit Page link. The Edit Page link activates the management options for the area and any content elements displayed in the area.

3. Hover over the person listing you want to update and click the down arrow to display the Listing Management options drop-down list as shown in Figure 2-5.

4. Click the Edit option from the Listing Management options drop-down list.

5. On the Change Settings page, make the necessary updates to the listing. The Change Settings page is divided into four tabs organizing the listing attributes. The information that can be changed about a person listing includes the following:

    a. On the General tab, you can update general listing information. The name, description, and location information that was entered during the creation of the person listing can be updated. To update the name, click the Select Person link and enter search options for the person you wish to locate, and then add the name to the Selected Account Name list by clicking the Add button. Only one name can reside in the Selected Account Name list. Once the name you need is in the Selected Account Name list, click the OK button to return to the Change Settings page.

    b. On the Publishing tab, you can update publishing start and expiration dates and approval status information. Publishing dates are used to determine when the listing should be available to users. By default, the start date is set to the date the listing is created, and the expiration date is left blank. This makes the listing available from the time it was created for an unlimited duration. These dates can be updated to limit the availability of the listing. The approval status is used to identify whether the listing is approved for use. Listings will not be available for portal users if they are not in an approved status. When areas are configured so that approvals to listing elements are not required, all listings default to an approved status. If areas are configured so that listing approvals are required, the listings will be given a pending status when they are created and must be approved before available for use. Listing statuses can be Pending (waiting for approval), Approved (available for access), Rejected (not to be displayed), and Archive (flagged for later archival).

    c. On the Display tab, you can change the group information and audiences that were selected when the listing was created. You can also update the image reference that was set when the person listing was created and specify an icon image. The icon image is displayed next to links for the listing on the area.

       d. On the Search tab, you can specify whether the listing should appear in search
   results. By default, when a listing is created, this option is set to yes.

  6. Once all changes have been made to the listing, click the OK button.

The changes to the person listing are saved, and you are returned to the area that contained
the listing.

Deleting Listings

To delete an existing listing or person listing:

  1. Navigate to the area containing the listing that needs to be deleted.

  2. From the Actions list in the area, click the Edit Page link.

  3. Hover over the listing you want to delete and click the down arrow to display the
Listing Management options drop-down list as shown in Figure 2-5.

  4. Click the Delete option from the Listing Management options drop-down list.

  5. Confirm the deletion of the listing by clicking the OK button on the displayed message
box.

The listing is deleted and the area is refreshed to reflect the change.

■**Note** Deleting a listing will permanently remove it from SharePoint. If you wish to make the listing
unavailable but not delete it, you should change the listing's approval status.

Managing Grouping and Ordering of Listings

Groupings are used to organize listings that are displayed in an area, and ordering allows you
to specify the display order of the listings within each grouping. In the "Adding Listings" and
"Editing Listings" sections earlier, we discussed how to assign listings to groupings. In this section, we will discuss managing grouping values and managing the order of listing elements
within groupings.

To access the management tools for grouping and ordering, you click the Edit Page link
in the Actions section. This will make the page management options available including the
Manage Grouping and Ordering link below the Listings web part. When you click this link,
you are taken to the Grouping and Ordering page as shown in Figure 2-6. The Grouping and
Ordering page lists all listings, regardless of status, and allows for the assignment of groupings
and the management of the order of the listings within the groupings.

To change a listing's grouping from the Grouping and Ordering page, simply select the
new grouping value from the Group drop-down list. This will move the listing under the new
grouping.

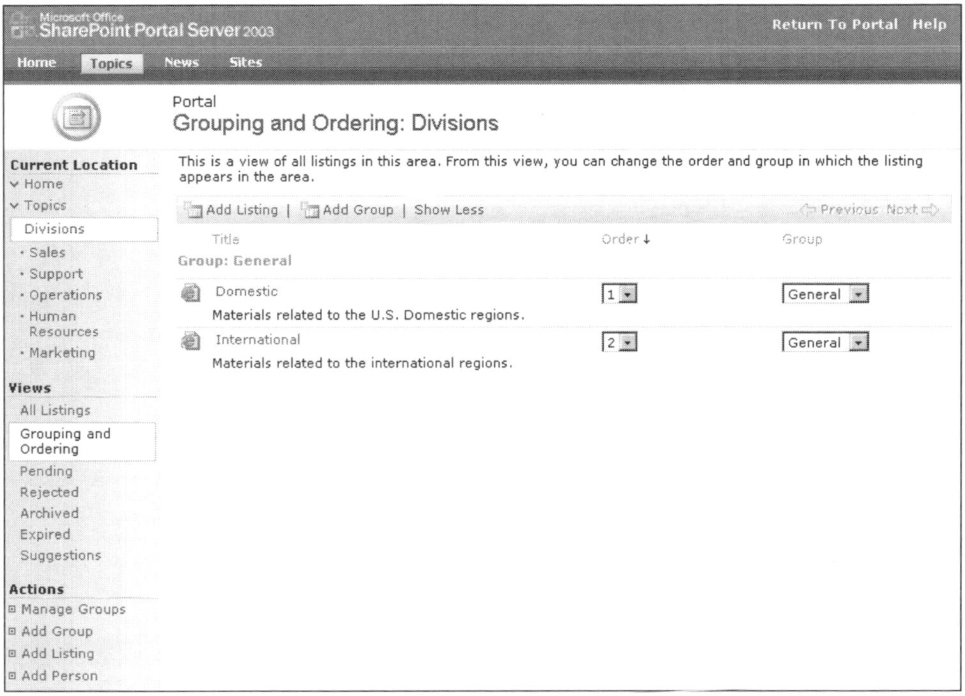

Figure 2-6. *Grouping and Ordering page*

Within each grouping, the default listing order is dependent on the area's listing order setting. We discussed this setting in the "Editing Properties of an Area" section earlier. If the area is configured for listings to be manually ordered, which is the default setting for an area, the listings will be listed in the order that they were created. If the area is configured for listings to be sorted alphabetically, then the listings will be displayed in alphabetical order. To change the order of listings within the groupings on the Grouping and Ordering page, simply select the new ordering value from the Order drop-down list for the listing. This will move the listing to the new ordered location within the grouping.

■**Note** Content Managers, Web Designers, and Administrators have the ability to manage grouping and ordering by default. While Contributors do have the ability to view the Grouping and Ordering page, they will not be able to change these values.

Adding New Groupings

New groupings can be added by performing the following steps:

1. On the Grouping and Ordering page, click the Add Group option.

2. On the Create Group page, enter the title for the new group and click the OK button.

The group is added to the Groupings list, and you are returned to the Grouping and Ordering page.

Editing Existing Groupings

Existing groups are edited through the Change Group Order page. To edit an existing grouping:

1. On the Grouping and Ordering page, click the Manage Groups link in the Actions list.

2. On the Change Group Order page, the available groups are listed in the order that they are displayed in the area. To change the order of the groups, you can update the Position from Top value. When this value is changed, the groups are reordered to reflect the change that was made.

3. To edit the group name, hover over the group name you wish to change and click the down arrow to display the Grouping Management options as shown in Figure 2-7.

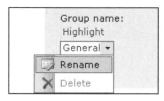

Figure 2-7. *Grouping Management options*

4. Click the Rename option from the Grouping Management options drop-down list.

5. On the Rename Group page, update the title for the group and click the OK button.

The group name will be updated, and you are returned to the Change Group Order page.

Deleting Existing Groupings

To delete a grouping:

1. On the Grouping and Ordering page, click the Manage Groups link in the Actions list.

2. On the Change Group Order page, hover over the group name you wish to delete and click the down arrow to display the Grouping Management options as shown in Figure 2-7.

3. Click the Delete option from the Grouping Management options drop-down list. The Delete option will only be available for groupings that were created by users. The default groupings created for the list cannot be deleted. They can only be renamed.

4. Confirm the deletion of the group by clicking the OK button on the displayed message box.

The group will be deleted and the Change Group Order page is refreshed to reflect the change. It is important to note that the default groupings for the listings (Highlighted, General, and Expert) cannot be deleted. These items can only be renamed. Only additional groups that are added can be deleted.

Special Areas

There are four areas that are automatically created as part of a SharePoint portal. Two of these areas are provided as starting points for creating a portal, while the other two provide specific capabilities for the portal. These four areas are the Home area, Topics area, News area, and Sites area. We will discuss the purpose for each of these areas and the unique capabilities they provide. This discussion will be based on the default layout of these areas. If a portal administrator has made any major alterations to these areas, the information provided here may differ slightly from your portal. However, in most cases, even when these areas have been updated, they will still contain the capabilities and attributes listed in this section.

Home Area

The Home area is the home page of the portal. This area is designed to be the primary entry point or gateway into the portal. When a portal is created, the home area contains News Listings, Events, and Links for You web parts. News Listings presents all current news available in the News area. (We will discuss the News area later in this section.) The Events list allows you to make key company event information available to portal users. This may include seminars being hosted, company holidays, and any other noteworthy events. We will discuss Event lists in more detail in Chapter 5. Links for You presents all content elements that have been targeted to you. Content in portal areas and WSS sites can be targeted to portal audiences. We discussed targeting listings to audiences earlier in this chapter and will discuss targeting other types of content to users in subsequent chapters. With the inclusion of these two web parts, the home page becomes the first stop to learn about current news and events related to the company and to get to information that has been identified as being important for you. Figure 2-8 shows a standard SharePoint portal home page.

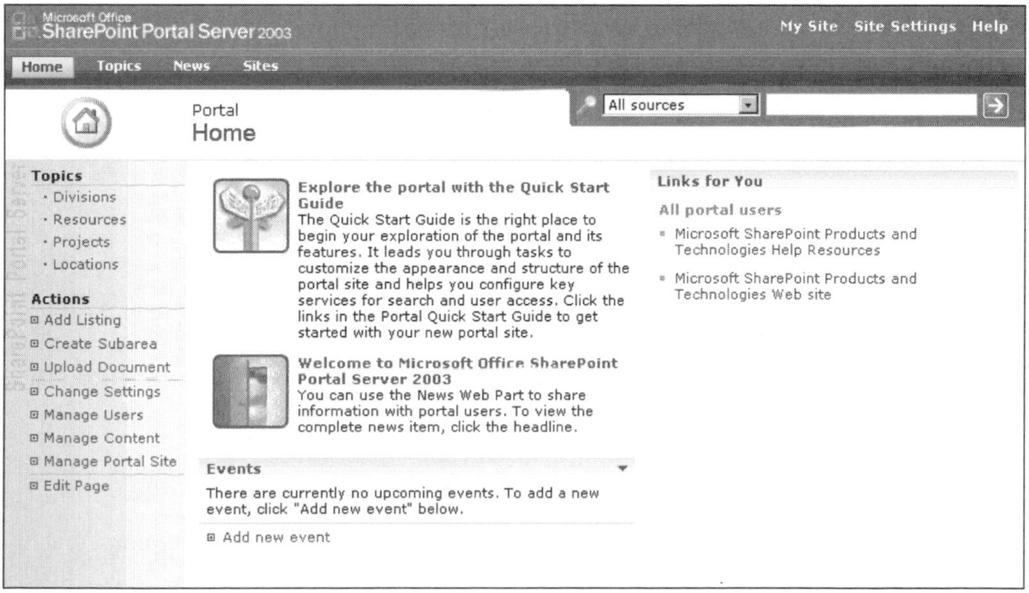

Figure 2-8. *Home page*

The Home area can be updated in the same way as any other area in the portal. Given this, portal administrators can change the web parts that are available and update the home page to include the information that provides the most value. We will discuss updating portal pages and managing web parts in Chapter 7.

One unique characteristic to be aware of on the Home area is that the Current Area Navigation works slightly differently. In all other areas, the Current Area Navigation shows the current area's hierarchy. On the Home area, the Current Area Navigation displays the subareas contained in the Topics area of the portal. This is done because the Topics area is designed to contain a topical organization of enterprise information. However, if the Topics area is deleted from the portal or hidden from the portal navigation, the Current Area Navigation will revert back to listing the subareas of the Home area.

Topics Area

The Topics area is designed to be the starting point for creating and organizing information by subject area. It is designed to provide an overview of the structure of the portal site and allow for easy browsing through materials managed by the portal. This is done through the use of the Browse by Topic web part listed in the Topics area. The Browse by Topic web part lists the map of the areas contained within the Topics area. It does this by listing all subareas under the current area with all of the subareas' children as well. Figure 2-9 shows the organization of the Topics area.

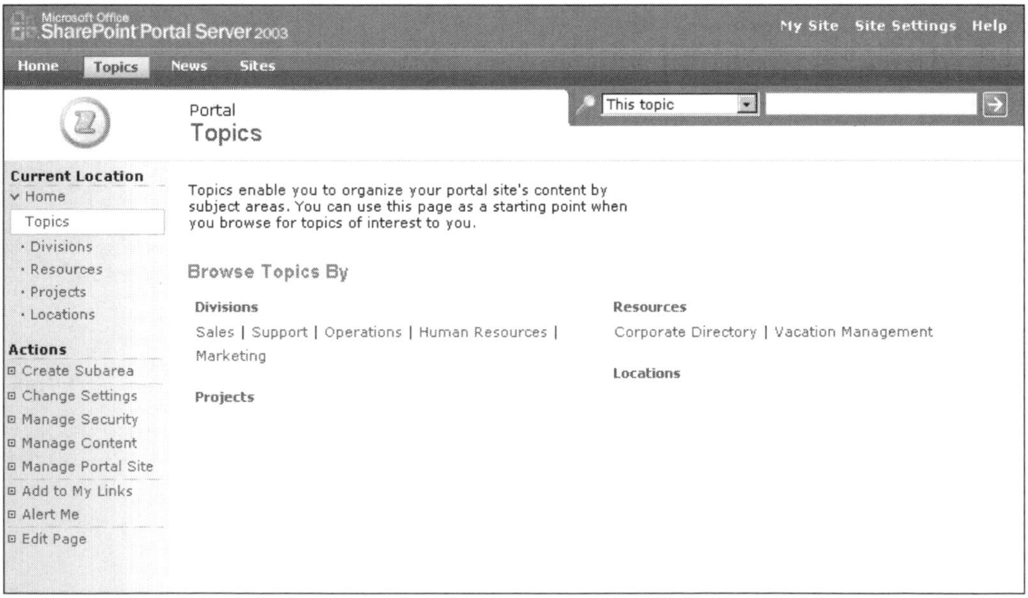

Figure 2-9. *Topics area*

As with the Home area, a portal manager responsible for the Topics area can change its layout and remove the Browse by Topic web part, but by default, this area provides a map of topic areas available to users within the portal.

News Area

The News area is provided as a location where news information can be disseminated to the organization. News items are very similar to listings in that they can reference existing content in the enterprise or can contain content created in the News area for the sole purpose of being listed as news.

By default, news items are presented on the portal home page through the News Listings web part, but the News Listings web part can be added to any area, making the portal news available in that area. News items are managed through the News area in the same way that listings are managed in any other portal area. If news needs to be broken down into subgroupings, subareas can be created under the News area. By default, Company News, Press Announcements, and External News subareas are available under the News area. The News area contains the News Areas web part, which lists news elements located within the subareas under the News area. Figure 2-10 shows the organization of the News area.

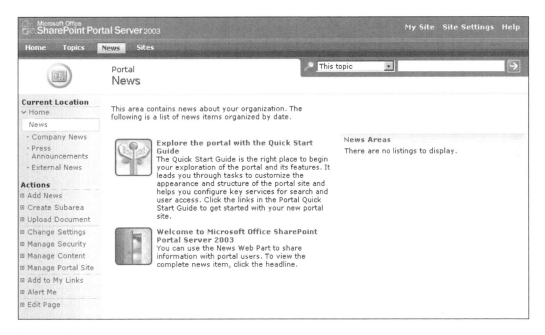

Figure 2-10. *News area*

Adding News Items

To add a news item to the News area:

1. Navigate to the News area by clicking News in the Area Listings Bar.

2. From the Actions list in the area, click the Add News link.

3. On the Add News page:

   a. Enter the title of the news item. This is the name by which the news item will be displayed in the portal area. You can also add a description, which if entered is displayed directly beneath the title in the portal area.

b. Enter the content for the news item. News item content is either in the form of a reference to a web-based or network file or as text entered for use as the news item content. To reference existing materials, select the Link to Existing Content option and enter the full web address or UNC path to the desired content. To create a listing by entering text, select the Add News Listing by Entering Text option and click the Open Text Editor button. The text editor is presented in which you can enter the content for the news item. Once the information is entered, click the OK button to return to the Add News page.

c. Enter date information for the news item. A start date for when the news item should be available to users is needed. This date defaults to the current date and can be changed. An expiration date for the news item can also be added. The expiration date when entered determines when the news item should no longer be available.

d. Select a group for the news item from the Group drop-down list. Groups are used to organize news items.

e. Optionally, you can enter the path to an image file. For news items, using the Add News Listing by Entering Text option, this graphic is displayed at the top of news content when it is viewed.

f. Select the location for the news item. By default, the news item will be placed in the News area. This should typically not be changed. If the news item is placed in an area other than the News area or an area located under the News area, it will be added as a normal portal listing. The news item location information is updated by clicking the Change Location link and then selecting all of the areas in which the news item should exist. News items can be placed in multiple locations. Once the news item locations are selected, click the OK button to close the Change Location window and return to the Add News page.

g. Optionally, you can select audiences for the news item. By selecting audiences, you target items to a specific group of people. While audiences do not determine what users have the right to access the news (access is determined by the area security), they do identify the individuals for which the item is important. When audiences are selected, the news item will appear in the targeted web parts and in the Targeted links section of My Site for users who are members of the audience. Defining audiences is a way to highlight or emphasize information for select portal users.

4. Once the news item information has been entered, click the OK button.

The news item is saved, and you are returned to the News area. The news item will be displayed in the news list.

Editing News Items

To edit existing news items:

1. Navigate to the News area by clicking News in the Area Listings Bar.

2. From the Actions list in the area, click the Edit Page link. The Edit Page link activates the management options for the area and any content displayed in the content area.

3. Hover over the news item you want to update and click the down arrow to display the News Management options as shown in Figure 2-11.

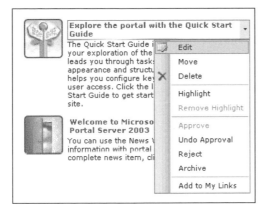

Figure 2-11. *News Management options*

4. Click the Edit option from the News Management options drop-down list.

5. On the Change Settings page, make the necessary updates to the news item. The Change Settings page is divided into four tabs organizing the news item attributes. The information that can be changed includes the following:

    a. On the General tab, you can update general news item information. The title, description, content, and location information entered during the creation of the news item can be updated. However, changing the location of the news item to an area other than the News area or a subarea under the News area will result in the news item becoming a listing within that area. When the news item references external content, a list of related items is also presented. This is a list of other news items and listings in the portal that reference the same document. This related-items list can be used to easily locate other listings and news that may need to be updated.

    b. On the Publishing tab, you can update publishing start and expiration dates and approval status information. Publishing dates are used to determine when the news item should be available to users and includes the dates entered when the news item was created. The approval status is used to identify whether the news item is approved for viewing. News items will not be available for portal users if they are not in an approved status. When the News area is configured so that approvals are not required, all news items default to an approved status. If the news area is configured so that news item approvals are required, the news listings will be given a Pending status when they are created and must be approved before they are available for use. News item statuses can be Pending (waiting for approval), Approved (available for access), Rejected (not to be displayed), and Archive (flagged for later archival).

    c. On the Display tab, you can change the group information and audience listings that were set when the news item was created. You can also update image information entered when the item was created and specify an icon image. The icon image is displayed next to links for the news item when the news item is listed on the News or Home areas.

    d. On the Search tab, you can specify whether the news item should appear in search results. By default, when a news item is created, this option is set to yes.

6. Once all changes have been made to the news item, click the OK button.

The changes to the news item are saved, and you are returned to the News area.

Changing the approval status information and the ability to move the news item to another area are options that are also made available directly through the News Management options drop-down list shown in Figure 2-11. To move a news item to a different location:

1. Navigate to the News area by clicking News in the Area Listings Bar.

2. From the Actions list in the area, click the Edit Page link. The Edit Page link activates the management options for the area and any content displayed in the content area.

3. Hover over the news item you want to move and click the down arrow to display the News Management options as shown in Figure 2-11.

4. Click the Move option from the News Management options drop-down list.

5. On the Move Listing page, click the Change Location option and select the new location for the news item. Then click the OK button to save the changes.

The news item is moved to the new location, and you are returned to the News area. If the news item is moved to an area other than the News area or a subarea under the News area, it is treated as a normal portal listing.

To change the approval status of a news item from the News Management options drop-down list, follow these steps:

1. Navigate to the News area by clicking News in the Area Listings Bar.

2. From the Actions list in the News area, click the Edit Page link.

3. Hover over the news item you want to change the status of and click the down arrow to display the News Management options as shown in Figure 2-11.

4. Click the desired approval status from the News Management options drop-down list. The options that are available include Approved, Undo Approval, Reject, and Archive. The option representing the current approval status of the news item will be disabled in the drop-down list.

The news item approval status is updated, and the area is refreshed to reflect the change.

■Note News items, like listings, in anything other than an approved status are not visible in the news list when viewing the page. In order to make these items visible, you must click the Edit Page link in the Actions section. This will make unapproved news items available for management.

Deleting News Items

To delete an existing news item:

1. Navigate to the News area by clicking News in the Area Listings Bar.

2. From the Actions list in the News area, click the Edit Page link. The Edit Page link activates the management options for the area and any content displayed in the content area.

3. Hover over the news item you want to delete and click the down arrow to display the News Management options as shown in Figure 2-11.

4. Click the Delete option in the News Management options drop-down list.

5. Confirm the deletion of the news item by clicking the OK button on the displayed message box.

The news item is deleted and the News area is refreshed to reflect the change.

Sites Area

The Sites area provides a consolidated list of all WSS and Internet/intranet sites associated with the portal. We call this list of sites the *site listing*. The Sites area is used to manage and organize site listings. We will discuss creating and managing WSS sites in Chapter 3.

By default, the Sites area provides several views of site listings. These views allow you to search for sites, browse through sites based on site attributes, browse through sites identified as spotlight sites, and browse through those that were most recently added. Figure 2-12 shows the default layout of the Sites area.

Figure 2-12. *Sites area*

Sites are listed in the site directory based on site listings. Site listings are references to web sites (intranet/Internet/WSS) that define the details about how and where a site should be referenced within a SharePoint portal. When WSS sites are created from within the Sites area, a listing is automatically created for the site. However, additional site listings can be added, and existing site listings can be edited or deleted through tools available in the Sites area.

The site management tools are made available in the Actions section of the Sites area page. The Actions section will contain several different management options in this area from those we discussed in standard areas. These additional options include the following:

- *Create Site*: Used to create new WSS sites and define how these sites should be listed in the portal. We will discuss creating WSS sites in Chapter 3.

- *Add Link to Site*: Used to create new portal site listings that point to existing WSS or web sites.

- *Manage Sites*: Allows you to manage existing site listings.

- *Customize List*: Allows you to change the properties of the Site Listings list. The Site Listings list is a custom SharePoint Portal list that can be updated to meet your organization's specific needs. This link allows you to access the management options for this SharePoint list.

- *Edit View*: Available when a view is selected from the Select View section. This option takes you to the Edit View page, where you can customize the selected view of the site listings. We will discuss customizing views in Chapter 4.

Along with the site management options, the Sites area also includes resources that allow you to easily organize and find sites. This area includes five tools that support this:

- *Search for Sites*: The Search for Sites section in the Sites area allows you to search for sites based on information within the site. To perform a site search, enter the search text into the Search for Sites text field and click the green arrow. This will perform a search for any sites containing the information you had entered. This search performs a standard portal search for sites so the results are presented in the standard portal search results page. We will discuss using the portal search and the portal search results page in the "Portal Search" section later in this chapter.

- *Browse Sites By*: The Browse Sites By section in the Sites area groups sites by their available attribute values. A site attribute is a defined characteristic by which sites can be categorized. By default, sites have division and region attributes that can be associated to them. This allows you to select division and region values for each site listing. The site listings will then be grouped based on the values selected. While division and region are provided by default, portal administrators can add new attributes for use in categorizing site listings. Using the Browse Sites By tools, you can click any of the listed site attribute values to view a list of sites grouped under the attribute value. Site attributes are set when the site listing is created. These attribute values can later be updated by editing the site listing. We will discuss editing site listings later in this chapter.

- *Spotlight Sites*: The Spotlight Sites section lists sites that have been flagged as spotlight sites. Flagging a site as a spotlight is done to make certain sites stand out. A site might be listed in the spotlight section if it contains some content or applications needed by a majority of portal users, if the site contains some new capabilities of note, or for any other reason that you decide a site should be listed as a spotlight site. It is important to keep the list of spotlight sites small so that the list only includes several sites of note. The spotlight attribute is set when the site listing is created. The spotlight attribute can also be changed by editing existing site listings. We will discuss creating and editing site listings later in this section.

- *Newest Sites*: The Newest Sites list in the Sites page lists the five most recently created sites. These sites are grouped by the time period in which they were added, including Today, Yesterday, This Week, This Month, and Earlier. This provides an easy way to find out what new resources are being made available to users through SharePoint.

- *Sites I Have Created*: The Sites I Have Created list in the Sites page lists all of the sites that you, the logged-on user, have created. These sites are grouped by their approval status and ordered based on when they were created, with the most recently create sites at the top. These tools allow you to easily navigate to sites that you have created. It can also be used to review the current approval status of the site you have created to determine whether it is available for use by portal users. We will discuss site approvals in more detail in Chapter 3.

Site Listings

Site listings are the references to WSS sites and web sites that are listed in the Sites area. These listings allow SharePoint to track information about sites and make these sites accessible through the portal. When new WSS sites are created using the Create Site option in the Sites area, a site listing is automatically created for this new site. Site listings can also be created for existing sites, and all existing site listings can be updated through the Sites area.

Creating a Site Listing for an Existing Site

To create a new listing for a WSS or web site that already exists:

1. Navigate to the Sites area by clicking Sites in the Area Listings Bar.

2. In the Sites area, click the Add Link to Site link from the Actions list.

3. On the Add Link to Site page, enter the information about the new site listing. This information will include the following:

   a. In the Site Link section, enter the title for the site listing. This is the name used within SharePoint to reference the site. The site can be a WSS site or any other available web site. You must also enter the URL to the site. The URL must include the full http:// path to the site. You can also enter a site description and owner information, and identify whether the site should appear in the Spotlight list. Site attribute values are also set in this section. As we discussed earlier, by default there are two site attributes: Division and Region. However, if others have been added, they will appear here as well. We will discuss adding and managing attributes in more detail later in this chapter.

   b. In the Search Results section, you identify whether the site and information on the site should be included when portal users perform searches.

c. In the Areas section, you specify the areas under which the listing will be displayed. You can select multiple areas under which the listing will be made available. Any listing created, regardless of the location selected, will appear in the Sites area. If you do not select an area under which the site should be listed, it will only appear in the Sites area.

4. Click the OK button once all the necessary information has been entered.

The new site listing is created, and you are returned to the Sites area.

Edit an Existing Site Listing

You can edit an existing site listing by following these steps:

1. Navigate to the Sites area by clicking Sites in the Area Listings Bar.

2. On the Sites page, click the Manage Sites link in the Actions section.

3. The existing site listings are displayed in the Content section of the Sites page. Hover over the site listing that you wish to edit and click the down arrow to display the Site Listing Management options as shown in Figure 2-13.

Figure 2-13. *Site Listing Management options*

4. Click the Edit Item option from the Site Listings Management options drop-down list.

5. On the Edit Site Listing page, the title, URL, description, owner, spotlight, and attribute values you had entered when the site listing was created are displayed. You can make any edits necessary to this information and then click the Save and Close option.

The site listing changes are saved, and you are returned to the Sites area.

Delete an Existing Site Listing

You can delete an existing site listing by following these steps:

1. Navigate to the Sites area by clicking Sites in the Area Listings Bar.

2. On the Sites page, click the Manage Sites link in the Actions section.

3. The existing site listings are displayed in the Content section of the Sites page. Hover over the site listing that you wish to delete and click the down arrow to display the Site Listings Management options as shown in Figure 2-13.

4. Click the Delete Item option from the Site Listings Management options drop-down list.

5. Confirm the deletion of the site listing by clicking the OK button on the displayed message box.

Note Deleting a site listing does not delete the actual site, only the selected reference to the site. We will discuss deleting WSS sites in Chapter 3.

Managing Attributes for Site Listings

As we previously discussed, site listing attributes are used to categorize site listings in the Sites area. By default, there are two attributes available for categorizing site listings: Division and Region. We set these attributes when the site listing is created or edited.

Editing Site Listing Attribute Values

You can edit the attribute values as follows:

1. Navigate to the Sites area by clicking Sites in the Area Listings Bar.

2. On the Sites page, click the Customize List link in the Actions section.

3. On the Customize Sites page in the Columns section, click the name of the attribute you wish to change.

4. On the Change Column page in the Optional Settings for Column section, edit the values listed in the Type Each Choice On a Separate Line text area. Once all of the options have been appropriately updated, click the OK button.

The site listing attribute values will be updated, and you will be returned to the Customize Sites page.

Note If you edit values that are currently in use in the site listings, you must update the listings that contain the edited values. For example, if we change the Finance option under Divisions to read Accounting, sites that had been assigned the value of Finance will still have a value of Finance. You must edit each listing having a division value of Finance and change this value to Accounting.

Adding New Site Listing Attributes

As we previously discussed, you can add new attributes by which sites can be categorized. To add a new attribute:

1. Navigate to the Sites area by clicking Sites in the Area Listings Bar.

2. On the Sites page, click the Customize List link in the Actions section.

3. On the Customize Sites page in the Columns section, click the Add a New Column link.

4. On the Add Column page, enter the information for the new site listing:

    a. In the Name and Type section, enter the name and type information for the attribute. The Name option specifies the name that will be displayed for the attribute. The Type option indicates the type of attribute being added. For site attributes, the type should typically be a Choice List. Select Choice List for this value.

    b. In the Optional Settings for Column section, replace the Enter Choice # text in the Type Each Choice on a Separate Line text area with the valid choices for the attribute values. In the Default Value text box, enter the choice text to use as a default value for the attribute. If no default value should be specified, then leave this text box empty.

5. Once you have entered all of the necessary information, click the OK button to save the information.

The new attribute information is saved, and you are returned to the Customize Sites page. The site listing is a special SharePoint list and can be managed in a similar way to other standard and custom lists in SharePoint. The Customize Sites page is the list customization page for the site listings list. For more information on managing lists and adding or editing list columns, see Chapter 4.

Portal Search

SharePoint Portal Server provides index and search capabilities that allow users to search for and find sites, documents, people, and other WSS site elements (such as lists or calendars) that are pertinent to their needs. Users can perform a simple search or an advanced search.

Performing a Simple Search

A simple search is performed by typing search words into the search box in the Search Tools section of any area and then clicking the green arrow. You can narrow the scope of content to search by changing the content source value. A *content source* is a defined set of information sources such as WSS sites, portal locations, file shares, or Exchange sources. By default, the simple search will search across all content sources. By selecting a specific content source, you can narrow the search to only look across a specific set of information.

When text is entered into the search box, the content sources are scanned for inclusion of the entered words. For example, if **vacation schedule** is entered into the search box, all selected content sources will be scanned for the word "vacation" and the word "schedule" anywhere in the content, and any results containing either word are returned. If you wish to search for a phrase instead of just words, place the phrase in quotes in the search box. Continuing our example, if **"vacation schedule"** is entered into the search box, content containing this phrase, not just the individual words, will be returned.

Performing an Advanced Search

Clicking the magnifying glass in the Search Tools section of any area takes you to the Advanced Search page. The portal advanced search allows you to find content using more refined search options and criteria. The advanced search allows for the selection of specific types of items (such as documents, lists, or people) as well as item properties containing specific values (such as the author being Tony Smith or title containing Yearly Budget). Figure 2-14 shows the Advanced Search page.

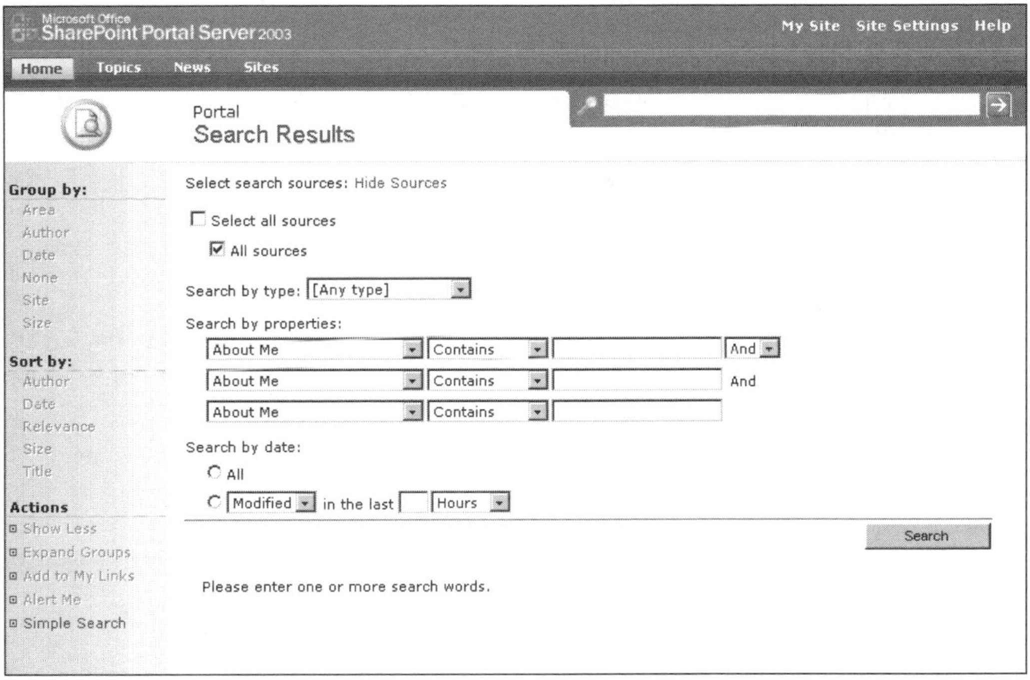

Figure 2-14. *Advanced Search screen*

To perform an advanced search:

1. Go to the Advanced Search screen by clicking the magnifying glass in the Search Tools section of any area.

2. Select the content sources across which to search. By default, All Sources will be selected. The All Sources option will cause the search to be performed across all available content sources.

3. Select the Search by Type value that identifies the type of items being searched for. You can search for area items, areas, document libraries, documents, lists, people, picture libraries, or pictures.

4. Enter the Search by Properties information. This identifies the attributes of the items to search across and the values to search for. When specifying search properties, you must select the type of constraint to use. For example, if you are looking for all materials authored by Tim, you would select the Author property and choose the Contains constraint, and then type **Tim** into the search box.

5. If you want to search by more than one constraint, select And or Or after the entered search constraint and then enter a new constraint in the next constraint line. The And option identifies that content should only be returned if both constraints are met, while the Or option specifies that content should be returned if either of the constraints is met.

6. If you wish to restrict your search based on when items were created or last modified, set the Search by Date values. This is done by selecting the radio button in front of the option and then selecting Modified to search for items last modified within the entered timeframe or selecting Created to search for items created within the entered timeframe. Then enter the timeframe value and unit.

7. Once all search requirements have been entered, click the Search button to perform the search.

The search results page will be presented containing references to all items satisfying the search criteria.

Working with Search Results

Whether you perform an advanced search or a simple search, the results that meet the search criteria are listed on the search results page. Search results can be organized into the following views:

- *By Site*: This is the default view. Results are grouped by the site in which the content resides and sorted by relevance.

- *Simple List*: Results are sorted by relevance.

- *By Author*: Results are grouped by author, with the authors sorted by relevance and the results within each author grouping sorted by relevance.

- *By Date*: Results are grouped by timeframes based on when they were last modified and then sorted by relevance.

- *By Area*: Results are grouped by area in which the content resides and sorted by relevance.

Search results are listed with the name of the item returned along with the author, date the item was last modified, beginning text from item, the link to the item, and the options for the item. The options for the item include the following:

- *Add to My Links*: Adds a link to the content element to your My Site. We will discuss My Links in the "My Site" section later in this chapter.

- *Alert Me*: Allows you to set up an alert for the item. Alerts are set up so that you are notified when changes to the item occur. We will discuss alerts in more detail in Chapter 7.

- *Item Details*: Shows additional details about the item. These additional details include the creation date, size, revision number, and content source.

To reduce the amount of information displayed for each search result, you can click the Show Less link from the Action list. This will collapse the search result elements so that only the name of the item, author, date last modified, and element options are displayed. To reset the search results list so that it shows the original amount of information, click the Show More link in the Actions list.

Changing Search Result Grouping

By default, when search results are grouped by site, author, date, or area, only the most relevant result within each grouping is displayed. The other results are collapsed or hidden on the page. To expand the results within a specific grouping, you can click the See More Results link at the bottom of the grouping. This will expand the group so that all search results contained within it are visible. To expand the search results for all of the groups listed on the search results page, you can click the Expand Groups link in the Actions section of the page. Search results can later be collapsed by either clicking the Hide Results link at the bottom of a grouped results list to collapse the specific group or clicking the Collapse Groups link from the Actions section of the page to collapse the results for all groups.

Change Search Results Sorting

While search results are sorted by relevance initially, you can specify different sort options. Selecting different sort options will not change the groupings; however, the groupings will be reordered into the new sort order and items within each of the groupings will also be ordered into the new sort order. To change the sorting of results on the search results page:

1. Click the Advanced Search Link from the Actions list in the search results page.

2. The advanced search elements will be added at the top of the screen, and the sorting options will be made available in the left-hand menu. The options available for sorting results are Author, Date, Relevance (default sorting value), Size, and Title.

3. Click the new Sort By value. This will sort the items by the value selected.

4. An up or down arrow will be listed next to the Sort By value selected. This arrow depicts whether the items are sorted in ascending (up arrow) or descending (down arrow) order. This order can be changed by clicking the Sort By value a second time. When this is done, the arrow direction will change, and the results will be placed in the reverse order.

My Site

My Site is your personal SharePoint web site. It provides a location where you can organize and manage your work. You can also use it as a location to share your own information and your own views of information with others.

To access your My Site, click the My Site link from the Portal Toolbar. The first time you access your My Site, it will be created and configured for you. My Site has two separate views, or presentations. The private view is designed to allow you access to your own My Site materials, and the public view is designed to allow other users to access your My Site information. Each view has different restrictions and provides different levels of access to the information in your My Site.

Private View

When you go to your own My Site, you are presented with the private view of your information. This view contains your My Site information and is meant to be organized in a way that makes it easy for you to leverage the information presented. Figure 2-15 shows a default My Site private view.

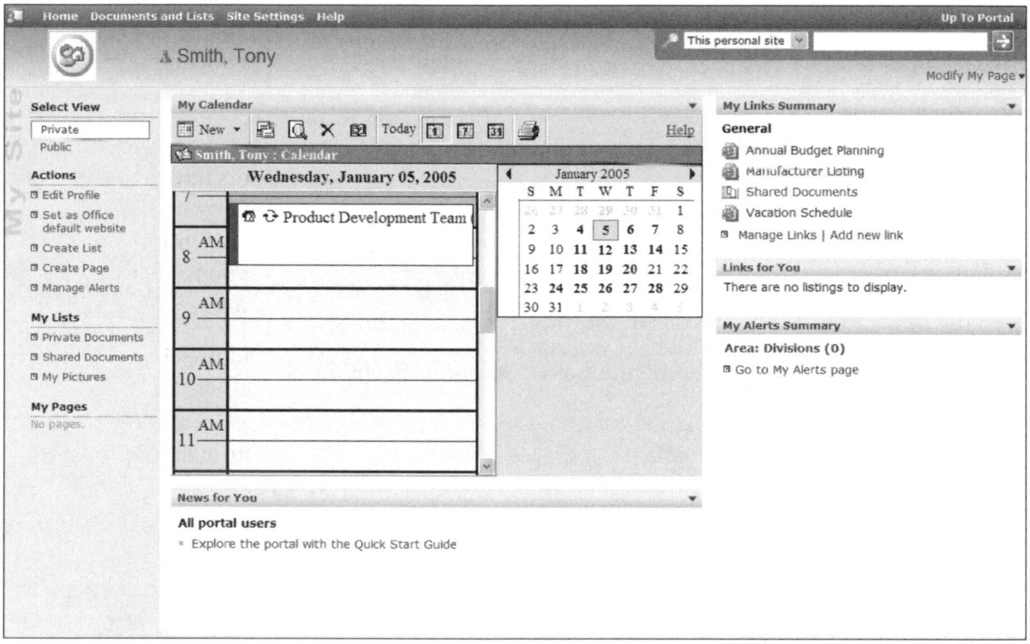

Figure 2-15. *My Site private view*

When you first access your My Site, the private view will include the following:

- *My Calendar*: Links to your Microsoft Outlook calendar allowing for events listed on your calendar to be viewable in your My Site.

- *News for You*: Lists current news items that have been targeted to audiences to which you are a member.

- *My Links Summary*: Lists areas and content in the portal that you have added to your My Links. Adding references to the My Links section is done by clicking the Add to My Links option in the Action section of any portal page or from the management options of a specific content item.

- *Links for You*: Lists content in the portal that has been targeted to audiences to which you are a member. We have discussed how audience assignments are set for areas and listings in this chapter. In the following chapters, we will describe how audiences are assigned to other types of portal content as well.

- *My Alerts Summary*: Lists all alerts that you have created against content in the portal. Alerts allow you to be notified when information in the portal or in a WSS site is changed. We will discuss alerts more in Chapter 7.

- *Private Documents*: Listed in the My Lists section of the left menu, Private Documents is a document library available only for you. This library can be used to store documents that no other users should have access to. You can think of this library similarly to your home or user drive on a network. It is a place you can save information where it will not be accessible by others. If absolutely necessary, permissions can be updated on this library to give other required users access to the documents contained within it. However, if other users need access to documents stored within your My Site, you would typically place these items in the Shared Documents library instead of giving other portal users access to your Private Documents library. We will discuss document libraries in more detail in Chapter 6.

- *Shared Documents*: Listed in the My Lists section of the left menu, Shared Documents is a document library available in your My Site that other portal users have access to. You have the ability to grant users any necessary level of permissions to this library. You can define those that just have read access as well as those that can contribute or manage information in this library. This library is designed as a place for you to share your information with others. We will discuss document libraries in more detail in Chapter 6.

- *My Pictures*: Listed in the My Lists section of the left menu, My Pictures is a picture library available for you to share pictures and photos with others. Like the Shared Documents library, the security on this library can be configured to allow any portal users to have the appropriate levels of permissions. We will discuss picture libraries in more detail in Chapter 6.

You can create other pages, document libraries, and lists; add web parts; and organize information in your My Site in the way that allows you to best use the information stored and referenced here. To create pages, document libraries, and lists, refer to Chapters 4 through 6.

In order to provide you with easy access to any items created in My Site, the search options provide an additional searching content source beyond those provided in the rest of the portal. The My Site search provides a This Personal Site content source. This is the default option for searching when in My Site, and it allows your search to be limited to content stored within your My Site. This content source is available when you search your own My Site, but it is not available when you are viewing other users' My Sites.

Through your My Site, you have the ability to edit your user profile. Your user profile contains information about you that SharePoint uses when referencing you in the portal. Much of the information in your profile is pulled from your organization's Active Directory and cannot be edited through SharePoint. The SharePoint technical administrator can determine the user profile details that can be edited by portal users. Individuals can then edit these profile details through their My Site. To edit profile information:

1. On your My Site private view page, click the Edit Profile link from the Actions list.

2. On the Edit My Profile page, update the profile items that must be changed. By default, you have the ability to update About Me (a brief description about you), Picture URL (reference to a picture of you), Home Phone, Cell Phone, Fax, and Assistant.

3. Once the information has been properly updated, click the Save and Close option.

The profile information is updated, and you are returned to your My Site.

Public View

Whenever your information is listed somewhere in the portal as a contact within an area, the owner or editor of documents or other content, or through a personal listing, your name is listed as a link that references your My Site. When other portal users go to your My Site, they are presented with your site's public view. The public view of your My Site is used to share information with others. This view allows you to organize portal content in the way that you want other portal users to find and view this information. Figure 2-16 shows a typical public view of a My Site.

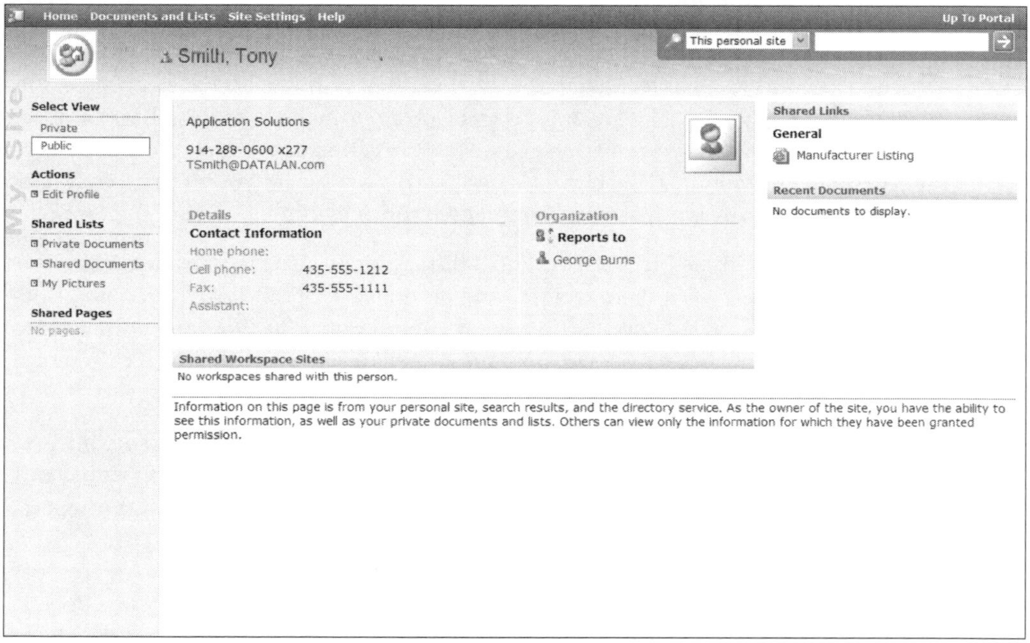

Figure 2-16. *My Site public view*

By default, the public view includes the following:

- *User Profiles*: Presents the profile information about the My Site owner. This includes the contact information about the user.

- *Shared Links*: Lists references to portal materials that the site owner has made available to others.

- *Recent Documents*: Lists documents in the portal and WSS that have been recently updated by the My Site owner.

As the owner of your My Site, you can create additional pages, document libraries, and lists; add additional web parts; and organize the information in the public view of your My Site to reflect the way you want others to access this information. Creating these other objects and customizing pages are discussed in Chapters 4 through 7.

CHAPTER 3

■ ■ ■

Using Windows SharePoint Services Sites

Windows SharePoint Services (WSS) provides the core document management, document collaboration, information storage, and application platform capabilities for a SharePoint environment. While the SharePoint Portal Server (SPS), through areas, alerts, and enterprise searching, provides the tools necessary to organize and locate information, Windows SharePoint Services sites are the foundation on which the information is stored and managed. WSS sites provide locations where groups of people can work together and share information. These sites can be used to collect team knowledge and enable individuals to effectively work with this knowledge.

As an application development platform, Windows SharePoint Services provides many of the building blocks needed to construct Information Worker applications. WSS also tightly integrates with the other Office System products, enabling WSS-based applications to be easily extended to include a wide range of capabilities.

Several different types of components can be used to store and manage information, facilitate collaboration, and provide workflow, reporting, and other application-centric capabilities through WSS sites. These components include the following:

- *Lists*: WSS includes a variety of standard lists and the ability to create custom lists. Both standard and custom lists can be modified to meet specific information management needs. We will discuss lists in detail in Chapters 4 and 5.

- *Libraries*: Document, picture, and form libraries are available in WSS to manage documents, images, and web forms. Attributes can be associated to files in libraries in order to facilitate organizing and retrieving these materials. We will discuss libraries in more detail in Chapter 6.

- *Discussion boards*: Discussion boards are forums used to discuss topics. Comments can be posted on a discussion board and then replies can be made to these postings. We will examine discussion boards in more detail in Chapter 5.

- *Surveys*: Surveys provide the ability for team members to be polled on specific subjects. You can specify a list of questions to be answered and then the results can be compiled. We will discuss surveys in Chapter 5.

- *Web parts*: A web part is an application component that can be displayed and managed through web part pages in SharePoint. WSS site pages are web part pages that can host web parts. Web parts are components that provide application functionality within SharePoint. We will discuss web parts in more detail in Chapter 7.

In this chapter, we will familiarize you with the general layout and structure of WSS sites. We will describe how to create and maintain sites and how to use the various features of these sites including templates, search tools, and site statistics. We will also discuss how to manage the various aspects of WSS sites including site security.

Sites

WSS sites provide the information management capabilities, collaboration services, and application platform that make up the foundation of a SharePoint environment. Sites include a variety of components and services to enable these capabilities. Three different categories of sites are available within WSS for managing and hosting information:

- *Team sites*: Designed to facilitate team collaboration. These sites provide the capabilities necessary to allow groups of individuals to work together on projects and initiatives.

- *Document workspaces*: Used to facilitate the creation of documents. These sites include the capabilities needed to allow multiple people to collaborate around the development and management of materials.

- *Meeting workspaces*: Used to manage meetings. These sites include the capabilities necessary to help plan meetings, share information between meeting attendees, organize materials presented during meetings, and track postmeeting action items.

SharePoint includes several site templates for use when creating any of these types of sites. A template is a starting point or default set of capabilities organized to meet a specific need. You can create a site based on a template in order to automatically provide a starting set of capabilities for the site. You can then, if necessary, customize the created site to better meet specific needs. The default set of site templates available for creating team sites, document workspaces, and meeting workspaces is designed to provide the most common functionality needed when sites are created.

As we mentioned previously, several types of components are available in WSS that provide the core capabilities of WSS sites. These components act as the building blocks for most WSS-based solutions. Table 3-1 lists the components available in the WSS team sites, document workspaces, and meeting workspaces.

Table 3-1. *Site Component Options*

	Team Site	Document Workspace	Meeting Workspace
Libraries			
Document library	✓	✓	✓
Form library	✓	✓	✓
Picture library	✓	✓	✓
Lists			
Agenda			✓
Announcements	✓	✓	✓
Contacts	✓	✓	✓
Decisions			✓
Issues	✓	✓	✓
Links	✓	✓	✓
Objectives			✓
Tasks	✓	✓	✓
Text box			✓
Things to bring			✓
Custom lists	✓	✓	✓
Discussion Boards			
Discussion board	✓	✓	✓
Surveys			
Survey	✓	✓	✓
Web Pages			
Basic page	✓	✓	
Web part page	✓	✓	✓
Sites and workspaces	✓	✓	✓

Configuring and using each of these components will be discussed in subsequent chapters.

Site Layouts

In order to help you better understand the three types of WSS sites, we will discuss their layouts and structure. We will also discuss the standard site templates that are available when creating these sites and the capabilities in these templates. This will give you the information you need to determine the sites to use depending on the situation. It will also help you decide which site templates to choose when creating a new site.

When we discuss the site types and the associated site templates, we can break our discussion into two parts. In the first, we will discuss team sites and document workspaces. We can group these two types of WSS sites together because the layout and capabilities provided by both are very similar. In the second part of our discussion, we will explore meeting workspaces. Meeting workspaces need to be discussed separately because their structures and capabilities are significantly different from those provided in team sites and document workspaces.

Team Sites and Document Workspaces

Team sites and document workspaces are very similar in form and function. Both team sites and document workspaces are designed to allow groups of people to work together. Team sites support project-centric work in which people are working together on short-term, limited-duration projects or on long-standing, ongoing initiatives. Due to this function, team sites are the most general-purpose sites available in WSS and can be used for a variety of information management and collaboration needs.

Document workspaces are designed to provide the tools necessary for people to work together when creating documents. These workspaces include resources to support the management of the document creation process and the materials that go into the development of these documents.

Team sites and document workspaces have the following structure:

- *Site Toolbar*: Located at the top of the site, the Site Toolbar contains site management links, help links, and navigation options. The list of links in this area will include the following:

  - *Home:* The Home link will take you to the site's home page, which is the initial screen presented when the site is first accessed. An example of a team site home page can be seen in Figure 3-3 later in this chapter.

  - *Documents and Lists*: The Documents and Lists link gives you access to the list of components that have been created within the site. This will include all libraries, lists, discussion boards, and surveys.

  - *Create*: The Create link gives you access to the component creation page. This page allows you to create any type of library, list, page, or site available for use in team sites or document workspaces.

- *Site Settings*: The Site Settings link gives you access to the administration options for the site. This is where you go to perform administrative tasks like updating the site name and description, creating templates, managing security, etc. The options available to you in this area are determined by your security rights within the site. We will discuss security rights in more detail in the "Managing Site Security" section later in this chapter.

- *Help*: The Help link provides online context-sensitive assistance for SharePoint capabilities.

- *Up To*: The Up To link is located at the far right of the Site Toolbar. This link provides access to the site's parent. For sites that are nested within other sites, called subsites, this link will take you up to the parent site. For top-level WSS sites, this link will take you to the SharePoint portal home page.

- *Search Tools*: Located in the upper right of the site just below the Site Toolbar, the Search Tools allow you to search for information located within the current site. Unlike the Search Tools in portal areas, the Search Tools in a WSS site will only search across content located within the current site. These searches do not span the entire site hierarchy or the entire portal as do the search capabilities provided in portal areas. The WSS search tools are also context sensitive, allowing them to be used to search across only a specific library or list as well. This is done by performing a search from within the library's or list's page. We will discuss these types of searches in the "WSS Site Search" section.

■**Note** There are third-party tools available that can replace the WSS site search capabilities with portal-like search tools. These tools allow for search options to work consistently within portal areas and WSS sites.

- *Quick Launch*: Located in the left-hand section of a site, the Quick Launch list provides easy access to components that are available within the site. Only components that have been configured to be displayed in the Quick Launch list will appear here.

- *Content*: Located to the right of Quick Launch list and below the Site Toolbar, the Content section is the main body of the site page. This section will contain the elements you want to make available through the site. This may include documents, lists, web parts, etc. For team sites, the content section is divided into left and right zones where content elements can be placed. This allows content on the site to be organized into a two-column structure. Figure 3-1 shows the Content section structure for a team site. For document workspaces, the content section is divided into a top zone, a left zone, and a right zone. This allows content in the top zone to span the entire content section, and then below this zone content can be organized into a two-column structure. Figure 3-2 shows the content section structure for a document workspace.

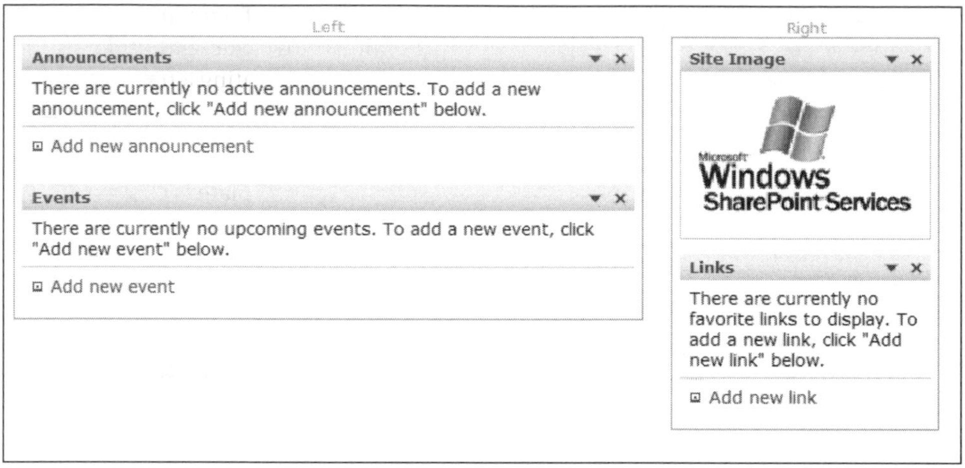

Figure 3-1. *Team site Content section*

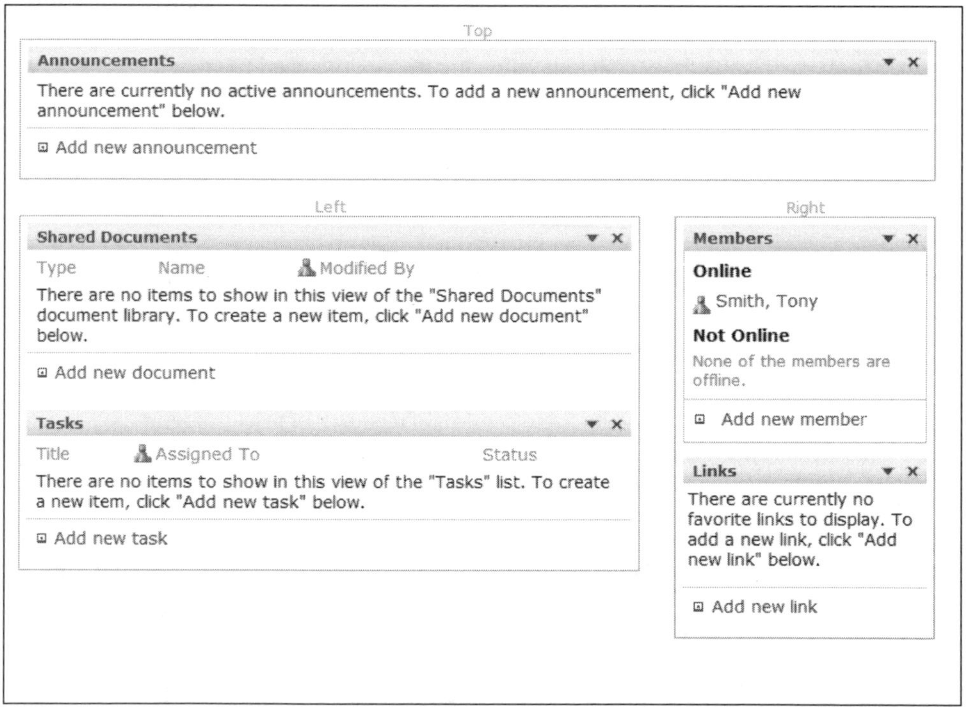

Figure 3-2. *Document workspace Content section*

The content that will be located in these types of sites will vary based on the template you select and the changes you make to the created site. Two default site templates are available for creating new team sites and one default site template for creating document workspaces.

Before we discuss creating sites, we need to show you the default set of templates that are available, the layouts of these templates, and the capabilities they provide so that you will be able to select the template that will best meet your needs when creating a new site.

Team Site Template

The first Team Site template available is called the Team Site. This template is designed to provide the most common set of capabilities used when creating a site that will be used to facilitate general project-type collaboration or information sharing. The site created when using this template is depicted in Figure 3-3.

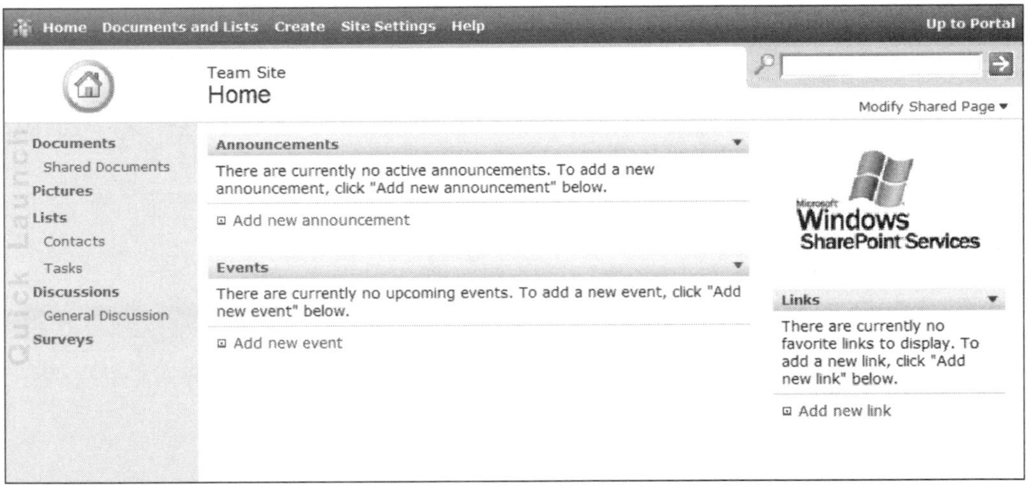

Figure 3-3. *Team site*

This template includes the components listed in Table 3-2.

Table 3-2. *Team Site Template Components*

Item	Type	In Quick Launch	In Content Area
Libraries and Lists			
Announcements	Announcements list	No	Yes (left zone)
Contacts	Contact list	Yes	No
Events	Events list	No	Yes (left zone)
General Discussion	Discussion board	Yes	No
Links	Link list	No	Yes (right zone)
Shared Documents	Document library	Yes	No
Tasks	Task list	Yes	No
Web Parts			
Site Image	Image web part	N/A	Yes (right zone)

Blank Site Template

The second Team Site template available is called Blank Site. This template is used to create a blank team site that only contains a Site Image web part. Figure 3-4 depicts a default blank site.

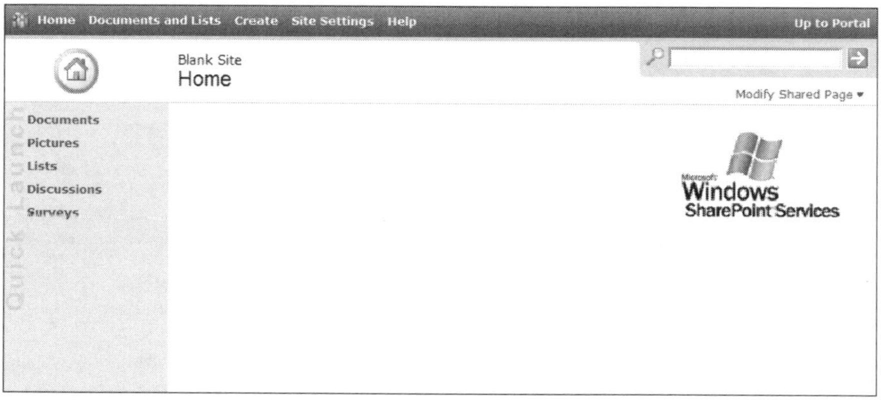

Figure 3-4. *Blank site*

A blank site is designed to provide you with an empty site that you can tailor to meet your specific needs. The blank site should be used when most of the items in the Team Site template are not applicable to your situation. This allows you to create a site to meet your needs without having to remove unnecessary components.

Document Workspace Template

There is only one default document workspace template, which appears in Figure 3-5.

This template provides the most common set of capabilities needed when creating a site to manage the collaborative effort around creating a document. Document workspaces created from the Document Workspace template include the components listed in Table 3-3.

Table 3-3. *Document Workspace Template Components*

Item	Type	In Quick Launch	In Content Area
Libraries and Lists			
Announcements	Announcements list	No	Yes (top zone)
Contacts	Contact list	Yes	No
Events	Events list	Yes	No
General Discussion	Discussion board	Yes	No
Links	Link list	No	Yes (right zone)
Shared Documents	Document library	No	Yes (left zone)
Tasks	Task list	No	Yes (left zone)
Web Parts			
Members	Web part	N/A	Yes (right zone)

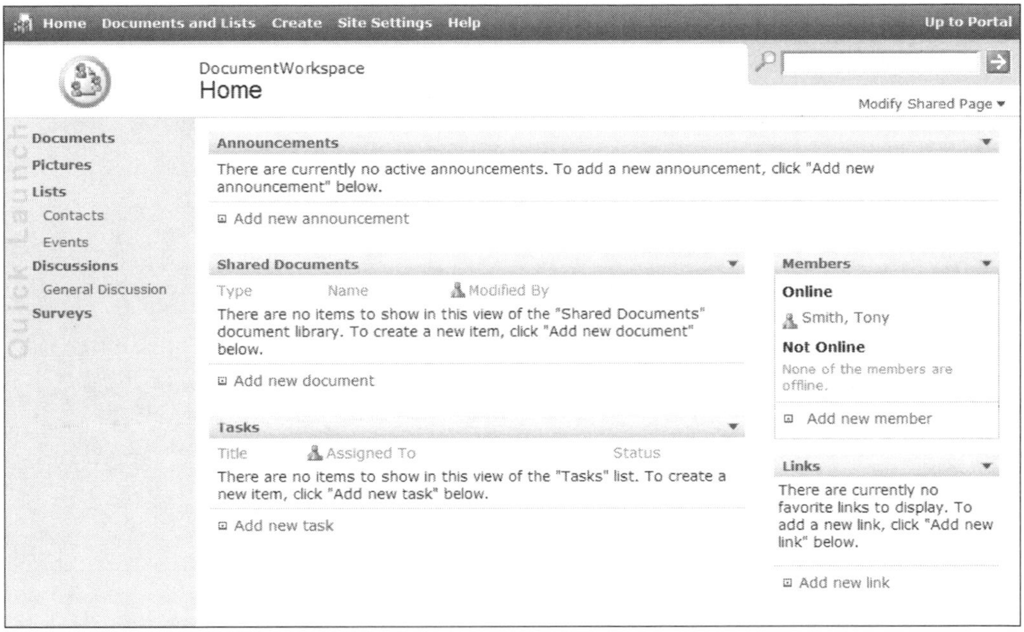

Figure 3-5. *Document workpace*

■**Note** When creating sites from any template, it is always a good practice to remove any components from the site that you do not want others to use. This will not only eliminate the possibility of people using components that are not intended for use, but also help keep the site layout and structure as organized and easy to use as possible.

Meeting Workspaces

Meeting workspaces are WSS sites designed to organize meeting materials and facilitate meeting planning and follow-up. Prior to a meeting, a meeting workspace can be used to collect and organize needed documents, create the agenda, and track and manage attendee lists and responses. During a meeting, the site can be used to gain access to materials being presented, track identified action items, and log decisions made. Finally, after a meeting the site can be used to publish meeting minutes, post any follow-up materials, and track the progress made against assigned action items.

Meeting workspaces have very different layouts from team sites and document workspaces. Figure 3-6 depicts the default layout of a meeting workspace.

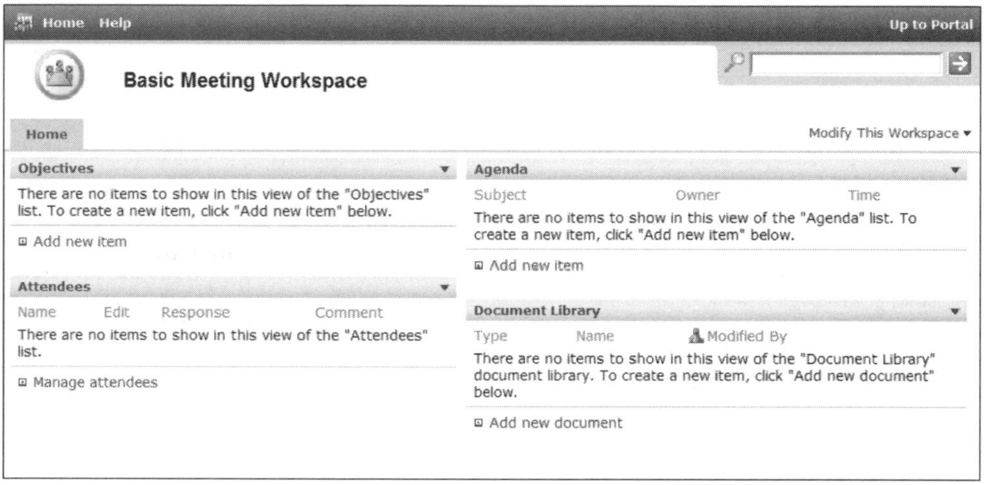

Figure 3-6. *Basic meeting workspace*

Meeting workspaces have the following structure:

- *Site Toolbar*: Located at the top of the workspace, the Site Toolbar contains help links and navigation options. The list of links in this section includes the following:

  - *Home*: The Home link will take you to the workspace's home page, which is the initial screen presented when the workspace is first accessed. An example of a meeting workspace home page is displayed in Figure 3-6.

  - *Help*: The Help link provides online context-sensitive assistance for SharePoint capabilities.

  - *Up To*: The Up To link is located at the far right of the Site Toolbar. This link provides access to the site's parent. For sites that are nested within other sites, or subsites, this link will take you to the parent site. For top-level sites, this link will take you to the SharePoint portal home page.

- *Search Tools*: Located in the upper right of the site just below the Site Toolbar, the Search Tools allow you to search for information located within the current meeting workspace. Unlike the Search Tools in portal areas, the Search Tools in a site will only search across content located within the current site. These searches do not span the entire site hierarchy or the entire portal like those available in portal areas.

■**Note** As with team sites and document workspaces, third-party tools are available for meeting work-spaces that can replace the site search capabilities with portal-like search tools. These tools allow for the search capabilities to work consistently in portal areas and WSS sites.

- *Page List*: Located below the Site Toolbar and Search Tools, the Page List is a tab-like list of all pages available within the current site. The first page listed in the Page List is the home page, which references the default page of the site.

- *Content*: Located below the Page List, the Content section is the main body of the site page. This section contains the elements being made available through the site page. This may include documents, lists, web parts, etc. For meeting workspaces, the Content section is divided into a left zone, a center zone, and a right zone. This allows content to be organized into a one-, two-, or three-column structure. Figure 3-7 shows the Content section layout for a meeting workspace.

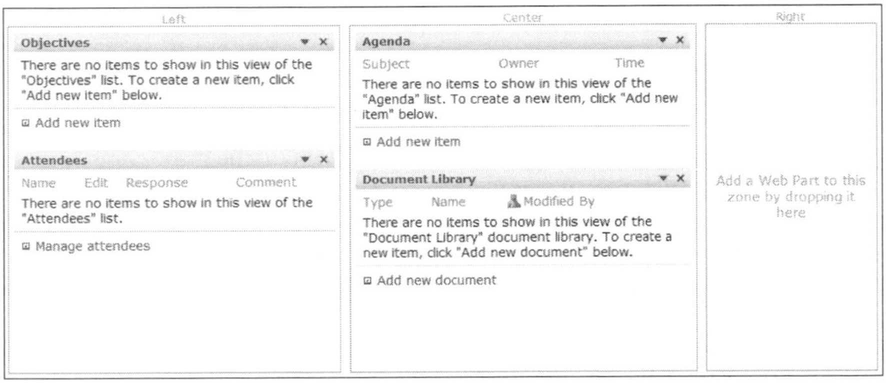

Figure 3-7. *Meeting workspace Content section*

There are five default templates for creating meeting workspaces. These templates are designed to provide the components typically used to support a variety of types of meetings. The sites created from these templates can then be tailored by adding and removing components, rearranging components, and adding or removing pages.

Basic Meeting Workspace Template

The Basic Meeting Workspace template is used to create general-use meeting workspaces. Sites created from this template contain the most commonly used resources for facilitating a meeting. The basic meeting workspace is the most general-purpose meeting site in WSS. Figure 3-6 depicts a workspace created from the Basic Meeting Workspace template. This template includes the components listed in Table 3-4.

Table 3-4. *Basic Meeting Workspace Template Components*

Item	Type	Page	Location on Page
Libraries and Lists			
Agenda	Agenda list	Home	Center zone
Attendees	Attendees list	Home	Left zone
Document Library	Document library	Home	Center zone
Objectives	Objectives list	Home	Left zone

Blank Meeting Workspace Template

The Blank Meeting Workspace template provides an empty meeting workspace site. Sites created using the Blank Meeting Workspace template will not contain any components. The Blank Meeting Workspace template is provided for when you need to create a new meeting workspace that is not similar to any of the available meeting workspace templates. This template allows you to add the components necessary to support your specific needs without having to remove unnecessary items.

Decision Meeting Workspace Template

The Decision Meeting Workspace template is provided to support meetings being held to make a set of decisions. Sites created from this template contain the most common resources necessary to support the decision-making process. The decisions made are then tracked within the site. Figure 3-8 depicts the default layout of a workspace created from the Decision Meeting Workspace template.

The default decision meeting workspace contains the components listed in Table 3-5.

Table 3-5. *Decision Meeting Workspace Template Components*

Item	Type	Page	Location on Page
Libraries and Lists			
Agenda	Agenda list	Home	Center zone
Attendees	Attendees list	Home	Left zone
Decisions	Decisions list	Home	Center zone
Document Library	Document library	Home	Center zone
Objectives	Objectives list	Home	Left zone
Tasks	Task list	Home	Center zone

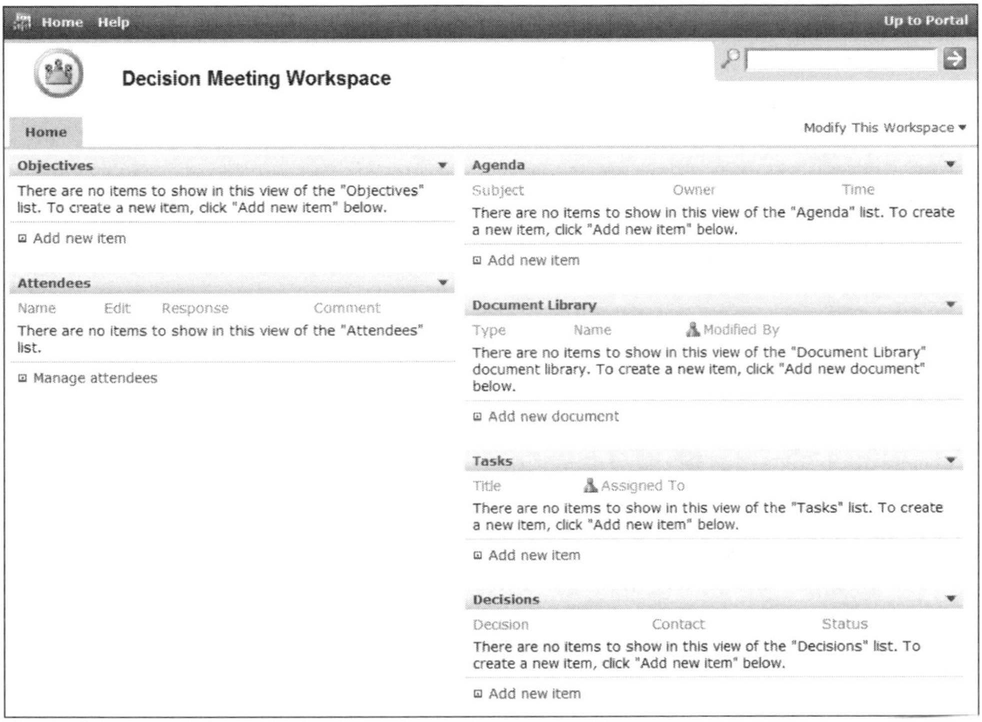

Figure 3-8. *Decision meeting workspace*

Social Meeting Workspace

The Social Meeting Workspace template provides the resources typically needed to facilitate meetings related to social gatherings. This might include anything from a company holiday party or picnic to a baby shower. Figure 3-9 depicts the default layout of a workspace created from the Social Meeting Workspace template.

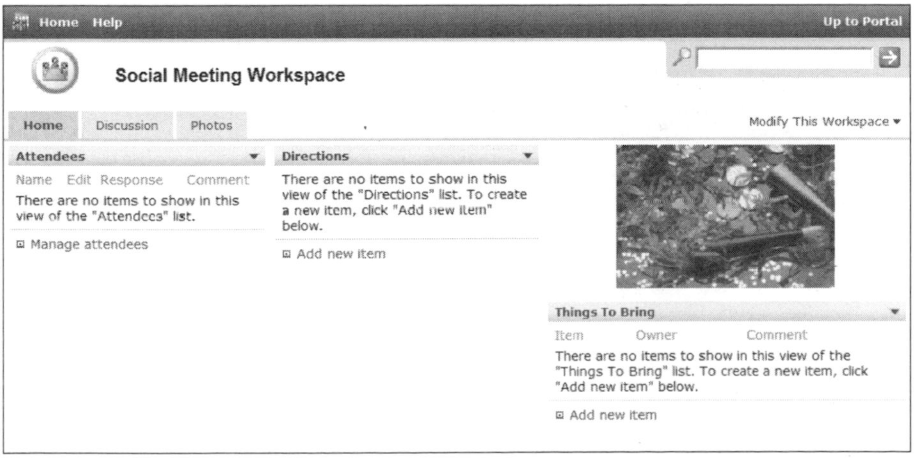

Figure 3-9. *Social meeting workspace*

The default social meeting workspace contains the components listed in Table 3-6.

Table 3-6. *Social Meeting Workspace Template Components*

Item	Type	Page	Location on Page
Libraries and Lists			
Attendees	Attendees list	Home	Left zone
Directions	Text Box list	Home	Center zone
Discussion Board	Discussion board	Discussion	Left zone
Picture Library	Picture library	Photos	Left zone
Things to Bring	Things to Bring list	Home	Right zone
Web Parts			
Image	Image web part	Home	Right zone

Multipage Meeting Workspace

The Multipage Meeting Workspace template is used as a starting point for creating meeting workspaces that will contain more than one page. While you can always add pages to a site created from any of the other meeting workspace templates, the Multipage Meeting Workspace template creates a site with two additional pages already included. The structure and default components available as part of the Multipage Meeting Workspace template are identical to those provided in the Basic Meeting Workspace template. The only difference in this template is the inclusion of the two additional, initially empty pages. Figure 3-10 depicts the default layout of a workspace created using the Multipage Meeting Workspace template.

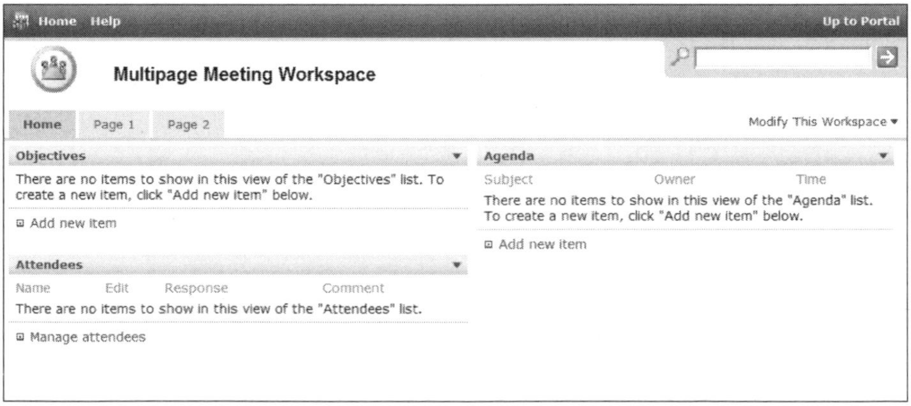

Figure 3-10. *Multipage meeting workspace*

The default multipage meeting workspace contains the components listed in Table 3-7.

Table 3-7. *Multipage Meeting Workspace Template Components*

Item	Type	Page	Location on Page
Libraries and Lists			
Agenda	Agenda list	Home	Center zone
Attendees	Attendees list	Home	Left zone
Objectives	Objectives list	Home	Left zone

Recurring Meeting Workspace

The Recurring Meeting Workspace template provides a meeting workspace that contains separate sites for the individual meetings held as part of a recurring meeting event. These workspaces are only available when meetings are created using the Events list (see Chapter 5) or through Microsoft Outlook 2003 as part of setting up a new recurring Outlook meeting. The recurring meeting workspace can be based on any of the meeting workspace templates we have already discussed or any custom meeting workspace templates that you create. When these workspaces are created, they have a left-hand bar similar to those on team sites and document workspaces. This left-hand bar lists the dates of each meeting included in the recurring meeting schedule. By clicking one of these listed dates, you can access the workspace for that date. Figure 3-11 depicts the default layout of the recurring meeting workspace. We will describe creating these workspaces in the "Creating Sites" section later in this chapter.

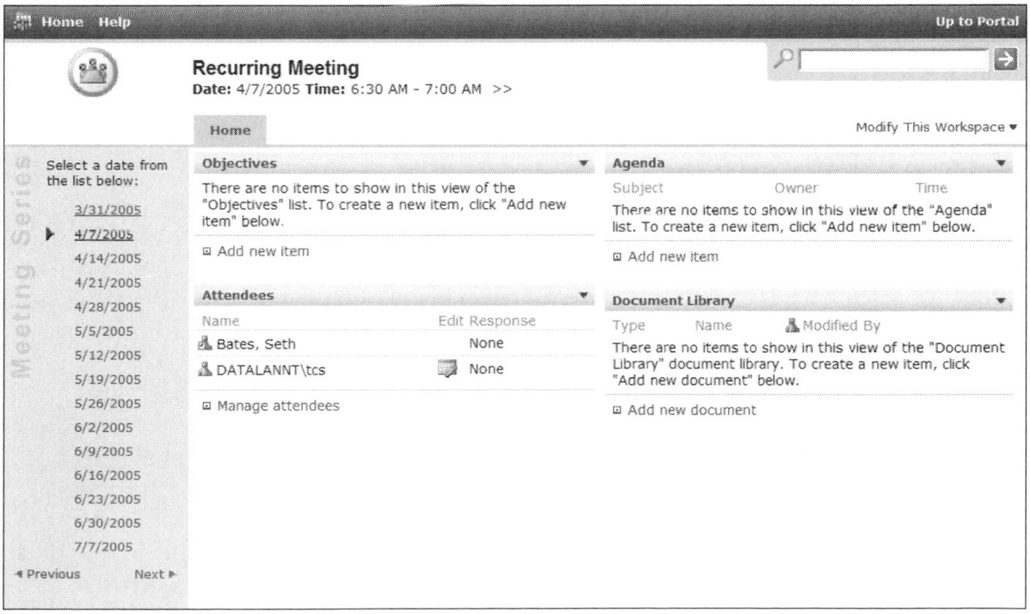

Figure 3-11. *Recurring meeting workspace*

All of the team site, document workspace, and meeting workspace templates provide starting-point structures for a variety of collaboration needs. You can tailor sites created from any of these templates to meet your specific needs. You can also create your own templates that can be used when creating new sites. We will discuss customizing sites in Chapter 7.

When creating a site, you should pick the template that will best meet your needs. For example, if you are creating a new site that will contain information about your company's lines of business, you may decide to use a Multipage Meeting Workspace template. This type of template would allow you to dedicate a tab to the materials for each line of business. This is just one example of how a meeting workspace could be used for something other than a meeting. All of the team site, document workspace, and meeting workspace templates have this potential. The key to selecting the right template is identifying the one with the layout and structure that best suits your specific needs.

Navigating Through WSS Sites

In Chapter 2 we discussed site listings, which enable portal areas to reference web resources. Site listings that reference WSS sites provide the navigational links between a SharePoint portal and WSS sites. Clicking these site listings in the portal areas will take you to the associated team site, document workspace, or meeting workspace.

Navigation within WSS sites varies based on the site type. Navigation within team sites and document workspaces works the same; however, navigating in meeting workspaces works very differently.

Navigating Through Team Sites and Document Workspaces

Team sites and document workspaces are very similar in layout and structure. The navigation between components within these types of sites and to subsites nested below these sites is handled in the same way.

From a team site or document workspace home page, you can navigate to components contained within the site in one of three ways. First, for any element listed in the Content area of the site, you can click the header of the item, such as clicking the Announcements header in a team site. This will take you to the selected item's detail page. The second method used to navigate to site items is to click the name of the item in the Quick Launch list. This will also take you to the selected item's detail page; however, this option is only available for items that have been configured to display in the Quick Launch list. The third method available for navigating to site elements is to click the Documents and Lists link in the Site Toolbar. This link takes to you the Documents and Lists page, which lists all libraries, lists, discussion boards, and surveys currently available in the site. You can then click the name of any of the listed items to view the detail page for that item. We will discuss working with each of the different types of components available in WSS sites in Chapters 4 through 7.

Additional site pages in a team site or document workspace are stored as documents in a document library. In order to navigate to additional site pages, you must navigate to the document library containing the pages and then click the page listed in the document library. An alternative method would be to place a document library view web part on the site home page. This will make the other site pages available on the site home page. We will discuss document libraries in more detail in Chapter 6. Given that additional site pages are handled in this way, they are not often used. Instead, content is more frequently broken out into a nested site hierarchy.

Subsites

It is very common for team sites and document workspaces to have additional team sites, document workspaces, or meeting workspaces nested within them. For example, a human resources site may have a subsite dedicated to providing HR benefit details. Another example would be a client site that contains individual project sites for the client. As we have mentioned previously, when sites are nested within other sites, they are called subsites. There are three main ways to navigate to subsites contained within a site, the first of which is as follows:

1. Navigate to the site containing the subsites.

2. Click the Documents and Lists link on the Site Toolbar.

3. On the Documents and Lists page, click the Sites, Document Workspaces, or Meeting Workspaces link in the left navigation bar.

4. On the Sites and Workspaces page, click All under Select a View to see all sites and workspaces located under the current site, and then click the name of the subsite you wish to view.

This will present the selected subsite's home page. The second way to navigate to a subsite is only available for individuals having access to the Site Settings pages. To navigate to subsites in this method:

1. Navigate to the site containing the subsites.

2. Click the Site Settings link on the Site Toolbar.

3. On the Site Settings page, click the Manage Sites and Workspaces link in the Administration section.

4. On the Manage Sites and Workspaces page, click the name of the subsite you wish to view.

This will present the selected subsite's home page. The third way to navigate to a subsite is through the use of a subsite viewer web part that would be placed in the Content section of the site. This is by far the more common method for providing subsite navigation capabilities within a site. However, no subsite viewer is provided in a default SharePoint deployment. A third-party subsite viewer web part would need to be installed. Many third-party components are available that provide this capability, several being freely distributed. A SharePoint technical administrator would need to install these for use in your WSS sites. You would then be able to add this web part to the content section of your site. We will discuss adding web parts to WSS site pages in Chapter 7.

Navigating Through Meeting Workspaces

The layout of meeting workspaces is different from the layout of team sites and document workspaces. Subsequently, navigating within meeting workspaces works differently as well. Quick Launch and the Documents and Lists options are not available in meeting workspaces, so the primary method for navigating between components in a meeting workspace is done by clicking the title of the component in the Content section of the workspace. Since almost all items making up a meeting workspace will reside on one of the workspace pages, this method works well.

When additional pages are available in meeting workspaces, these pages are referenced in the workspace's Page list. To navigate to these pages, simply click the page name in the Page list. Given that pages are handled in this manner, it is more common for additional pages to be used in meeting workspaces than in team sites or document workspaces.

Subsites

Meeting workspaces can also have subsites located underneath them. However, this typically does not occur as frequently as with team sites or document workspaces. Navigating to subsites in meeting workspaces is similar to navigating to them from team sites and document workspaces as we described previously. The main difference is that there is no Documents and Links option on the home page of a meeting workspace, so navigating to subsites through this link is not available. Given this, there are only two main ways to navigate to subsites within a meeting workspace. The first way is as follows:

1. Navigate to the meeting workspace containing the subsites to view.

2. From the site, click the Modify This Workspace link at the top right of the Content section and then select Site Settings from the Modify This Workspace menu, shown in Figure 3-12.

Figure 3-12. *Modify This Workspace menu*

3. On the Site Settings page, click the Manage Sites and Workspaces link in the Administration section.

4. On the Sites and Workspaces page, click the name of the subsite you wish to view. Figure 3-13 shows the Sites and Workspaces page.

This will present the selected subsite's home page.

The second way to navigate to a subsite is through the use of a subsite viewer web part that would be placed in the Content section of the meeting workspace. As with team sites and document workspaces, this is by far the most common method for providing subsite navigation capabilities. There are many third-party components available that provide this capability, several being freely distributed. A SharePoint technical administrator would need to install these and make them available for use in WSS sites. We will discuss adding web parts to WSS site pages in Chapter 7.

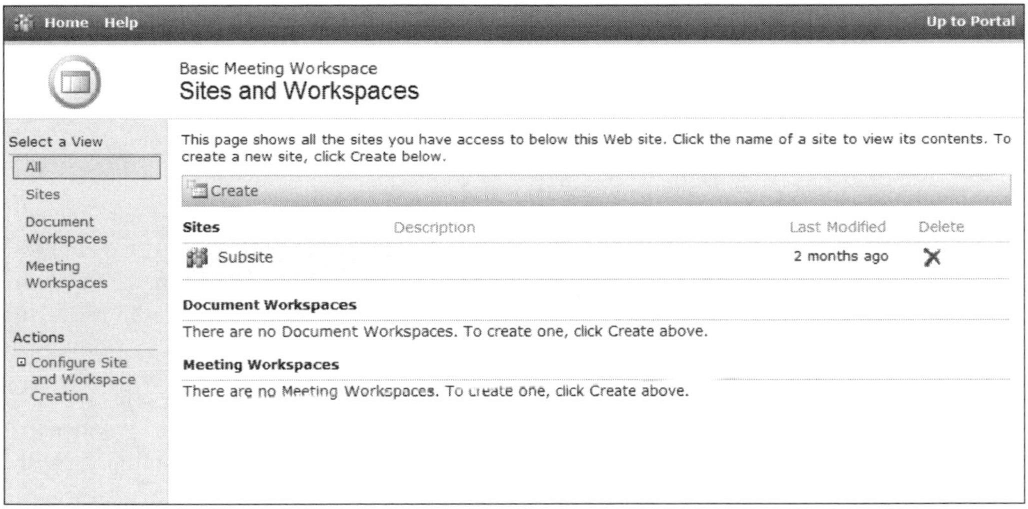

Figure 3-13. *Sites and Workspaces page*

Creating Sites

When we talk about creating and managing WSS sites, we need to break our discussion down into two topics: top-level sites and subsites. A top-level site is a WSS site created from within the portal. Its only parent locations are portal areas in which listings are available that point to the site. A subsite is a WSS site that is created within another WSS site. WSS sites can be nested to create any desired SharePoint structure.

■**Note** As we discussed in Chapter 1, we are assuming that you are using SharePoint Portal Server and Windows SharePoint Services together. If you had deployed only Windows SharePoint Services, then creating top-level sites is handled through the SharePoint Central Administration tools.

Creating Top-Level WSS Sites

One important decision to make when determining the layout of your SharePoint environment is the site structure. Determining this structure requires understanding how the portal will be used and requires planning to be done around the structure that will best support this use. As part of this planning, you need to consider the number of top-level WSS sites you will be creating. Each top-level WSS site has its own set of security rights, while subsites can inherit the rights of their parent site. When designing your SharePoint site structure, it is important to break top-level sites out logically, but it is equally important to keep the number of these sites manageable, since security must be administered for each.

You create top-level WSS sites the same way regardless of the type of WSS site you are creating. To create a top-level WSS site:

1. Navigate to the sites area in the portal by click the Sites link in the Area Listing Bar.

2. On the sites area, click the Create Site link in the Actions list.

3. On the New SharePoint Site page, follow these steps:

    a. In the Title and Description section, enter the title for the site. This is the name by which the site will be displayed in any site references including portal listings. You can also add a description that, if entered, is displayed directly beneath the title in the portal listings and at the top of the content section of the site.

    b. In the Web Site Address section, enter the URL name for the site. It is often good practice to make this the same as the site title. However, it is also good practice to not include any spaces in the URL, so if the site title is Business Planning, the URL name would be BusinessPlanning.

    c. In the Your E-mail Address section, your e-mail address should be automatically listed in the E-mail Address box. If it is not, you can type in your e-mail address. This e-mail address is used by SharePoint to send you information about the site. An example of this would be sending you notifications when users request access to the site.

    d. Once all the necessary information is entered, click the Create button.

4. On the Add Link to Site Page, follow these steps:

    a. In the Site Link section, you can specify whether the site should be listed in the site directory. This option is checked by default. The site title, URL name, and description will be listed in the Title, URL, and Description lines based on the information you entered into the New SharePoint Site page. It is good practice to not change these values. You can, however, specify optional site owner information to be associated with the site and then enter the values for any listed site attributes. As we discussed in Chapter 2, site attributes are used to help organize listings in portal areas. Finally, you can identify whether the site should be listed in the Spotlight Sites section of the sites area.

    b. In the Search Results section, you can identify whether the site and its content should be included in search results when searches are performed using the search options in portal areas. This is the default, so the site and its content are included in search results.

    c. In the Areas section, you can specify the portal areas where the site will be listed. You can select multiple areas. Areas are selected by clicking the Change Location link and then selecting all of the areas in which the site should be listed. Once all of the areas have been selected, click the OK button on the Change Location window to save the locations and return to the Add Link to Site page.

    d. Once all the necessary information has been entered on the Add Link to Site page, click the OK button.

5. On the Template Selection page, pick the template on which the site should be based. The template identifies the default layout of the site and the components included in the site. We discussed the format and components of the default templates earlier in this chapter. For information on any additional custom templates added by your organization and listed in this section, you will need to refer to your SharePoint administrator.

The site is created, and you are taken to the home page of the new site.

Creating Subsites

As we described earlier, any existing WSS team sites, document workspaces, or meeting workspaces can contain subsites. You can create any type of WSS site under existing sites by following these steps:

1. Navigate to the WSS site under which the new subsite should be created.

2. On the site home page, do one of the following as appropriate:

    a. For team sites and document workspaces, click the Create link on the Site Toolbar. Then on the Create Page page, click the Sites and Workspaces link under the Web Pages section.

    b. For meeting workspaces, click the Modify This Workspace link at the top right of the Content section and then select Site Settings from the Modify This Workspace menu, shown in Figure 3-12. Then on the Site Settings page click the Manage Sites and Workspaces link in the Administration section. On the Sites and Workspaces page, click the Create option. These steps, while more complicated than those described previously, will also work for accessing the New SharePoint Site page for team sites and document workspaces.

3. On the New SharePoint Site page, make these changes:

    a. In the Title and Description section, enter the title for the site. This is the name by which the site will be displayed in any site references. You can also add a description, which if entered is displayed at the top of the content section of the site.

    b. In the Web Site Address section, enter the URL name for the site. It is often good practice to make this the same as the site title. However, it is also good practice to not include spaces in the URL name, so if a site title is Business Planning, the URL name would be BusinessPlanning.

    c. In the Permissions section, specify whether the user access permissions for the subsite being created should be the same as the permissions of the parent site or whether unique permissions should be used. When you select to use the same permissions, security will be based on the permissions of the parent site. We will discuss changing site permissions in the "Managing Site Security" section later in this chapter.

    d. Once all the necessary information is entered, click the Create button.

4. On the Template Selection page, pick the template on which the site should be based. The template identifies the default format and components included in the site. We discussed the format and components of the default templates earlier in this chapter. For information on any additional custom templates listed, you will need to refer to the site administrator. Once the desired template is selected, click the OK button.

The subsite is created, and you are taken to the home page of the new subsite.

Creating Meeting Workspaces Through Outlook 2003

As we discussed earlier, meeting workspaces can be created as part of creating a new Outlook 2003 meeting request. This allows the Outlook meeting and the meeting workspace to be linked so that attendee information in the meeting workspace reflects the attendees of the Outlook meeting. It also allows for the meeting request in Outlook to reference the associated meeting workspace.

To create a new meeting workspace as part of creating a new Outlook meeting request:

1. In Outlook 2003, begin creating a new meeting request either by right-clicking a calendar time and selecting New Meeting Request or New Recurring Meeting, by clicking the down arrow on the New button in the Outlook button bar and selecting Meeting Request, or by selecting File ➤ New ➤ Meeting Request from the Outlook menu.

2. Enter the details about the meeting on the New Meeting form.

3. Click the Meeting Workspace button on the New Meeting form. This will present the Meeting Workspace task pane.

4. On the Meeting Workspace task pane, click the Change Settings link in the Create a Workspace section.

5. On the Create Meeting Workspace task pane, as shown in Figure 3-14, follow these steps:

    a. Select a location where the meeting workspace will be created. If the desired location is not in the Select a Location drop-down list, choose Other and then enter the URL to the required location in the Other Workspace Server window and click OK.

    b. Select a workspace template by choosing the Create a New Workspace option and selecting the desired Meeting Workspace template.

    c. Click the OK button.

6. On the Meeting Workspace task pane, click the Create button. The meeting workspace is created and a link to the meeting workspace is added to the meeting request. If the Outlook meeting is a recurring meeting, a recurring meeting workspace will be created.

7. Click the Send button on the Outlook meeting request to send this Outlook request to the attendees.

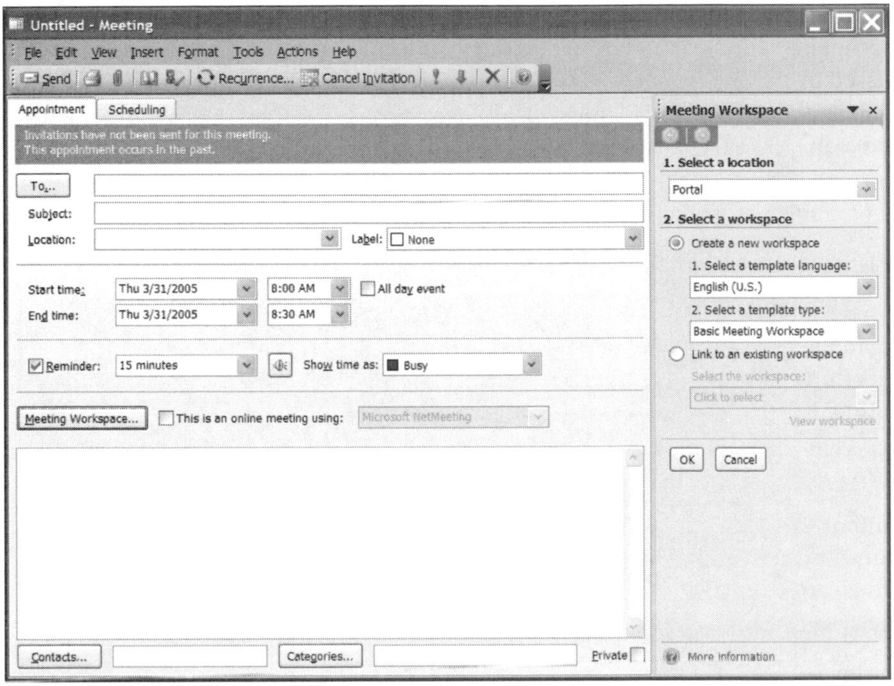

Figure 3-14. *Outlook meeting request with Meeting Workspace task pane*

When meeting requests are created in this way, the attendee list in the meeting site is linked to the Outlook meeting attendee list.

You can also link a new Outlook meeting to an existing meeting workspace. To do this, follow the same steps as earlier, except instead of selecting the Create a New Workspace option in the Meeting Workspace task pane, as in step 5b, select the Link to an Existing Workspace option and select the workspace from the Workspace drop-down list. Keep in mind that the Workspace drop-down list will contain the list of meeting workspaces that exist under the location selected in the Select a Location drop-down list. If there are no meeting workspaces under this location, the Select a Workspace drop-down list will not contain any values.

Creating a New Document Workspace from Office 2003

Document workspaces can be created from within the Microsoft Office 2003 Word, Excel, and PowerPoint programs. This is extremely helpful when the creator of a document decides that a document workspace is needed in order to further develop the document and, if necessary, collaborate with others during this update process. The document workspace can be created without leaving the program the creator is using. This minimizes work interruptions and makes creating document workspaces much more convenient for people who spend a signifi-cant amount of time working in Word, Excel, or PowerPoint.

To create a document workspace from within Office 2003:

1. In Word, Excel, or PowerPoint, select the Shared Workspace option from the task pane drop-down header. If the task pane is not open, you can open it by selecting View ➤ Task Pane from the program menu.

2. In the Shared Workspace task pane, as shown in Figure 3-15, do the following:

    a. Enter the name for the workspace in the Document Workspace Name field.

    b. Select the location where the workspace will be created from the Location for New Workspace drop-down list. If the location where you want to create this workspace is not listed, choose the (Type New URL) option and enter the location under which the new workspace will be created.

    c. Click the Create button.

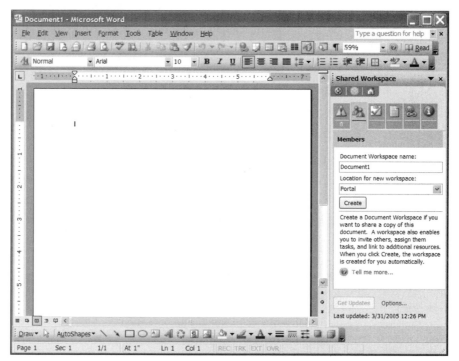

Figure 3-15. *Microsoft Word with Shared Workspace task pane*

3. If the document has not yet been saved, you will be asked to save the document.

The workspace is created and the document is placed in the workspace.

Create a New Document Workspace from a Document in a Site

Document workspaces can also be easily created for documents that already exist in a WSS site. At times, a document that exists within a site will need to be updated, and the update process will involve multiple people working on the document. While updates are being made to the document, you may wish to leave the current version available for site users. In this situation, you can create a new document workspace for this document. When the workspace is created, a copy of the document will be placed in the workspace. Within the workspace, you will be given the ability to post the document back to the original location once all the necessary updates have been made.

To create a new document workspace for an existing WSS document:

1. Navigate to the location in WSS where the document resides.

2. Hover over the document and select the Create Document Workspace option from the document's drop-down list.

3. On the Create Document Workspace page, click the OK button.

The new document workspace is created, and a copy of the selected document is placed in the workspace.

Once the version of the document in the workspace is finalized, you can publish it back to the original source document by selecting the Publish to Source Location option from the document's drop-down menu. We will discuss managing documents in more detail in Chapter 6.

■**Note** When you create a document workspace in this way and are planning to edit the document in the new document workspace, it is important to not edit the original source document. Publishing the document from the created document workspace back to the source document will overwrite any changes made to the source document. We will discuss managing documents in more detail in Chapter 6.

Managing Site Security

Similar to the way site group assignments determine the rights a user has in portal areas, site group assignments in WSS sites determine what rights users have in WSS sites. You can define users' rights within a site based on the level of access they require to the information contained within the site.

Security must be configured for all top-level WSS sites. By default, the only user who will have access to a newly created top-level site will be the person who created the site. When a subsite is created within an existing WSS site, you can define whether it should inherit the permissions of the parent site or whether it should have unique permissions. If you specify that the subsite should inherit permissions from the parent site, then security is not managed for the subsite; instead, the security will be based on the rights assigned in the parent site. If you use unique permissions, then the only user who will initially have access to the subsite will be the user who created the subsite.

There are four default site groups available in WSS sites:

- *Reader*: Has read-only access to the information contained within the site

- *Contributor*: Can add and edit content to lists and libraries in the site

- *Web Designer*: Can create lists and libraries, and customize pages in the site

- *Administrator*: Has full administrative access to all site resources

When creating your WSS sites, it is important to understand the security needs of the individuals who will be using the sites and assign them the appropriate security to allow them to work with the materials within the site.

Adding Users to Site Groups

For top-level sites and subsites that have been configured to use unique permissions, users who are part of the Administrators site group can change the permissions for the site. To add permissions on a top-level site or subsite that uses unique permissions:

1. Navigate to the site in which you need to change permissions.

2. Navigate to the Site Settings page using one of the following methods:

   a. For team sites and document workspaces, this is done by clicking the Site Settings link on the Site Toolbar.

   b. For meeting workspaces, this is done by clicking the Modify This Workspace link at the top right of the Content section and then selecting Site Settings from the Modify This Workspace menu.

3. On the Site Settings page, click the Manage Users link in the Administration section.

4. On the Manage Users page, click the Add Users option.

5. On the Add Users page, enter the domain user or group account information, or enter the e-mail address for the user you wish to add, select the site group memberships that you wish to assign to the user or group, and click the Next button.

6. If the user or group information was not found in Active Directory, an error screen will be displayed. If this screen is presented, click the browser Back button to return to the Add Users page, update the information so that it refers to a valid Active Directory user or group, and click the Next button.

7. If the user or group was found in Active Directory, then the Add Users page containing step 3 and step 4 is presented. On this page, verify the user's information and then determine whether an e-mail should be sent to the user notifying that person of the change in rights by checking or unchecking the Send E-mail option. If you wish to send a notification e-mail to the user, enter the text to be sent in the Subject and Body fields. Once the send e-mail option information has been appropriately set, click the Finish button.

■**Note** The information in the Confirm Users Information section in step 3 of the Add Users page should never need to be updated. This information is pulled from Active Directory as part of the user profile. If this information is not accurate, it should be appropriately updated in the Active Directory instead of being changed in the site.

The user or group is added to the selected site group, and you are returned to the Manage Users page.

You can also add users to site groups using the Members web part. This web part is available in team sites and document workspaces, but not in meeting workspaces. The Members web part displays the list of users and groups having access to the site. It also has a link that allows you to add new users. When you click the Add New Member link, if you are an administrator of the site, you are taken to the Add Users page as described in step 5 earlier. You would then follow the same steps to add the new users or groups and assign them to the appropriate site groups.

Note If you are not an administrator of the site and you click the Add New Members link in the Members web part, you will be prompted with a logon screen instead of being given access to the Add Users page.

Changing Existing Site Group Assignments

To change existing site group assignments for a top-level site or a subsite that uses unique permissions:

   1. Navigate to the site in which you need to change permissions.

   2. Navigate to the Site Settings page using one of the following methods as appropriate:

   a. For team sites and document workspaces, this is done by clicking the Site Settings link on the Site Toolbar.

   b. For meeting workspaces, this is done by clicking the Modify This Workspace link at the top right of the content section and then selecting Site Settings from the Modify This Workspace menu.

   3. On the Site Settings page, click the Manage Users link in the Administration section.

   4. On the Manage Users page, check the boxes in front of the site group assignments that you will be updating and click the Edit Site Groups of Selected Users option. If you are updating a single site group assignment, you can simply click the name of the assigned user or group.

   5. On the Edit Site Group Membership page, update the site group assignment by checking and unchecking the site group options and then clicking the OK button to save the changes.

The updates to the site group assignments are saved. The Manage Users page is displayed, and the updates made are reflected in the site group assignment list.

Deleting Existing Site Group Assignments

To remove an existing site group assignment for a top-level site or a subsite that uses unique permissions:

   1. Navigate to the site in which you need to delete permissions.

   2. Navigate to the Site Settings page using one of the following methods as appropriate:

   a. For team sites and document workspaces, this is done by clicking the Site Settings link on the Site Toolbar.

    b. For meeting workspaces, this is done by clicking the Modify This Workspace link at the top right of the Content section and then selecting Site Settings from the Modify This Workspace menu.

3. On the Site Settings page, click the Manage Users link in the Administration section.

4. On the Manage Users page, check the boxes in front of the site group assignment(s) that you will be removing and click the Remove Selected Users option.

5. Confirm the deletion of the site group assignment by clicking the OK button on the displayed message box.

Changing Permission Inheritance for a Subsite

As we have discussed, when you create a subsite you have the ability to identify whether the subsite should have its own unique permission definitions or whether it should inherit permissions from its parent site. After the site has been created, you have the ability to change this setting if the security requirements around the subsite change. To change the permission inheritance settings for a subsite:

1. Navigate to the site in which you need to change permission inheritance.

2. Navigate to the Site Settings page using one of the following methods as appropriate:

    a. For team sites and document workspaces, this is done by clicking the Site Settings link on the Site Toolbar.

    b. For meeting workspaces, this is done by clicking the Modify This Workspace link at the top right of the Content section and then selecting Site Settings from the Modify This Workspace menu.

3. On the Site Settings page, click the Go to Site Administration link under the Administration section.

4. On the Site Administration page, click the Manage Permission Inheritance link in the Users and Permissions section.

5. On the Manage Permission Inheritance page, select either the Use the same permissions as the parent site option or the Use unique permissions option based on whether you want to have the site inherit permissions from the parent or use unique permissions. Then click the OK button.

6. If you changed the permission inheritance option to Use the same permissions as the parent site, then you must click OK in the message box warning you that changing the site to inherit permissions can cause you or others to not be able to use the site.

The permission inheritance for the site is updated, and you are returned to the Site Administration page.

Setting Site Creation Permissions

It is not uncommon for you to need to allow nonadministrators to create subsites within an existing site. This can occur for many reasons, such as when you want users to create workspaces for projects or when you want users to create and manage meeting workspaces under a team site. An example of this would be having a yearly budgeting project site that is used to create departmental and overall company budgets for the upcoming year. You may want to allow site users to have the ability to create meeting workspaces under the yearly budgeting site that can be used to manage the meetings held during the budgeting process.

Another example of when you would want users to create subsites within an existing site would be when you have a request for proposal (RFP) response site used to store and track information around RFP responses your company is creating. In this scenario, you may want site users to have the ability to create a team site under the RFP site whenever a new RFP is received. This subsite will then be used to manage the materials and the collaboration efforts concerning the creation of the RFP response.

Defining who has the ability to create subsites is done by an administrator of a WSS site. The administrator will select the site groups that should have the ability to create subsites in the current WSS site. This assignment will also allow these individuals to create subsites within any sites inheriting permissions from the site where this permission was granted. To assign site creation rights to a site group in a site:

1. Navigate to the site in which you need to assign site creation permissions.

2. Navigate to the Site Settings page using one of the following methods as appropriate:

    a. For team sites and document workspaces, this is done by clicking the Site Settings link on the Site Toolbar.

    b. For meeting workspaces, this is done by clicking the Modify This Workspace link at the top right of the content section and then selecting Site Settings from the Modify This Workspace menu.

3. On the Site Settings page, click the Configure Site and Workspace Creation link under the Administration section.

4. The Modify Site and Workspace Creation screen lists the site groups eligible for being granted site creation rights; by default, these groups are Contributors and Web Designers. Click the checkbox in front of the site groups that should be given subsite creation rights and click the OK button.

The specified groups are granted site creation rights, and you are returned to the Site Settings page.

Changing Site Group Permissions

As we discussed in Chapter 2, with portal site groups, administrators of WSS sites can change the permissions of existing site groups and create additional site groups tailored to meet specific site security needs. In some cases, you may need to tailor the permissions of existing site groups to meet specific security needs within a site. In other situations, you may want to create new site groups that provide a specific set of permissions within the site. It is always better to create a new site group instead of editing the default ones provided, but there are situations where this is not practical.

Editing Existing Site Group Permissions

To edit the permissions of an existing site group:

1. Navigate to the site in which you need to change site group permissions.

2. Navigate to the Site Settings page using one of the following methods as appropriate:

   a. For team sites and document workspaces, this is done by clicking the Site Settings link on the Site Toolbar.

   b. For meeting workspaces, this is done by clicking the Modify This Workspace link at the top right of the content section and then selecting Site Settings from the Modify This Workspace menu.

3. On the Site Settings page, click the Go to Site Administration link under the Administration section.

4. On the Site Administration page, click the Manage Site Groups link under the Users and Permissions section.

5. On the Manage Site Groups page, click the name of the site group for which you will be changing the permissions.

6. On the Members Of page, click the Edit Site Group Permissions option.

7. On the Edit Site Group page, update the listed permissions by checking or unchecking permission options for the site group. Once the desired permission options are set, click the Submit button.

The permissions of the site group are updated, and you are returned to the Members Of page.

Creating New Site Groups

To create new site groups:

1. Navigate to the site in which you need to create a new site group.

2. Navigate to the Site Settings page using one of the following methods as appropriate:

   a. For team sites and document workspaces, this is done by clicking the Site Settings link on the Site Toolbar.

   b. For meeting workspaces, this is done by clicking the Modify This Workspace link at the top right of the Content section and then selecting Site Settings from the Modify This Workspace menu.

3. On the Site Settings page, click the Go to Site Administration link under the Administration section.

4. On the Site Administration page, click the Manage Site Groups link under the Users and Permissions section.

5. On the Manage Site Groups page, click the Add a Site Group option.

6. On the Add a Site Group page, do the following:

   a. In the Site Group Name and Description section, enter the name for the new site group. You can also enter an optional description. The description is presented next to the name when the site group is listed for selection in the site security management pages.

   b. In the Rights section, check the checkboxes in front of all permissions that the site group should have.

   c. Once all of the necessary information has been entered, click the Create Site Group button.

The new site group is created, and you are returned to the Manage Site Groups page.

Deleting Existing Site Groups

To delete an existing site group:

1. Navigate to the site in which you need to delete a site group.

2. Navigate to the Site Settings page using one of the following methods as appropriate:

   a. For team sites and document workspaces, this is done by clicking the Site Settings link on the Site Toolbar.

   b. For meeting workspaces, this is done by clicking the Modify This Workspace link at the top right of the Content section and then selecting Site Settings from the Modify This Workspace menu.

3. On the Site Settings page, click the Go to Site Administration link under the Administration section.

4. On the Site Administration page, click the Manage Site Groups link under the Users and Permissions section.

5. On the Manage Site Groups page, check the checkbox in front of the site group to delete and click the Delete Selected Site Groups option.

6. On the delete confirmation screen, click the OK button.

The site group is deleted, and the site group list is updated on the Manage Site Groups page to reflect the change.

Managing Cross-Site Groups

Cross-site groups are used in WSS sites when you want to group a list of users together who are not represented by an Active Directory group, and assign rights to that group within multiple sites under the same site collection. We call the group of sites nested within a single top-level site a site collection. For example, you may have a site called Proposals in your Sales area, and within this Proposals site you create subsites for each proposal the sales group creates. For our example, we will assume that there are set teams of people who work together on proposals, and that only the team working on a proposal should have access to that proposal's site. In this scenario, you can create a cross-site group for each proposal team and use this group to assign rights to proposal sites when they are created.

Cross-site groups are available for use within all sites contained in the same site collection. Cross-site groups can be assigned to normal site groups the same way you would assign active directory users or groups to site groups. Cross-site groups do not by themselves have rights within sites the way normal site groups do. They must be assigned to a normal site group in order for them to be granted rights within a site.

Creating Cross-Site Groups

You can create and manage cross-site groups from any site contained in the same site collection as long as you are at least a Contributor within the site. To create a new cross-site group:

1. Navigate to any site within the site collection where you are at least a Contributor.

2. Click the Site Settings link on the Site Toolbar.

3. On the Site Settings page, click the Go to Site Administration option in the Administration section.

4. On the Site Administration page, click the Manage Cross-Site Groups option in the Users and Permissions section.

5. On the My Cross-Site Groups page, click the New Cross-Site Group menu option.

6. On the new Cross-Site Group page, make the following changes:

    a. In the Name and Description section, enter the name for the site group. You can also enter an optional description.

    b. In the Owners section, select the user or group that will own the cross-site group. The owner is the user or group that can make updates to the cross-site group properties and membership. You can either select yourself, some other user, or the members of the cross-site group.

    c. Click the Create button.

The cross-site group is created, and the creator is added as a member of the group.

Editing Cross-Site Groups

Cross-site group owners have the ability to update the properties of their groups, including the group name, description, and owner. To update the properties of a cross-site group:

1. Navigate to any site within the site collection where you are at least a Contributor.

2. Click the Site Settings link on the Site Toolbar.

3. On the Site Settings page, click the Go to Site Administration option in the Administration section.

4. On the Site Administration page, click the Manage Cross-Site Groups option in the Users and Permissions section.

5. On the My Cross-Site Groups page, click the name of the cross-site group to edit.

6. On the Members Of page, click the Change Cross-Site Group Settings option.

7. On the Change Cross-Site Group Settings page, make any necessary updates to the name, description, or ownership information. Then click the OK button.

The updates you made to the cross-site group are saved, and you are returned to the Members Of page.

Changing Cross-Site Group Membership

To change the members of a cross-site group that you own:

1. Navigate to any site within the site collection where you are at least a Contributor.

2. Click the Site Settings link on the Site Toolbar.

3. On the Site Settings page, click the Go to Site Administration option in the Administration section.

4. On the Site Administration page, click the Manage Cross-Site Groups option in the Users and Permissions section.

5. On the My Cross-Site Groups page, click the name of the cross-site group to update.

6. On the Members Of page, add or remove members as follows:

    a. *To add members*: Click the Add Members option. Then on the Add Users Page enter the active directory account information for the user to add and click the Next button. Then click the Finish button on the Add Users Confirmation page.

    b. *To remove members*: Click the checkbox in front of the account to remove and click the Delete Selected Members option. Click OK on the deletion confirmation window.

You are returned to the Members Of page, and the members list is updated to reflect the memberships changes made.

Deleting Cross-Site Groups

To delete existing cross-site groups that you own:

1. Navigate to any site within the site collection where you are at least a Contributor.

2. Click the Site Settings link on the Site Toolbar.

3. On the Site Settings page, click the Go to Site Administration option in the Administration section.

4. On the Site Administration page, click the Manage Cross-Site Groups option in the Users and Permissions section.

5. On the My Cross-Site Groups page, click the checkbox in front of the cross-site groups to delete, and click the Delete Selected Cross-Site Groups option.

6. Click OK on the deletion confirmation message box.

The selected cross-site groups are deleted, and the My Cross-Site Groups page is updated to reflect the change.

Changing General Site Details

The information that you enter about the site when it is created, such as the title and description, can be changed later. You can also change other types of information about the site, such as the theme. These changes allow you to configure the site to meet the specific needs it is being created to fulfill or to allow you to update the site over time as these needs change.

Updating Site Title and Description

To update the site title and description information that was entered when the site was created:

1. Navigate to the site in which you need to update the site title and description.

2. Navigate to the Site Settings page using one of the following methods as appropriate:

   a. For team sites and document workspaces, this is done by clicking the Site Settings link on the Site Toolbar.

   b. For meeting workspaces, this is done by clicking the Modify This Workspace link at the top right of the Content section and then selecting Site Settings from the Modify This Workspace menu.

3. On the Site Settings page, click the Change Site Title and Description link in the Customization section.

4. On the Change Site Title and Description page, update the site title and description information as needed, and then click the OK button.

The changes made are applied to the site, and you are returned to the Site Settings page.

■**Note** While you can change the site title and description, you cannot change the site URL. This means that if the link to the Finance site is http://server1/sites/finance, and you decide to change the title of the Finance site to Accounting, you will access the Accounting site through the original http://server1/sites/finance URL.

Updating Site Themes

A site theme defines the font and color schemes for a site. Themes allow complete color and font configurations to be stored together and applied through a single step. This ensures aesthetic consistency within the site. By default, individuals in the Web Designers and Administrators site groups have the ability to change site themes.

To change the theme on a site:

1. Navigate to the site in which you need to change the theme.

2. Navigate to the Site Settings page using one of the following methods as appropriate:

   a. For team sites and document workspaces, this is done by clicking the Site Settings link on the Site Toolbar.

   b. For meeting workspaces, this is done by clicking the Modify This Workspace link at the top right of the Content section and then selecting Site Settings from the Modify This Workspace menu.

3. On the Site Settings page, click the Apply Theme to Site link in the Customization section.

4. On the Apply Theme to Web Site page, select the theme to be applied from the list and click the Apply button.

The selected theme is applied to the site, and you are returned to the Site Settings page.

Deleting Sites

There are two ways to delete existing sites. The first is to delete the site from within that site's Site Settings page. To delete an existing site in this way:

1. Navigate to the site you wish to delete.

2. Navigate to the Site Settings page using one of the following methods as appropriate:

   a. For team sites and document workspaces, this is done by clicking the Site Settings link on the Site Toolbar.

   b. For meeting workspaces, this is done by clicking the Modify This Workspace link at the top right of the Content section and then selecting Site Settings from the Modify This Workspace menu.

3. On the Site Settings page, click the Go to Site Administration link under the Administration section.

4. On the Site Administration page, click the Delete This Site link under the Management and Statistics section.

5. On the Delete Web Site page, click the Delete button.

The site is deleted and you are taken to the Your Web Site Has Been Deleted page.

The second way to delete a site is from the Sites and Workspaces page of the site's parent. Given that you delete the site from within its parent, this method only works for deleting subsites. It cannot be used to delete a top-level site. To delete sites in this way:

1. Navigate to the parent of the subsite you wish to delete.

2. Navigate to the Sites and Workspaces page as we discussed in the "Navigating Through WSS Sites" section.

3. Click the Delete icon for the listed subsite to delete.

4. On the Delete Web Site page, click the Delete button.

The site is deleted, and you are returned to the Sites and Workspaces page. Sites can only be deleted when they do not contain subsites. If there are subsites nested under the site being deleted, you will be prompted with an error when you try to delete the site.

■**Note** Deleting a site permanently removes the site and all of its content.

Site Templates

As we discussed earlier in this chapter, when you create a new site or subsite, you select a template as part of the creation process. The site template defines the initial set of components to include in the site being created and defines the layout of the components in the new site. The template also defines the structure and configuration of the components within the site and whether any content, such as list values and documents, should be added to the new site being created.

Creating Site Templates

The templates we discussed earlier are default templates provided to create team sites, document workspaces, and meeting workspaces. Once you create a new site based on one of the available templates and then tailor the site to meet your specific needs, you can save the updated site as a new template that can be used when additional sites are created. Anyone who is a member of the Administrator site group can create and manage site templates.

The templates that you will be creating will be made available when sites are created within the same site collection where the site template was created. As we mentioned previously, we call the group of sites nested within a single top-level site a site collection.

An example of how site templates are used can be seen when you have a top-level site called Budget Planning which contains a subsite called 2005 Budget. You can then update the 2005 Budget site to reflect the layout needed to support yearly budget planning and so it includes the components needed to support yearly budget planning. We will discuss creating components and editing page layouts in Chapters 4 through 7. Once the 2005 Budget site has the desired structure and content, you can save it as a template. This template will then be available when other new sites are created within the Budget Planning site collection. By saving the 2005 Budget site as a template, you save yourself and others the future effort of having to perform the same customizations you made to the 2005 Budget site when additional yearly budget sites are required. It also allows you to provide others with a starting point for creating yearly budget sites that include the layout and components they will need within these sites. This helps to ensure that all of the yearly budget sites have a consistent structure and that the structure contains the resources needed to properly support the budget planning process.

Note While our discussions about creating and managing site templates focus on templates that are only available within the site collection where they were created, templates can also be created and made available for when you create top-level sites and subsites in any site collection. A technical SharePoint administrator must save and register templates so they can be used in this way.

To create a site template for use in the current site collection:

1. Navigate to the site you wish to save as a site template.

2. Navigate to the Site Settings page using one of the following methods as appropriate:

   a. For team sites and document workspaces, this is done by clicking the Site Settings link on the Site Toolbar.

   b. For meeting workspaces, this is done by clicking the Modify This Workspace link at the top right of the Content section and then selecting Site Settings from the Modify This Workspace menu.

3. On the Site Settings page, click the Go to Site Administration link under the Administration section.

4. On the Site Administration page, click the Save Site as Template link under the Management and Statistics section.

5. On the Save Site as Template page, make the following changes:

   a. In the File Name section, enter the name that will be used to save the template.

   b. In the Title and Description section, enter the title for the template. This is the name the template will appear as when you select a template during the site creation process. You can also enter an optional description for the template.

   c. In the Include Content section, you can specify whether the content within the selected site should be included in the site template. Content includes any documents or list data that exists in the selected site. To include the content in the template, check the Include Content checkbox.

   d. Once all necessary information is entered on the Save Site as Template page, click the OK button.

Note When you choose to include content, this will only include content within the current site. It does not include subsites of the current site or content within these subsites.

6. On the Operation Completed Successfully page, click the OK button.

A copy of the site is saved as a template, and you are returned to the Site Administration page. The new site template will now be available in the Template Selection page when people create new sites within the same site collection.

Editing Site Templates

To edit a site template, you simply edit the site you originally used to create the site template or create a new site from the existing template and then make the edits to that site. Once the changes have been made to the site, you create the new template by following the steps described previously. You can then delete the old template from the Site Templates Gallery. We will discuss deleting templates in the "Deleting Site Templates" section later in this chapter.

Even though you cannot edit existing template files, you can edit the properties of these files. The properties that can be edited include the file name, title, and description. To edit this information for an existing site template:

1. Navigate to the top-level site under which the template is available.

2. Navigate to the Site Settings page using one of the following methods as appropriate:

    a. For team sites and document workspaces, this is done by clicking the Site Settings link on the Site Toolbar.

    b. For meeting workspaces, this is done by clicking the Modify This Workspace link at the top right of the Content section and then selecting Site Settings from the Modify This Workspace menu.

3. On the Site Settings page, click the Go to Site Administration link under the Administration section.

4. On the Top-Level Site Administration page, click the Manage Site Template Gallery link under the Site Collection Galleries section.

5. On the Site Template Gallery page, click the Edit icon next to the name of the template you wish to edit.

6. On the Site Template Gallery edit page, make any necessary updates to the template's file name, title, and description, and then click the Save and Close option.

The changes are saved, and you are returned to the Site Template Gallery page.

Deleting Site Templates

While you cannot remove the default site template provided, you can delete any custom site templates created. To delete an existing custom site template:

1. Navigate to the top-level site under which the template is available.

2. Navigate to the Site Settings page using one of the following methods as appropriate:

    a. For team sites and document workspaces, this is done by clicking the Site Settings link on the Site Toolbar.

   b. For meeting workspaces, this is done by clicking the Modify This Workspace link at
      the top right of the Content section and then selecting Site Settings from the Mod-
      ify This Workspace menu.

3. On the Site Settings page, click the Go to Site Administration link under the Administration section.

4. On the Top-Level Site Administration page, click the Manage Site Template Gallery link
   under the Site Collection Galleries section.

5. On the Site Template Gallery page, click the Edit icon next to the name of the template
   you wish to edit.

6. On the Site Template Gallery edit page, click the Delete option.

7. Click the OK button on the delete confirmation window.

The template is deleted, and you are returned to the Site Template Gallery page.

WSS Site Search

When you navigate to a WSS site, the Search Toolbar is available similarly to the way it is in portal
areas; however, searching within WSS sites works very differently from searching in portal areas.
First, there is no advanced search option available in WSS sites. The only search available is equiv-
alent to the portal area simple search we discussed in Chapter 2. WSS site searches will also only
search for information within the current site. They will not look across information stored in any
other portal location. They also do not include information stored in any subsites.

The WSS search is context sensitive within the site. If a search is performed from the site
home page, all libraries and lists within the site are included in the search. When the search is
performed from within the page of a specific library or list, only content in that library or list
will be included in the search.

To perform a WSS search, you type the words to search for into the search box in the
Search Tools section of the WSS site page and click the green arrow. Documents or list items
located in the site that meet the entered search criteria will be listed.

Site Statistics

Site statistics are provided for WSS sites in order to allow you to review how your site is being
used by site users and to monitor the resources that your site is using. Statistical information
about user access and resource consumption is available to users who are part of the Administrators site group for the site.

■**Note** For site statistic options to be available, a technical administrator of the SharePoint environment
must have enabled them for use in the SharePoint environment.

Site Usage Statistics

Site usage data is available to allow you to evaluate how people are using your site. The types of access that are available for review include the following:

- *Number of Hits per Page*: Includes details about how many times pages and documents within your site have been accessed

- *User Access Statistics*: Includes information about how often each user is accessing the site

- *Operating System Access Statistics*: Includes information about the operating systems being used to access the site

- *Browser Access Statistics*: Includes information about the browsers being used to access the site

- *Referrer URL Statistics*: Includes the list of URLs users accessing the site navigated from when going to this site

For each of these types of information, you can look at monthly statistics or daily statistics. Monthly statistics will provide the following information:

- The total number of times the page has been accessed

- The number of times the page was accessed in the most recent month it was accessed

- The date the page was last accessed

- The number of times the page was accessed on the last day it was accessed

Figure 3-16 shows a standard monthly Number of Hits per Page Site Usage Report.

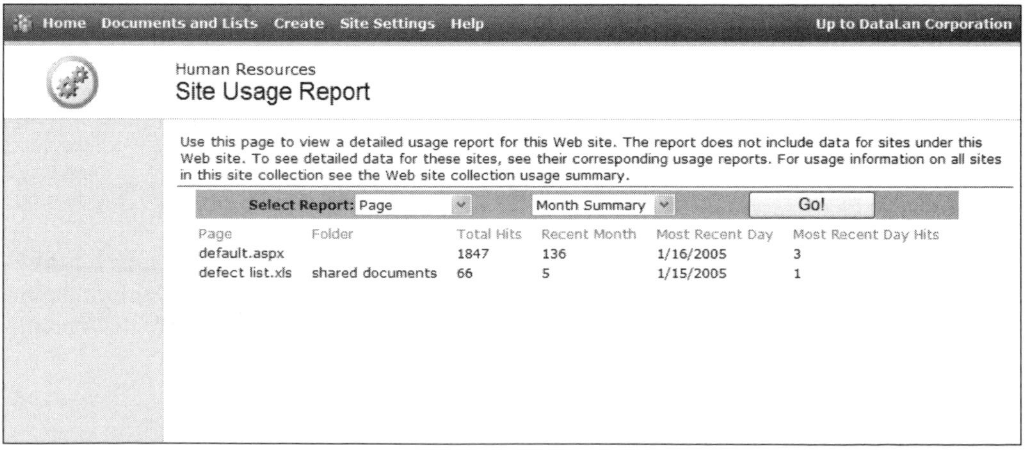

Figure 3-16. *Monthly Number of Hits per Page Site Usage Report*

Daily statistics provide a daily breakdown of access volumes. Figure 3-17 shows a daily User Access Statistics Site Usage Report.

Home   Documents and Lists   Create   Site Settings   Help   Up to DataLan Corporation

Human Resources
Site Usage Report

Use this page to view a detailed usage report for this Web site. The report does not include data for sites under this Web site. To see detailed data for these sites, see their corresponding usage reports. For usage information on all sites in this site collection see the Web site collection usage summary.

Select Report: User   Daily   Go!

User	Jan 16	Jan 15	Jan 14	Jan 13	Jan 12	Jan 11	Jan 10	Jan 9	Jan 8	Jan 7	Jan 6	Jan 5	Jan 4	Jan 3	Jan 2	Jan 1	Dec 31	Dec 30	Dec 29	Dec 28	Dec 27	Dec 26	Dec 25	Dec 24	Dec 23	Dec 22	Dec 21	Dec 20	Dec 19	Dec 18	Dec 17
datalannt\nhe	0	0	0	2	0	0	0	0	0	0	0	0	0	0	0	0	0	0	0	0	0	0	0	0	0	0	0	0	0	0	0
datalannt\spsimport	3	8	4	4	4	4	3	8	4	4	4	4	4	3	8	4	4	4	4	4	3	8	4	4	4	4	4	3	8	4	

Figure 3-17. *Daily User Access Statistics Site Usage Report*

Viewing Site Usage Statistics

To view usage statistics for a site:

1. Navigate to the site in which you want to view site usage information.

2. Navigate to the Site Settings page using one of the following methods as appropriate:

   a. For team sites and document workspaces, this is done by clicking the Site Settings link on the Site Toolbar.

   b. For meeting workspaces, this is done by clicking the Modify This Workspace link at the top right of the Content section and then selecting Site Settings from the Modify This Workspace menu.

3. On the Site Settings page, click the Go to Site Administration link under the Administration section.

4. On the Site Administration page, click the View Site Usage Data under the Management and Statistics section.

5. On the Site Usage Report page, select the type of report from the Select Report dropdown list, select either Monthly Summary or Daily, and click the Go button.

The selected report statistics are displayed.

Site Collection Usage Statistics

Site collection usage information provides some basic statistics about a site collection. As we mentioned earlier, a site collection is made up of all sites contained within the same top-level site. Site collection usage statistics allow you to understand, at a high level, how your site collection is used and how many resources the site collection is using within the SharePoint environment. The statistics that can be viewed include the following:

- *Storage Information*: Provides basic information about the storage space used by the site collection. This includes the current space used, percent of space used by web discussions, and maximum storage allowed for the site.

■**Note** Site storage allocation limits can be configured to define the maximum amount of space a site or site collection can use. These settings must be configured by a technical administrator of the SharePoint environment.

- *User Information*: Lists the number of users who have been added to the site collection and provides any user account restriction details.

- *Activity Information*: Provides basic access statistics for the site collection including the total number of times information within the site collection has been accessed and bandwidth used on the last day the site was accessed.

Figure 3-18 depicts site collection usage information.

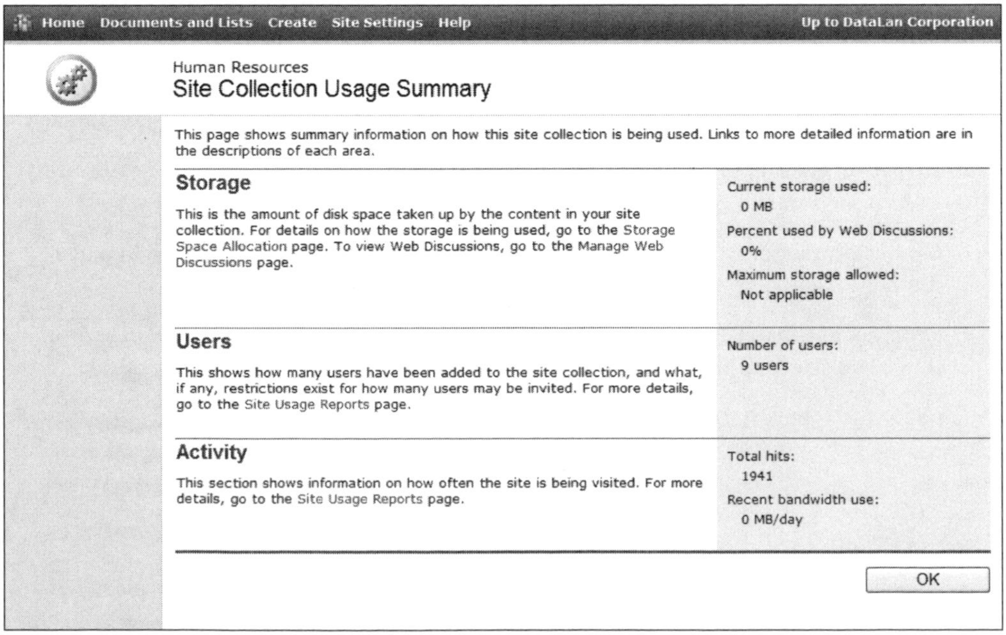

Figure 3-18. *Site Collection Usage Summary*

An example of how the site collection usage statistics and the site usage statistics could be used together would be when site administrators want to understand how effective their sites are and where work should be spent to increase site effectiveness. Administrators can look at the site collection usage statistics to see how many hits their site collections are receiving. If administrators notice a specific site collection is not being accessed as much as others, they can review the site usage statistics for the sites within that site collection to determine the sites not being used. This will help them identify areas where work within the environment may be needed.

Viewing Site Collection Usage Statistics

To view the site collection usage information:

1. Navigate to the top-level site under which you want to view site collection usage information.

2. Navigate to the Site Settings page using one of the following methods as appropriate:

   a. For team sites and document workspaces, this is done by clicking the Site Settings link on the Site Toolbar.

   b. For meeting workspaces, this is done by clicking the Modify This Workspace link at the top right of the Content section and then selecting Site Settings from the Modify This Workspace menu.

3. On the Site Settings page, click the Go to Site Administration link under the Administration section.

4. On the Top-Level Site Administration page, click the View Site Collection Usage Summary link under the Site Collection Administration section.

The Site Collection Usage Summary screen is presented, listing the site collection usage information.

Site Hierarchy

From a top-level site, you can view the entire hierarchy within a site collection. This allows you to view the entire structure of a site collection without having to manually traverse the sites in the site collection. To view the site hierarchy:

1. Navigate to the top-level site under which you want to view the site hierarchy.

2. Navigate to the Site Settings page using one of the following methods as appropriate:

   a. For team sites and document workspaces, this is done by clicking the Site Settings link on the Site Toolbar.

   b. For meeting workspaces, this is done by clicking the Modify This Workspace link at the top right of the Content section and then selecting Site Settings from the Modify This Workspace menu.

3. On the Site Settings page, click the Go to Site Administration link under the Administration section.

4. On the Top-Level Site Administration page, click the View Site Hierarchy link under the Site Collection Administration section.

The View Site Hierarchy page is presented listing the URLs and titles for all sites in the current site collection. You can go directly to any of the listed sites by clicking the site's URL. Figure 3-19 depicts a site hierarchy.

Figure 3-19. *Site hierarchy*

Storage Space Allocation

WSS sites include the ability to view storage space allocations within a site collection. You have the ability to view the amount of space used by all components within a site hierarchy, including all libraries and lists. This allows you to identify how space is being used throughout the site and can be used to help locate sites using excessive amounts of storage or site components not being used to store any information. Figure 3-20 depicts storage space allocation information.

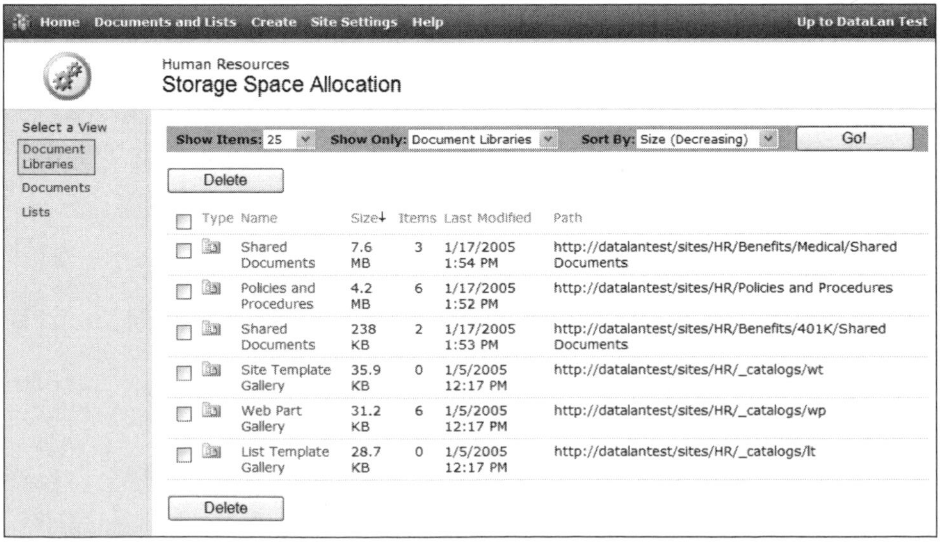

Figure 3-20. *Storage space allocation*

Viewing Storage Space Allocation

To view storage space allocation information:

1. Navigate to the top-level site under which you want to view the storage space allocation information.

2. Navigate to the Site Settings page using one of the following methods as appropriate:

    a. For team sites and document workspaces, this is done by clicking the Site Settings link on the Site Toolbar.

    b. For meeting workspaces, this is done by clicking the Modify This Workspace link at the top right of the Content section and then selecting Site Settings from the Modify This Workspace menu.

3. On the Site Settings page, click the Go to Site Administration link under the Administration section.

4. On the Top-Level Site Administration page, click the View Storage Space Allocation link under the Site Collection Administration section.

5. On the Storage Space Allocation page, select the number of items, type of items, and sort information to display.

    a. Show Items can be set to 25, 50, or 100 and determines the number of items to display allocation information for at a time.

    b. The Show Only drop-down list allows you to select the type of items that will be listed. You can choose to list document libraries, documents, or lists.

    c. The Sort By drop-down list allows you to select the sort method for the items being displayed. You can choose to sort information using these options: Size (Decreasing), Size (Increasing), Date (Decreasing), or Date (Increasing).

6. Once the Show Items, Show Only, and Sort By options are set properly, click the Go! button.

The storage allocations for the items selected are displayed. These items are sorted based on the Sort By value that was selected. You can click any of the listed items to access them.

CHAPTER 4

■■■

Custom Lists and Data

In SharePoint, Microsoft has simplified the storage of information into the basic concept of a *list*. Much of the data that you contribute to or consume is based on the fundamental idea that it is contained in a list of similar information. Each of the lists in SharePoint can have its own unique set of attributes that describe an item in the list. WSS comes with many standard list templates and the capability to create your own custom lists based on the data that best describes the information you are trying to capture.

The most frequently used way of tracking any information in SharePoint is through the use of a custom list. Using a custom list allows you to store information in a structured representation of the data that you design. Lists in SharePoint also allow you to control how the information is displayed, who has the ability to alter or view the information, and whether new content must be approved before it appears in the list. The ability to customize lists allows SharePoint content structure and data to be maintained by business users rather than having to rely on your IT staff.

Creating Custom Lists

There are multiple ways to create a custom list in SharePoint. The quickest way is to choose the Custom List option on your site's Create page. You will also notice an option on the Create page that will enable you to create a custom list using the Datasheet view rather than the standard view that the Custom List option uses. The Datasheet view will be described in the "Managing Views" section later in this chapter.

To create a new custom list, follow these steps:

1. Navigate to a Windows SharePoint Services site, or create a new site as described in Chapter 3.

2. Click the Create link on the top menu bar.

3. On the Create page, click the Custom List link in the Custom Lists section.

4. On the New List page, enter a name and description for the list.

5. Select Yes under the Navigation options if you want to show a link to this list on the Quick Launch menu of the site.

6. Click the Create button.

You have now created a custom list that contains a single data column called Title. Figure 4-1 shows a list like the one you have just created. Later in this chapter, in the "Managing Custom Lists" section, we will describe how to customize this list by configuring additional columns and discuss ways of managing information in the list.

Figure 4-1. *A new custom list*

Working with Custom Lists

Now that you have a list to work with, you need to provide content in that list. In addition to adding, editing, and deleting items, it is important to know how to find the information in a list so that you can locate the items in an efficient manner.

A quick way to find items is using the search bar near the top of the list screen. When on the home page of a site, this search bar finds information throughout the site, but when used on the list screen, it only shows results found in the current list. The list screen is displayed by clicking the name of the list on the Quick Launch menu of the site's home page or from the Documents and Lists page by clicking the Documents and Lists link on the site's top menu.

Adding, Editing, and Deleting Items

Before you can explore how to use other features of a list, you must first know how to add items.

To add items to a list, follow these steps:

1. Click the New Item link on the list page.

2. On the New Item page, enter a title. Title is the only column of data in the list when it is created. Later we will add more columns to the list, and there will be more than just a title to enter on the New Item page.

3. Click the Save and Close link.

Editing and deleting items is performed by first displaying the item's context menu. Displaying a context menu in SharePoint is not performed by right-clicking the mouse as it is in many other programs, but rather by hovering the mouse over the item in the list so that the item becomes highlighted and a small inverted triangle appears on the right-hand side of the item. Once this triangle appears, click it to display the list item's context menu, as shown in Figure 4-2.

This context menu gives you the View Item option, which shows a read-only display of all of the information about this item. Not all information about an item is necessarily displayed on the list page, so viewing an item ensures that you see all data related to an item.

The item's context menu also gives you the ability to edit the item by performing the following steps:

1. Activate the item's context menu by hovering over the item with your mouse and clicking the inverted triangle.

2. Click the Edit Item link in the context menu.

3. On the Edit Item page, change the title.

4. Click the Save and Close link.

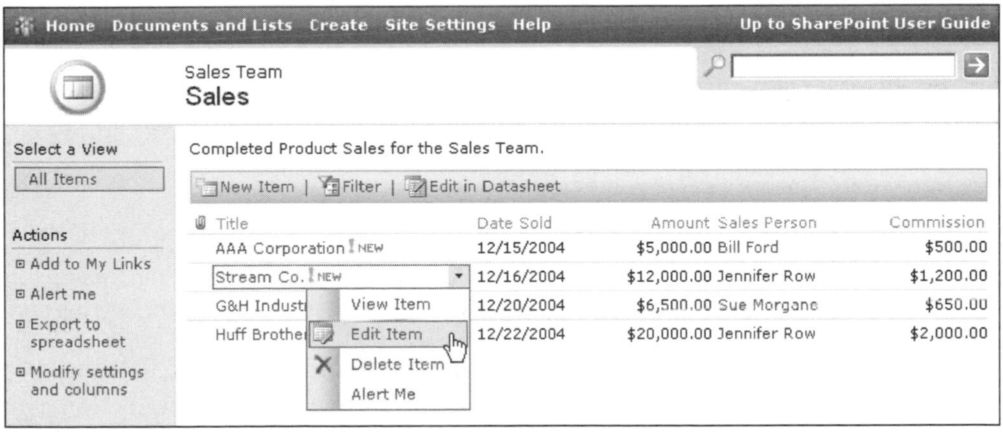

Figure 4-2. *A list item's context menu*

You may have noticed many places so far that allow you to delete a list item. The context menu, the View Item page, and the Edit Item page all have links allowing you to delete the item. After clicking these links, you are requested to confirm that you wish to delete the item.

■**Caution** Once you select OK on the confirmation for deleting the item, the information it contains is physically deleted from SharePoint. It is not possible to recover the list item without assistance from your IT staff.

Attachments

Lists have the ability to store files attached to a particular list item. Including attachments allows users to access documents and files that are related to the list item in one location. Enabling this ability for a list is described in the "Managing Custom Lists" section later in this chapter. To attach a file to an existing list item in a list with attachments enabled:

1. Activate the item's context menu by hovering over the item with your mouse and clicking the inverted triangle.

2. Click the Edit Item link in the context menu.

3. On the Edit Item page, click the Attach File link in the toolbar.

4. Click the Browse button.

5. On the Choose File dialog box, select a file and click the Open button.

6. On the Edit Item page, click the OK button. Repeat steps 3 through 6 to attach multiple files to the list item.

7. Click the Save and Close link in the toolbar.

After step 6, the file you chose will be shown under the Attachments heading on the Edit Item page. It is important to note that the file is not actually attached to the list item until you click the Save and Close link, which saves changes to the data. You can remove attachments from a list item by selecting the Delete link that is displayed next to the attachment on the Edit Item page. This also requires you to click the Save and Close link before the attachment is actually removed from the list item.

Filtering and Sorting the List

Lists can contain hundreds of items or more, which can quickly make it difficult to find the items you are looking for when browsing the list. SharePoint lists provide ways of filtering and sorting information that you are probably already familiar with.

Sorting the items can prove to be a valuable asset when visually scanning a list for a particular item. The name of each data column that supports sorting will appear as a link on the list page. To sort by a specific column, simply click that link. The list will redisplay with the column you selected sorted in ascending order (for example, A to Z and 1 to 10). Clicking another column name will re-sort the list with that new column's information in ascending order. If you click a column name that is already sorting in ascending order, the list will redisplay with that column sorted in descending order (for example, Z to A and 10 to 1). You can tell what column a list is sorted on by a small arrow that will appear directly beside the column name of the column that is the basis for the sorting of the list. This arrow will be pointed down when the list is sorted in ascending order, and it will be pointed up when the list is sorted in decending order.

Another feature of SharePoint lists is the ability to filter the list items based on selected column values. This powerful feature allows you to take a list containing hundreds of items and reduce the items shown to you to only the ones that meet the criteria you are looking for.

To filter a list, perform the following steps:

1. Click the Filter link on the list page.

2. Drop-down lists will appear above the column titles for each column in the list. These drop-down lists will contain all of the possible values that are being used in the selected column for the list.

3. Click the drop-down list for the Titles column and select a value.

4. The list will refresh and only show you items that contain your selected value for the title.

5. Click the Change Filter link to modify the filtering.

6. Select a new value from the Title column's drop-down list or select (All) to remove the filter from the Title column.

7. The list will refresh with the new filter you have selected.

8. Steps 6 and 7 can be repeated using different columns in the list in order to apply multiple filters simultaneously.

A funnel-shaped icon will be displayed next to the column name of any column that currently has a filter applied to it. Filtering is not supported for every type of column. For example, columns based on Multiple lines of text and Hyperlink or Pictures types, which are described in the "Managing Columns" section later in this chapter, do not support filtering.

Filtering a list can let you quickly condense list information to just the items you are looking for. Imagine a list of product sales with columns containing the product, sales amount, date, and salesperson. If you have hundreds or thousands of sales, the list becomes too long to look through for sales by a specific salesperson, but with filtering you can quickly filter on a specific salesperson by selecting that salesperson's name in the appropriate column. The sales list will refresh, showing you only the sales by that person. Furthermore, you can sort that filtered list by date and have a very beneficial view of the data as shown in Figure 4-3.

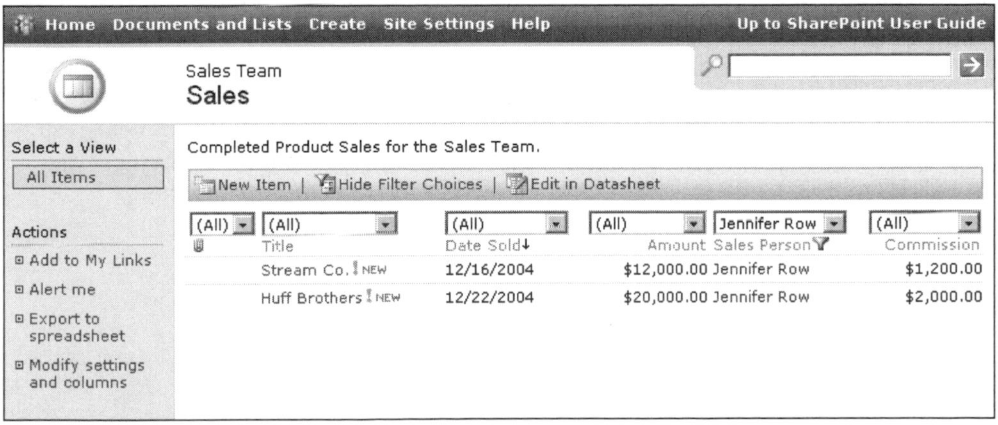

Figure 4-3. *Filtering and sorting list items*

Even more powerful is the ability to use these views, or combinations of sorting, filtering, and other criteria, by simply selecting them rather than entering the criteria every time you look at the list.

Using Views

List views are important because they allow list items to be presented in the way that users can best work with the information. Views determine the information displayed on the screen, including columns shown, the order that items are displayed, and the style used to present the items. When in a list, the view can be selected from the left menu. From the examples earlier, you can see that by creating a new list, a view called All Items was also created, and since it is the only view available, it is the currently selected view. This can also be seen in Figure 4-3.

Users with the appropriate permissions in SharePoint can create additional views for a list that display the same list with different filtering, sorting, grouping, or summations. When the list has multiple views, they will each be available via a link on the left menu bar, allowing you to easily switch between them. Once you have selected a view that most closely represents the information you want to see, you can further filter and sort the list items displayed by using the filtering and sorting functionality we have already discussed. The creation of these views will be discussed in the "Managing Views" section later in this chapter.

Faster Data Manipulation Using the Datasheet

A more advanced way to edit the items in a list is to use the Datasheet view. SharePoint integrates with Office 2003 to provide an easy way for you to edit multiple items in a list quickly without having to go to each individual item's Edit Item page separately. In order for the Datasheet view to work, you need Office 2003 installed on the computer you are using to access the list. Your browser security settings must also allow ActiveX components to run in order for the Datasheet view to operate properly.

To edit items in the Datasheet view, simply click the Edit in Datasheet link on the toolbar of the list. The list will change to an Excel-like display as shown in Figure 4-4. This display will allow you to easily manipulate multiple items in the list quickly by utilizing familiar productivity features such as copy/paste.

The Datasheet view provides rudimentary spreadsheet abilities such as creating summations via the toolbar. A context menu via a right-click on the Datasheet view provides you easy access to options for adding and deleting rows or columns. The context menu also provides the ability to auto-fill cells or for you to pick cell values from a list of previously entered values in the column. When you need to modify or approve multiple list items, the Datasheet view proves much more valuable than individually selecting and updating each list item.

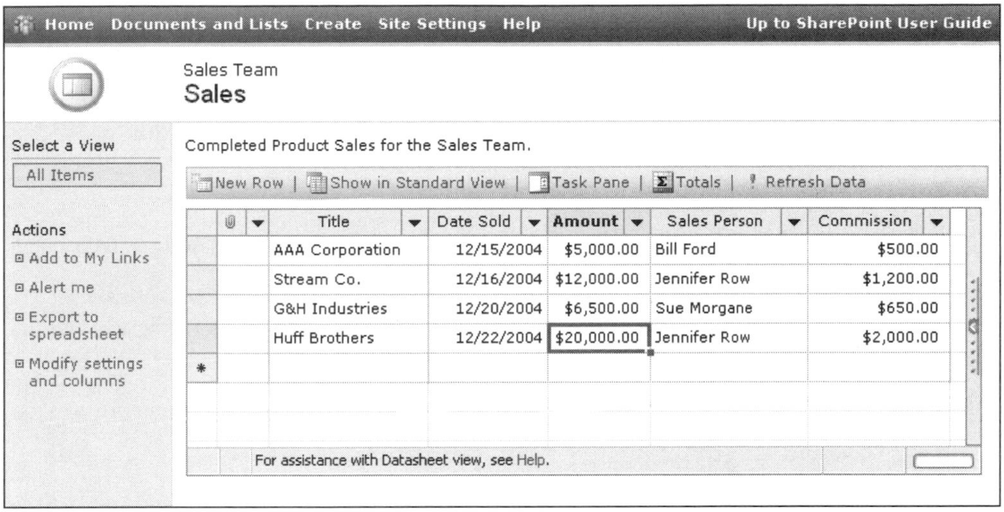

Figure 4-4. *The Datasheet view*

Managing Custom Lists

The power of using custom lists to store information in a site is the ability to customize the list to meet any structured information sharing need. Lists allow you to determine not only what data is stored in the list, but also how it is stored, how it is displayed, when it is displayed, and who has the ability to view, create, or edit that information.

■**Note** Creating and managing a list requires that you have the proper permissions. By default, you must be in the Administrator or Web Designer site groups in order to have access to creating and customizing lists.

All management of a list begins by selecting the Modify Settings and Columns link from the Actions menu on the list screen. Clicking this link takes you to the Customize List screen where the options are categorized into General Settings, which includes security; Columns, where you determine how the information is stored; and Views, where you customize the ways in which other users can see the information.

Settings

The General Settings options allow you to change basic aspects of the list that make it easier for other users to understand the purpose of the list as well as provide navigation and basic workflow options. The General Settings screen is also where you would specify whether users are allowed to attach files to a list item.

To edit the general settings of a list, follow these steps:

1. On the list screen, click the Modify Settings and Columns link in the Actions list on the left menu.

2. On the Customize List screen, click the Change General Settings link under the General Settings category.

Table 4-1 describes the list settings you can edit in order to customize the behavior of a list.

Table 4-1. *General Settings for SharePoint Lists*

Setting	Description
Name	The name used to identify the list through your SharePoint site. This should be short but descriptive enough so that users know the purpose of the list from the name alone.
Description	More elaborate explanation of the lists' purpose. This is displayed on the Documents and Lists screen to help users find the information they are looking for as well as on the list screen to communicate the purpose of the list to users.
Navigation	Determines whether a link for the list is displayed on the Quick Launch bar on the left side of the site's home page. Selecting Yes allows users to easily see that your list exists and quickly navigate to it.
Content Approval	Selecting Yes to enable the Content Approval option means that users do not see newly added items until a user with Manage List permission (Administrator or Web Designer group members normally) approves the item. See the "Content Approval" section next for more information on approving items for entry in a list.
Attachments	Determines whether users can add files as an attachment to the list item. Select Enable Attachments to allow users to attach one or more files to items in the list.
Item-Level Permissions	Provides the ability to limit the items that users can view or edit. Read access options allow you to specify whether users can view all items in the list or only the items they have created. Edit access options allow you to specify whether users can edit all items or the items they have created, or restrict edit access entirely. Users who have the Manage List permission can see and edit all items and are unaffected by item-level permissions.

Content Approval

Approving items for entry in a list does not occur in the Customize List screen; nevertheless, it is an important part of managing list content when it is enabled. Once content approval is enabled in the general settings for a list, the actual approval and rejection occurs on the list screen. Enable content approval when you do not want users seeing information until an approver has had the opportunity to review it.

Items in a list with content approval enabled will contain an additional option in their context menu as you can see in Figure 4-5. Items that have not been approved by a user with the Manage List permission will not appear in the list to most users of the site. Users who do not have this permission will not see their new items in the All Items view until after an approver has reviewed it.

Enabling content approval also creates two new views for the list to help users work with the list items. The first is called Approve/Reject Items and is intended for users with the Manage List permission to use in order to quickly display the list items categorized by status. This view is displayed in Figure 4-5. In this manner, approvers can easily see pending items and take the appropriate approval action. Users without this permission will not be able to access the Approve/Reject Items view.

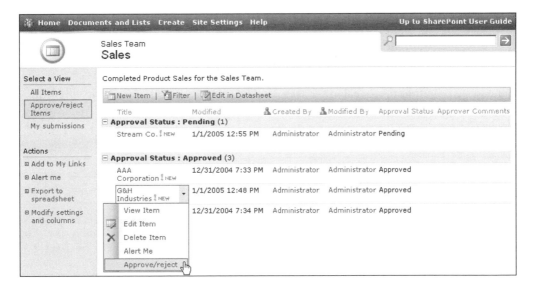

Figure 4-5. *Item approval*

To approve or reject newly added list items:

1. As a site administrator or web designer, navigate to a list that has the Content Approval option enabled.

2. Select the Approve/Reject Items view by clicking the link in the views list on the left.

3. Activate the context menu of the item you wish to approve or reject by hovering over the Title column with your mouse and clicking the inverted triangle.

4. Click the Approve/Reject link in the context menu.

5. Select the appropriate approval status for the item. Pending leaves the item in the current state, neither approved nor rejected. The Approved option makes the item visible to all users of the list. Rejected marks it as rejected so that the creator can modify the item but it remains hidden from other users of the list.

6. Enter a comment explaining the content approval decision especially when rejecting an item, so that the creator can understand why the item was rejected.

Users who have added items to the list should select the My Submissions view to see whether any of their items have been rejected. This view displays to users all items they have created and categorizes them based on their approval status. If an item is rejected by the content approver, any comments entered by the approver are displayed in the My Submissions view so that the submitter can make corrections or add another item.

■**Note** Items added by a user that has the Manage List permission are automatically approved and will immediately appear to all users who can normally view items in the list.

Security

An important decision when managing your list is who will have access to it. Different levels of access range from viewing items to deleting items and can be even as powerful as allowing other users to manage the list properties and settings themselves.

Table 4-2 describes the list security that is applied to the standard SharePoint site groups when you first create a list.

Table 4-2. *Default List Security*

Site Group	Security
Administrator	Can perform all functions in a list including viewing list items, modifying list items, managing list settings, and changing permissions.
Web Designer	Can view, add, modify, and delete items in the list. A member of this group also has the ability to modify the list's general settings and structure as well as approve/reject items, but cannot change the security settings of the list even if that member was the one who created the list.
Contributor	Can view, add, modify, and delete items in the list.
Reader	Can only view items. Readers are not allowed to add, edit, or otherwise modify the content of the list.

■**Note** SharePoint displays links to many actions that a user does not necessarily have the permissions to use. When users without the proper permissions attempts to click these links or complete the action, they will be prompted for an account and password that has the correct permissions. This is not an error like many users believe, rather it is how SharePoint security works in many places.

As you can see from Table 4-2, the only users with the ability to change list security are those in the Administrator site group. If you are a site administrator, Web Designer members may request changes to security for the lists that they have created since they cannot modify the security themselves.

As an administrator, you have many options for changing list permissions. Access can be granted based on site groups or domain users. Furthermore, permissions for users can be determined by basic list permission groups or more granular advanced permission settings.

To add users to the list security, perform the following steps:

1. On the List screen, click the Modify Settings and Columns link in the Actions list on the left menu.

2. On the Customize List screen, click the Change Permissions for this List link under the General Settings section.

3. On the Change Permissions screen, click the Add Users link on the toolbar.

4. On the Add Users screen, enter the e-mail address or user name of the user or users you wish to add in the Users box. You can also give access to the list to a site group that does not yet have permission by entering the site group name in the Users box.

5. If you do not know the exact e-mail addresses or user names of the people you want to give access to, you can click the Address Book button. This button will open up the same address book you should be familiar with from Outlook. From the address book you can search for people in both corporate and personal address lists. When you have found a user you wish to grant access to for the list, select that user in the list and click the To button. After you have done this for all of the users you wish to add, click the OK button.

6. Select the permission group that you want your new users to have access to. For more granular security, click the Advanced Permissions link. The advanced permissions allow you to choose specific permissions from all available access types that you can grant to another user.

■**Note** When you add multiple users at the same time, they can only have the same permissions. If you need to give different permissions to each user or group, you must perform these steps for each distinct set of users and permissions you need to create.

---

7. Click the Next button.

8. On steps 3 and 4 of Add Users, enter any additional information about the users and specify whether you want SharePoint to notify them about their new ability to access this list.

9. Click the Finish button.

You will now notice that the users you have added show up in the list of users with access to the list along with the permissions you specified. You should also notice that a new message and link appear near the top of the Change Permissions screen. This message tells you that the list no longer has the same permissions as the site it is on. The link provides you with an easy way to reset the permissions to the same security that the site is using.

To modify list permissions for a site group, perform the following steps:

1. On the List screen, click the Modify Settings and Columns link in the Actions list on the left menu.

2. On the Customize List screen, click the Change Permissions for this List link under the General Settings section.

3. On the Change Permissions screen, check the boxes next to the Contributor and Reader site groups. We will change permissions for both of these groups at the same time. If you only wish to change the permissions for a single group, you can click the name of that site group.

4. Click the Edit Permissions of Selected Users link on the toolbar.

5. For this example, we will allow the Readers and Contributors groups to add and edit list items but not to delete items. To do this, click the Advanced Permissions link.

6. Check the boxes next to View List Items, Add List Items, and Edit List Items.

7. Click the OK button.

The Change Permissions screen will refresh, and you will now notice that the Contributor and Reader permissions are both displayed as being custom. Expanding the custom permission by clicking the plus sign allows you to view the specific permissions for these site groups.

Managing Columns

The power of custom lists resides in the ability to design the structure determining how your information will be stored and presented. SharePoint refers to the individual data fields in your list as *columns*. Each column has a specific type of data associated with it. These types include text, numbers, currency, and many others that allow SharePoint to enforce formatting and allow for other business rules on the data such as minimum and maximum values for number entry.

The complete list of column types can be seen in Figure 4-6.

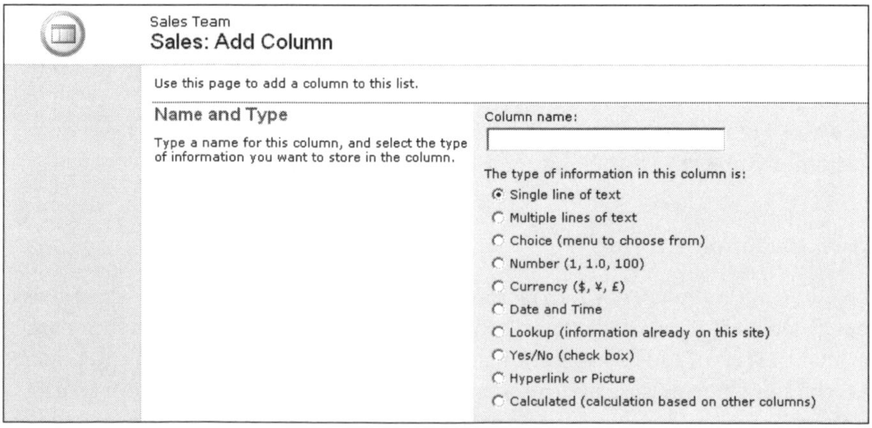

Sales Team
Sales: Add Column

Use this page to add a column to this list.

Name and Type

Type a name for this column, and select the type of information you want to store in the column.

Column name:

The type of information in this column is:
- ○ Single line of text
- ○ Multiple lines of text
- ○ Choice (menu to choose from)
- ○ Number (1, 1.0, 100)
- ○ Currency ($, ¥, £)
- ○ Date and Time
- ○ Lookup (information already on this site)
- ○ Yes/No (check box)
- ○ Hyperlink or Picture
- ○ Calculated (calculation based on other columns)

Figure 4-6. *Column types on the Add Column screen*

SharePoint provides you with an easy way to determine the number, type, order, and settings for each column in your list. To add a column to a list, perform the following steps:

1. On the List screen, click the Modify Settings and Columns link in the Actions list on the left menu.

2. On the Customize List screen, click the Add New Column link under the Columns section.

3. On the Add Column screen, enter a short descriptive name for the column.

4. Choose the column type for the information that will be entered into this column.

5. Specify any settings under the optional settings section. The settings that appear in this section are dependent on the column type and will dynamically change if you select a different column type. These settings are described in detail in upcoming sections.

6. Check the boxes next to Add to default view. This makes the information visible on the default view when users are displaying this list. Views are covered in detail later in this chapter.

7. Click the OK button.

When these steps are completed, you are taken back to the Customize List screen and your new column can be seen in the Columns section. To edit a column, simply click the name of the column in the Columns section. The settings for the column will be available for modification in the Change Column screen.

■**Caution** When changing the column type, SharePoint will warn you that you could experience data loss. For example, changing a Single line of text column to a Number will result in SharePoint dropping any values that contain character data (for example, "abc123") since it does not know how to interpret them strictly as numbers. SharePoint takes it another step further, permitting certain column types to be changed only to certain other column types. For example, you cannot change a Single line of text column to a Lookup since it cannot reconcile the data between the two types. Likewise, once a Multiple lines of text column is created, it cannot be changed to any other type. Be sure to plan out the design of your list well to avoid having to make these changes when users have already populated the list with data.

To delete a column, perform the following steps:

1. On the Customize List screen, click the name of the column under the Columns section.

2. On the Change Column screen, click the Delete button at the bottom of the screen.

3. When prompted to confirm that you wish to delete the column and all of the data that it contains, click the OK button.

■**Caution** Once you select OK on the confirmation for deleting the item, the column is physically deleted from SharePoint. All of the data in that column is deleted from SharePoint as well. It is not possible to recover the data without assistance from your IT staff, so be absolutely sure that the information in that column is no longer needed before confirming that it should be deleted.

Once you have created many columns to hold all of the information for a list, you may find that you want to modify the order in which they are displayed to the user. More important columns may need to be placed earlier in the order or related items placed nearer to each other. Modifying the order of the columns affects how they appear when a user adds, edits, or views a list item.

To modify the order of the columns, perform these steps:

1. On the Customize List screen, click the Change the Order of the Fields link under the Columns section.

2. On the Change Field Order screen, change the position of a column by selecting a number in the drop-down list next to it in the list. A smaller number moves the column closer to the top of the display, while a larger number moves it farther down. As you change the sequence number for a column, other sequence numbers will automatically change to maintain the same number of sequence numbers in the proper order.

3. Repeat step 2 until the columns' order numbers are in the correct sequence that you want them displayed to the user.

4. Click the OK button.

As you saw while performing the previous steps, there are many different column types, and each has its own settings and functionality. We will now take you through each type in detail so you can make the most productive use of this SharePoint functionality when creating the structure for your lists.

Single Line of Text

Use the Single line of text type when the column should contain any textual information, including numbers, punctuation, and symbols, without carriage returns. Examples include names, phone numbers, and titles. This column type will display to the user as a text box, allowing entry of text on one line. Table 4-3 lists the optional settings for a Single line of text column.

Table 4-3. *Optional Settings for Single Line of Text Columns*

Setting	Description
Description	Displayed on the Add and Edit Item screens to help users understand what information they should enter.
Required Information	Specifies whether users must enter information in this column in order to add or edit an item.
Maximum Characters	The largest number of characters that users can enter. This value can be from 1 to 255 (the default).
Default Value	The initial value for the column when users create a new list item. This can be specific text or a value calculated from a formula. For more information on using calculations and formulas, see the calculated column type and formula discussion in the "Calculated" section later in this chapter.

Multiple Lines of Text

Use the Multiple lines of text type when the column should contain any long textual informa-tion that can span more than a single line of entry with no maximum length or if you need rich text editing capabilities. Examples include addresses, comments, and directions. This column type will display to the user as a text area, allowing entry of text on more than one line. Table 4-4 lists the optional settings for a Multiple lines of text column.

Table 4-4. *Optional Settings for Multiple Lines of Text Columns*

Setting	Description
Description	Displayed on the Add and Edit Item screens to help users understand what information they should enter.
Required Information	Specifies whether users must enter information in this column in order to add or edit an item.
Number of Lines to Display	The height of the text area, in lines, that is displayed when users add a new item.
Allow Rich Text	Determines whether a toolbar is displayed on the text area, which allows users to alter the look of the text with features such as bold, italics, underline, alignment, indentation, numbered lists, and colors.

Choice

Use the Choice type when you want to present a list of predetermined values to the user. Examples could include state, status, and department. You can determine how the choices are displayed to the user by selecting a display type from the optional settings. Table 4-5 lists the optional settings for a Choice column.

Table 4-5. *Optional Settings for Choice Columns*

Setting	Description
Description	Displayed on the Add and Edit Item screens to help users understand what information they should enter.
Required Information	Specifies whether users must enter information in this column in order to add or edit an item.
Choices	Type the predetermined list of choices here, making sure each choice is on a separate line.
Display Type	Determines how the choices will be displayed to users. Possible types are drop-down list, radio buttons, and checkboxes. Choosing checkboxes allows users to select multiple values for this column.
Allow Fillins	If you choose Yes for this option, users can type in a value that is not in the predetermined choice list.
Default Value	The initial value for the column when users create a new list item. This can be a specific choice or a value calculated from a formula.

Number

Use the Number type when the column should contain only numerical data, including percents. SharePoint will not allow character information in this column type, which allows you to perform mathematical operations on the information in this column when using views. Views and how to do these mathematical operations are discussed in detail later in this chapter. Examples include quantity, discount, and age. Table 4-6 lists the optional settings for a Number column.

Table 4-6. *Optional Settings for Number Columns*

Setting	Description
Description	Displayed on the Add and Edit Item screens to help users understand what information they should enter.
Required Information	Specifies whether users must enter information in this column in order to add or edit an item.
Limits	Allows you to specify the minimum and maximum value that users can enter. If users enter a value outside of this range, they are shown a message with the limits displayed so that they can correct the information.
Decimals	Determines how many decimal places to display. If set to Automatic, the decimal is displayed differently for each value entered. If set to a specific number, the decimal is displayed at that position for every value; thus a decimal of 2 displays the value 5 as 5.00.
Default Value	The initial value for the column when users create a new list item. This can be a specific value or a value calculated from a formula.
Percentage	If you check this option, all values are displayed as and behave like percents.

■**Caution** When changing a Number column that contains data to a percentage, SharePoint determines the percentage value using decimals so that the value 0.5 becomes 50%. As a result, the value 50, which users could have entered intending 50%, becomes 5000% when you change a Number column from a non-percentage to a percentage.

Currency

Use the Currency type when the column should contain only monetary values. Examples include cost, salary, and payment. This column type behaves very similarly to the number column by allowing mathematical operations in views. Table 4-7 lists the optional settings for a Currency column.

Table 4-7. *Optional Settings for Currency Columns*

Setting	Description
Description	Displayed on the Add and Edit Item screens to help users understand what information they should enter.
Required Information	Specifies whether users must enter information in this column in order to add or edit an item.
Limits	Allows you to specify the minimum and maximum value that users can enter. If users enter a value outside of this range, they are shown a message with the limits displayed so that they can correct the information.
Decimals	Determines how many decimal places to display. If set to Automatic, the decimal is displayed differently for each value entered. If set to a specific number, the decimal is displayed at that position for every value; thus a decimal of 2 displays the value 5 as 5.00.
Default Value	The initial value for the column when users create a new list item. This can be a specific value or a value calculated from a formula.
Currency Format	Allows you to choose a country to determine the currency type and how the values are displayed with currency symbols.

Date and Time

Use the Date and Time type when the column should contain either date values or both date and time values. Examples include paid date, due date, and start time. Unfortunately, Share-Point does not provide the ability to enter a time value without a date. Table 4-8 lists the optional settings for a Date and Time column.

Table 4-8. *Optional Settings for Date and Time Columns*

Setting	Description
Description	Displayed on the Add and Edit Item screens to help users understand what information they should enter.
Required Information	Specifies whether users must enter information in this column in order to add or edit an item.
Format	Determines whether the values for this column contain only a date or both a date and time.
Default Value	The initial value for the column when users create a new list item. This can be the current date and time when the item is added, a specific date and time, or a value calculated from a formula.

■**Caution** SharePoint does not provide the ability to enter only time values. If you select only a time for a Date and Time column without entering a date and save the changes, the time value you chose will not be saved.

Lookup

Use the Lookup type when the column should contain a list of choices for the user to select from. The difference between this type and the Choice type is that the Lookup type determines the choices dynamically by presenting the values from another list on the same site. It also allows you to create a column whose choices are the list of users for the site. A Lookup column is always displayed as a drop-down list when entering the data as shown in Figure 4-7. The values are presented as links on the list screen allowing you to quickly see the list item associated with the given lookup value. Table 4-9 lists the optional settings for a Lookup column.

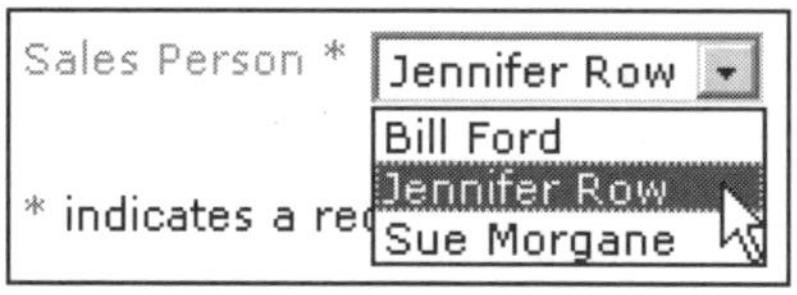

Figure 4-7. *A Lookup column*

■**Note** Presence Information requires that your technical IT administrator has installed Microsoft's Live Communications Server and Windows Messenger in your organization. These products are not part of a standard SharePoint deployment.

Table 4-9. *Optional Settings for Lookup Columns*

Setting	Description
Description	Displayed on the Add and Edit Item screens to help users understand what information they should enter.
Required Information	Specifies whether users must enter information in this column in order to add or edit an item.
Source List	The list whose list items will be used as choices in this column. Options include all other lists in the site as well as a special list called User Information that contains all of the users of the site.
Source Column	The column in the source list that will contain the values to be used as choices in this list.
Presence Information	If the User Information option is selected as the source list, this optional setting is presented. Check this to include the presence and messaging interface next to the selected users. This interface provides integration with Windows Messenger features.

Yes/No

Use the Yes/No type when the column should contain a simple on or off value. Examples include active and reviewed. This column type will display to the user as a checkbox. Table 4-10 lists the optional settings for a Yes/No column.

Table 4-10. *Optional Settings for Yes/No Columns*

Setting	Description
Description	Displayed on the Add and Edit Item screens to help users understand what information they should enter
Default Value	The initial value for the column when users create a new list item

Hyperlink or Picture

Use the Hyperlink or Picture type when the column should contain either a link to someplace else or an image that should be displayed with the list item. Examples include logos and web site links. Table 4-11 lists the optional settings for a Hyperlink or Picture column.

Table 4-11. *Optional Settings for Hyperlink or Picture Columns*

Setting	Description
Description	Displayed on the Add and Edit Item screens to help users understand what information they should enter.
Required Information	Specifies whether users must enter information in this column in order to add or edit an item.
Format	Used to determine whether the value should be displayed as a link that users can click or an image that gets displayed on the list or View Item screens. When entering an image, users cannot upload a file; instead they must enter a URL to the image.

Calculated

Use the Calculated type when the column should not allow users to determine the value but rather should calculate the value based on a formula that can include other list item column data. Examples include discount amount, current date period, and net sale price. This column type will not display to users in the Add Item screen, but the calculated value will display in the list and View Item screens. Table 4-12 lists the optional settings for a Calculated column.

Table 4-12. *Optional Settings for Calculated Columns*

Setting	Description
Description	Displayed on the Add and Edit Item screens to help users understand what information they should enter.
Formula	The calculation used to determine the value for the column.
Data Type	The type of data that the Calculated column will create. Available data types are text, number, currency, date and time, and yes/no. Other optional settings are available according to the data type selected, similar to optional settings for the corresponding column types; for instance, the number data type allows you to select decimals and percentage.

The ability to create list columns that display the results of logical, mathematical, and other operations on list data makes SharePoint lists extremely customizable. In addition to the Calculated column type, calculations can be used to determine the default value for other column types.

The formula is what determines the resulting value for the Calculated column. A formula is made up of functions, operators, constants, and references to other columns. Functions are predefined calculations that require you to specify parameters and return a result. SharePoint categorizes the available functions into the categories discussed in Table 4-13.

Table 4-13. *Types of Functions in SharePoint*

Category	Description
Date and Time	Works with dates and date columns. An example is DATEDIF(), which calculates the amount of a specified time unit between two dates.
Financial	Performs calculations for loans, investments, and other financial data. An example is FV(), which calculates a future value of an investment given a period, payments, and interest rate.
Information	Functions in this category return True or False if a value matches the information type requested. Examples include ISNUMBER(), ISTEXT(), and ISBLANK().
Logical	Applies logic to parameters. An example is IF(), which conditionally returns separate results based on the logical truth of a given value. Other examples include AND, OR, and NOT.

Category	Description
Lookup and Reference	The only function in this category is CHOOSE(), which allows the calculation to select a value from different choices based on a specified parameter.
Math and Trigonometry	A large group of functions that perform mathematical calculations. An example is SUM(), which returns the result from adding all of its parameters.
Statistical	Another large group of functions that perform statistics-based calculations. An example is STDEV(), which returns the standard deviation from the parameters passed to it.
Text and Data	This group of functions perform string manipulation and other data-specific calculations. An example is LEN(), which returns the number of characters that the text parameter contains. These functions also let you combine or compare values from different columns.

In addition to functions, SharePoint provides the ability to use operators in your formulas. Operators come in three types: arithmetic, comparison, and text. Arithmetic operators provide add (+), subtract (–), multiply (*), divide (/), and other operations that produce numeric results. Comparison operators result in a logical yes/no and include less than (<), greater than (>), equals (=), as well as others. The only text operator available is for concatenation (&), which results in the combination of two text values.

A very important aspect to creating powerful calculated columns is the ability to include references to other columns. You reference other columns by entering the column name in the formula. If SharePoint uses the column name for its own internal use, you may have to enclose the reference in brackets like this: [LastName]. When a calculation uses a column reference, it is referring to the value in the referenced column for the same list item on which the calculation is being performed. This allows you to perform functions on the columns or manipulate them with operators. Formulas can also include constants. Specific numbers, text, or dates that are entered into a formula are considered constants, since their value for the formula is not dependent on another function or column data.

■**Note** You cannot use column references in column default values. It is also not possible for calculations to use column values in rows other than the current row.

Figure 4-8 shows where a formula and return type are specified for a calculated column. Table 4-14 provides examples of formulas that will help you to better understand how functions, operators, constants, and columns can be combined to create beneficial calculated columns.

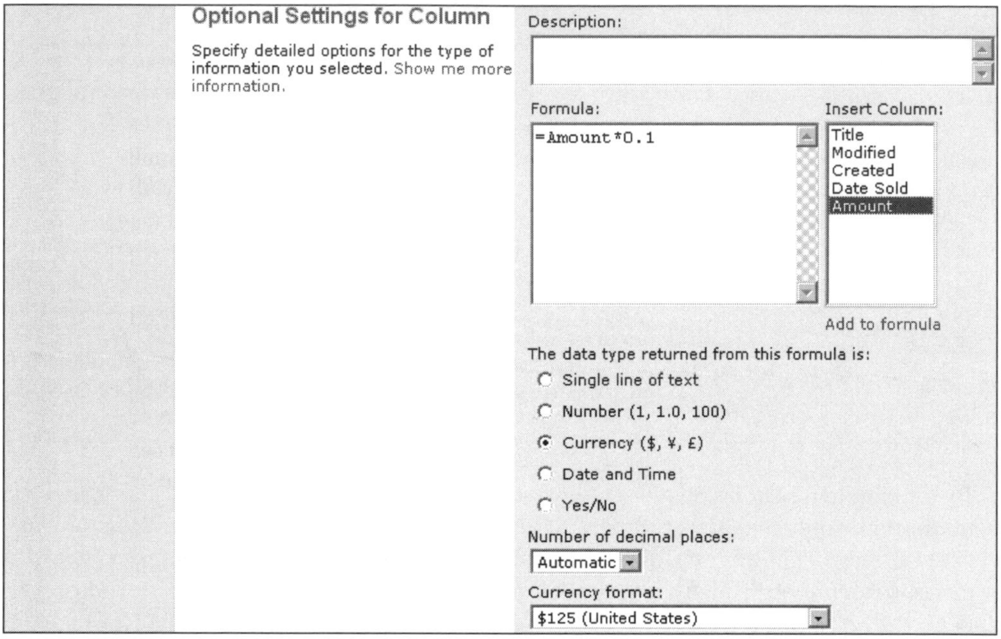

Figure 4-8. *Calculated column optional settings*

Table 4-14. *Example Formulas*

Formula	Description
=SUM(Num1, Num 2, Num 3)	Uses the SUM() function to add three columns that are referenced
=SUM(Num 1, Num 2)/ Num 3	Uses the SUM() function to add two columns and then divides that number by the value in a third column using the / operator
=LastName&","&FirstName	Uses the concatenation operator to create a full name column from separate LastName and FirstName columns
=IF(Cost>10, "High", "Low")	Uses the IF() function to return a constant text value of High if the Cost column is greater than 10 and a constant text value of Low if it is not
=TEXT(WEEKDAY(DueDate), "ddd")	Shows how to nest functions by using both the WEEKDAY() function to determine the day of the week as a number and the TEXT() function to convert that number to its three-letter abbreviation

SharePoint provides many more functions and operators for calculated columns than we have the space to cover in this chapter. For more information on calculated columns, see the SharePoint help files by clicking the Show Me More Information link under the Optional Settings section on the Add Column or Change Column screens.

Managing Views

Earlier in this chapter we mentioned the use of views, which are an integral part of creating and using a list. Views are a persisted display of the data in a list, and they are created to provide a quick way for your users to find the data they need in a way that is most meaningful to them. Views provide the filtering and sorting abilities that you can achieve normally through a list but also add grouping, mathematical operations on columns, the ability to show or hide certain columns, and more. As you will see later, views can be *public*, so that all users of the list see a link to the view, or *private*, so that only the user creating the view sees a link to the view on the list screen.

There are three types of views in SharePoint, each with its own abilities and settings that determine how the view displays data. The standard type is the most commonly used view. It displays items in a tabular display that contains grouping and style settings not found in the other view types. The datasheet type uses the Datasheet view discussed earlier to display the data in an Excel-like editable grid. The calendar type displays the list items in a calendar format based on date fields from the list item that you specify. Refer to Table 4-15 for the best uses for each view type.

Table 4-15. *The Different View Types*

Type	Purpose
Standard	Use the standard view type when you want list items displayed in a line-item or tabular format. The standard view allows grouping to provide an expandable and collapsible display of the list items. It also allows a style setting that you can use to present your list items as line items, tables, business cards, and other variations.
Datasheet	The datasheet type is best used when the data changes frequently and time spent updating items should be minimized. The user can switch to a Datasheet view while in a standard view, so the standard type is the better option for most of your views. Users must have Office 2003 installed in order to use the datasheet type.
Calendar	Use the calendar when the data is best suited to representation by dates. The calendar can be shown in a month, week, or daily view. Good examples for a calendar type are lists of events, tasks, and milestones where displaying by date allows users to interpret important or recent list items the same way they would look at an Outlook calendar.

■Tip The All Items view created with a new custom list is determined by the link you choose on the Create page. Choosing the Custom List link generates the All Items view as a standard view, while the Custom List in Datasheet View link creates the All Items view as a Datasheet view.

Standard and Datasheet Views

One of the primary selections when managing a view is deciding what data should be displayed. The view allows you to select just one column up to as many as all of them to be displayed. You are also given the ability to determine the order in which the columns are displayed in the view. The columns you have created for the list are not the only columns available for the view to display. The view can actually expose some columns that SharePoint uses to manage the list as well as columns related to item approval. Table 4-16 further describes the special columns that can be used in a view.

■**Caution** Modifying the order of the columns in the list settings does not change the order of columns in any views. You must edit the view and change the Position From Left value of each column to change how the view displays them.

Just like you can sort the list items in the normal list screen, a view allows you to determine what the default sort will be for users displaying the view. These settings only determine what the initial sort will be when the view is first displayed. Users can still sort the items even further via the standard functionality on the list screen. Compared to the normal sort, the view's sort functionality is more complex. In the list screen you can only sort by a single column, but a view can be sorted by up to two columns. The view also allows you to sort on columns that are not actually being displayed, including the special columns described in Table 4-16.

Table 4-16. *Special List Columns for Use in Views*

Column	Description
Attachments	Used to determine whether the list item contains attachments. When displayed in a view, this column will contain a paperclip icon if there are attachments associated with the list item. Setting the filter criteria to Yes or No allows you to filter based on this column.
Title (linked to Edit)	Displays the Title column as a link that takes the user to the Edit Item screen. This column is identical to the normal Title column when used for sorting and filtering.
ID	Contains a number that uniquely identifies a list item within a list.
Modified	The date and time that the list item was last edited. If the item was never edited, it contains the date and time the list item was created.
Created	The date and time that the list item was created.
Created By	The user who created the list item.
Modified By	The last user to modify the list item.
Approval Status	The status of the list item in the approval process. Possible values are Pending, Rejected, and Approved. This column is only available in lists that require approval.
Approver Comments	The comments entered by the approver during the approval process. This column is only available in lists that require approval.
Edit (link to Edit)	Displays a column containing an Edit icon as a link that takes the user to the Edit Item screen.
Title (link to View)	Displays the Title column as a link that takes the user to the View Item screen. This column is identical to the normal Title column when used for sorting and filtering.

■**Tip** The column used to sort the view does *not* need to be one of the columns being displayed.

Filtering in views is also similar to filtering in the list screen but provides enhanced functionality. One difference is the ability to combine multiple filters using AND and OR logical operators. The list screen provides only the ability to create a filter where the column value exactly matches the specified value. The view's filtering makes it easy to create filters that use other operators such as greater than, less than, is not equal to, begins with, and contains. By creating a combination of up to ten of these filters, you are able to create powerful filters that can simplify a large list to only the items meeting strict criteria.

There are also two special values that you can use when creating filters. Entering [**Today**] as the value for the filter uses the current date as the filter's criteria. Typing [**Me**] as the value for the filter causes SharePoint to use the current user as the criteria for the filter. These special values allow you to create views like My Items or Items Submitted Today. In addition to the columns you have created for the list, you can specify filter criteria for the special columns described in Table 4-16.

Another feature of a standard view is the ability to display the list items in a group-by-group fashion. Grouping only applies to standard views and not Datasheet views. You can select what column controls the grouping, and all list items with the same value in that column will be displayed together in expandable and collapsible groups. SharePoint allows for up to two levels of grouping. You are able to specify the sort order of the groups as well as their default behavior of being collapsed or expanded. All columns including the special columns in Table 4-16 can be part of a view's grouping criteria.

SharePoint views allow you to perform mathematical functions on the data in a given column. These are specified in the Totals section of the Manage View screen. The functions available to perform on a column depend on the column type. Many columns allow you to generate a count of the number of list items that contain a value in that column. Date columns allow you display the average, minimum, or maximum values that the column contains for all list items in the view. Number columns allow you to perform all of these functions as well as display the sum, standard deviation, and variance of the values. Totals can be generated from all columns including the special columns described in Table 4-16.

The view type is the most important option in determining how the list looks when displayed. The standard view type lets you choose from a list of styles that control exactly the manner in which the columns are displaying on the list screen. The view style is not available for a Datasheet view. Table 4-17 describes the different options available to you when choosing the style of your view.

Long lists of data that are not filtered down in views will reduce performance when viewed or make the list extremely long. Many users balk at the idea of scrolling down page after page in their browser in order to find the item they need to work with. In addition to the previously discussed features that reduce these situations, views also impose limits on the number of list items being displayed in the view. You are given the option of changing SharePoint's default limit of 100 items. You can choose to display only the specified number of list items, but this could cause users to be unaware of all of the data in the list. The other option is to allow users to page through the list items in batches of the specified number of list items. Choosing the paging option displays the number of the list items they are currently viewing as well as a Next link to see the next batch of list items, but no Previous link.

Table 4-17. *View Styles*

Style	Description
Basic Table	Displays each list item in a single row with each column in the view being displayed from left to right.
Boxed	List items are displayed in individual boxes, two boxes wide on the screen. Inside each box the column information is displayed vertically alongside the column labels. This style gives the appearance of business cards when the list contains contact information. Figure 4-9 shows the boxed view style.
Boxed (no labels)	Identical to the boxed style but without the column labels.
Newsletter	Displays the list items in rows, but in each row the Single line of text columns early in the view's column order are displayed horizontally like headlines. All additional columns in the view are displayed vertically underneath the headline columns without column labels.
Newsletter (no lines)	Identical to the newsletter style but without horizontal lines separating the individual list items.
Shaded	Identical to the basic table except that alternating items are displayed with a background color, making it easier to follow the columns from left to right for a particular list item.

Figure 4-9. *Boxed view style*

Tip When filtering a paged view the filter is applied to the entire list, not just the items on the currently displayed page.

To create a public standard view, follow these steps:

1. On the list screen, click the Modify Settings and Columns link in the Actions menu on the left.

2. On the Customize List screen, click the Add a New View link under the Views section.

3. On the Create View screen, click the Standard View link.

4. In the Name section, enter a name for the view and check the box to make this view the default view that others will use to access this list.

5. In the Audience section, select Create a Public View so that other users will be shown a link to this view.

6. In the Columns section, check the box next to each column that you wish to appear in the view. You can also specify the order in which the columns will be displayed in the view by modifying the numbers under the Position from Left heading.

7. In the Sort section, use the drop-down list to select the column that will be used to sort the list. Select whether the sorting should be performed in an ascending (A to Z, 1 to 10) or descending (Z to A, 10 to 1) manner. You can choose an additional sorting column that will be used if the initial sorting column contains duplicate values.

8. In the Filter section, you can choose to display only the list items that match a given criterion. Use the drop-down lists to select a column and an operation, and then type in a value in the text box. To create more than two filters, click the Show More Columns link.

9. In the Group By section, select a column to display the list items in groups determined by the values in the column. This section also allows you to determine how the groups are sorted and whether they are expanded or collapsed by default.

10. In the Totals section, choose any mathematical calculations you wish to perform on the list items and have displayed in the view. Count is the most common calculation and is a nice way to let users know how many list items are in the view they are displaying.

11. In the Styles section, choose the style for the view as described in Table 4-17. The default style is the basic table.

12. In the Limits section, select the number of list items that should be displayed and whether that should be a hard limit or the size of batches that the user can page through.

13. Click the OK button.

Calendar View

What we have discussed so far regarding views pertains mostly to the standard or datasheet types. The calendar view type contains different settings in order to generate a usable display.

While all of the columns of a list are available to display in a standard view, only the Title column is displayed in a calendar view. When creating a calendar view, there is no need to choose what columns to display; rather, you choose what columns the calendar dates are based on. The calendar view type gives two options for this. The first is to base the calendar on a single date, and SharePoint displays a list of the date columns in the list for you to choose from for this. The other option is to base the calendar on two date columns where each calendar entry begins on one column and ends on the date in the second column. This makes the calendar more useful when the list contains begin and end dates or assigned and due dates.

Another option for the calendar view type allows you to choose from three different calendar settings. These settings are a monthly, weekly, or daily view. The option you choose in the view is only the initial display when a user clicks the link to display the view. Once displaying the view, you are able to change the display by clicking the toolbar of the list or by clicking specific dates in the calendar.

The only other option that is available when creating a calendar view is a filter. The filter in a calendar view works identically to the filter in the standard and Datasheet view settings. There are no sorting, totals, groups, styles, or limits available in a calendar view.

To create a public calendar view, follow these steps:

1. On the list screen, click the Modify Settings and Columns link in the Actions menu on the left.

2. On the Customize List screen, click the Add a New View link under the Views section.

3. On the Create View screen, click the Calendar View link.

4. In the Name section, enter a name for the view and check the box if you want to make this view the default view that others will use to access this list.

5. In the Audience section, select Create a Public View so that other users will be shown a link to this view.

6. In the Columns section, select which date columns to base the calendar display on. You can choose to base it on a single date or to have the calendar display items with two dates that represent the start and end of the calendar entry.

7. In the Calendar Settings section, select the Month View to have the calendar initially display the current month to the user.

8. In the Filter section, you can choose to display only the list items that match a given criterion. Use the drop-down lists to select a column and an operation, and then type a value in the text box. To create more than two filters, click the Show More Columns link.

9. Click the OK button.

The calendar will now be available to select from on the list screen. Figure 4-10 shows a calendar view displayed by week for the previously mentioned Sales example.

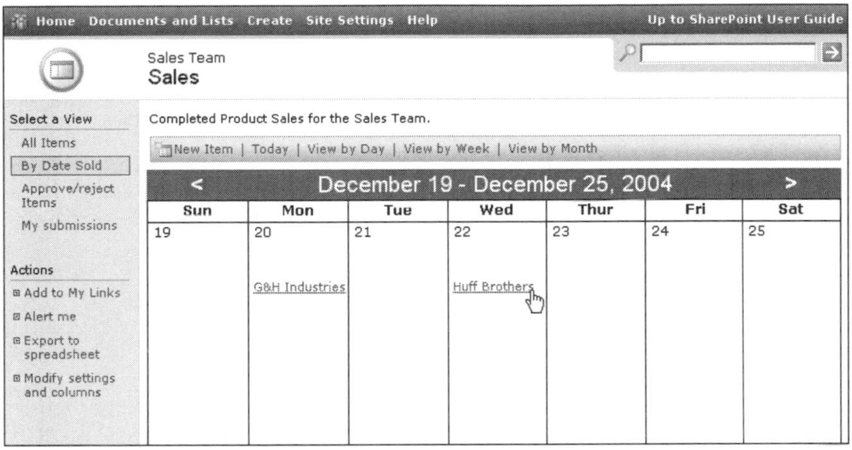

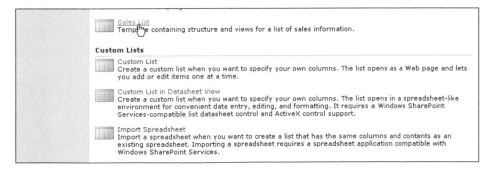

Figure 4-10. *Calendar view*

Creating a List Template

Often you need to create multiple lists with the same or similar columns, views, and settings. Whether you need to create these lists in the same site or create a similar list in multiple sites, it is extremely inefficient to go through the process of creating the list, adding columns, creating views, and all the other steps that go into making a useful list repeatedly for each instance where you need the list.

As an example, you may be tracking sales on a SharePoint site. International sales may include the same column and views that domestic sales would use, but also include additional columns or views that are not associated with domestic sales. It would be inefficient to create the domestic sales list with all of its columns and views and then duplicate the effort in order to create the international sales list.

To make it easier to quickly create lists that are similar in structure, SharePoint allows you to take any list and make a list template from it. You can even choose to have it maintain the content, or list items, in the template. Then, when you create a new list in the same site collection, you are able to select the list template you have created as shown in Figure 4-11. When the new list is created, it will contain the same columns, views, and settings as the original list and can also contain the same information.

Sales List
Template containing structure and views for a list of sales information.

Custom Lists

Custom List
Create a custom list when you want to specify your own columns. The list opens as a Web page and lets you add or edit items one at a time.

Custom List in Datasheet View
Create a custom list when you want to specify your own columns. The list opens in a spreadsheet-like environment for convenient data entry, editing, and formatting. It requires a Windows SharePoint Services-compatible list datasheet control and ActiveX control support.

Import Spreadsheet
Import a spreadsheet when you want to create a list that has the same columns and contents as an existing spreadsheet. Importing a spreadsheet requires a spreadsheet application compatible with Windows SharePoint Services.

Figure 4-11. *Create screen with a Sales List template*

To create a list template, follow these steps:

1. As a site administrator or web designer, navigate to a list screen.

2. Click the Modify Settings and Columns link in the Actions menu on the left.

3. Under General Settings, click the Save List as Template link.

4. Specify a file name, a simple title, and a more elaborate description for the template.

5. If you want the template to contain all of the data and attachments currently in the list, check the Include content checkbox.

6. Click the OK button.

At this point, the template is available for use when creating new lists as shown in Figure 4-11. After the template is created, a link that takes you to the list template gallery will be displayed. The list template gallery allows you to manage all of the list templates that you or other users create.

To get to the list template gallery from a site, follow these steps:

1. On the site's home page, click the Site Settings link on the top menu bar.

2. On the Site Settings screen, click the Go to Site Administration link under the Administration section.

3. If the site you are on is a subsite rather than a top-level site, click the Go to Top-level Site Administration link under the Site Collection Administration section; otherwise skip to step 4.

4. On the Top-level Site Administration screen, click the Manage List Template Gallery link under the Site Collection Galleries section.

Changing the file name, title, and description can be accomplished by clicking the edit icon for the appropriate template. Clicking the file name link allows you to download the template file from the SharePoint site. If you already have previously created template files, you can upload them into the list template gallery by clicking the Upload Template link in the toolbar and selecting the .stp file you want added to the gallery.

■**Tip** Template files (.stp) can be downloaded from SharePoint and uploaded into a different SharePoint site collection or even a different installation of SharePoint. This can be beneficial when creating a list structure that can be used in multiple installations of SharePoint in your organization.

Deleting the List

You may want to delete a list if the data is no longer needed, if the list was created on the wrong site, or for other reasons. The Customize List screen allows you to quickly delete a list from a site.

To delete a list, follow these steps:

1. On the list screen, click the Modify Settings and Columns link in the Actions list on the left menu

2. On the Customize List screen, click the Delete this List link under the General Settings category.

3. Click OK when prompted for confirmation that you wish to delete the list.

■**Caution** Once you select OK on the confirmation for deleting the list, the list and all of the information it contains is physically deleted from SharePoint. It is not possible to recover that list without assistance from your IT staff.

Adding a Listing to the Portal

Now that you have the ability to create custom lists to hold information that other users will want to find, you must make it easier for those users to find that information through the portal. As discussed in earlier chapters, the portal is instrumental in allowing users to easily find the information they are looking for. One of the best ways to allow users to find this information is to provide listings in the area or areas that best relate to the list.

Lists give you the ability to easily add listings to multiple portal areas from the Customize List screen. The functionality is virtually the same as adding a listing when in a portal area as described in Chapter 2.

To add listings for a list to the portal, perform the following steps:

1. On the list screen, click the Modify Settings and Columns link in the Actions list on the left menu.

2. On the Customize List screen, click the Select a Portal Area for this List link under the General Settings category.

3. On the Add Listing screen, the title, description, and content address are all prepopulated with the corresponding values from the list. You can modify these values if you want.

4. On the Add Listing screen, you can select a group to categorize the listing and provide the URL of an image to display with this listing.

5. On the Add Listing screen, click the Change Location link under the Location section.

6. On the Change location dialog box, expand the tree by clicking the plus signs and check the boxes next to all of the areas on which you want a listing for your list.

7. On the Change location dialog box, click the OK button.

8. On the Add Listing screen, select the audiences that you want this listing specifically targeted to.

9. Click the OK button to create the listings.

After you complete the preceding steps, listings for your list will have appeared in the selected portal areas. You are able to edit these portal listings the same way you learned how to edit portal listings in Chapter 2. Now users are able to easily find their way from the SharePoint portal to the list you have created.

Differences Between Portal Lists and Site Lists

Lists have a few slight differences when they are created in a SharePoint Portal Server 2003 area as opposed to a Windows SharePoint Services site. In order to work with lists in SPS, you will need to be in at least the Contributor site group for the area that the list resides on. Keep in mind that this does not mean an area that a listing for the list appears, but the actual area that houses the list.

Whereas on a WSS site you can get to the list from the Quick Launch navigation on the right or the Documents and Lists link on the top menu, these links do not appear for a SharePoint Portal Server 2003 area. If you are in at least the Contributor site group, there will be a Manage Content link in the Actions list on the left side of the screen. This link takes you to all of the existing lists (and libraries, which we will discuss in Chapter 6) and provides you with further links to create new lists the same way we create them earlier in this chapter.

The other major difference between SPS lists and WSS lists relates to security. You may remember that the WSS lists contained a link on the Customize List screen called Change permissions for this list so that you could modify security at the list level. This link does not appear for a list that is housed in a SharePoint Portal Server 2003 area. The following tip shows you how you can still modify security at the list level in a portal area.

■**Tip** Even though you are not given a link to modify security at the list level in a portal area, you can still accomplish this by typing the following URL in your browser:

http://*<Portal Name>*/*<Area Name>*/_layouts/1033/shropt.aspx?obj{*<List Identifier>*},list

Be sure to replace *<Portal Name>* with the name of your portal server, *<Area Name>* with the name of the area containing the list (if the list is on the Home area of the portal, do not specify an area name in this URL), and *<List Identifier>* with the unique ID associated with the list. An easy way to find the unique ID for the list is to copy it from the URL of the Customize List screen. After navigating to the Customize List screen, everything directly after 'List=" in the URL and between the braces is the unique ID.

Advanced Office 2003 Integration

There are many advanced features when using Office 2003 that allow you to manage list information. Most of these enhanced abilities are provided through Excel 2003 and allow you to view, edit, and manipulate list data from within an Excel spreadsheet instead of through the SharePoint site. We will describe some of the more useful features including exporting SharePoint list information into Excel, importing Excel data into a SharePoint list, and synchronizing data changes between the two.

Exporting SharePoint Lists to Excel

The ability to take existing lists in SharePoint Portal Server areas or Windows SharePoint Services sites and export the list items into a spreadsheet is fairly straightforward. This can be beneficial when providing the information to someone without access to the list or when you need to do what-if scenarios on the data without making permanent changes to the list.

To export a list to Excel, follow these steps:

1. Navigate to a SharePoint list you want to export.

2. Click the Export to Spreadsheet link in the Actions list on the left menu.

3. If you are prompted about opening or saving the Microsoft Office Excel Web Query File, click the Open button.

4. On the Opening Query dialog box in Excel, click the Open button to confirm that you want to run the query to export the information into the Excel spreadsheet.

5. If you already have Excel 2003 open, the Import Data dialog box will appear. Choose where to put the list. Options include a region on the current worksheet, a new worksheet, or a new workbook. If you did not have Excel 2003 running, the data will be put into a new workbook.

■**Note** When exporting list information to Excel, all list items displayed by the current view are exported. Items removed from the view by its filter setting are not included, but setting the temporary filter on the list screen has no effect on the data exported.

The Excel List

The new data that appears after performing the preceding steps is actually more than just values in a spreadsheet format. This information is treated as a list within Excel. You can tell that a region of cells in Excel is a list by the colored box surrounding the cells, the column headings that act as filters using drop-down menus, and the additional list actions available in the Excel menu under the Data option as shown in Figure 4-12. These list actions are also available by right-clicking the list in the spreadsheet or by displaying the List toolbar within Excel.

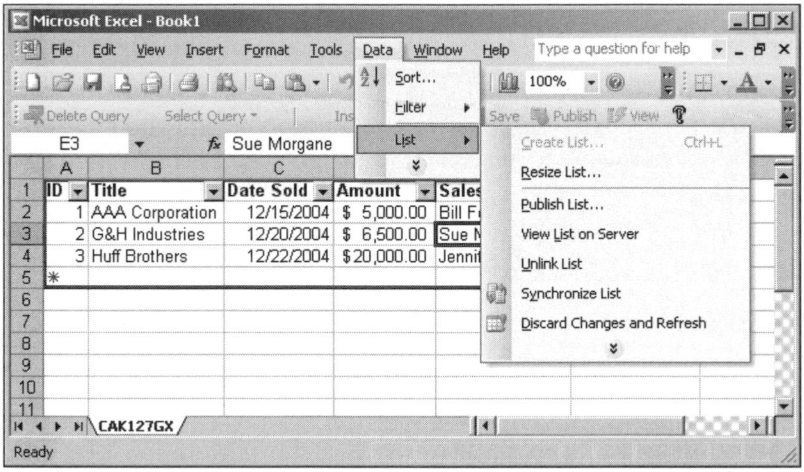

Figure 4-12. *An Excel List after exporting from SharePoint*

The power of the Excel List is that it is linked to the list in SharePoint that was used to create the spreadsheet. This allows you to make changes to the data in Excel and have those changes applied to the list in SharePoint, or vice versa. Of the available Excel List actions, the following are the most important to the integration with SharePoint:

- View List on Server

- Unlink List

- Synchronize List

- Discard Changes and Refresh

The View List on Server action launches your browser and displays the default view of the linked SharePoint list.

The Unlink List action removes the link between the Excel List and the SharePoint list. After unlinking the lists, data changes can no longer be synchronized between them. You may do this when you have completed your what-if scenarios or data editing and no longer want the Excel sheet used as an interface for changing the SharePoint list information. Once this unlinking is performed, the Excel List cannot be relinked to the same SharePoint list; you would have to export the SharePoint list again using the steps provided earlier.

The Synchronize List action is the most important of the advanced actions when using linked lists. This action sends any changes made to the Excel List to SharePoint and also updates the Excel List with any changes that users have made to the SharePoint list. Synchronizing the lists often ensures that everyone is viewing the latest information whether they are using SharePoint or the Excel sheet.

Sometimes a conflict occurs when you have edited a value in Excel and, before synchronizing, a user has edited the same value in the SharePoint list. The next time you choose to synchronize the lists, Excel will display the Resolve Conflicts and Errors dialog box. This dialog box displays each list item that has had conflicting changes made to it, highlights the conflict, and allows you to choose how to resolve it. For each conflict you can discard or apply your change. You can also choose to have Excel discard or apply your changes for all conflicts at once.

The Discard Changes and Refresh action retrieves the list information from the SharePoint list and uses it to repopulate the Excel List. Any changes you have made in the Excel List are overwritten by the list data from SharePoint.

Creating Custom Lists Using Excel

In the "Exporting SharePoint Lists to Excel" section, we described how to take an existing SharePoint list and manage the data in Excel. The integration between Office 2003 and Windows SharePoint Services also allows you to use an existing Excel sheet as the basis for creating a SharePoint list. There are two ways of doing this.

Import Spreadsheet

If you have followed the steps to create a custom list earlier in this chapter, you may have noticed an additional link on the site's Create page under the Custom Lists section. This Import Spreadsheet link is what provides the starting point when creating a custom list based on existing Excel data.

To create a custom list from existing Excel data, follow these steps:

1. Navigate to a SharePoint site where you want the list created.

2. Click the Create link on the top menu bar.

3. On the Create page, click the Import Spreadsheet link in the Custom Lists section.

4. On the New List page, enter a name and description for the list.

5. In the Import from Spreadsheet section, click the Browse button.

6. On the Choose File dialog box, locate and select the Excel file that contains your source data, then click the Open button.

7. On the New List page, click the Import button. The spreadsheet will open in Excel, and the Import to Windows SharePoint Services List dialog box will be displayed.

8. In the Import to Windows SharePoint Services list dialog box shown in Figure 4-13, select the range type. Range of Cells allows you to select the cells from the spreadsheet, while List Range and Named Range allow you to select an existing range using the Select Range drop-down.

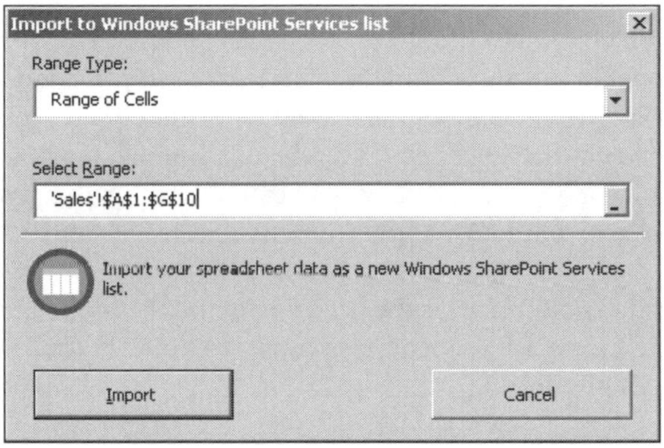

Figure 4-13. *The Import to Windows SharePoint Services list dialog box*

9. Click the Import button.

■**Note** The Import to Windows SharePoint Services list dialog box will not allow you to import values that already are linked to another SharePoint list.

Publish List

The second way to create a custom list using existing Excel data is by publishing the list from within Excel. Before you can publish the list, your Excel data must be converted to an Excel List. To convert your values to an Excel List:

1. Highlight the range of values by clicking the top-left value and dragging the mouse to the bottom-right value.

2. Under the Data menu, choose the List submenu and click the Create List action.

3. On the Create List dialog box, click the My List has Headers checkbox if your values include column headers.

4. Click the OK button.

Once your values are formatted as an Excel List, you are able to publish them as a custom list to a SharePoint site. To publish the list, follow these steps:

1. Select the Excel List.

2. Under the Data menu, choose the List submenu and click the Publish List action.

3. On the Publish List to SharePoint Site dialog box, enter the URL of the SharePoint site where the list should be created.

4. Select the checkbox labeled Link to the New SharePoint List. This makes the Excel List and SharePoint list linked as described earlier.

5. Enter a name and description for the list.

6. Click the Next button.

7. On the Publish List to SharePoint Site dialog box, verify the columns and data types that will be created. If there is a problem, cancel the publishing and make changes to the spreadsheet.

8. Click the Finish button.

After performing the preceding steps, a dialog box will display giving you a link to the new custom list in SharePoint. If you checked the Link to the New SharePoint List box, the lists will be linked allowing you to perform the actions described in the Excel List discussion earlier. This includes synchronizing changes between the Excel List and the new SharePoint list.

Advanced Datasheet Features

Earlier in this chapter, we discussed the use of the Datasheet view for enhanced editing of list data. The Datasheet view contains numerous features that allow for integration with Office 2003 products. These features, described in Table 4-18, can be found by clicking the Task Pane link in the Datasheet view's toolbar. The task pane will appear on the right side of the Datasheet view and consists of a toolbar and Office Links section as shown in Figure 4-14.

Table 4-18. *Datasheet Task Pane Office Links*

Feature	Description
Export and Link to Excel	Exports the list information in the same manner as the Export to Spreadsheet link on the Actions menu. The lists are linked, allowing you to synchronize data between Excel and SharePoint.
Print with Excel	Exports the list information to Excel and displays the Print dialog box, allowing you to quickly print out the list items.
Chart with Excel	Exports the list information to Excel and displays the Chart Wizard dialog box, allowing you to create graphs and charts based on the list items.
Create Excel PivotTable Report	Exports the list information to Excel and displays the PivotTable Field List dialog box and toolbar. The PivotTable allows you to select from the columns in the SharePoint list and create PivotTable reports with the capability to alter rows and columns interactively to display data detail in different ways.
Export to Access	Exports the list information into a new Access table in either a new or existing Access database. When doing this, the list and Access database are not linked and cannot be synchronized between the two.
Create Linked Table in Access	Creates a new Access-linked table in either a new or existing Access database. The linked table is synchronized with the SharePoint list. Any changes made in Access are also visible in the SharePoint list and vice versa.
Report with Access	Creates a new Access linked table in either a new or existing Access database and then generates an Access report based on the information in the linked table.

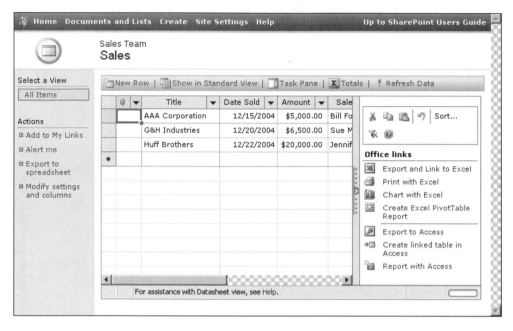

Figure 4-14. *The DataSheet view's task pane*

■**Note** For more information on Office 2003 features like PivotTables and Access Reporting, please see the product documentation.

CHAPTER 5

■■■■

Template Lists

Creating custom lists for all of your information needs, while powerful and flexible, can become time consuming. To address this, SharePoint comes with built-in standard lists that you can use as templates. These lists greatly reduce the amount of time it takes to design and build all of the facilities you will use to manage data in your Windows SharePoint Services sites and SharePoint Portal Server areas. Many of these templates include enhanced integration with Office 2003 products.

As well as an existing structure of list columns, these list templates come with a number of views intended to make the list items more manageable for your users. These lists still allow you to modify the structure by adding new columns, modifying the settings of existing columns, or removing extra columns that are not appropriate for your list's needs. Managing the views and settings of a list created from a template is performed in the same way you would for a custom list. Refer to Chapter 4 for more details on accomplishing these actions. This chapter will also refer to lists that have been added to a web part page on a site or portal. How to do this is discussed in detail in Chapter 7.

Standard Lists

SharePoint provides many list templates that are available to use whether you are creating a list in the portal, a team site, a document workspace, or a meeting workspace. These standard lists apply to most situations involving team collaboration and information management. Many of these standard list templates include additional capabilities and integration with other Office System products that you do not get from building custom lists. By understanding these unique features, you can choose the right list and customize it further to make the best use of SharePoint technologies.

We will describe each of these lists and their unique capabilities in this chapter. Before getting into these details, we will give you the steps needed to create a new standard list. To create a new standard list in a Windows SharePoint Services team site or document workspace:

1. Click the Create link on the Site Toolbar.

2. On the Create screen, click the link of your desired template under the Lists section.

3. On the New List screen, enter a name and description for the list.

4. Under the Navigation section, select Yes if you want a link to the list displayed on the Quick Launch menu of the site's home page.

5. Click the Create button.

To create a new standard list in a SharePoint Portal Server area:

1. Click the Manage Content link from the Actions list on the left.

2. On the Document and Lists screen, click the Create link on the toolbar.

3. On the Create screen, click the link of your desired template under the Lists section.

4. On the New List screen, enter a name and description for the list.

5. The Navigation section does not apply to a standard SPS area as there is no Quick Launch menu displayed. You can therefore ignore this option.

6. Click the Create button.

To create a new standard list in a meeting workspace, see the "Meeting Workspace Lists" section later in this chapter.

Links

The Links list template creates a list you should use when you want to provide a list of links to both external and internal web pages. The list contains a single view, called All Links, which displays all list items along with an Edit column for editing a list item. The columns in the Links list template are shown in Table 5-1.

Table 5-1. *Links List Columns*

Column	Type	Notes
URL	Hyperlink or Picture	The web address for the link along with the text that should be shown as the name
Notes	Multiple lines of text	Long description of the link

Links lists prove most useful when you add them to the home web part page of the site. (Adding web parts to a page is discussed in Chapter 7.) Displaying your links list on the home page of the site provides users with an easy way to find other web sites relevant to the information in the team site. For example, a site for the company sales team could benefit from links to the corporate web site and sales entry system. Figure 5-1 shows the links list displayed on the home page of a team site.

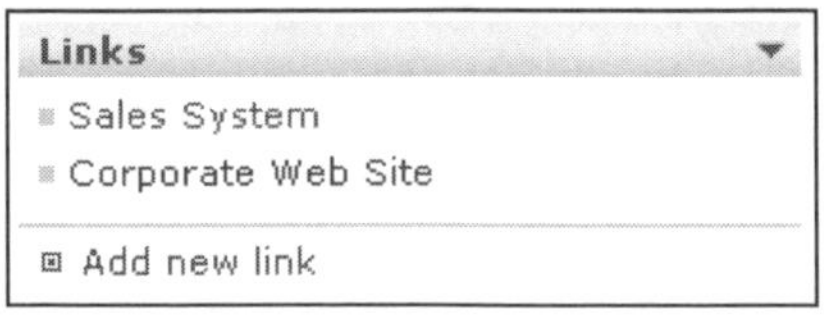

Figure 5-1. *A links list displayed on a site*

Changing List Item Order

There is no ability to change the order of the list items in a custom list; however, this feature is part of many template lists. The Links list template is one of these lists. This feature is controlled by a setting that can be configured for each view created for the list. When managing a view in the links list, there will be an additional option under the Sort section that lets you turn on and off this feature, which allows users to manually order the items in the list.

To change the order of the links in a links list:

1. Navigate to the links list screen.

2. On the links list screen, click the Change Order link on the toolbar.

3. On the Change Order screen, set the order by changing the numbers in the Position from Top column with smaller numbers being towards the top of the list.

4. Click the OK button.

■Note When you click a link in the links list, the link opens in the current instance of the browser; therefore you leave the context of your portal. Without technical customization, you cannot have the links launch in a new window unless you right-click the link and choose the Open in New Window option in your browser.

Announcements

The Announcements list template allows you to easily create a list of items intended to inform site users of important messages. The list contains a single view called All Items, which displays the title of the announcement as well as the last time it was modified. The columns in the Announcements list template are shown in Table 5-2.

Table 5-2. *Announcements List Columns*

Column	Type	Notes
Title	Single line of text	Short text that is used as a heading for the announcement.
Body	Multiple lines of text	Longer text message of the announcement.
Expires	Date and Time	The date when the list item is no longer relevant. This allows views to filter using this date and display only the most recent items.

Like the links list discussed earlier, the announcements list is often added to the home web part page of a site. Having the announcements list, as shown in Figure 5-2, as one of the first lists displayed on a site allows you to increase your ability to keep users up to date on the latest related news.

Figure 5-2. *The announcements list displayed on a site*

■**Note** The default view used when the announcements list is added to a web part page filters on the Expires column with an expression of Expires is greater than or equal to [Today]. This helps keep the list of announcements displayed short, as list items are not displayed once the Expires date passes.

Contacts

The Contacts list template is helpful in maintaining contact information for people that your site users may need to reach. This could include other team members, client contacts, or vendor information. The contacts list, shown in Figure 5-3, contains a single view called All Contacts, which by default displays the last name, first name, company, business phone, home phone, and e-mail address of each contact. The columns in the Contacts list template are shown in Table 5-3.

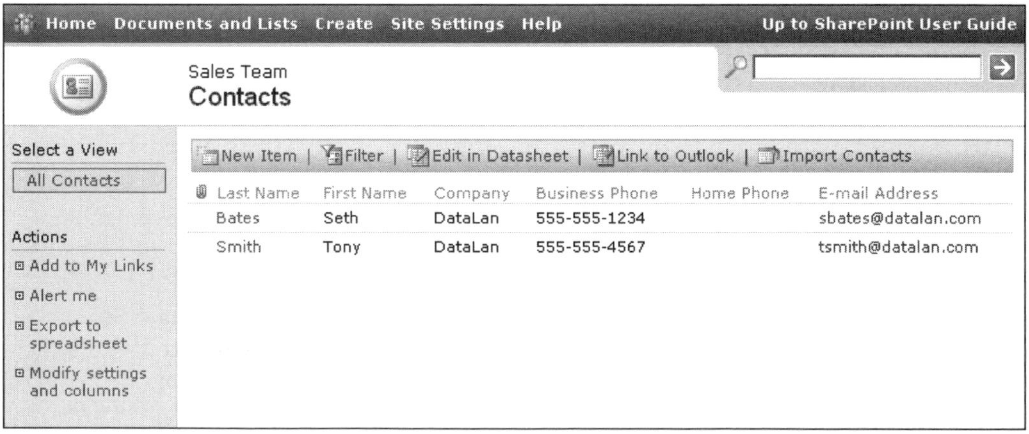

Figure 5-3. *The contacts list screen*

Table 5-3. *Contacts List Columns*

Column	Type	Notes
Last Name	Single line of text	
First Name	Single line of text	
Full Name	Single line of text	Full Name is not calculated from Last Name and First Name columns.
E-mail Address	Single line of text	Accepts any text as no validation is done on the value entered, ensuring that it is a proper e-mail address format. If the value is a proper e-mail address, it is displayed as an e-mail link.
Company	Single line of text	
Job Title	Single line of text	
Business Phone	Single line of text	Accepts any text as no validation is done on the value entered, ensuring that it is a proper phone number format.
Home Phone	Single line of text	Accepts any text as no validation is done on the value entered, ensuring that it is a proper phone number format.
Mobile Phone	Single line of text	Accepts any text as no validation is done on the value entered, ensuring that it is a proper phone number format.
Fax Number	Single line of text	Accepts any text as no validation is done on the value entered, ensuring that it is a proper phone number format.
Address	Multiple lines of text	
City	Single line of text	
State	Single line of text	
Postal Code	Single line of text	Accepts any text as no validation is done on the value entered, ensuring that it is a proper postal code format.
Country	Single line of text	
Web Page	Hyperlink	Link to corporate or personal web page.
Notes	Multiple lines of text	

Exporting Contacts

The Contacts list template provides many ways in which to integrate your contact information with other applications that use contacts. SharePoint allows you to both import and export contact information from your Windows Address Book. Exporting allows the contacts in your list to be available in such applications as Outlook. Contacts must be exported individually from SharePoint. To export a contact:

1. Navigate to the contacts list screen.

2. On the contacts list screen, open the context menu of the contact you wish to export.

3. Click the Export Contact link.

4. When you are prompted that you are downloading a file, click the Open button.

   a. If you have Outlook installed, a New Contact window will appear with information populated from the SharePoint contact. Click the Save and Close button on the toolbar.

   b. If you do not have Outlook installed, a Contact Properties window will appear. Click the Add to Address Book button and the properties will become editable. Click the OK button to add the contact to your address book.

5. The contact will now appear in your address book.

Importing Contacts

Exporting contacts is useful when the contact information has already been added to your SharePoint list and you would like that information locally. More often, when initially creating a contacts list, you may have that information in your local address book or in an enterprise Global Address List and want to import it into the SharePoint contacts list. The contacts list screen allows you to perform an import from these sources if you have Office 2003 installed.

Tip You can only import contacts that contain an e-mail address. Contacts without e-mail addresses will not be available in the list of contacts to import.

To import contacts, perform the following steps:

1. Navigate to the contacts list screen.

2. On the contacts list screen, click the Import Contacts link on the toolbar.

3. On the Select Users to Import dialog box, select an address list from the Show Names From The drop-down list. This will contain all local address books along with enterprise address lists for your organization.

4. Select a user or group from the list. Selecting a group will import all members of the group into the contacts list.

5. Click the Add button.

6. Repeat steps 3 through 5 for each user you wish to import into your SharePoint contacts list.

7. Click the OK button.

8. The list will refresh and contain the newly imported contacts.

■**Caution** There is no synchronization between exported or import contacts and SharePoint contacts lists. If you make modifications to the contact in SharePoint, it will not be modified in your address book and vice versa. You must make the modification in both places or export/import the contact again. See the next section, "Linking Contacts Lists with Outlook," for more enhanced Outlook integration.

Linking Contacts Lists with Outlook

In addition to importing and exporting contacts to your Windows Address Book, SharePoint allows you to link the contacts list with Outlook 2003. Linking a SharePoint contacts list with Outlook creates a contacts folder in Outlook that displays contact information retrieved from SharePoint. The list of contacts is read-only when in Outlook, so all modifications must be performed in the SharePoint contacts list. This ensures that the information is centrally managed yet still available for use by everyone within Outlook.

To link a contacts list with Outlook:

1. Navigate to the contacts list screen.

2. On the contacts list screen, click the Link to Outlook link on the toolbar.

3. You are prompted that Outlook does not recognize the site that the contacts list is on, and it asks you to verify that you want to add the contacts list to Outlook. Click the Yes button.

4. The linked list will display as a new folder in the Other Contacts section of your Outlook contacts as shown in Figure 5-4.

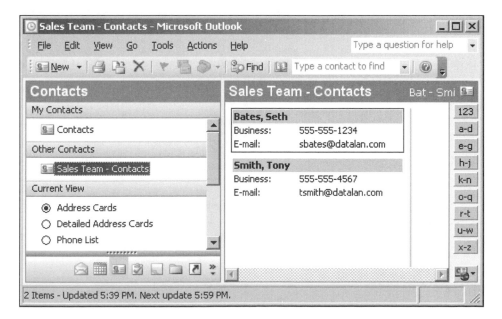

Figure 5-4. *A linked contacts list in Outlook*

If you edit a contact in Outlook that has been linked from SharePoint, you are told that the item is read-only. Outlook allows you to save a copy of the contact in your default contacts list where you can make changes, but the items are not linked to SharePoint. The best place to make changes to the contact information is in the SharePoint contacts list, as the new information will be presented each time you open the list in Outlook. Outlook caches a local copy of the contacts list so that, even if you are not able to connect to SharePoint, you can still see the contact information as of the last time you viewed the list from Outlook.

■**Caution** If you have Office 2003 installed and still cannot import/export or link contact information, your installation may not be complete. Have an administrator ensure that the Windows SharePoint Services Support component of Office 2003 has been installed and that Outlook is your default e-mail client.

Events

The Events list template is one of the most feature-rich list templates available, allowing you to maintain lists of events within a team site or portal area. Some common uses for the Events list template include tracking meetings, deadlines, or milestones. The Events list template is further enhanced by features such as recurring events and integration with SharePoint workspaces and Outlook 2003, all of which are discussed in the upcoming text. Events list items are based on dates and include the columns shown in Table 5-4.

Table 5-4. *Events List Columns*

Column	Type	Notes
Title	Single line of text	
Begin	Date and Time	Starting time for the event.
End	Date and Time	Ending time for the event.
Description	Multiple lines of text	Long text description of the event.
Location	Single line of text	Where the event will take place.
Recurrence	Special	Controls whether the event occurs multiple times and when. See the "Recurrence" section.
Workspace	Special	Links to an associated meeting workspace if one has been created for the event.

The Events list template contains several default views, allowing the users to display the list items in various ways. These views are listed in Table 5-5. Remember that, just like all lists, you can still customize the events list, shown in Figure 5-5, by adding or editing fields and creating additional views to display the events in more meaningful ways to your users.

Table 5-5. *Events List Views*

View	Description
All Events	The default view, it displays all items in the list. Recurring events are displayed as a single list item.
Calendar	Displays all events in a calendar view type, allowing the user to graphically see the events in the list.
Current Events	Displays all events that occur on the current date and any dates in the future. Each instance of a recurring event is shown separately.

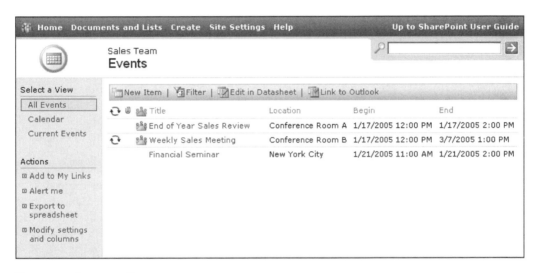

Figure 5-5. *The events list*

Recurrence

A unique aspect of items in the events list is the ability to mark them as recurring events. A recurring event is one that happens more than once over a time period, like a weekly sales meeting. When creating a new event in the events list or editing an existing event, you are given the ability to determine its recurrence.

The event's recurrence is determined by a time period, a pattern, and a date range. Each time period is associated with its own available pattern settings that let you precisely determine how often the event occurs. These time periods and patterns are shown in Table 5-6. The date range consists of a start date and an ending. Available ending types for a recurring event are a specific date, a number of occurrences, or an option for no end date to the recurrence.

Table 5-6. *Recurrence Time Periods and Patterns*

Time Period	Pattern
Daily	Every X days (example: every 2 days)
Weekly occurs	Every X weeks and on which days of the week the event (example: every 1 week on Monday, Wednesday, and Friday)
Monthly	Day X of every Y month (example: day 1 of every 3 months)
	or
	The ordered weekday of every X month (example: the second Monday of every 2 months)
Yearly	None

Recurring Events in Views

When an event is recurring, the first column in the All Events view will contain an icon with two circular arrows. You can see an example of this in Figure 5-5. The special column used for this is the Recurrence column, which is available when managing views.

A recurring event is displayed as a single list item in the All Events view, but the Current Events view displays each occurrence of a recurring event as a separate list item. You can display each occurrence of a recurring event separately in your custom views using a new view type, Standard View with Expanded Recurring Events, inherent only to events lists.

As discussed in Chapter 4, creating a new view takes you to a screen displaying the available view types. When you create a new view in an events list, there will be a link for the Standard View with Expanded Recurring Events view type. This view type only allows you to specify column, filter, style, and item limit settings but displays each occurrence of a recurring event separately in the list. This can be seen in Figure 5-6, which is displaying the same list shown in Figure 5-5 but using the Current Events view.

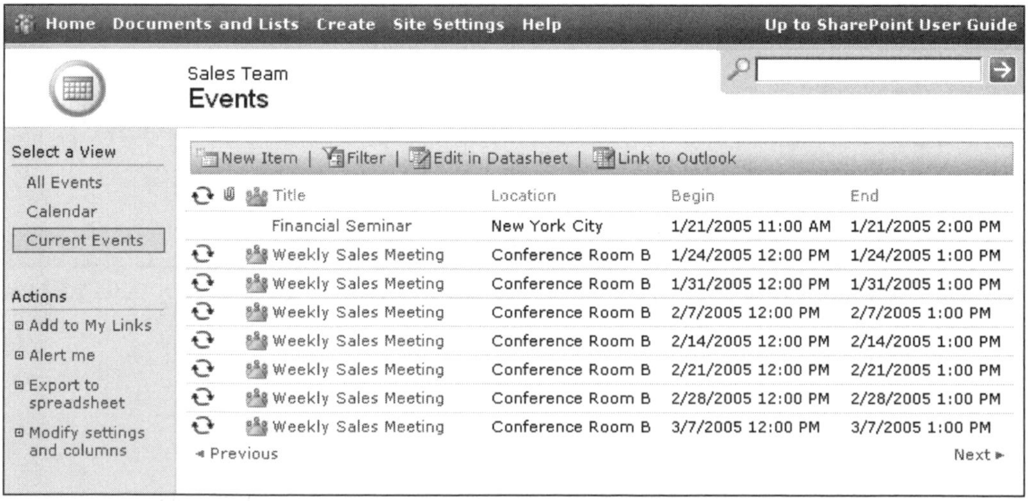

Figure 5-6. *The Current Events view displays each event occurrence.*

When you choose to view a recurring event from the Calendar view, the Current Events view, or any other view that displays expanded recurring events, you are looking at an individual occurrence of that event. You can notice the difference by the options in the toolbar of the View Item or Edit Item screens. When you are viewing an occurrence, there will be an additional link in the toolbar called Edit Series. In this case, the Edit Item link allows you to edit the specific occurrence of an event that you are currently viewing, while the Edit Series link allows you to make modifications to the recurring event that the item is an instance of. Clicking the Edit Series link takes you to the same screen that you would go to when choosing the Edit Item link from the context menu of a list item in a standard view like the All Events view.

■**Note** Editing a single occurrence of a recurring event will cause a new recurring events list item to be created based on the updated information. The new event is still associated with the original series but will be presented separately in views based on the standard view type such as All Events.

Exporting Events

Like the contacts list, the events list allows you to export list items from SharePoint. The events list exports events list item information in a calendar information file that Outlook can then import. Events must be exported individually from SharePoint, and recurring events can only be exported one occurrence at a time. To export an event:

1. Navigate to the events list screen.

2. On the events list screen, open the context menu of the event you wish to export.

3. Click the View Item option.

4. On the Item screen, click the Export Event link in the toolbar.

5. When you are prompted that you are downloading a file, click the Open button.

6. A new Outlook appointment window will appear with information populated from the SharePoint event. Click the Save and Close button on the toolbar.

7. The event will now appear in your default calendar.

■**Caution** There is no synchronization between exported events and SharePoint events lists. If you make modifications to the event in SharePoint, it will not be modified in your Outlook calendar and vice versa.

Linking Events Lists with Outlook

Another feature of the Events list template that is not available from custom lists is the ability to view the events information through Outlook 2003. Similar to the link feature in a contacts list, linking a SharePoint events list with Outlook creates a new calendar in Outlook. The list of events is read-only when in Outlook, so all modifications must be performed in the SharePoint events list. This ensures that the information is the same when displayed in both places. Linking events lists with Outlook can allow you to easily view a calendar of events such as your company's training schedule or scheduled client visits.

To link an events list with Outlook:

1. Navigate to the events list screen.

2. On the events list screen, click the Link to Outlook link on the toolbar.

3. You are prompted that Outlook does not recognize the site that the events list is on, and it asks you to verify that you want to add the events list to Outlook. Click the Yes button.

4. The linked list will display as a calendar in the Other Calendars section of Outlook as shown in Figure 5-7. To display your calendars within Outlook, select the Calendar option from the Go application menu.

Figure 5-7. *A linked events list in Outlook*

You cannot edit an event in Outlook that has been linked from SharePoint. Outlook allows you to save a copy of the event to your default calendar where you can then make changes. The only place to make global changes to the events information is in the SharePoint events list, as the new information will be displayed each time you view the calendar in Outlook. Other users of the events list will also see the most up-to-date information, ensuring that the latest changes are available to every user. Outlook caches a local copy of the events list calendar so that even if you are not able to connect to SharePoint, you can still see the event information as of the last time you viewed the calendar from Outlook.

■**Caution** If you have Office 2003 installed and still cannot access events list information, your installation may not be complete. Have an administrator ensure that the Windows SharePoint Services Support component of Office 2003 has been installed.

Workspaces

A useful feature of the events list is the ability to integrate directly into meeting workspaces from the events list items. The meeting workspaces you read about in Chapter 3 can be created from events in the events list, resulting in additional navigation and information available in both the meeting workspace and events list item.

When adding or editing an event, you will see a workspace checkbox near the bottom of the screen. Checking this box will create a meeting workspace and associates the workspaces with your event. You are able to create a new meeting workspace or associate the event with an already existing workspace under the current site if a workspace was already created without the use of the events list.

To create a meeting workspace for an existing events list item:

1. Navigate to the events list screen.

2. On the events list screen, activate the context menu for an event and click the Edit Item link.

3. On the Item screen, check the Workspace checkbox.

4. Click the Save and Close link on the toolbar.

5. On the New or Existing Meeting Workspace screen, if a meeting workspace already exists under the current site, a Create or Link section will be displayed. Make sure the Create a New Meeting Workspace option is selected. Selecting the Link to an Existing Meeting Workspace option allows you to associate the event with a meeting workspace you have already created by selecting it from the list.

6. The title and web address is already populated using the name of the event. Enter a description.

7. Click the OK button.

8. On the Template Selection page, select the Meeting Workspace template to use for this event. These templates are described in Chapter 3.

9. Click the OK button.

After following these steps, you are brought to the newly created meeting workspace. The meeting workspace's integration with the events list can be seen underneath the title of the workspace. The date and time of the event is retrieved from the events list and a Go to Events link is displayed, allowing you to quickly navigate back to the list. Also, you are automatically added to the attendees list, discussed later in this chapter, as the organizer of the meeting.

If you click the Go to Events link so that the events list is displayed, you will see that the list item now displays an icon of a meeting in the All Events view. This can be seen earlier in Figures 5-5 and 5-6. A link is also displayed in the View Item screen for the event. Clicking either the icon or link takes you to the meeting workspace shown in Figure 5-8.

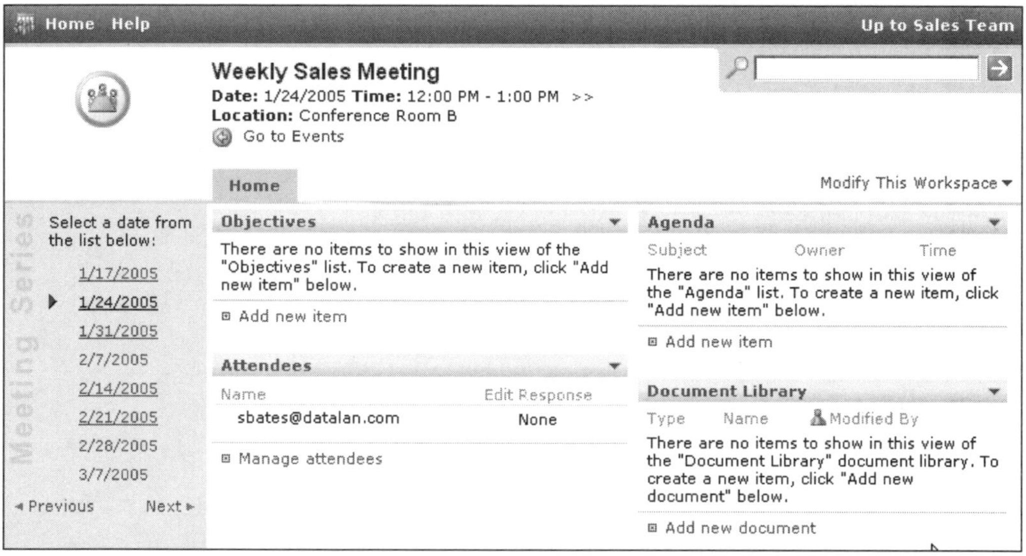

Figure 5-8. *A meeting workspace created from a recurring event*

Workspaces in Series

Creating a meeting workspace for a recurring event adds an additional level of functionality to the meeting workspace. The workspace is created using the same steps given in the previous section, but when the workspace is displayed, you will notice a new navigation menu on the left. This navigation menu, shown in Figure 5-8, allows you to navigate to different displays of the workspace based on each occurrence of the event.

These instances of the workspace are said to be "in series" as they are all related to the same event. Content added to one instance of the series does not necessarily display in other instances. This is determined by a setting in the workspace lists. This setting is described in the "Meeting Workspace Lists" section later in this chapter.

■**Tip** You can specify that lists share content between series by changing an option in their List Settings screen. How to do this in detail is shown later in the "Meeting Workspace Lists" section of this chapter.

Tasks

The Tasks list template is one of the most commonly used templates in team collaboration sites. The tasks list is used to assign and manage tasks for site users. The columns in the Tasks list template are shown in Table 5-7. Remember that you can customize the columns, including the available options for Choice columns, in order to tailor your list to your current business terminology.

Table 5-7. *Tasks List Columns*

Column	Type	Notes
Title	Single line of text	
Priority	Choice	Default options include High, Normal, and Low
Status	Choice	Default options include Not Started, In Progress, Completed, Deferred, and Waiting on someone else
% Complete	Number	Only allows numbers from 0 to 100
Assigned To	Lookup	Choose from users of the current WSS site or SPS area
Description	Multiple lines of text	
Start Date	Date and Time	
Due Date	Date and Time	

■**Note** If the site's security is based on Active Directory groups, individual users will not be displayed in Lookup columns like Assigned To until they have visited the site.

The Tasks list template contains many different default views designed to provide users with easy ways in which to display the tasks they are interested in. These views are listed in Table 5-8.

Table 5-8. *Tasks List Views*

View	Description
All Tasks	The default view, it displays all items in the list.
My Tasks	Displays title, status, priority, % complete, and due date for all of the current user's tasks. This is accomplished by using a filter of Assigned To is equal to [Me].
Due Today	Displays title, assigned to, status, priority, and % complete for all of the tasks due on the current date. This view uses a filter of Due Date is equal to [Today].
Active Tasks	Displays title, assigned to, status, priority, % complete, and due date for all active tasks. Active tasks are determined by a filter of Status is not equal to Completed.
By Assigned To	Similar to the All Tasks view except that it sorts the list items based on the Assigned To column.

The item-level security described in Chapter 4 is particularly useful to ensure that users cannot modify tasks that are not their responsibility. SharePoint does not provide the ability to link a tasks list to your tasks in Outlook. Aside from the extra views that the template gives you, there is no functionality on the tasks list screen, as shown in Figure 5-9, which is not available when using custom lists. You could build a list identical to the tasks list by using the features available for custom lists, but it is provided to make creating this common list type easier.

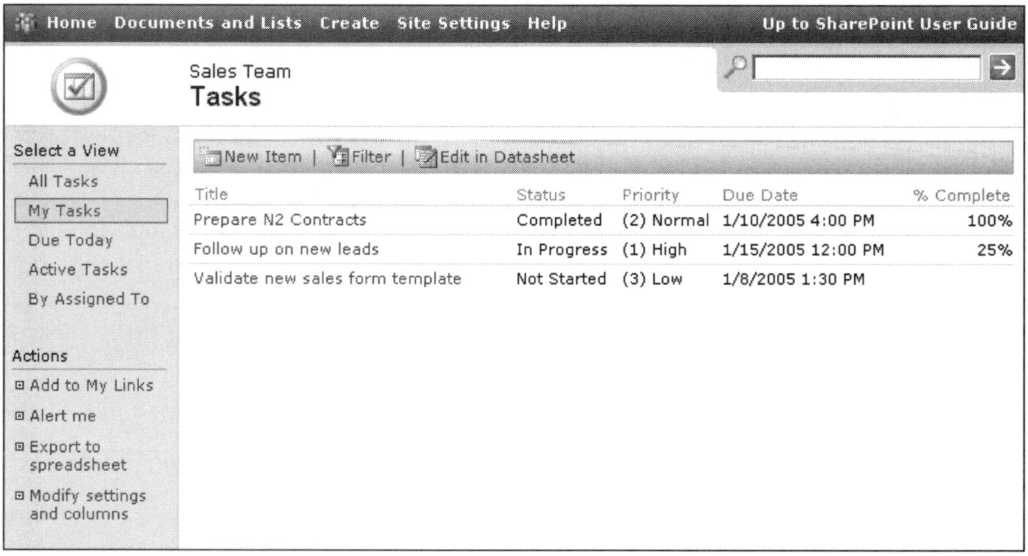

Figure 5-9. *The tasks list*

■**Note** A drawback of storing your tasks in multiple tasks lists on SharePoint sites is that there is no built-in way to see all of your tasks in a single list. There are third-party products that address this issue by providing rollup functionality of all of your tasks in SharePoint.

Issues

Similar to the Tasks list template, the Issues list template is useful for creating a list of items where a user must take action. The issues list is best suited as a list of risks that must be mitigated or business opportunities that must be managed. The columns in the Issues list template are shown in Table 5-9.

Table 5-9. *Issues List Columns*

Column	Type	Notes
Title	Single line of text	
Assigned To	Lookup	Choose from users of the current WSS site or SPS area.
Status	Choice	Default options include Active, Resolved, and Closed.
Category	Choice	Default options include Category1, Category2, and Category3. Make sure to edit these options when creating your issues list.
Priority	Choice	Default options include High, Normal, and Low.
Comment	Multiple lines of text	
Due Date	Date and Time	

Like some other list templates, the Issues list template contains default views designed to provide users with easy ways in which to display the issues more relevant to them. These views are listed in Table 5-10.

Table 5-10. *Issues List Views*

View	Description
All Issues	The default view, it displays all items in the list.
My Issues	Displays title, status, priority, category, and due date for all of the current user's tasks. This is accomplished by using a filter of Assigned To is equal to [Me].
Active Issues	Displays title, assigned to, status, priority, category, and due date for all active tasks. Active tasks are determined by a filter of Status is equal to Active.

The issues list comes with the ability to notify users via e-mail when they have been assigned a list item or when a list item they own has been modified. This is the only list template that contains this feature. To enable this notification, set Email Notification to Yes on the General Settings screen of the issues list.

Related Issues

The issues list allows for relationships between list items, which is not available with custom lists or other list templates. Each issue includes a list of related issues from the same list. These related issues are displayed on the View Item screen as links to the related issue's View Item screen. The View Item screen for an issue is displayed in Figure 5-10.

The Add Item and Edit Item screens allow you to manage this relationship. A special column called Add Related Issue is used to enter new related issues. This column is not displayed in any views and does not contain data itself; it is only used to enter the related Issue ID on the Add Item or Edit Item screen. Adding related issues must be done one at a time, saving the list item for each related issue. A remove link is provided alongside each related issue in the Edit Item screen, allowing you to remove that issue from the list of related issues for the currently displayed issue.

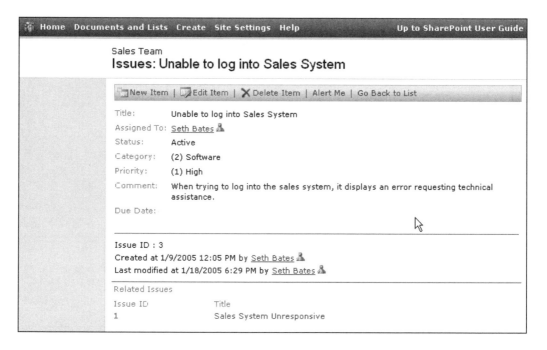

Figure 5-10. *An issue with related issues*

Current Issues

Editing list items in an issues list causes SharePoint to handle the underlying data differently than it does other lists. In all other lists, when you edit a value in a list, SharePoint saves the changes you have made to the existing list item. This is not how SharePoint handles the editing of issues. When you edit a list item in an issues list and save the changes, a new list item is created with the most recent information for the issue, and the history of the issue information is displayed on the View Item page. You then have multiple list items that are really the same issue.

The issues list does not display all copies of each issue, only the most recent list item. This is accomplished by using a special column called Current. This column is not displayed to the user; instead SharePoint uses this column to mark which list item for an issue is the most recent. All views in the Issues list template contain a filter of `Current is equal to Yes`, which causes the view to only display the most recent versions of the issues.

■**Tip** Always remember to include the `Current is equal to Yes` filter when creating views for an issues list unless you need to see all historical versions of the issues.

Reports

Another aspect unique to the issues list is the inclusion of built-in reports. Although the standard reports are fairly simple in nature, they can prove to be very helpful in managing and monitoring a potentially large issues list such as a software defect tracking list or help desk call tracking list. The Issues list template comes with four issues list reports. Each report has its own specific settings, as shown in Table 5-11, that allow you to filter the data that will be presented in the report.

Table 5-11. *Issues List Reports*

Report	Description	Settings (Available Filters)
Issues by category	Displays the number of issues in each category	Category Status
Issues by person	Displays the number of issues in each category for each user	Assigned To Status
Issues created over a date range	Displays the number of issues created on dates in a date range	Start Date End Date Category
Issues for a date range	Displays the number of issues that exist on dates in a date range	Start Date End Date Category Assigned To Status

To view a report, perform the following steps:

1. Navigate to the issues list screen.

2. On the Issues screen, click the View Reports link in the Actions list.

3. On the Issues–Reports screen, click the link of the report type that you want to view.

4. On the Report screen, change the settings in the list on the left to set how the report will filter the issues for the report.

5. Click the Create Report button and a report will display similar to the one shown in Figure 5-11.

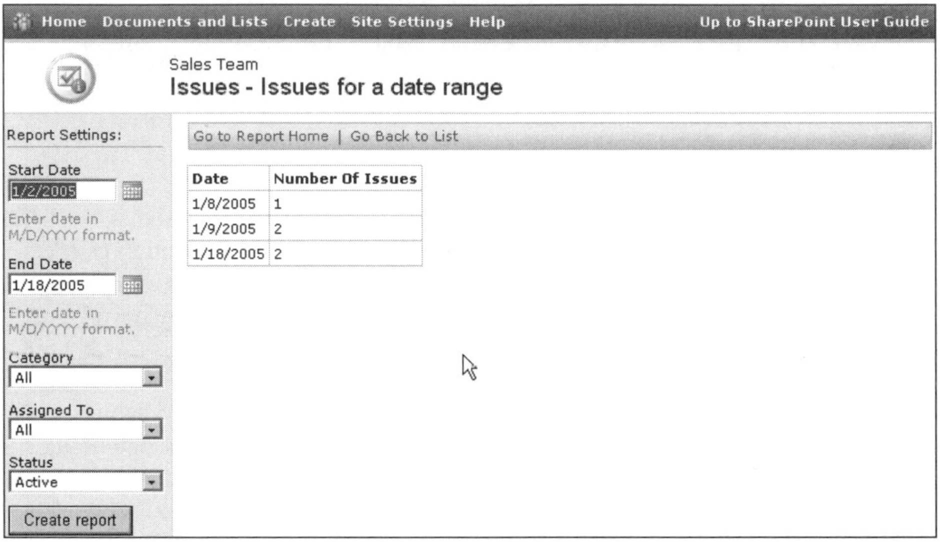

Figure 5-11. *Report showing issues for a date range*

Meeting Workspace Lists

In addition to the standard lists discussed previously, meeting workspaces provide more list templates not available in Windows SharePoint Services team sites or document workspaces. These additional list templates are designed to enhance a meeting workspace that is focused on organizing and managing a meeting event. While they do not have the additional integration with Office 2003 that some of the standard lists have, the meeting workspace lists do have some features not found in other lists.

Creating lists in a meeting workspace is a little different from creating them in team sites or document workspaces. Meeting workspaces do not include the Create link that is prominently displayed at the top of team sites to allow easy creation of lists. Instead, you must create new lists via the Modify This Workspace link. This link, and the related Modify Shared Page link that you see in a team site or document workspaces, is used to manage web parts and web part pages. Web parts and web part pages are discussed in more detail in Chapter 7.

To create a new list in a Windows SharePoint Services meeting workspace:

1. Click the Modify This Workspace link on the top-right side of the workspace.

2. From the context menu that is displayed, click the Add Web Parts link.

3. On the Create Lists pane, drag the type of list that you want to create onto the web part page and the list is created. If the list template you want is not displayed on the pane, click the Show All Lists link and continue with these steps.

4. On the New List screen, enter a name and description for the list.

5. Click the Create button.

Lists for Meetings in Series

If you followed the preceding steps to create a list using the Show All Lists link, you may have noticed a new setting when creating a list as well as a setting that is shown in team site lists which is missing in workspaces. Since there is no Quick Launch menu for a meeting workspace like there is in a team site, there is no Navigation section on the New List page when creating new lists.

Instead of the Navigation section, a section titled Share List Items Across All Meetings (Series Items) is displayed. Selecting Yes for this setting makes the list and its contents shared among workspaces in the same series. Workspaces created for recurring events as described in the "Events" section earlier in this chapter are able to use this setting. Each workspace created for the recurring event is said to be in the same series.

When you select to share the item, any item added to a list in one workspace in the series will be displayed to users of all workspaces in the series. This setting is available for all lists created in a meeting workspace, not just the list templates described in the upcoming sections.

If you do not select Yes for Sharing List Items Across Meetings in a recurring meeting workspace, lists will have an additional link in the toolbar. This link will allow you to display list items for the current meeting occurrence or display a consolidated view of list items from all occurrences of the meeting workspace. The link in the toolbar toggles between This Meeting and All Meetings.

Agenda

The Agenda list template creates a list that should be used in meeting workspaces to manage the topics to be discussed and when during the meeting they will be the focal point. The columns in the Agenda list template are all text columns rather than being more specific column types such as Date and Time. The columns in the Agenda list template are shown in Table 5-12.

Table 5-12. *Agenda List Columns*

Column	Type	Notes
Subject	Single line of text	
Owner	Single line of text	Text column type allows any text entry rather than selection of site users like other list templates provide.
Time	Single line of text	Text column type allows any text entry rather than specific date and time values.
Notes	Multiple lines of text	

The agenda list contains two views to allow users to best review and manage the meeting agenda. These views are described in Table 5-13.

Table 5-13. *Agenda List Views*

View	Description
All Items	The default view, it displays all items in the list. Items are displayed with a custom style that shows the Notes column underneath the other three columns in the list.
My Items	Displays items that the current user has created. This is accomplished by using a filter of Created By is equal to [Me].

Changing List Item Order

Many of the meeting workspace list templates, including the Agenda list template, allow you to change the order of the items in the list. This is available to all views of the list where you have specified to allow users to order items in the Sort section of the List screen. This functionality can also be seen in the Links list template described in the "Links" section near the beginning of this chapter.

To change the order of the links in an agenda list:

1. Navigate to the agenda list screen.

2. On the agenda list screen, click the Change Order link on the toolbar.

3. On the Change Order screen, set the order by changing the numbers in the Position from Top column with smaller numbers being towards the top of the list.

4. Click the OK button.

■**Note** Changing the list item order changes the order of the items for all views of a list. There is no way to change the order of the list items differently for each view.

Decisions

The Decisions list template creates a list that can be used to record decisions made during the course of a meeting. This allows decisions made during the course of the meeting to be recorded as they are made and makes these decisions available for review after the meeting. The columns in the Decisions list template are shown in Table 5-14.

Table 5-14. *Decisions List Columns*

Column	Type	Notes
Decision	Single line of text	
Contact	Single line of text	Text column type allows any text entry rather than selection of site users.
Status	Choice	Default options include Final, Pending Approval, and Proposed.

The decisions list contains two different views in which users can display decisions list items. Like many other meeting workspace lists, the views in the Decisions list template allow the user to change the display order of the list items. These views are described in Table 5-15.

Table 5-15. *Decisions List Views*

View	Description
All Items	The default view, it displays all items in the list.
My Items	Displays items that the current user has created. This is accomplished by using a filter of Created By is equal to [Me].

Objectives

The Objectives list template is used to create a list of goals for the meeting. Most meeting workspace templates contain an objectives list built from the Objectives list template. The objectives list is an extremely simple list with only a single column, shown in Table 5-16, and a single view that displays all list items. As with most other meeting workspace list templates, the objectives list provides the ability for the user to change the display order of the list items.

Table 5-16. *Objectives List Column*

Column	Type
Objective	Multiple lines of text

Text Box

The Text Box list template creates a highly specialized yet very simple list. A list item for the text box list consists of a single text field as shown in Table 5-17.

Table 5-17. *Text Box List Column*

Column	Type
Text	Multiple lines of text

The list also contains a single view called All Items that displays every item in the list. The uniqueness of this list, though, is that only a single list item exists in the list. After adding a list item using the Add New Item link, the list no longer allows the addition of new items. Instead, the list contains an Edit Text link that allows the user to alter the text of the only list item in the list. Since the list contains only a single list item, there are far fewer options available when managing the list. The Customize List screen does not allow you to add or edit columns or views, and the Change General Settings screen does not display settings for attachments or approval of list items.

The purpose of the text box list is to allow the user to insert text onto the meeting workspace page. Since the text column is a Multiple lines of text type, the text that the user enters can be decorated with colors, alignment, bolding, font size, and other rich text aspects as shown in Figure 5-12. You can also see the text box list in use by creating a social meeting workspace. The social meeting workspace contains a directions list that is created from the Text Box list template.

Figure 5-12. *The text box list used to customize a meeting workspace*

Things to Bring

The Things to Bring list template creates a list of items necessary for the meeting and who is responsible for them. This list can be beneficial in both corporate and social meeting workspaces to manage who is responsible for meeting necessities. The columns in the Things to Bring list template are shown in Table 5-18.

Table 5-18. *Things to Bring List Columns*

Column	Type	Notes
Item	Single line of text	
Comment	Single line of text	
Owner	Single line of text	Text column type allows any text entry rather than selection of site users.

The things to bring list contains the two views most common in meeting workspace lists, allowing users to see all of the list items or the list items they created. Like many other meeting workspace lists, the views in the Things to Bring list template allow the user to change the display order of the list items. These views are described in Table 5-19.

Table 5-19. *Things to Bring List Views*

View	Description
All Items	The default view, it displays all items in the list.
My Items	Displays items that the current user has created. This is accomplished by using a filter of Created By is equal to [Me].

Attendees

The Attendees list template allows members of the Administrator site group to manage people who will be involved in a meeting. The attendees list is created automatically when you create a meeting workspace. The list maintains a list of people who are invited to the meeting, along with an attendance type and response. The columns in the Attendees list template are shown in Table 5-20.

Table 5-20. *Attendees List Columns*

Column	Type	Notes
Name	Single line of text	
Comment	Multiple lines of text	
Response	Choice	Options include None, Accepted Tentative, and Declined. The attendees list does not allow you to change these options.
Attendance	Choice	Options include Required, Optional, and Organizer. The attendees list does not allow you to change these options.

■**Note** There can only be one attendees list in a meeting workspace. If you add another attendees list, both lists will display the same information.

Managing the Attendees List

The attendees list does not display an Add Item link on the list screen like most other lists. There also is no context menu for any columns, preventing you from editing any of the attendees. In order to add, edit, or delete attendees, you must first click the Manage Attendees link displayed on the toolbar of the list screen as shown in Figure 5-13. The list will then display a built-in view that includes an Add Attendee link on the toolbar and a context menu on the Name column. This context menu provides the View Item, Edit Item, and Delete Item options found in all other lists.

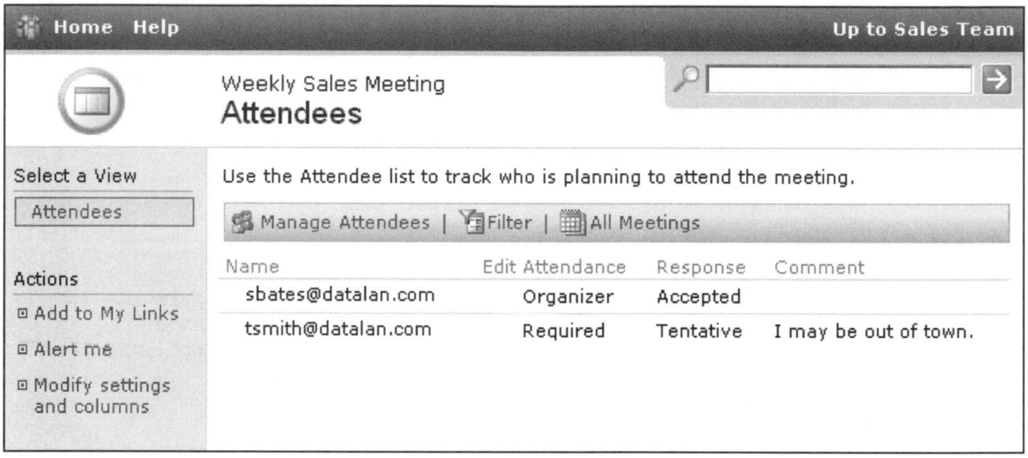

Figure 5-13. *The attendees list screen*

Caution Adding people directly to the attendees list does not automatically give them access to the meeting workspace. Make sure you add them as users of the workspaces in order to provide them with the proper access.

To add an attendee directly to the attendees list:

1. Navigate to the meeting workspace.

2. On the meeting workspace screen, click the Manage Attendees link on the attendees list.

3. On the attendees list screen, click the Add Attendee link on the toolbar.

4. On the New Item screen, enter the e-mail address or user name for the new attendee.

5. If you do not know the exact e-mail address or user name of the person you want to add, you can click the Address Book button. This button will open up the same address book you should be familiar with from Outlook. From the address book, you can search for the user in both corporate and personal address lists. When you have found a user you wish to grant access to for the list, select that user in the list and click the OK button.

6. Set the attendance type of required, optional, or organizer for the new attendee.

7. Click the Save and Close link on the toolbar.

■**Tip** You cannot delete the attendees list from a meeting workspace. If you do not want the attendees list to display, you can hide the web part on the workspace's web part page. See Chapter 7 for further information on managing web parts and web part pages.

Special Lists

There are two more lists provided for use in WSS sites and SPS areas that have not yet been discussed in this chapter. These two lists are highly specialized to perform very specific management of their list items that you cannot get through either custom lists or any of the other list templates. The Discussion Board and Survey list templates manage and present their list items in a manner that is specific to their own purpose.

Discussion Boards

If you have ever used an Internet news group or web site discussion forum, then SharePoint's Discussion Board list template will be familiar to you. The purpose of a discussion board is to organize messages around similar topics. New messages can be created as well as replies to existing messages. The columns of a discussion board list include the user-editable columns shown in Table 5-21 as well as some special columns that SharePoint uses to manage how the list items are related and displayed.

Table 5-21. *Discussion Board List Columns*

Column	Type
Subject	Single line of text
Text	Multiple lines of text

The Created and Created By columns normally found in other lists do not exist in a discussion board list. Instead, there are Posted At and Posted By columns that perform the same functions but are more accurately named for this type of list. There is also a Reply column that can be used in a user-created view to display an icon that, when clicked, allows a user to reply to the current discussion thread.

The discussion board comes with two views that show the discussion messages in distinct ways. Each user often has their own preference for viewing discussion forums in one of the two views described in Table 5-22.

Table 5-22. *Discussion Board List Views*

View	Description
Threaded	The default view, it displays list items (messages) and their replies grouped together. These groupings are called *threads* and are shown in Figure 5-14. This view contains a unique link in the toolbar labeled Expand/Collapse, which allows you to expand or collapse the thread groupings.
Flat	Displays all list items in the discussion board as separate list items. The subject, who it was posted by, and modified date are displayed as well as the message itself, which is collapsed and can be viewed by clicking the plus sign next to the subject.

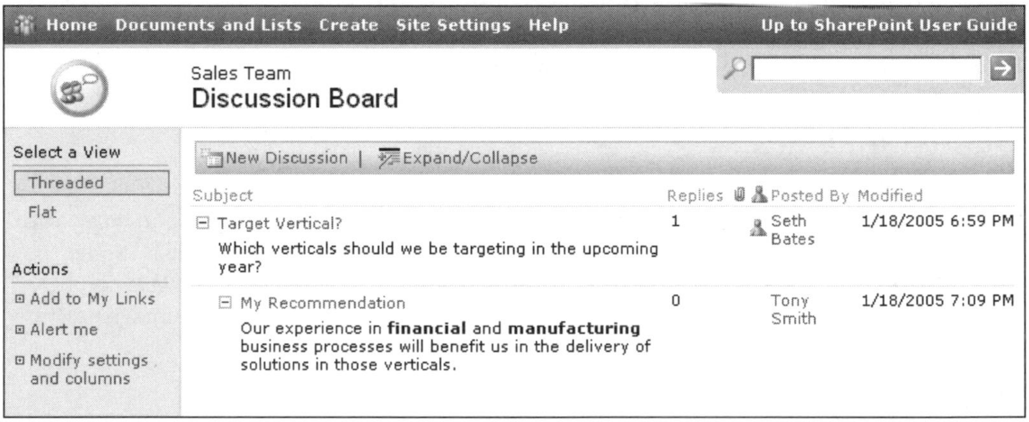

Figure 5-14. *The discussion board displaying the threaded view*

Using the Discussion Board

Aside from reading the message in a discussion board, you will want to do two things: create new discussion threads and reply to existing threads. To create a new discussion thread, click the New Discussion link on the toolbar of the discussion board screen. Enter a subject and text, and then click the Save and Close link just as you would when creating new list items in other list types.

To reply to an existing thread, you can click the Reply icon if it is presented in the view currently displayed. If the Reply column is not displayed, choose Reply from the context menu of a list item in the appropriate thread. Both methods take you to a New Item screen where the subject is populated with the subject of the thread you are replying to. Enter a message and click the Save and Close link to create a new message in the thread.

Tip When replying to a thread, you can change the subject line even though it is filled in for you. Share-Point will still know which thread the message belongs to.

Surveys

The Survey list template allows you to create lists that are presented to users as a question-naire. Although the underlying technology is the same as with other lists, the survey list is highly customized to make managing, responding, and reporting results match what you would expect when working with a survey. Surveys are an easy way to gain feedback from users. A survey added to a human resources site could poll employees about medical benefits satisfaction or preferences for a holiday party location.

To create a new survey, perform the following steps:

1. Click the Create link on the top menu of the site.

2. On the Create screen, click the Survey link under the Surveys section.

3. On the New Survey screen, enter a name and description for the survey.

4. Under the Survey Options section, specify whether users' names should be displayed with their responses and if a user should be able to respond to the survey more than once.

5. On the Add Question screen, enter the text for the question and choose an answer type. The answer types are almost identical to column types when adding columns to a list in Chapter 4.

6. Specify the optional settings for the current question. The settings available are deter-mined based on the answer type you selected.

7. If you want to add another question, click the Next Question button and repeat steps 5 and 6.

8. If you do not wish to add any more questions to the survey, click the Finish button.

Instead of managing the columns, in a survey you manage the questions. Managing ques-tions is extremely similar to managing columns in a custom list. Clicking the Modify Survey and Questions link on the survey screen will take you to the Customize Survey screen, allowing you to manage the survey. Here, under the Questions section, you can add, edit, and rearrange sur-vey questions in the same manner that you manage columns in other lists.

Surveys come with standard views as shown in Table 5-23. You do not have the ability to edit these views or add new views.

Table 5-23. *Survey Views*

View	Description
Overview	The default view, it displays the name, description, time created, and the number of responses for the survey.
Graphical Summary	For each question, this displays the percentage of respondents giving each answer.
All Responses	This view is similar to the All Items view found in other lists. It shows a list item for each user who has responded to the survey. It contains the familiar context menu, allowing you to view, edit, or delete a list item.

■Tip If you want users in the Reader site group to respond to a survey, you must configure the security on the survey. The default settings do not allow these users to add items, thus prohibiting them from responding to the survey.

Rating Scale

Instead of having column types like the other lists we have discussed, survey questions have answer types, which are managed in the same way as column types in other lists. Along with the types provided for columns, answer types include a new type called Rating Scale. The Rating Scale, shown in Figure 5-15, is displayed as a grid in which the user selects a value from a range for each row. Optional settings for the Rating Scale type are shown in Table 5-24.

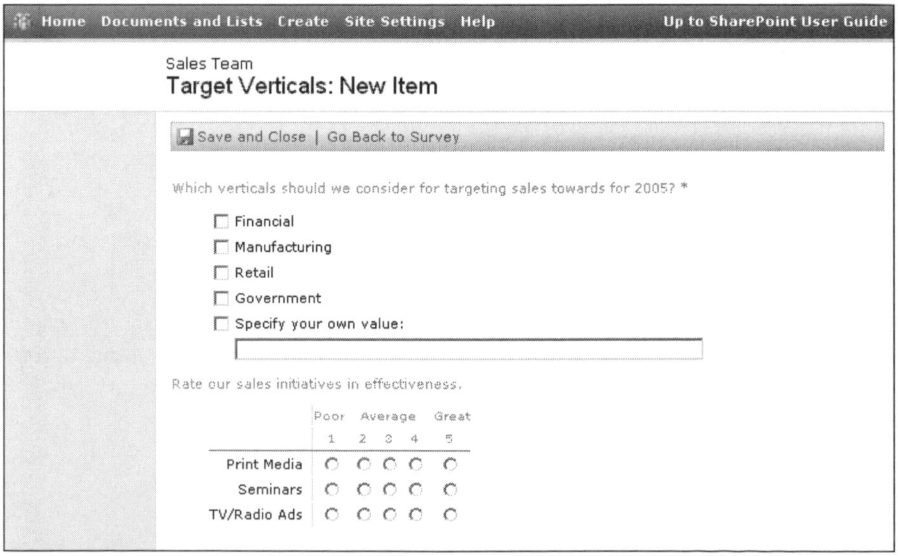

Figure 5-15. *Responding to a survey*

Table 5-24. *Optional Settings for Rating Scale Answer Types*

Setting	Description
Required	Specifies whether users must answer this question in order to submit their responses for the survey.
Choices	Indicates the labels for the grid rows. These choices determine the number of rows displayed.
Number Range	Determines the number of columns in the grid, or the number of options the user can select from to answer each row.
Range Text	Specifies the column heading. There are three range text entries: one for the left side, one for the right side, and one for the middle of the grid.
N/A Option	Specifies whether an option of N/A is available as an answer.
N/A Option Text	Specifies the heading for the N/A option column.

Responding to a Survey

For the survey to be useful, you will need to respond to the questions that were created and likely have others respond as well. Responding to a survey is similar to the experience of creating a new list item in other lists.

To respond to a survey:

1. Navigate to the survey list screen.

2. On the survey list screen, click the Respond to This Survey link in the toolbar. If you have already responded and the survey does not allow multiple responses per user, you will be presented with an error message.

3. On the New Item screen, shown in Figure 5-15, enter answers for each question with an asterisk, as these are required to save your response.

4. Enter answers for any nonrequired questions you want.

5. Click the Save and Close link on the toolbar.

After responding to the survey, you are taken to the Survey Overview view where you can see how many responses there are so far. You can now use the views created by the list to see a breakdown of the responses to each question or to see who has responded to the survey.

Advanced Office 2003 Integration

Throughout this chapter we have discussed various ways in which template SharePoint lists integrate with Office 2003 products. In addition to importing contacts, exporting events, and linking contacts or events lists with Outlook, lists created from SharePoint list templates provide some additional integration with Office 2003 that we explored in our discussion of custom lists in Chapter 4.

Exporting SharePoint Lists to Excel

The exporting of list information from custom lists into Excel discussed earlier in Chapter 4 also applies to template SharePoint lists. This provides you with an easier interface with which to modify large amounts of data in the list. Once in Excel, you can make numerous changes to the information and then commit all of the changes to the SharePoint list at the same time. This allows you to make updates while ensuring that SharePoint users are viewing a complete list of updated information rather than a partially completed list that would be shown if you were editing items individually within SharePoint.

To export a list to Excel, follow these steps:

1. Navigate to a SharePoint list you want to export.

2. Click the Export to Spreadsheet link on the Actions list on the left menu.

3. If you are prompted about opening or saving the Microsoft Office Excel Web Query File, click the Open button.

4. On the Opening Query dialog box in Excel, click the Open button to confirm that you want to run the query to export the information into the Excel spreadsheet.

5. If you already have Excel 2003 open, the Import Data dialog box will appear. Choose where to put the list. Options include a region on the current worksheet, a new worksheet, or a new workbook. If you did not have Excel 2003 running, the data will be put into a new workbook.

■**Note** When exporting list information to Excel, all list items displayed by the current view are exported. Items removed from the view by its filter setting are not included, but setting the temporary filter on the list screen has no effect on the data exported.

The Excel List

After performing the preceding steps to export a list to Excel, the data that appears in the Excel spreadsheet is formatted as an Excel List. The cells of an Excel List are denoted by the colored box surrounding the cells, the column headings that act as filters using drop-down menus, and the additional List actions available in the Excel menu under the Data option. The context menu, available by right-clicking the list in the spreadsheet, and the List toolbar also provide these actions.

The Excel List is what gives you the ability to make changes to the data within Excel and apply those changes to the SharePoint list. The Excel List can also receive changes that SharePoint users have made to the SharePoint list. The Excel List provides the following actions for you to manage the connection between the SharePoint list and Excel List:

- *View List on Server*: Opens the SharePoint list in your browser

- *Unlink List*: Severs the connection between the Excel List and the SharePoint list

- *Synchronize List*: Sends information updates to and from the SharePoint list and provides the ability to resolve data conflicts

- *Discard Changes and Refresh*: Cancels data updates made within Excel and retrieves the list information from SharePoint

Advanced Datasheet Features

In Chapter 4, we described the use of the Datasheet view for editing custom list data. The Datasheet view is also available for use with the standard and meeting workspace lists discussed in this chapter. The Datasheet view contains numerous features that allow for integration with Office 2003 products. Clicking the Task Pane link in the Datasheet's toolbar will display a list of Office integration features that are described in Table 5-25.

Table 5-25. *Datasheet Task Pane Office Links*

Feature	Description
Export and Link to Excel	Exports the list information in the same manner as the Export to Spreadsheet link on the Actions menu. The lists are linked, allowing you to synchronize data between Excel and SharePoint.
Print with Excel	Exports the list information to Excel and displays the Print dialog box, allowing you to quickly print out the list items.
Chart with Excel	Exports the list information to Excel and displays the Chart Wizard dialog box, allowing you to create graphs and charts based on the list items.
Create Excel PivotTable Report	Exports the list information to Excel and displays the PivotTable Field List dialog box and toolbar. The PivotTable allows you to select from the columns in the SharePoint list and create PivotTable reports with the capability to alter rows and columns interactively to display data detail in different ways.
Export to Access	Exports the list information into a new Access table in either a new or existing Access database. When doing this, the list and Access database are not linked and cannot be synchronized between the two.
Create Linked Table in Access	Creates a new Access-linked table in either a new or existing Access database. The linked table is synchronized with the SharePoint list. Any changes made in Access are also visible in the SharePoint list and vice versa.
Report with Access	Creates a new Access-linked table in either a new or existing Access database and then generates an Access report based on the information in the linked table as shown in Figure 5-16. This can be a valuable method for printing list information.

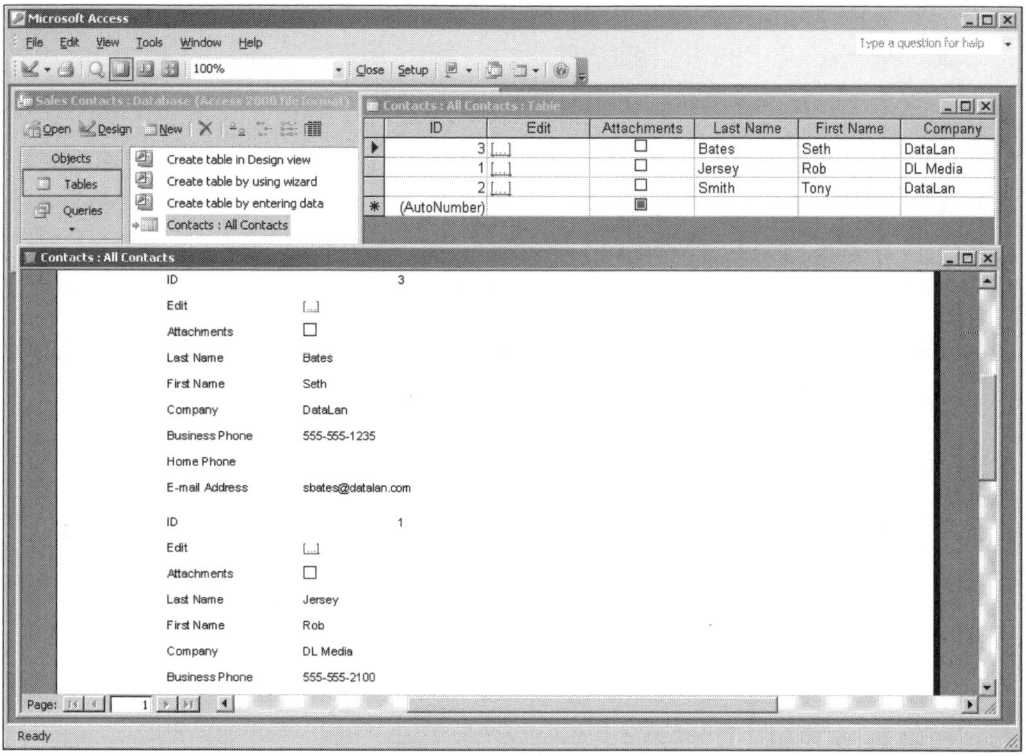

Figure 5-16. *Using the Report with Access feature to create a contacts list report*

CHAPTER 6

■ ■ ■

Libraries

In the previous two chapters, we discussed lists, which are one of the main components SharePoint uses to store information. As you saw, SharePoint provides a great deal of flexibility in storing and managing raw data using custom and template lists. In addition to raw data management, an Information Worker solution often needs to store and maintain documents.

Information workers spend countless hours creating, approving, and publishing various documents that are used to directly impact business processes and decisions. SharePoint provides most traditional document management capabilities including version control, content approval, searching, and document metadata.

SharePoint's document management is based on libraries. Using a library is very similar to using a list, as many of the display and management features are the same. Columns, views, and other familiar elements of SharePoint lists can also be found in a library. Libraries expand on list capabilities by providing the necessary document management features mentioned previously.

SharePoint libraries are categorized into these three different types:

- *Document library*: Stores most file types and provides integration into Office 2003 products such as Word 2003 and Excel 2003

- *Form library*: Specialized library for storing XML-based forms like those created by the new Office 2003 product InfoPath

- *Picture library*: Contains additional features around the storage and management of image file types

Document Library

Of the three types of libraries that SharePoint provides, the document library is the general-purpose library for managing files. You can think of a document library as a SharePoint list, with columns, views, settings, and permissions, except that each of the list items has a file associated with it. The document library also includes document management capabilities like check-in, check-out, versioning, and folder structures not found with lists. Features of a library that are identical to a list will only be briefly described in this chapter; for more details, please refer back to Chapter 4.

Creating Document Libraries

There is more than one way that you can create a custom document library in SharePoint. The quickest way is to choose the Document Library option on your site's Create page. To create a new document library, follow these steps:

1. Navigate to a Windows SharePoint Services site or create a new site as described in Chapter 3.

2. Click the Create link on the top menu bar.

3. On the Create page, click the Document Library link in the Document Libraries section.

4. On the New Document Library page, enter a name and description for the library.

5. Select Yes under the Navigation section if you want to show a link to this library on the Quick Launch menu of the site's home page.

6. In the Document Versions section, select Yes if you want the library to provide version-control features for the documents. This is discussed in the "Managing Document Libraries" section later in this chapter.

7. In the Document Template section, select the template file type for the library. Document templates are also discussed in the "Managing Document Libraries" section later in this chapter.

8. Click the Create button.

You have now created a document library that contains a single data column called Title. Viewing the library provides the file name, type, and modification information of each document. Figure 6-1 shows a library like the one you have just created.

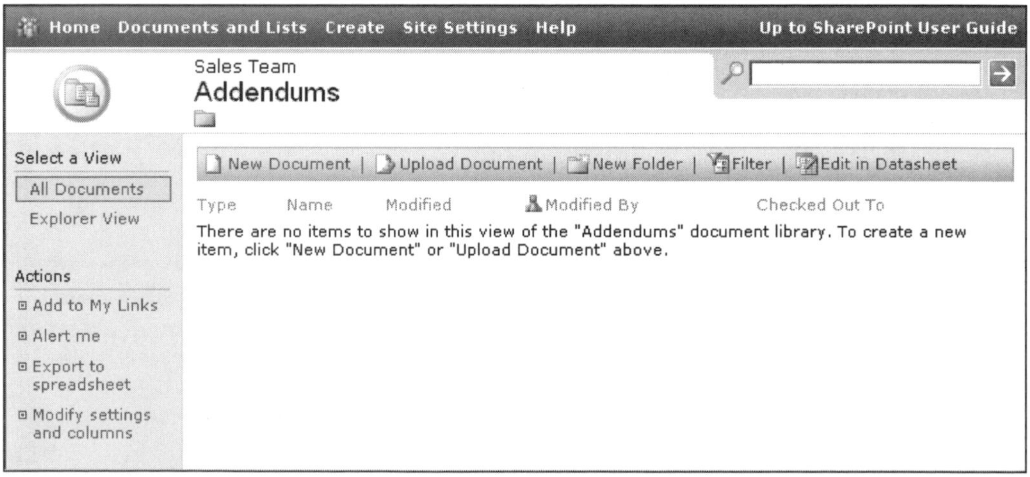

Figure 6-1. *A new document library*

Working with Document Libraries

As we have said, libraries contain many of the same features found in lists. This is because SharePoint libraries are built on the same general principles as lists. Although working with the libraries will seem very similar to working with lists, there are many new ways of adding and maintaining information in a document library, which we will describe.

Using Views

Views function the same way in a library as they do in lists. They determine what information is presented to the user and in what format. On the library screen, the view is selected from the left menu under the Select a View heading.

By default, two views are created for a document library. The first is called All Documents and displays the file name, type, and modification information for all documents in the library.

The second view, called the Explorer View, provides an interface similar to the Windows Explorer that is used to view and manage files on your computer. Documents and folders are shown as icons in this view. Many of the options for working with documents are exactly like the options available in Windows Explorer such as presenting the documents in list, detail, and icon displays. Right-clicking the Explorer View area presents the same functionality as right-clicking in Windows Explorer. Creating new folders and documents, cut/copy/paste, renaming, and other file system features are all available through this special document library view shown in Figure 6-2.

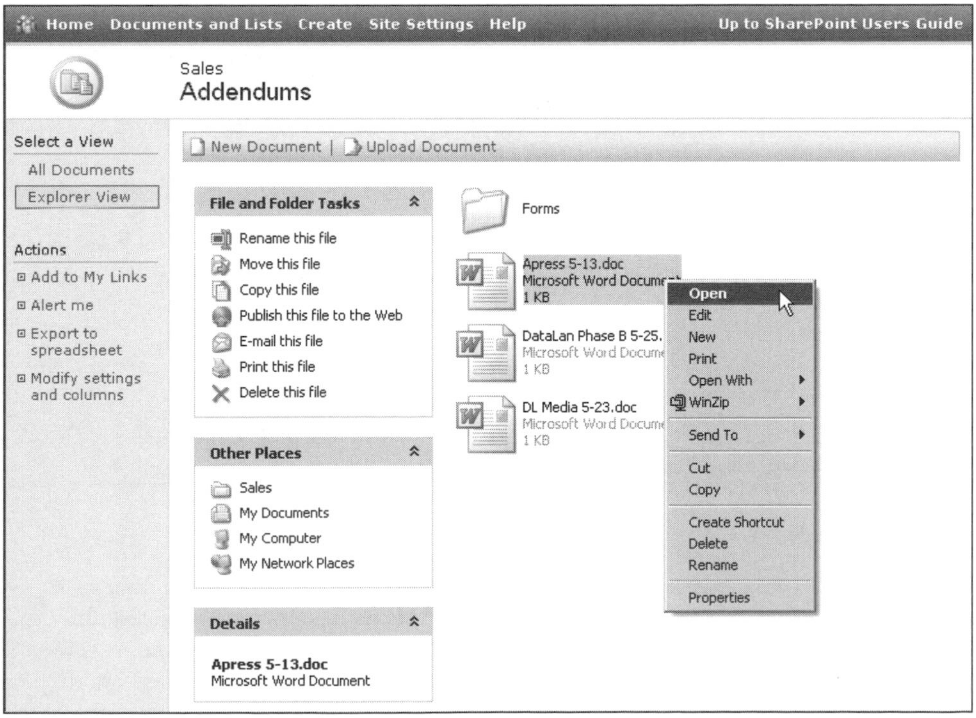

Figure 6-2. *The Explorer View*

■**Caution** The Explorer View requires that a technology called WebDAV is properly configured on your computer. If the Explorer View does not display properly, your IT administrator will need to ensure that you have WebDAV properly installed and configured.

Users having permission to manage a library can create new views each with its own way of presenting the document information. Each of these views will be available in the left menu after being created. Remember that you can apply filters and sorting after choosing an appropriate view as described in Chapter 4.

Filtering and Sorting Documents

Since libraries are built on the same underlying principles as lists, you are able to manipulate the documents as you would list items. This includes filtering and sorting the documents being displayed on the library screen.

Filtering is accomplished by clicking the Filter link on the toolbar of the library screen. Drop-down lists are then presented above each filterable column in the library. Selecting a value in these drop-down lists will filter the library so that only documents with the selected values are displayed. A funnel icon next to a column heading indicates that a filter is currently being applied to documents based on that column. To remove a filter, select the (All) option in the drop-down list.

Sorting the documents in a library is accomplished by clicking the column heading. Initially a column will sort in ascending order. Clicking that same column heading again will re-sort the library based on a descending order for that column, while clicking a different heading will sort the library based on the newly selected column. A small icon of an arrow next to the column heading indicates which column the library is sorting on and the direction.

Folders

You have the ability to create folders in document libraries. This lets you structure the way that documents are stored within a single document library. The structure of folders is a hierarchy similar to that of other familiar file systems like local and shared network drives.

To create a new folder in a document library:

1. Navigate to the Document Library screen.

2. On the Document Library screen, click the New Folder link on the toolbar.

3. On the New Folder screen, enter a name for the folder.

4. Click the Save and Close link.

The folder will appear in the library just like a document but will have an icon that looks like a tabbed manila file folder, similar to the Windows Explorer folder icon. Navigating through folders in a document library is quite simple. To view the documents in a folder, simply click the name of the folder in the library. The currently displayed folder is shown underneath the document library's name near the top of the page. When you are viewing the documents inside a folder, there will be an additional link on the toolbar. This link, simply titled Up, will take you out of the current folder that you are viewing and display the contents of the parent folder in the hierarchy.

■**Tip** Instead of using folders to organize a document library, have the manager of the document library create custom columns you can use to categorize the documents. This is generally seen as the more appropriate way to organize documents in SharePoint and supports more robust searching.

Folders have a unique set of options available in their context menus. These options include editing and deleting the folder. To edit a folder:

1. Click the Edit Properties link in the context menu of the folder.

2. On the Edit Folder page, change the Name. This is the only editable folder information.

3. Click the Save and Close link.

To delete a folder, select Delete from the folder's context menu and click OK when prompted for confirmation. The Edit Folder screen also contains a link on the toolbar to delete the folder.

■**Caution** Once you click OK on the confirmation dialog box for deleting the folder, the folder and all of the documents within it are physically deleted from SharePoint. It is not possible to recover the documents without assistance from your technical SharePoint administrator. Third-party products are available that can add recycle bin functionality to SharePoint, allowing easier recovery.

Adding Documents

Once a document library exists, you need to know how to get your documents into the library before others can work with them. There are two main ways to accomplish this from within the SharePoint document library. The first is to use the New Document link to create a new file from the document library's document template. Setting the library's document template, the default being a Microsoft Word document, is discussed in the "Managing Document Libraries" section later in this chapter. To create a new document in a document library:

1. Click the New Document link on the toolbar of the library page.

2. If a warning message is displayed regarding opening documents, click the OK button.

3. In the application that opens, create your document.

4. Select to save the document. If the application is an Office application, you will be shown the Save As dialog box, allowing you to save the document directly into the document library.

5. Close the application.

■**Caution** The New Document link requires that you have Microsoft Office 2003 installed.

Using the New Document link is a good way to add new documents to the document library. For documents that already exist, the document library provides a way to upload the document from your local computer or network into the document library. This is accomplished from the Upload Document link in the library using these steps:

1. Click the Upload Document link on the toolbar of the library page.

2. On the Upload Document screen, shown in Figure 6-3, click the Browse button.

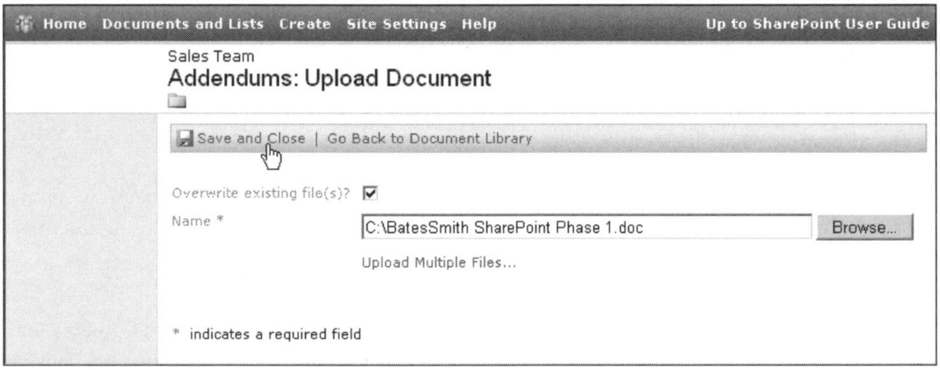

Figure 6-3. *Uploading a document*

3. On the Choose File dialog box, select the file you want to upload by navigating the drive and folders on your local computer or network.

4. Click the Open button.

5. On the Upload Document screen, edit any additional property information that is available for the library.

6. Click the Save and Close link on the toolbar.

■**Caution** There are restrictions on the file types that can be uploaded into a SharePoint document library. For example, EXE files are not permitted by default. Uploading one of these files will result in an error being displayed. The list of disallowed types is managed by your technical SharePoint administrator.

If you have Office 2003 installed on your computer, another link will be presented to you on the Upload Document screen. This link, Upload Multiple Files, allows you to select and upload more than the single file at a time that you are able to do on the default Upload Document screen. A restriction when uploading multiple files is that you are unable to set any metadata information on the files as they are uploaded like you can when uploading a single file. The metadata information can be entered after the documents are uploaded. How to do this is described in the "Editing Document Properties" section later in this chapter.

Clicking the Upload Multiple Files link displays your file system view as shown in Figure 6-4. Local drives, network shares, and networked computers and their folders are shown on the left. The right side of the screen lists the files in the currently selected drive or folder. Each file is displayed with a checkbox, thereby allowing you to select multiple files. Check off all of the files you want to upload and click the Save and Close link from the toolbar to upload all of these files into your document library.

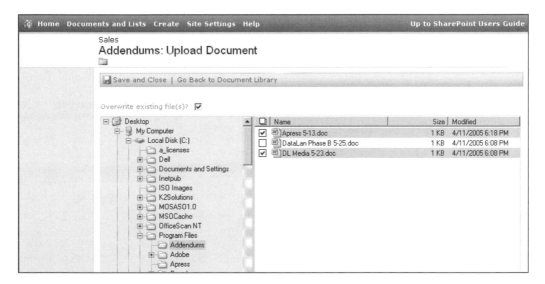

Figure 6-4. *Uploading multiple files*

Editing Documents

The context menu displayed for a document, just like context menus for list items, provides the entry point into working with your documents. This includes editing a document's content. If the file type is a recognized type, like from an Office application, the context menu will include an Edit in <Application> choice. For instance, Word documents will have the option Edit in Microsoft Office Word in their context menu. Selecting this choice will open the document in the native application. After making any changes to the file, saving the file will save the new document back to the document library.

Check-Out and Check-In

After opening a document for editing from a document library and saving your changes, other users can immediately view the modifications by opening the document themselves. At times you will want to make changes that are not seen by others until you are ready. There are also times when you want to save some changes to the document but have not completed all of the changes you need to make before others make further modifications. The way to solve these situations is through a control mechanism like the check-in and check-out capability of SharePoint.

To edit a document by checking it out:

1. Activate the document's context menu by hovering over the file name with your mouse and clicking the inverted triangle.

2. Click the Check Out link in the context menu. The document is now checked out to you.

3. Activate the document's context menu again and click the Edit in <Application> link.

4. Change the content of the file and save the document back into the library.

5. Repeat steps 3 and 4 until you are ready for others to see your changes.

6. Activate the document's context menu and click the Check In link.

7. On the Check In screen, shown in Figure 6-5, add comments describing the changes that were made to the document.

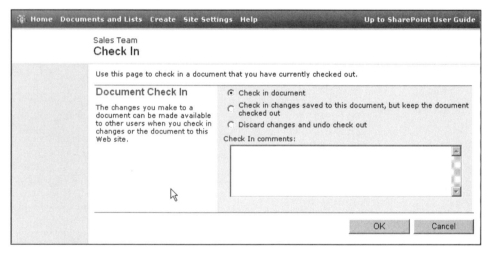

Figure 6-5. *The Check In screen*

8. Click the OK button.

Until you check the document in, other users will not see the latest content while viewing the document library. If they choose to view the document, they will see it as it looked before you checked it out, even if you have saved the document back to the document library. This allows you to make incremental updates, saving the document each time, and then checking it in when you have completed all of your changes. When the document is checked out to you, other users are unable to make edits to it until you have checked the document back in.

Users in the administrator site group have the ability to check in documents that other users have checked out. This is important in the event that urgent modifications must be made to the document, the user who has the document checked out leaves your company, or another similar situation occurs. If you are the administrator, you will be able to select Check In from the context menu of the checked-out document. On the Check In screen, select the appropriate option to keep or discard changes that were made to the document. After clicking the OK button, a confirmation warning will be displayed stating the user who has the document checked out along with the date and time they checked it out. Clicking Yes on the warning dialog box checks in the document, allowing other users to gain access to the most recent version.

Editing Document Properties

In addition to the actual file content, you may also need to edit the document properties in the library. The document properties include the document file name, title, and any additional columns that the document library designer has created to help categorize the document in the library.

The context menu for each document contains two links to allow you to work with the document properties, also called metadata. Click View Properties in the context menu to display a screen of document properties including the creator of the document and when it was created, along with who edited the document last and when it was edited. From this screen, you can edit the properties by clicking the Edit Item link on the toolbar. Another way to edit the item properties is the Edit Properties selection in the document's context menu. Either of these two options displays a screen that allows you to change the document's file name, title, and other custom metadata. To edit a document's properties from the Document Library screen:

1. Activate the document's context menu by hovering over the file name with your mouse and clicking the inverted triangle.

2. Click the Edit Properties link in the context menu.

3. On the Edit Properties page, change the file name, title, or other properties.

4. Click the Save and Close link.

Document Workspaces

Creating and using document workspaces was discussed, along with Windows SharePoint Services sites, in Chapter 3. Document libraries provide an additional way to create document workspaces that integrates them with a document in the library. You can use this approach to easily create a separate workspace devoted to the collaborative creation of a specific document. This can prove useful when many people are collectively contributing to the production of a complex document such as a contract, a proposal response, or a company policy file.

To create a document workspace for a document:

1. Navigate to the Document Library screen.

2. Activate the document's context menu by hovering over the file name with your mouse and clicking the inverted triangle.

3. Click the Create Document Workspace link in the context menu.

4. On the Create Document Workspace page, click the OK button.

Once you have completed the preceding steps, your new document workspace will be displayed as shown in Figure 6-6. Notice the Shared Documents document library that was created contains the document from which you created the workspace. You will be automatically added to the site users and displayed in the Members web part. To allow others to work collaboratively with you, add new users to the site as described in Chapter 3. This allows you to set different permissions for the workspace from the permissions that exist for the original document library. While a large group of users may be able to view the original document library, you may only want a small subset of those users to have access to the workspace in order to edit the document. You are able to create lists, add other supporting documents, and use other SharePoint features in order to collaborate on the document modifications.

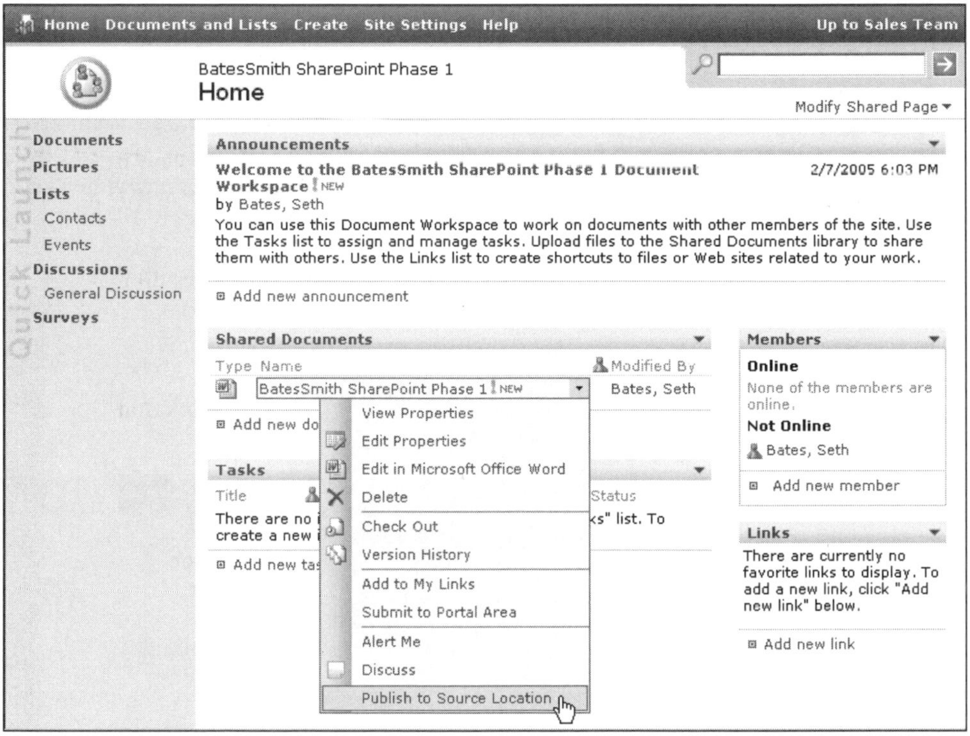

Figure 6-6. *A document workspace created from a document library*

Once you have made the necessary changes to the document, you can publish it back to the initial document library from which you created the workspace. To do this, perform the following steps:

1. In the document workspace, activate the document's context menu by hovering over the file name with your mouse and clicking the inverted triangle.

2. Click the Publish to Source Location link in the context menu. This is shown in Figure 6-6.

3. On the Publish to Source Location page, click the OK button.

4. On the Confirmation page, click the Home link on the top menu to return to the document workspace.

To return to the workspace from the parent WSS site, click the Document Workspaces link under the See Also section of the Documents and Lists page of the site. For more information regarding navigating subsites, refer to the "Navigating Through WSS Sites" section of Chapter 3.

Versions

Like many other document management platforms, SharePoint document libraries have the ability to store each instance of a saved document as a separate version. Enabling document versioning is done through the management features of the document library. This setting is available on the General Settings screen of the library as explained in the "Managing Document Libraries" section later in this chapter.

A document library that has document versioning enabled allows you to view previous versions of a document from the Versions Saved screen. To view a previous version of a document in a library with versioning enabled:

1. Activate the document's context menu by hovering over the file name with your mouse and clicking the inverted triangle.

2. Click the Version History link in the context menu.

3. On the Versions Saved page, shown in Figure 6-7, click the Modified link that represents the version you wish to view.

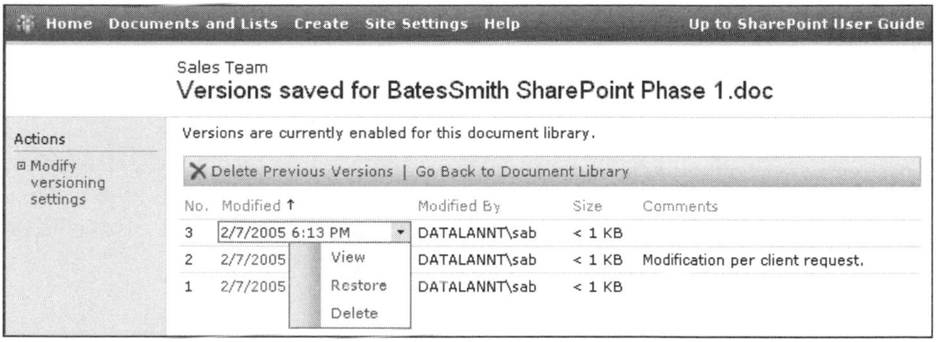

Figure 6-7. *Document version history*

There are some peculiarities to note when viewing versions of a document. The document version may open inside of the browser window rather than in the native application. If this happens, make sure to click the back button on the browser in order to return to the document library. Closing the window will close not only the document, but also the browser window you were using to view the library. Another potential, and sometimes confusing, browser behavior is caching the versions while you view them. While viewing older versions of a document, if another user edits the document, the links on the Version History screen may not display the appropriate versions. Using a new browser window to display older document versions will solve this issue.

The Versions Saved screen provides the ability to restore an older version of the document, thereby making it the current version. You may need to do this if you discover that newer versions had incorrect information added to them and you wish to revert to a version with accurate information. To restore a version:

1. Navigate to the Versions Saved screen for the document.

2. Activate the context menu for the version you wish to restore and click the Restore link.

3. When prompted for confirmation, click the OK button.

4. A new version of the document will be created from the selected version and set as the current version.

Deleting versions can be done in two ways. If you want to delete all historical versions of the document, without deleting the document itself, click the Delete Previous Versions link on the toolbar of the Versions Saved screen. If you want to delete a single version, use the Delete link in the context menu of the version you wish to remove.

■**Tip** If a document is checked out, a new version is not created every time you save the document. A new version will only be created once the document is checked in. Conversely, if you do not check out the document, each time the document is saved a new version is created.

Faster Data Manipulation Using the Datasheet

The Datasheet capabilities found in a list are also provided for document libraries. This integration with Office 2003 allows an easy way for you to edit the metadata of multiple documents in a list without having to go to each document's Edit Item page separately. This can be especially useful for updating metadata after performing a multiple file upload.

■**Note** In order for Datasheet mode to work, you need Office 2003 installed on the computer you are using when accessing the library. Your browser security settings must also allow ActiveX components to run in order for the Datasheet view to operate properly.

To edit document information in Datasheet mode, click the Edit in Datasheet link on the toolbar of the library. The library changes to a spreadsheet display, allowing you to quickly change multiple data values. Spreadsheet abilities such as creating summations are available via the toolbar. A context menu via a right-click of the Datasheet view provides you with the ability to add and delete rows or columns. The context menu also provides the ability to auto-fill cells or for you to pick cell values from a list of previously entered values in the column. When you need to modify the metadata of multiple documents in the same library, the Datasheet view is more efficient than navigating to each individual Edit Item page.

Managing Document Libraries

Just like lists, the power of a document library resides in your ability to customize the way it stores and presents information to the user. Many of the management features of a library are identical to those found in custom lists.

■**Note** Creating and managing a library requires that you have the proper permissions. By default, you must be in the Administrator or Web Designer site groups in order to have access to creating and customizing libraries.

All management of a library begins by selecting the Modify Settings and Columns link from the Actions list on the library screen. Clicking this link takes you to the Customize Library screen where the options are categorized into General Settings; Columns, where you determine how the document metadata is stored; and Views, where you customize the ways in which other users can see the documents.

General Settings

The General Settings screen allows you to determine the functionality available to users of the library and allows you to alter the general characteristics of the library.

To edit the general settings of a library, follow these steps:

1. Navigate to the Document Library screen.

2. On the Document Library screen, click the Modify Settings and Columns link in the Actions list on the left menu.

3. On the Customize Library screen, click the Change General Settings link under the General Settings category.

Table 6-1 describes the library settings you can edit in order to customize the behavior of a document library.

Table 6-1. *General Settings for SharePoint Document Libraries*

Setting	Description
Name	Specifies the name used to identify the library through your SharePoint site.
Description	Gives a more elaborate explanation of the library's purpose. This is displayed on the Documents and Lists screen and the library screen.
Navigation	Determines whether a link for the library is displayed on the Quick Launch bar on the left side of the site screen.
Content Approval	Allows you to enable the Content Approval feature so that users do not see newly added items until a user with Manage List permission (members of the Administrator or Web Designer groups normally) approves the item.
Document Versions	Enables versioning that causes the library to maintain separate copies of a document each time it is saved to the library.
Document Template	Allows you to enter the URL of a document in the site that should be used as the template for all new documents created in the library through the New Document option.

Document Template

Every document library uses a template in order to determine what type of file is created when the user clicks the New Document link on the toolbar of the library screen. Initially, the document template is selected when the document library is created as shown in Figure 6-8.

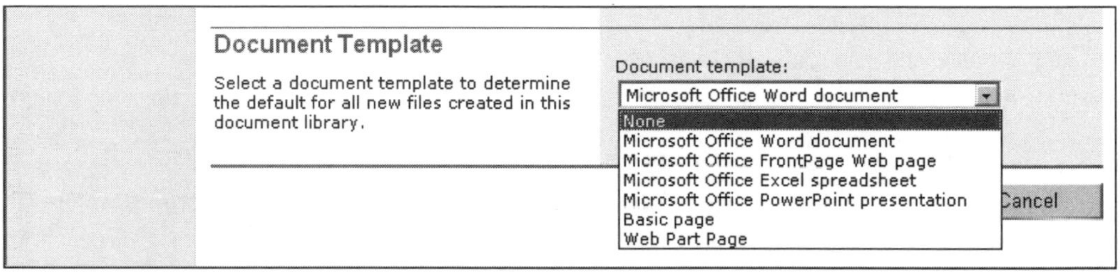

Figure 6-8. *Document template*

Available document template options are as follows:

- *None*: No template is used; however, a Word document is created when the user clicks the New Document link in the library.

- *Word document*

- *FrontPage web page*

- *Excel spreadsheet*

- *PowerPoint presentation*

- *Basic Page*: A SharePoint Basic Page (see Chapter 7) is created in the library when the user clicks the New Document link.

- *Web Part Page*: A SharePoint Web Part Page (see Chapter 7) is created in the library when the user clicks the New Document link.

Once the document library has been created, you can customize the document template it is using. Since the document template initially is just a blank new document of the type specified as the document library template option, you may want to add content to standardize how the documents in the library look. For instance, you may want to add headers and footers with the company logo to a Word document template in a document library for contracts, or a corporate About Us slide to a PowerPoint document template in a library for corporate presentations. To edit the document template:

1. On the Document Library screen, click the Modify Settings and Columns link in the Actions list on the left menu.

2. On the Customize Library screen, click the Edit Template link next to the Document Template heading under the General Settings section.

3. If a warning message is displayed regarding opening documents, click the OK button.

4. When the document template opens in its native application, make the changes you desire.

5. Save the document template from the application menu or toolbar, and then close the application.

A document library also allows you to use an existing document as the document template. The document must be placed in the same document library where it will be used as a template. You cannot use a document in another document library on the current or any other site. To set the document template for a library to a specific document in the library:

1. On the Document Library screen, click the Modify Settings and Columns link in the Actions list on the left menu.

2. On the Customize Library screen, click the Change General Settings link under the General Settings category.

3. On the Change General Settings screen, enter the URL to the document under the Document Template section. This should be in the following format: `<Document Library>/Forms/<File Name>`. An example would be Policies/Forms/VacationTime.doc, where Policies is the name of the document library and VacationTime.doc is the file name. Documents must exist in the Forms directory of the document library in order to be used as templates. Adding a document into the Forms directory of the document library is discussed in the "Advanced Office 2003 Integration" section later in this chapter.

4. Click the OK button.

■**Note** Changing the document template will not affect existing documents in a document library, only new documents created using the New Document option after the template has changed.

Content Approval

When content approval is enabled for a document library, a newly added document is not displayed to all users, even in the All Documents view, until someone with the Manage List permission has approved the document. The process, which begins on the library screen, is identical to the content approval process in lists.

Libraries with content approval enabled will contain two new views intended to help content approvers work with the documents. The first is called Approve/Reject Items and is intended for users with the Manage List permission to display the documents categorized by status. In this manner, approvers can easily see pending documents and take the appropriate approval action. Users without this permission will receive a login dialog box when trying to access the Approve/Reject Items view.

Users who have added documents to the library can use the My Submissions view to see the current state of their documents. This view displays all documents the user has created, categorized by their approval status. When approving or rejecting a submission, the content approver can enter comments explaining their action. These comments can be seen in the My Submissions view so that the submitter can make corrections or take other appropriate steps.

■**Note** Documents added by a user who has the Manage List permission are automatically approved and will immediately appear to all users who can normally view documents in the library.

Security

Managing the security of a document library is performed identically to managing the security of lists. By default the library inherits the security of the site or area that it is on. If you are in the administrator site group, you have the ability to modify the security using the same users, site groups, and site group permissions that we described in detail in Chapter 4.

To modify library permissions security in a WSS site:

1. On the Library screen, click the Modify Settings and Columns link in the Actions list on the left menu.

2. On the Customize Library screen, click the Change Permissions for this Document Library link under the General Settings section.

3. Proceed by adding, modifying, and deleting users and site groups based on the "Security" section in Chapter 4.

The advanced permissions available in a library are identical to those found in a SharePoint list with one notable addition. A Cancel Check-Out permission can be given to a site group or user to allow them to undo check-out actions by other users.

Managing Columns

The ability to design your own structure to provide users with information about your documents is often a key to the efficient use of your document library. SharePoint provides you with the ability to add library metadata, called columns, of various data types including formatting rules about the information that can be stored in these columns.

Adding and managing columns in a library is done exactly like it is for lists. The data types, optional settings, and management process are identical. Refer to "Managing Columns" in Chapter 4 for more details on the available column types and how to add or edit columns. Adding columns to document libraries and maintaining the information makes it easier for users to locate documents relevant to their needs.

Managing Views

We have already discussed several document library views earlier in this chapter. One such view is the All Documents view, which is available by default when a document library is created. Once the library is created, you are able to create your own custom views to customize the way in which the documents are displayed to users. The same types of views available for lists are also available in libraries: standard, datasheet, and calendar.

The sorting, filtering, grouping, styles, and totals that are settings for list views apply to libraries as well. These options and how to add, edit, and configure views is described in detail in the "Managing Views" section of Chapter 4. Library views have an additional setting available under the Folders section that allows you to determine whether the view displays the folder structure or instead shows all files regardless of which folder they are contained in. The Styles section has an additional style available called Document Details, which displays each document in a separate box with its modification and size information shown.

Libraries also have a different set of special columns that are available for use in views. These columns are shown in Table 6-2 and can provide value when displaying them in your custom views.

Table 6-2. *Special Document Library Columns for Use in Views*

Column	Description
Type	Determines the file type of the document. When used in views, the type is displayed as a familiar icon representing the file type.
Name (linked to document with edit menu)	Displays the file name as a link that opens the document. Also provides the context menu for editing and managing a document.
Name (linked to document)	Displays the file name as a link that opens the document.
Modified	Indicates the date and time that the document or its metadata was last edited. If the document was never edited, it contains the date and time the document was created.
Modified By	Indicates the last user to modify the document.
File Size	Specifies the size of the document (in kilobytes).
ID	Contains a number that uniquely identities a document within a library.
Created By	Indicates the user who added the document to the library.
Created	Specifies the date and time that the document was added to the library.
Checked Out To (link to username to user details page)	Indicates the user who currently has the document checked out.
Approval Status	Specifies the status of the document in the approval process. Possible values are Pending, Rejected, and Approved. This column is only available in libraries that require approval.
Approver Comments	Displays the comments entered by the approver during the approval process. This column is only available in libraries that require approval.
Edit (link to Edit)	Displays a column containing an icon as a link that takes the user to the Edit Item screen.

Creating a Library Template

As was described in the "Creating a List Template" section of Chapter 4, you often find yourself needing to use the same library structure for multiple libraries. Also, you may want to use the same library structure in multiple sites. It would be an inefficient use of time for you to manually create the columns and views for multiple instances of similar libraries.

Imagine having separate sites for each department in your company. Each department has policy and procedure documents they want stored in document libraries within their sites. The columns and views for each document library are similar, so it is a good practice to create a single document library and save this library as a template.

To create a library template:

1. As a member of the site Administrator or Web Designer site groups, navigate to a library screen.

2. Click the Modify Settings and Columns link in the Actions menu on the left.

3. Under General Settings, click the Save Document Library as Template link.

4. Specify a file name, a simple title, and more elaborate description for the template.

5. If you want the template to contain the documents currently in the library, check the Include content checkbox.

6. Click the OK button.

A template for this site collection is now created based on the document library. This template will be available in the Document Libraries section of the Create page. When you want to create a document library that is based on the template, choose the template on the Create page rather than choosing the Document Library link.

Deleting the Library

There may be times when deleting a library is necessary. This is accomplished on the Customize Library screen.

To delete a library, follow these steps:

1. On the library screen, click the Modify Settings and Columns link in the Actions list on the left menu.

2. On the Customize Library screen, click the Delete this Document Library link under the General Settings category.

3. Click OK when prompted for confirmation that you wish to delete the library.

■**Caution** Once you click OK on the confirmation dialog box for deleting the library, the library and all of the documents it contains are physically deleted from SharePoint. It is not possible to recover the documents without assistance from your IT staff.

Adding a Listing to the Portal

Portal listings can be created that link to a document library, allowing users to quickly find the documents important to them. These listings are created from the document library itself in a manner very similar to creating listings for lists. It provides the ability to create multiple listings on various portal areas simultaneously.

Adding a listing to the portal can be done via the Select a Portal Area for this Document Library link on the Customize Library screen. See the "Adding a Listing to the Portal" section of Chapter 4 for more details on adding a listing.

You can also add a listing to the portal that links to a specific document. To do this, select the Submit to Portal Area from the document's context menu while viewing the library. The Add a Listing screen will be displayed and behave as described in Chapter 4. This feature is also available when uploading a document by selecting the Add a Listing for this Document checkbox on the Upload screen.

Differences Between Portal Document Libraries and Site Document Libraries

Libraries in the portal and libraries in a WSS site have a few differences. Portal areas do not contain the Quick Launch menu or Documents and Lists link found in a WSS site. Instead, a Manage Content link is available in areas in the Actions list on the left side of the screen for users in at least the Contributor site group. This link takes you to a screen with links to all of the existing lists and libraries and the ability to create new ones.

Document libraries created in a portal area contain different default columns from those created in WSS sites. While document libraries created in sites initially only contain a Title column, document libraries created in SPS areas contain the columns shown in Table 6-3.

Table 6-3. *Default Area Document Library Columns*

Column	Type	Notes
Title	Single line of text	
Owner	Single line of text	Text column type allows any text entry rather than selection of portal users.
Description	Multiple lines of text	
Status	Choice	Default options include Rough, Draft, In Review, and Final.

The other major difference between SPS libraries and WSS libraries is that the link on the Library screen called Change Permissions does not appear for a library that is housed in a SharePoint Portal Server 2003 area. The following tip shows you how you can still modify security at the library level in a portal area.

■**Tip** Even though you are not given a link to modify security at the library level in a portal area, you can still accomplish this by typing the following URL in your browser:

http://<*Portal Name*>/<*Area Name*>/_layouts/1033/shropt.aspx?obj{<*Library Identifier*>},list

Be sure to replace <*Portal Name*> with the name of your portal server, <*Area Name*> with the name of the area containing the list (if the list is on the Home area of the portal, do not specify an area name in this URL), and <*Library Identifier*> with the unique ID associated with the library. An easy way to find the unique ID for the library is to copy it from the URL of the Customize Library screen. After navigating to the Customize Library screen, everything directly after "List=" in the URL and between the braces is the unique ID.

Form Library

A new application in the Office 2003 suite is InfoPath 2003. InfoPath is a form creation and submission tool that lets a designer create a form for data entry, and users can then fill out this form. After a user fills out the form, the data can be saved to XML files, databases, or other data management tools where it can then be analyzed and incorporated into related business processes. An example is a purchase order in which employees enter information regarding items they wish to buy like quantity, cost, and reason for purchase, and after being submitted, the information is reviewed by their manager or purchasing coordinator.

SharePoint includes integration for InfoPath forms through the use of form libraries. A form library is very similar to a document library except that the template used in the library is an InfoPath form. Instead of uploading documents, the library's responsibility is to provide a repository for completed forms and give users the ability to review the responses.

■**Note** For additional information on how to use Microsoft Office InfoPath 2003, please see the help files that come with the product or visit http://office.microsoft.com.

Creating Form Libraries

Creating form libraries can be accomplished by publishing an InfoPath form using InfoPath or through the library creation process within a Windows SharePoint Services site or portal server area.

To create a new form library from within a WSS site, follow these steps:

1. Navigate to a Windows SharePoint Services site or create a new site as described in Chapter 3.

2. Click the Create link on the top menu bar.

3. On the Create page, click the Form Library link in the Document Libraries section.

4. On the New Form Library page, enter a name and description for the library.

5. Select Yes under the Navigation section if you want to show a link to this library on the Quick Launch menu of the site's home page.

6. In the Form Versions section, select Yes if you want the library to provide version-control features for the form files. This is discussed in detail in the "Managing Form Libraries" section later in this chapter.

7. In the Form Template section, select a template form from the available templates. WSS only comes with the Blank Form template, but we will discuss how to obtain other templates in the "Managing Form Libraries" section later in this chapter.

8. Click the Create button.

You have now created a form library based on the form template you selected. Viewing the library provides the file name, type, modification information, and custom form fields of each submitted form. Figure 6-9 shows a library like the one you have just created.

Figure 6-9. *A new form library using the Sales Report form template available from the Microsoft Office 2003 Web Parts and Components package*

Working with Form Libraries

In order to work with form libraries, you need to have a working knowledge of using Microsoft Office InfoPath. From a user's perspective, opening an InfoPath form, entering appropriate information in the fields presented, and then saving the form is all that is necessary. Form libraries allow you to save and organize related forms in one place while being able to view data from the forms without opening each individual form.

Using Views

By now you are familiar with the concept of views and their use in determining the way in which the items are displayed to the users of the list or library. When a form library is created, it comes with default views as shown in Table 6-4.

Table 6-4. *Form Library Views*

View	Description
All Forms	The default view displays the file name, modification information, and form data for all items in the library.
Explorer View	Displays an interface that allows you to view and manage forms similar to how files are managed with Windows Explorer. This view is also used in document libraries.
Merge Forms	Allows you to combine the data from multiple forms into a single form. This view is only available with certain form templates that allow data merging like the Sales Report template.
My Forms	Displays the type, file name, and modification information for all of the current user's forms. This is accomplished by using a filter of Created By is equal to [Me].

As is the case with other views in lists and libraries, the view contains filtering and sorting information. In addition to the view's filtering and sorting, you are able to apply additional filtering and sorting on the library screen as described in the "Using Views" section for document libraries earlier in this chapter.

Adding Forms

Adding forms to a forms library can be accomplished in two ways. The first, and most common, is to create a new form by using the form library's template. This provides a quick way to fill out form information and lets you make the most out of the form library's integration with InfoPath. To create a new form:

1. Click the Fill Out This Form link on the toolbar of the form library screen.

2. When InfoPath opens, as shown in Figure 6-10, enter the appropriate data in the fields on the InfoPath form.

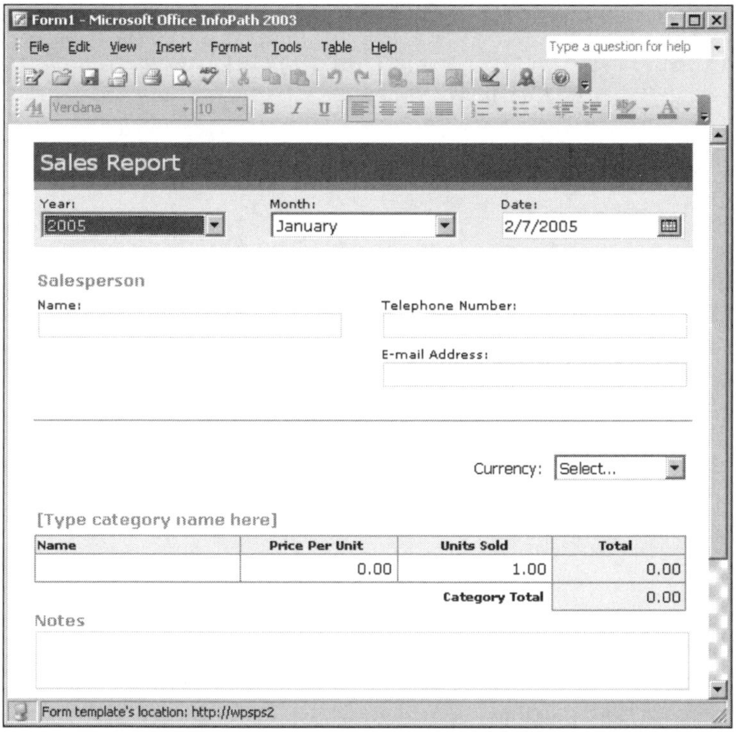

Figure 6-10. *Filling out a form with InfoPath*

3. Select to save the document from the menu or toolbar of InfoPath.

4. On the Save As dialog box, which will display the form library as the destination, change the name of the file.

5. Click the Save button.

6. Close InfoPath.

You are also able to upload a form into the form library. Uploading a form that was not created based on the library's template is allowed, but you will not receive the complete integration with the library that is provided. To upload forms, simply click the Upload Form link on the toolbar of the library screen. The Upload Form screen will appear and function identically to the Upload Document screen in document libraries. Follow the same process used there by clicking the Browse button, selecting a file, and then clicking the Save and Close link to upload the form.

Editing Forms

After you either create a new form or upload an existing form to the library, you are able to edit the form's data. To edit the information in the form, the context menu available in the library includes an Edit in Microsoft Office InfoPath option. Selecting this option will open the form in InfoPath, allowing you to make modifications and save it back to the library.

The check-out and check-in features of document libraries also apply to form libraries. To prevent others from working on the same form that you are editing, it is best to check out the form first. After making all of your changes using InfoPath, save the form back to the library and check it in so that other users see that changes have taken place. Until you check the form in, other users of the library will not see the updates you made even if you have saved the form back to the library. This allows you to keep the form checked out until you are ready for others to see your modifications.

Edit Form Properties

In addition to editing the InfoPath forms themselves, you can edit the custom properties created for the form library to further describe each form. This is accomplished from the Edit Properties link in the context menu of each form in the library. Changing the title and file name of the form is accomplished on the Edit Properties screen.

■**Note** You can only edit custom form properties from the Edit Properties screen, not the data in the form itself.

Merge Forms

Libraries created from InfoPath form templates that allow form merging provide an additional view called Merge Form. This Merge Form view allows you to combine the data from separate forms into a single form. Many of the form templates discussed in the "Form Templates" section later in this chapter contain the form merging capabilities. This could be useful to consolidate such things as purchase orders, timesheets, and sales reports. To merge forms in a form library:

1. On the Library screen, click the Merge Forms view in the Select a View list on the left.

2. On the Merge Forms view, check the checkbox in the Merge column for each form you want to combine.

3. Click the Merge Forms link on the toolbar.

4. InfoPath will open and combine the data from the forms selected. Make any additional updates to the information.

5. Select to save the document from the menu or toolbar of InfoPath.

6. On the Save As dialog box, which will display the form library as the destination, change the name of the file.

7. Click the Save button and then close InfoPath.

■**Note** Merging forms does not delete the original forms; it creates a new form with the combined data from the multiple source forms.

Folders and Versions

Just as we discussed earlier in this chapter with regard to document libraries, you can create folders in form libraries to help you organize your forms. The adding, editing, and deleting of folders is performed using the same steps as with a document library, so refer to the "Folders" section of "Working with Document Libraries" earlier for further instructions.

Version history features are also available when versioning is enabled for the form library. Viewing the Version History screen via the form's context menu along with restoring, deleting, and viewing versions is accomplished using the same steps written in the "Versions" section of "Working with Document Libraries."

Managing Form Libraries

Many settings and options used when managing form libraries are identical to those of lists and document libraries. Please refer back to the "Managing Document Libraries" section in this chapter or the "Managing Custom Lists" section in Chapter 4 for detailed instructions for managing library metadata, views, settings, and templates.

General Settings

The Change General Settings screen available from the Customize Library page allows you to specify general settings of the library. The settings available for the form library are similar to the document library settings. Table 6-5 describes these form library settings.

Table 6-5. *General Settings for SharePoint Form Libraries*

Setting	Description
Name	Indicates the name used to identify the library through your SharePoint site.
Description	Provides a more elaborate explanation of the library's purpose. This is displayed on the Documents and Lists screen and the library screen.
Navigation	Determines whether a link for the library is displayed on the Quick Launch bar on the left side of the site screen.

Setting	Description
Content Approval	Allows you to enable the Content Approval feature so that users do not see newly added forms until a user with Manage List permission (members of the Administrator or Web Designer groups normally) approves the item.
Form Versions	Enables versioning, which causes the library to maintain separate copies of a form each time it is saved to the library.
Form Template	Allows you to enter the URL of an InfoPath form in the site that should be used as the template for all new forms in the library.

Form Templates

In the same manner that a document library contains a template file used when creating new documents, form libraries have an InfoPath file used as a template when users click the Fill Out this Form link on the toolbar of the form library screen. You specify which form template is used by the library during its creation. SharePoint comes with only a blank form as a template. The blank form requires you to use InfoPath to create the fields and layout that the form will use.

Microsoft has made available an addition to Windows SharePoint Services called the Microsoft Office 2003 Web Parts and Components. When this is installed on the SharePoint server, a large number of prebuilt form templates become available in form libraries. These templates include the following:

- Absence Request

- Expense Report

- Invoice

- Purchase Order

- Status Report

- Travel Request

■Tip The Microsoft Office 2003 Web Part and Components provides added functionality and Office integration for users, including numerous form library templates. Your technical SharePoint administrator can obtain this add-in from the Microsoft web site or from http://www.sharepointextras.com.

After a form library has been created, you can customize the template from the Customize Library screen. This is especially useful if you chose the Blank Form template when creating the library with the intention of designing it from scratch. To edit the form template using InfoPath 2003:

1. On the Library screen, click the Modify Settings and Columns link in the Actions list on the left menu.

2. On the Customize Library screen, click the Edit Template link next to the Template heading under the General Settings section.

3. When the document template opens in InfoPath, make the changes you desire in Design Mode. Refer to InfoPath documentation for instructions on using the InfoPath product.

4. Save the document template from the application menu or toolbar, and then close InfoPath.

Managing Columns and Views

At first glance it seems that only a Title column is available when a form library is created. This is true in a sense, but the form library is tightly integrated with the form template you chose when creating the form library. This allows the library to display the data fields from the form as columns in the library's views.

For example, creating a form library using the Absence Request form displays employee name, department manager, time requested, and other data from the form. As users fill out these forms and save them to the library, the data they entered into the forms can be displayed in the library screen. This allows you to see their responses without opening each individual form.

When creating custom views, the form library contains the same special columns available in document libraries. The creation information, modification information, and file size of the form are present. As a result of the integration between the form library and the InfoPath forms, views can also use the form's data fields to perform sort, filter, group, and totaling functionality.

▨Tip Displaying, filtering, grouping, and totaling InfoPath form fields in form library views is a simple yet extremely effective way for users to arrange and display the completed InfoPath forms.

Relink Forms

When InfoPath forms are filled out, they contain a link to the template that was used to create them. If there are forms in a form library that are not linked to the form library's template, the library allows you to relink these forms with the template. The form will not be linked to the template if it is uploaded rather than created by using the Fill Out this Form toolbar link, or if the form or its library has been moved from a different site in SharePoint. To relink forms in a form library:

1. On the Library screen, click the Modify Settings and Columns link in the Actions list on the left menu.

2. On the Customize Library screen, click the Relink Forms to this Form Library link under the General Settings section.

3. On the Relink Forms screen, check the checkbox in the Relink column next to each form that you wish to relink to the form template.

4. Click the Relink Forms link on the toolbar.

■**Caution** Ensure that your technical SharePoint administrator has installed Service Pack 1 for Windows SharePoint Services and you have the latest service pack for InfoPath 2003 before attempting to relink forms. An issue with the original version of SharePoint 2003 has the potential to cause data corruption in your forms when performing a relink operation.

Other Library Management

Remaining management features of SharePoint form libraries are performed exactly like their counterparts in document libraries and lists. The following management tasks can all be accomplished using the descriptions and steps found earlier in this chapter or in the "Managing Lists" section of Chapter 4:

- Content approval

- Library security

- Library template management

- Deletion of libraries

- Addition of library listings to the portal

Picture Library

Picture libraries build upon the file management features introduced earlier by the document library. They have the same mechanisms for displaying the file information including views, folders, filtering, and sorting. Picture libraries then add many image-specific features and integration into other applications not available with a document library. These added features make pictures libraries the ideal place to store your image files in SharePoint.

Appropriate uses of picture libraries include storage of corporate marketing graphics, presentation diagrams, product photographs, and company event slideshows. Features of a picture library that are identical to a list or document library will be briefly mentioned here and then referenced to the appropriate chapter for more details.

Creating Picture Libraries

There are multiple links from which you can create a picture library in SharePoint. The quickest way is to choose the Picture Library option on your site's Create page.

To create a new picture library, follow these steps:

1. Navigate to a Windows SharePoint Services site or create a new site as described in Chapter 3.

2. Click the Create link on the top menu bar.

3. On the Create page, click the Picture Library link in the Picture Libraries section.

4. On the New Picture Library page, enter a name and description for the library.

5. Select Yes under the Navigation section if you want to show a link to this library on the Quick Launch menu of the site.

6. In the Picture Versions section, select Yes if you want the library to provide version-control features for the images. This is discussed in the "Managing Picture Libraries" section later in this chapter.

7. Click the Create button.

You have now created a picture library containing the default set of columns and views associated with the picture library template. Viewing the library provides the file name, type, file size, and picture dimensions of each image. Figure 6-11 shows a library like the one you have just created.

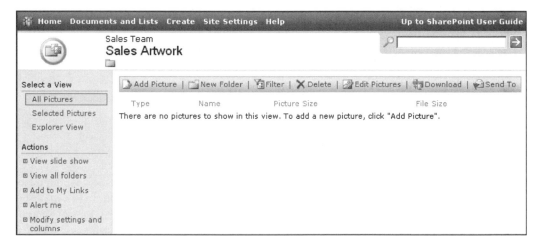

Figure 6-11. *A new picture library*

Working with Picture Libraries

Now that you are familiar with both lists and document libraries, it should be easy to learn the basics of using a picture library. There are some unique features that provide added value to picture libraries that we will discuss.

Using Views

One of the first things you notice about a picture library is the unique ways in which the library can display the files. Views for picture libraries provide some image-specific function-ality that makes looking for images easier.

When a picture library is created, it comes with three default views. One of these views is the Explorer View, which we discussed with document libraries, and it works the same way here. The other two default views, All Pictures and Selected Pictures, actually contain three different display styles for showing the image files. You can select the display style in the View list on the left side of the Picture Library screen. The display styles are described in Table 6-6.

Table 6-6. *Display Styles for Picture Library Views*

Display	Description
Details	Displays the images similarly to the standard view type in which each item is displayed on a row-by-row basis showing data about the item. Default data displayed in this view is type, file name, picture size, and file size. A thumbnail version of the selected image is displayed on the left side of the page.
Thumbnails	Displays small versions of all images in the view with the file name below the picture as shown in Figure 6-12. Clicking the image takes you to the View Properties screen for the picture.
Filmstrip	Displays tiny versions of all images in the view horizontally along the top and a larger version of the selected image below. The file name and description of the selected image is also shown. Changing which image is selected displays the newly selected image in the larger display. Clicking the large image takes you to the View Properties screen for the picture.

Figure 6-12. *The thumbnails display in a picture library*

The All Pictures view uses the preceding display styles and shows all pictures in the library. The Selected Pictures view displays a subset of the pictures in All Pictures. Each file in All Pictures has a corresponding checkbox next to it. Checking the checkbox for one or more of the images and then switching to the Selected Pictures view shows only those pictures you had selected in the All Pictures view. These selections are remembered when you leave the library or site and return. The selecting pictures functionality is needed for downloading or editing pictures, as discussed later in this chapter. If you have no pictures selected before choosing the Selected Pictures view, a message will be displayed stating that there is nothing for it to display.

Filtering and Sorting Pictures

Using the filtering and sorting features of a picture library is performed almost identically to the same features in other lists and libraries. The only difference is that column headings used for sorting and displaying filters are not shown on all of the different display styles for the views. The only display style that contains these headings is the Details type. In order to sort the pictures being displayed, you must first change to the Details type. Once on the Details type, use the column headings to sort the list of pictures as you would any other library or list. Now you can switch to the Thumbnails or Filmstrip display style, and they will use the sorting you specified earlier.

The Filter button is displayed on the toolbar of all three display styles. It also uses column headings to allow you to determine which columns are being filtered, so clicking the button will take you to the Details display style. Once on this display style you can set filtering the same way we have discussed in the "Filtering and Sorting the List" section of Chapter 4. After setting your filters, changing to the Thumbnails or Filmstrip display style will show those types using the filters you selected on the Details type.

Folders

Just as we discussed earlier in this chapter with regard to document and form libraries, you can create folders in picture libraries to help you organize your images. The adding, editing, and deleting of folders is performed using the same steps as you would in these other libraries.

The Picture Library does have an additional folder feature not found in the other two library types. A link is provided in the Actions list that allows you to display a hierarchical view of all folders in the library and quickly navigate to any of them. To do this, perform these steps:

1. Navigate to the Picture Library screen.

2. On the Picture Library screen, click the View All Folders link in the Actions list on the left.

3. On the View Folders screen, shown in Figure 6-13, the hierarchy of folders in the picture library will be displayed in the Folders section.

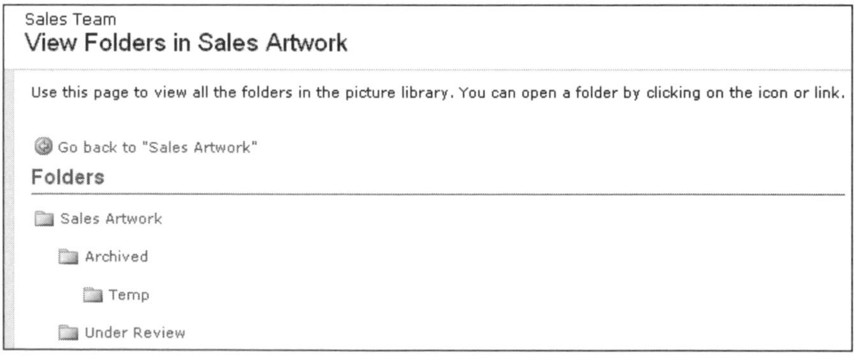

Sales Team
View Folders in Sales Artwork

Use this page to view all the folders in the picture library. You can open a folder by clicking on the icon or link.

Go back to "Sales Artwork"
Folders

- Sales Artwork
  - Archived
    - Temp
  - Under Review

Figure 6-13. *The All Folders screen for a picture library*

4. Click the name or icon of a folder to quickly navigate to that folder's contents.

▓**Tip** Although the link does not exist in the Actions list of a document or form library, you can still get to the View Folders screen by entering the URL yourself or creating your own link to the following page:

http://*<Site URL>*/_layouts/1033/folders.aspx?List={*<List Identifier>*}

Replace *<Site URL>* with the URL to the site or area containing your library and *<List Identifier>* with the unique ID associated with the library. An easy way to find the unique ID for the list is to copy it from the URL of the Customize List screen if you have the proper permissions. After navigating to the Customize Library screen, everything directly after "List=" in the URL and between the braces is the unique ID.

Adding Pictures

Adding pictures to the library is similar to uploading documents in a document library. Unlike a document library, there is no link allowing you to create new pictures; you are only able to upload previously existing picture files. Rather than being performed from an Upload link, this is accomplished from the Add Picture link in the library using these steps:

1. Click the Add Picture link on the toolbar of the library page.

2. On the Add Picture screen, click the Browse button.

3. On the Choose File dialog box, select the image file you want to upload by navigating the drive and folders on your local computer or network.

4. Click the Open button.

5. Back on the Add Picture screen, click the Save and Close link on the toolbar.

If you have Office 2003 installed on your computer, another link will be presented to you on the Add Picture screen. This link, Upload Multiple Files, starts the Microsoft Office Picture Manager application, which comes with Office 2003. The Picture Manager provides you with the ability to organize and edit image files. To upload using the Picture Manager:

1. Click the Add Picture link on the toolbar of the library page.

2. On the Add Picture screen, click the Upload Multiple Files link.

3. When Microsoft Office Picture Manager opens, use the Picture Shortcuts area on the left to locate and select the folder containing the image files you want to upload.

4. In the Thumbnail area in the middle of the application, select the images you want to upload. Select multiple images by pressing and holding the Ctrl key while selecting the files.

5. In the Upload Settings area, select to send either the original pictures or to optimize the images for viewing on the web. Optimizing the images reduces the size of the file but also decreases the quality of the image.

6. Click the Upload and Close button.

7. On the Uploading Pictures screen, click the Go Back To link to return to the picture library.

Editing Pictures

Editing pictures in a picture library is another feature that utilizes the integration with Microsoft Office Picture Manager. If you do not have Office 2003, specifically Picture Manager, installed, you will not be able to edit the files in a picture library without using another application outside of SharePoint and uploading them again.

There are many ways to begin the process of editing pictures. The context menu on the Details display contains an Edit Picture option that allows you to edit that specific picture. The toolbar displayed on a picture library view contains an Edit Pictures link that allows you to edit all of the selected pictures at once. The View Properties and Edit Properties screens discussed later include an Edit Picture link on the toolbar. To edit multiple pictures, follow these steps:

1. Navigate to the Picture Library screen.

2. On the Picture Library screen, select at least one picture by checking the corresponding checkbox.

3. Click the Edit Pictures link on the toolbar.

4. When Microsoft Office Picture Manager opens, as shown in Figure 6-14, use the features it provides to modify your images. These features are mostly found under the Picture menu.

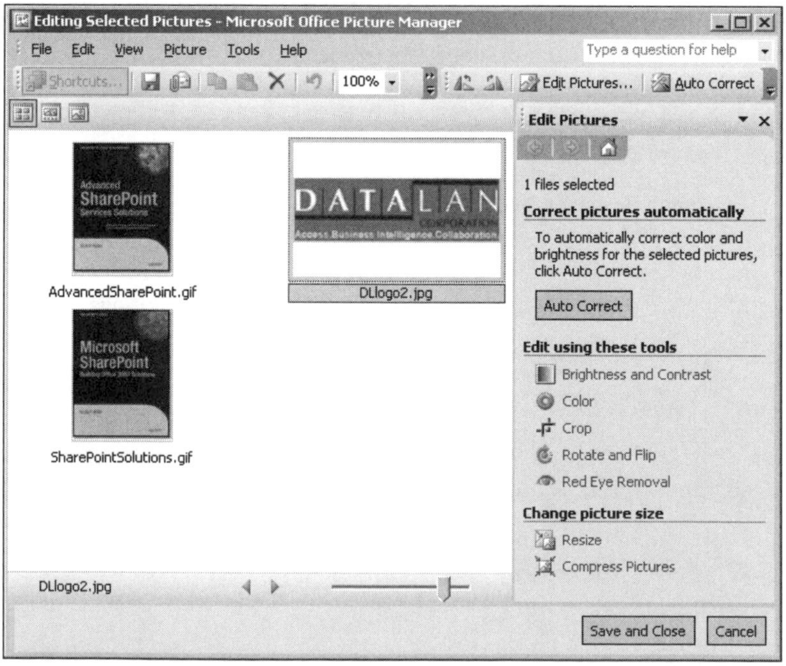

Figure 6-14. *Microsoft Office Picture Manager*

5. Click the Save and Close button.

6. On the Editing Pictures screen, click the Go Back To link to return to the picture library.

> ■**Note** For further information on how to use Microsoft Office Picture Manager, please see the help files that come with the product or visit `http://office.microsoft.com`.

Check-Out and Check-In

Picture libraries allow you to check out and check in the files in order to determine when other users of the library are able to view updated files. This feature is identical to the check-out process used in document and form libraries; however, the only display style that contains a context menu for each library item is the Details display of a standard view like All Pictures. You can also use the check-out and check-in links on the toolbar of the View Properties screen.

Edit Picture Properties

Picture properties allow users to more easily find and maintain relevant images. Therefore, it is important to make sure these properties accurately describe the associated picture. These properties are displayed in the library views to describe the pictures.

The Edit Properties screen contains the ability to change this information. There are several ways to access the Edit Properties screen. The Details display style of library views provides a context menu for each picture, and this context menu presents links to both the View Properties screen and the Edit Properties screen. The View Properties screen, shown in Figure 6-15, contains a link to the Edit Properties screen on the toolbar.

Figure 6-15. *The View Properties screen*

The Edit Properties screen for a picture library displays a large image of the picture along with editable data for the default and custom properties that are maintained for each picture in the picture library. After editing any of this information, click the Save and Close link to commit your changes back to the library.

Versions

Pictures libraries allow versioning and provide the same interface into versions as do document and form libraries. The Version History screen allowing you to view, restore, and delete previous versions is available. For details on using versioning, see the "Versions" section under "Document Libraries" earlier in this chapter. The one versioning difference with picture libraries is the location where you can gain access to the Version History screen. Only the Details display style gives you the context menu for each picture that contains the Version History link.

Download

A missing feature from document libraries is the ability to easily download one or more documents to your local file system or network drives. Not only does the picture library come with this functionality, but it does so using two different methods.

The simpler method of the download feature lets you download a single picture at a time. No integration with Office 2003 is necessary for this feature to work. You will find the download feature available in the context menus displayed in the Details display style. To download a single picture file, perform the following steps:

1. Navigate to a Details display of the Picture Library screen.

2. Activate the document's context menu by hovering over the file name with your mouse and clicking the inverted triangle.

3. Click the Download Picture link in the context menu.

4. On the File Download dialog box, click the Save button.

5. On the Save As dialog box, navigate to the directory in which to save the file and click the Save button.

The more advanced approach to downloading the picture files allows you to download multiple files at the same time. This is accomplished with integration into the Microsoft Office Picture Manager application installed with Office 2003. While downloading via this method, you are able to choose from multiple image sizes that the downloaded pictures will be saved as. This allows you to create thumbnails of the pictures easily. Access to this feature is provided through the Download link on the toolbar of the picture library. To download multiple pictures from a picture library:

1. Navigate to the Picture Library screen.

2. On the Picture Library screen, select at least one picture by checking the corresponding checkbox.

3. Click the Download link on the toolbar.

4. On the Download Pictures screen, shown in Figure 6-16, select the size that you want the image files to be saved as.

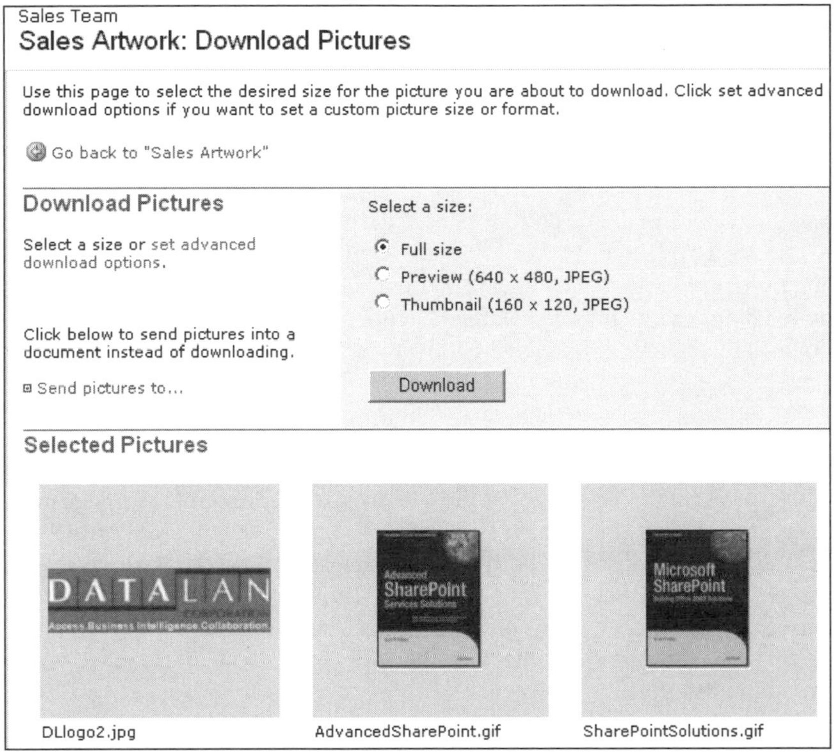

Figure 6-16. *Downloading images from a picture library*

5. Click the Download button.

6. On the Download Pictures dialog box, click the Browse button.

7. Navigate to the directory in which to save the file and click the OK button.

8. Back on the Download Pictures dialog box, click the Save button.

Downloading picture files in this manner provides you with many options. You may have noticed the Set Advanced Options link on the Download Pictures screen. Clicking that link presents you with the options shown in Table 6-7.

Table 6-7. *Download Advanced Options*

Option	Notes
File Format	Allows you to determine the file format of the image when it is saved. Available options are JPG, TIF, BMP, GIF, and PNG formats.
Picture Size	Allows you to resize the image that is saved. You are able to choose from a list of predefined dimensions, specify custom dimensions, or specify a percentage of the original size.

The Download Pictures dialog box contains three options including the directory where the files will be saved. The second is the ability to rename the files with a standard prefix and incrementing number like August1, August2, August3, etc. The last option allows you to open the downloaded pictures into Microsoft Office Picture Manager where you can continue to work with them.

Send To

Another unique and valuable feature of picture libraries is the option to send selected pictures to an Office 2003 application. This includes the useful capability to send the image in an e-mail message via Outlook. In addition to being available as a link on the toolbar of the Picture Library page, the Send To feature can be accessed through a link on the Download Pictures screen shown in Figure 6-16. SharePoint once again uses its integration with the Microsoft Office Picture Manager application to accomplish this. You are able to send the pictures to either a currently open or a new document for the applications shown in Table 6-8, each with its own available options.

Table 6-8. *Send To Application Options*

Application	Options
Outlook	Allows you to include the pictures as attachments or inline previews as well as specify an image size and layout style
Word	Allows you to resize the image before sending it
PowerPoint	Allows you to resize the image before sending it
Excel	Allows you to resize the image before sending it

To e-mail pictures to another user:

1. Navigate to the Picture Library screen.

2. On the Picture Library screen, select at least one picture by checking the corresponding checkbox.

3. Click the Send To link on the toolbar.

4. On the Send Pictures dialog box, shown in Figure 6-17, select Microsoft Office Outlook message.

Figure 6-17. *Sending pictures to another application*

5. Click the Send button.

After performing the preceding steps, a new Outlook message window will appear that includes the pictures you selected from the Picture Library. The Send Pictures dialog box also allows you to insert the picture into an open Office document by presenting you with a list of the currently open files. This can save you time when adding images to Office documents.

■**Caution** The Send To, multiple-file Download, and other useful features require you to have Microsoft Office Picture Manager installed and ActiveX controls supported. This application is part of the Office 2003 installation.

Slide Show

Another unique way to work with picture libraries is to display a slide show, which is useful for presentations or leisurely browsing of the images in the library. Available in the Actions list of the Picture Library screen is the View Slide Show link. Clicking this launches a pop-up window with a large rendition of the first image in the library along with a set of media controls on the right. These controls let you start, pause, and stop the slide show along with moving to the previous or next image in the library.

The slide show is not started until you press the play link, at which time the page will begin displaying pictures from the library at five-second intervals. Along with each image, the file name, description, and date the picture was taken is also presented.

Managing Picture Libraries

The tasks and options used when managing picture libraries are so similar to those of lists and document libraries that we will not go into detail about most of them here. Please refer back to the "Managing Document Libraries" section in this chapter or the "Managing Custom Lists" section in Chapter 4 for detailed instructions for managing library columns, views, settings, and templates.

General Settings

As is the case with all other libraries and lists, the General Settings screen allows you to determine the basic behavior of the picture library. Table 6-9 describes the library settings you can edit in order to customize the behavior of a picture library.

Table 6-9. *General Settings for SharePoint Picture Libraries*

Setting	Description
Name	Indicates the name used to identify the library through your SharePoint site
Description	Provides a more elaborate explanation of the library's purpose displayed on the Documents and Lists screen and the library screen
Navigation	Determines whether a link for the library is displayed on the site's Quick Launch bar
Content Approval	Allows you to enable the Content Approval feature so that users do not see newly added items until a user with Manage List permission (members of the Administrator or Web Designer groups normally) approves the item
Picture Versions	Enables versioning, which causes the library to maintain separate copies of a picture each time it is saved to the library

Managing Columns

Adding and managing the columns used to define the library's information structure is accomplished the same way in a picture library as in other libraries and lists. The same column types as in other libraries exist for use when collecting information about each picture so you can refer to the detailed description of these in Chapter 4. The default picture library columns are shown in Table 6-10.

Table 6-10. *Default Picture Library columns*

Column	Type
Title	Single line of text
Date Picture Taken	Date and Time
Description	Multiple lines of text
Keywords	Multiple lines of text

Managing Views

As mentioned earlier, views have additional features in picture libraries. They also are missing some of the features of other library and list types. Upon creating a view in a picture library, you will see that the Create View screen does not have an option for creating a Datasheet view, as the Datasheet view features are not available in picture libraries.

Unique to a picture library is the view style called Picture Library Details. This view style is what allows a user to choose from the display styles described earlier. These display styles provide for viewing thumbnails and previews of selected images while in the picture library.

Picture libraries also have their own set of special columns that are available for displaying, filtering, sorting, and grouping in views. These columns are shown in Table 6-11 and provide additional detail about the images when users are navigating the picture library.

Table 6-11. *Special Picture Library Columns for Use in Views*

Column	Description
Type (icon linked to document)	Determines the file type of the picture. When used in views, the type is displayed as a familiar icon representing the file type.
Name (linked to document)	Displays the file name as a link that opens the picture.
Name (linked to document with edit menu)	Displays the file name as a link that opens the picture. Also provides the context menu for editing and managing a picture.
Name (linked to display items)	Displays the file name as a link that displays the picture properties.
Picture Size	Indicates dimensions of the image.
File Size	Specifies the size of the picture (in kilobytes).
Created By	Indicates the user who added the picture to the library.
ID	Contains a number that uniquely identifies a picture within a library.
Modified By	Indicates the last user to modify the picture.
Modified	Specifies the date and time that the picture or its metadata was last edited.
Created	Specifies the date and time that the picture was added to the library.
Checked Out To (link to username to user details page)	Indicates the user who currently has the picture checked out.
Approval Status	Specifies the status of the picture in the approval process. Possible values are Pending, Rejected, and Approved. This column is only available in libraries that require approval.
Approver Comments	Shows the comments entered by the approver during the approval process. This column is only available in libraries that require approval.
Edit (link to Edit)	Displays a column containing an icon as a link that takes the user to the Edit Item screen.
File Type	Displays the file extension.
Picture Width	Specifies width dimension of the image (in pixels).
Picture Height	Specifies height dimension of the image (in pixels).
Thumbnail	Displays the thumbnail version of the image that SharePoint creates when a picture is uploaded.
Web Preview	Displays the preview version of the image that SharePoint creates when a picture is uploaded.

Other Library Management

Remaining management features of SharePoint picture libraries are performed exactly like their counterparts in document libraries and lists. The following management tasks can all be accomplished using the descriptions and steps found earlier in this chapter or in the "Managing Custom Lists" section of Chapter 4:

- Content approval

- Library security

- Library template management

- Deletion of libraries

- Addition of library listings to the portal

Advanced Office 2003 Integration

The Office 2003 suite of products is focused mainly on document creation, and thus contains many enhanced integration points with SharePoint libraries. Integration points between Office 2003 and picture libraries like editing, downloading, and sending pictures were discussed earlier in this chapter. While we will only briefly describe features that also exist for SharePoint lists, we will discuss in detail the additional library integration such as the ability to save directly into a library from Office products. We will also show you how to use the feature-rich Shared Workspace Task Pane to work with many aspects of a SharePoint site without using your browser.

Open and Save As Integration

Earlier in this chapter, we discussed various methods for uploading to and opening files from document libraries. These methods require the use of a browser to navigate to the site and perform the desired actions. Office 2003 provides enhanced integration between its File menu and SharePoint libraries. This integration allows you to save to a library directly from the File ➤ Save As dialog box in any of the following Office applications: Word, Excel, FrontPage, InfoPath, Project, OneNote, Outlook, PowerPoint, Publisher, and Visio.

Entering the URL of the document's site into the Save As dialog box displays the list of document libraries in that site. Once you select the document library in which to save the document and specify a file name, Office prompts you for custom column information that exists for the library. If the library includes columns of the same name as Office document properties, the document's metadata will be set based on the values specified in the Office document.

To save a file to a document library from within an Office 2003 application, follow these steps:

1. Select the Save As option from the File menu in the Office 2003 application.

2. On the Save As dialog box, enter the URL to the site in the File Name box and press Enter. The URL can be copied from the address bar of a browser window that is open to the site and should not contain everything up to the last backslash.

3. In the list of document libraries, double-click the desired library.

4. When the contents of the selected document library are displayed, enter a file name for your new document in the File Name box.

5. Click the Save button.

6. If there are custom columns for the selected document library, the Web File Properties dialog box will appear, allowing you to specify document metadata as shown in Figure 6-18. Enter the appropriate information about the document and click the OK button.

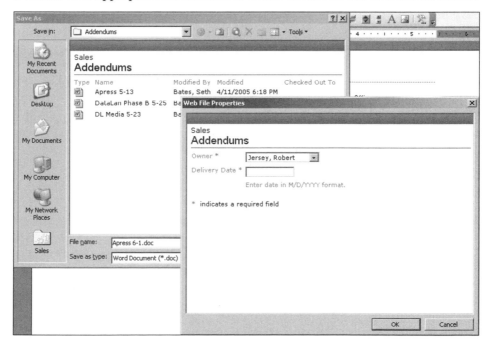

Figure 6-18. *Saving to a document library from Word 2003*

When discussing document templates earlier in this chapter, we stated that the document template must reside in the Forms folder of the document library. The easiest way to save a document into this folder is using the Save As integration with Office as outlined in the following steps:

1. Select the Save As option from the File menu in the Office 2003 application.

2. In the Save As dialog box, enter the URL to the site in the File Name box and press Enter. The URL can be copied from the address bar of a browser window that is open to the site and should contain everything up to the last backslash.

3. In the list of document libraries, double-click the desired library.

4. On the Save As dialog box, click the Views button on the toolbar. This button does not have a label but can be found to the left of the Tools button.

5. Select the Details option, which allows you to see the Forms folder that exists within the document library.

6. Double-click the Forms folder.

7. Enter a file name for your new template in the File Name box.

8. Click the Save button.

In addition to SharePoint's integration with the Save As action of Office products, libraries can be accessed using the Open action in the File menu. The process is very similar to the steps discussed earlier using Save As. Selecting the Open action and entering the URL to the site in the File Name box will display the document libraries that exist on that site. Selecting a document library will display the files of the proper type for the Office application you are using. You are then able to select one of these files to open within the application.

■**Tip** You can make it easier to access a SharePoint site or library within the Save As or Open dialog box of Office 2003 by adding it to the My Places list. When the site or library contents are displayed in the dialog box, select the Add to My Places action from the Tools button on the dialog box's toolbar. This will add an icon to the left area of the dialog box that you can use as a shortcut to access the site or library.

Shared Workspace Task Pane

One of the most lavish integration aspects between Office 2003 and SharePoint is the Shared Workspace Task Pane. The Shared Workspace Task Pane allows you to access and modify content in a SharePoint site from within Office without having to navigate to the site using your browser. The Shared Workspace Task Pane, shown in Figure 6-19, is available in the following Office 2003 applications: Word, Excel, Microsoft Project, OneNote, PowerPoint, and Visio.

The default behavior of these applications is to display the Shared Workspace Task Pane whenever opening a document from a SharePoint document library. You can also display the Shared Workspace Task Pane using the Task Pane option in the application's View menu. Once the Task Pane is displayed, select Shared Workspace from the list of task panes available when clicking the task pane's title.

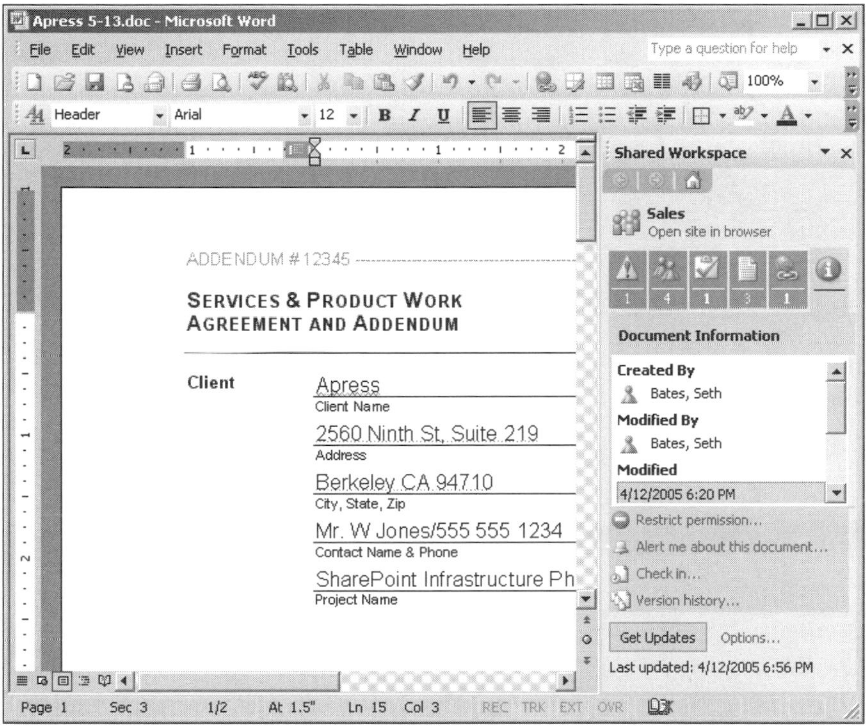

Figure 6-19. *The Shared Workspace Task Pane*

If the current document that is open does not reside in SharePoint, the Shared Workspace Task Pane allows you to create a document workspace for it. How to do this was previously discussed in the "Creating a New Document Workspace from Office 2003" section of Chapter 3.

When the open document in Office is contained within a SharePoint document library, the Shared Workspace Task Pane provides a link that will open the site in a browser window and an Update button to refresh the site contents, and also displays the following tabs of information:

- *Status*: Displays the checked-out status of the document and whom the document is checked out to. It also displays a link that allows you to check in the document if it is checked out.

- *Members*: Displays the users of the site. Also provides links to add new users or create a new e-mail message to the users of the site to facilitate collaboration.

- *Tasks*: Displays tasks from the tasks list on the site. You are also able to add, edit, and delete tasks; mark tasks as completed; and create alerts for the tasks list. Alerts are discussed in Chapter 7.

- *Documents*: Shown in Figure 6-20, this tab displays the documents within the library where the currently open document is stored. This tab provides the ability to add, delete, and open documents as well as create folders and alerts for the library. Alerts are discussed in Chapter 7.

Figure 6-20. *The Documents tab of the Shared Workspace Task Pane*

- *Links*: Displays links from the Links list on the site. You are also able to add, edit, and delete links, and create alerts for the links list. Alerts are discussed in Chapter 7.

- *Document Information*: Displays creation and modification information for the document. This tab also includes the custom columns for the library, allowing you to set the document's metadata values. Check-in, check-out, and complete version history management is included on this tab, allowing you to completely manage a document from within Office without needing to open the site in a browser.

All of the preceding tabs include a Get Updates button that retrieves the latest information from SharePoint and refreshes the task pane. These tabs also include an Options link where you can configure task pane behavior including automated updates to the information displayed in the task pane.

■**Note** The Documents tab of the Shared Workspace Task Pane only displays documents within the same library as the currently open document, not all documents stored in the site. The Tasks and Links tabs only display information from the tasks and links lists created from default SharePoint site templates.

Creating Form Libraries Through InfoPath Form Publishing

Earlier in this chapter, we described how to create form libraries from SharePoint. When following this method, you are limited when choosing the form template to those installed on the SharePoint environment. Creating custom InfoPath 2003 forms is a powerful way to capture and store information in SharePoint.

In order to facilitate the use of custom InfoPath forms in form libraries, InfoPath provides the Publishing Wizard, which lets you create a new form library based on a custom form. This allows you to integrate the library and InfoPath together by specifying which InfoPath fields are displayed as columns in the library. Displaying these fields as form library columns allows users to easily view InfoPath data in the library without opening each individual form. An option is also available to publish a form to an existing library, thereby making it the template.

To publish an InfoPath form to a new SharePoint form library, follow these steps:

1. Select the Publish option from the File menu in InfoPath.

2. On the Publishing Wizard dialog box, click the Next button.

3. Select to publish the form to a SharePoint form library and click the Next button.

4. Select the Create a New Form Library option and click the Next button.

5. Enter the URL of the site where you want your InfoPath form to reside and click the Next button.

6. Enter a name and description for the new form library and click the Next button.

7. Now you can specify which InfoPath fields should be displayed as columns within the form library.

   a. Click the Add button.

   b. On the Select a Field or Group dialog box, shown in Figure 6-21, select a field whose data you want displayed in the library.

   c. For the Column Name, you can rename the field to a more user-friendly value.

   d. Click the OK button.

   e. Repeat step 7 until you have all of the desired fields listed.

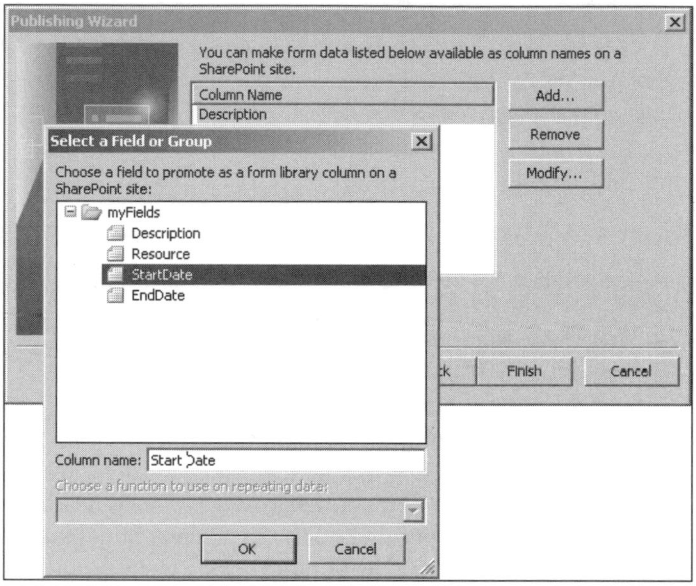

Figure 6-21. *Adding form library columns in the Publishing Wizard*

8. Click the Finish button.

9. Click the Close button.

After completing the preceding steps, the new form library will exist on the site. When a user clicks the library's New Form link, your custom InfoPath form will be displayed, and the appropriate information can be entered and saved to the form library.

Exporting Library Metadata to Excel

In Chapters 4 and 5, we discussed how exporting list information to Excel can provide an easier interface for making multiple changes to the list data. This integration with Office 2003 is also available when working with the document or form libraries. Picture libraries do not allow exporting to Excel.

To export a document library to Excel, follow these steps:

1. Navigate to a SharePoint document library you want to export.

2. Click the Export to Spreadsheet link in the Actions list on the left menu.

3. If you are prompted about opening or saving the Microsoft Office Excel Web Query File, click the Open button.

4. On the Opening Query dialog box in Excel, click the Open button to confirm that you want to run the query to export the information into the Excel spreadsheet.

5. If you already have Excel 2003 open, the Import Data dialog box will appear. Choose where to put the list. Options include a region on the current worksheet, a new worksheet, or a new workbook. If you did not have Excel 2003 running, the data will be put into a new workbook.

■**Note** When exporting library information to Excel, all documents displayed by the current view are exported. Documents removed from the view by its filter setting are not included, but setting the temporary filter on the library screen has no effect on the data exported.

After performing the preceding steps to export a library to Excel, the data is formatted as an Excel List just like exporting a SharePoint list formats the data. Many library columns are read-only when working with the Excel List. You cannot edit file names, creation information, modification information, file sizes, or the ID column when working with the linked library in Excel. As described in more detail in Chapters 4 and 5, the Excel List provides the following actions for you to manage the connection between the SharePoint library and Excel List:

- *View List on Server*: Opens the SharePoint library in your browser

- *Unlink List*: Severs the connection between the Excel List and the SharePoint library

- *Synchronize List*: Sends information updates to and from the SharePoint library and provides the ability to resolve data conflicts

- *Discard Changes and Refresh*: Cancels data updates made within Excel and retrieves the library information from SharePoint

Advanced Datasheet Features

In Chapter 4, we described the use of the Datasheet view for editing custom list data. The Datasheet view is also available when working with document and form libraries. The Datasheet view contains numerous features that allow for integration with Office 2003 products. Clicking the Task Pane link in the Datasheet's toolbar will display a list of Office integration features including various export capabilities to both Excel worksheets and Access databases. For more detail about these capabilities, please refer to Chapter 4.

■ ■ ■

CHAPTER 7

Pages, Web Parts, and Alerts

Up to this point, we have discussed the organization and storage mediums for information in SharePoint. This included the basic organization and management of sites and areas. We also described the means for structuring and storing data in SharePoint lists and libraries. In discussing these topics, we have touched on basic presentation aspects of information like listings, areas, site templates, and views.

You will need to further customize the ways in which information is presented to allow others to effectively utilize portals and sites. SharePoint allows you to create pages in areas and sites in addition to those created by default like the home page in a team site. Both the default pages and additionally created pages can be customized with the provided rich-text-entry tools, by using components called web parts, or by using FrontPage 2003. Web parts are configurable components that provide a set of functionality similar to a small application. In this chapter, we will show you how to customize pages to include these web parts. We will discuss what web parts are provided by Windows SharePoint Services and SharePoint Portal Server 2003.

Once you have SharePoint portals and sites configured to include list data and documents, users will need to know when the information important to them has changed. Alerts are SharePoint's mechanism for notifying users that new information is available or existing information has been changed. The last part of this chapter will discuss using and managing alerts in both portals and sites.

Pages

Most sites and areas initially contain a single presentation page when created, the home page. For example, when creating a site from the Team Site template, the home page of the site is created with various web parts that display the announcements list, events list, and links list. Except for navigating to the list screens themselves, there is no other page created that can be customized to display lists, libraries, or web parts. The exception to this rule is the Multipage Meeting Workspace site template, which contains three pages upon creation.

SharePoint allows you to expand the sites by creating additional pages. These pages can then be customized to display information. The two types of pages that are available to add to your sites and areas are

- Basic Page

- Web Part Page

Basic Pages

The simplest page type is the Basic Page. The Basic Page is available in portal areas, team sites, and document workspaces. You cannot create this type of page in sites created from the various meeting workspace templates. This page is customized by using the Rich Text Editor, presented as a dialog box, to create a static display of decorated text and images. The Basic Page is useful for creating pages made completely from static content without needing any HTML knowledge. Uses include newsletters and user instructions.

Creating Basic Pages

When Basic Pages are created, they are stored in a document library. This means that before creating any new pages for a site or area, you must make sure that the site or area has a document library that can be used to store the pages. To create a Basic Page in a WSS site, follow these steps:

1. Navigate to a Windows SharePoint Services site or create a new site as described in Chapter 3.

2. Ensure that a document library exists that the new page can be created in. If not, follow the process described in Chapter 6 for creating a document library.

3. Click the Create link on the top menu bar.

4. On the Create page, click the Basic Page link in the Web Pages section.

5. On the New Basic Page screen, type a name for the page.

6. Under the Save Location section, select the document library where you want the page to reside.

7. Click the Create button.

Note Since SharePoint treats the creation of new pages similarly to creating a new document in a library, you only need to be in a site group that allows you to add new documents to a library in order to have the proper permissions for creating new pages. Using the default groups, this is any site group except for Reader.

Once the page is created, it will be shown and a dialog window will be displayed as you can see in Figure 7-1. This dialog window is the Rich Text Editor, which is what you use to create the content to be displayed on your new Basic Page. The Rich Text Editor is made up of two toolbars that provide enhanced text along with the design area. Using the text editor may be familiar to you, as most of the toolbar buttons are identical to those found in Microsoft Office products such as Word. Some of the features available in the Rich Text Editor are

- Fonts, including style, size, and color
- Text decorations like bold, italics, and underline
- Alignment and indentation
- Tables
- Images and hyperlinks

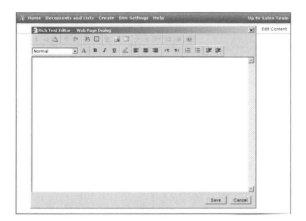

Figure 7-1. *A new Basic Page showing the Rich Text Editor*

After creating and formatting the information to present, click the Save button. This will set the page's content to what was created in the editor. The dialog window will disappear and the page will refresh, showing the content you have created.

Viewing and Editing Basic Pages

Once additional pages have been created for your site or area, you will want other users to be able to view them. Since the pages are actually stored as documents within a library, users can simply navigate to the library using the Quick Launch menu in a site or a listing in the portal. The drawback to this is that users need to know that they should look in a particular document library for pages.

One way to make it easier for users of your site to navigate to a Basic Page is by using the links list. Create a links list as described in Chapter 5 and display this list on the site's home page. (The Team Site template has a links list created and displayed by default.) Then add links to the links list that point to your added pages. When users view your site, they will then see a list of links on the home page, as shown in Figure 7-2, which can take them to the additional pages of content.

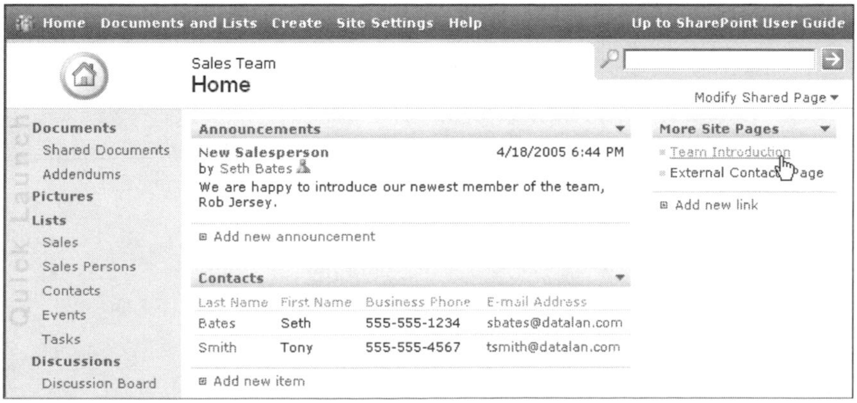

Figure 7-2. *A links list used to display additional site pages*

Another option for displaying the pages is displaying the List View Web Part for the document library on the home page of the site. This results in the pages contained in the document library being shown on the home page as links. See the "Web Parts" section later in this chapter for information on using the List View Web Part.

Editing the content of a Basic Page is just as simple as creating one since SharePoint provides an additional hyperlink on the page that enables you to edit the content. This hyperlink is only displayed to users who have the required permissions to edit documents in a library. By default, this includes members of the Contributor, Web Designer, and Administrator site groups. To edit the page content:

1. Navigate to the Basic Page screen.

2. On the Basic Page screen, click the Edit Content link on the top-right corner.

3. In the Rich Text Editor dialog box, modify the information displayed using the dialog box's toolbar buttons.

4. Click the Save button.

The page will refresh, displaying the new content you created using the Rich Text Editor. In addition to the navigation options previously mentioned, you can enter the URLs of other pages in the site into the Rich Text Editor. These URLs will then be displayed as links, allowing site users to easily navigate between content pages.

Web Part Pages

The other page type is called a Web Part Page. This page type is much more complex than the Basic Page and requires much more discussion around how to use and customize it. It is available in portal areas and all WSS site templates including meeting workspaces. In fact, portal areas and the home pages of sites are customized Web Part Pages.

Before we continue with Web Part Pages, we must first define the term for the components that are used to customize a Web Part Page, the web part. A web part is a modular component of functionality that provides additional features to the user when added to a Web Part Page. Some examples of this functionality are showing list items from a SharePoint list, allowing you to search a database, showing the user's Outlook Inbox, or displaying the users of a site. We will discuss web parts in more detail later in this chapter.

Creating Web Part Pages

Creating Web Part Pages is handled differently depending on the type of site or area you are creating them in. Creating a Web Part Page in either a portal area, team site, or document workspace is very similar to the way you create a Basic Page. Just like the Basic Page, a Web Part Page must be created within a document library in the same area or site.

An important configuration of the Web Part Page that you must select during the creation process is the layout of the Web Part Zones. Web Part Zones are regions where web parts can be added to the page. Different layouts can be used in order to allow users to arrange web parts in different numbers of columns and rows on the screen.

To create a Web Part Page in a WSS site as shown in Figure 7-3, follow these steps:

1. Navigate to a Windows SharePoint Services site or create a new site as described in Chapter 3.

2. Ensure that a document library exists that the new page can be created in. If not, follow the process described in Chapter 6 for creating a document library.

3. Click the Create link on the top menu bar.

4. On the Create page, click the Web Part Page link in the Web Pages section.

5. On the New Web Part Page screen, type a name for the page.

6. Under the Layout section, select the layout of Web Part Zones for the page. This cannot be changed through the site once the page is created.

7. Under the Save Location section, select the document library where you want the page to reside.

8. Click the Create button.

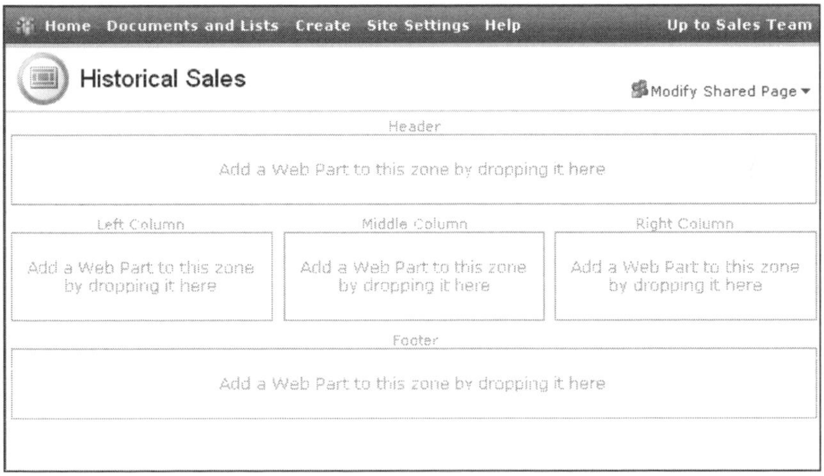

Figure 7-3. *A new Web Part Page with the header, footer, and three-column layout*

■**Note** Since SharePoint treats the creation of new pages for a site similarly to creating a new document in a library, you only need to be in a site group that allows you to add new documents to a library in order to have the proper permissions for creating new pages. Using the default groups, this is any site group except for Reader.

For creating the Web Part Page in a portal area, the only change to the steps earlier is that you initiate the process by clicking the Manage Content link in the Actions list, and then click the Create button on the toolbar. You will then be at step 4 in the list of earlier steps. Since portal areas contain a document library when they are created, it is unnecessary to create one before creating the Web Part Page, although it helps to organize pages in their own libraries.

Within a meeting workspace, Web Part Pages are created a little differently. The pages are not stored in a document library like they are on team sites, portal areas, or document workspaces. You also cannot select the layout of the Web Part Zones for pages added to a meeting workspace, as they are always created with a three-column layout as described in Chapter 3. Web Part Pages appear as tabs on the meeting workspace, shown in Figure 7-4, which allow users to quickly change from page to page while within the workspace.

Figure 7-4. *A new workspace Web Part Page*

To create a Web Part Page in a WSS meeting workspace, follow these steps:

1. Navigate to a Windows SharePoint Services meeting workspace or create a new meeting workspace as described in Chapter 3.

2. Click the Modify This Workspace link near the top-right corner of the screen and click the Add Pages option.

3. On the Pages pane, enter a name for the page. This name will appear on the tab within the meeting workspace.

4. Click the Add button.

■**Note** Creating new Web Part Pages for a meeting workspace is restricted to users in the Web Designer and Administrator default site groups. If you are not in one of these groups, the Modify This Workspace link will not appear.

Viewing Web Part Pages

Users of a team site may initially be unaware that there are additional Web Part Pages for a site since, like Basic Pages, they reside in a document library with no navigation to them provided by the site. You can use the same links list idea described under Basic Pages to present links for the Web Part Pages to other users of your site. Simply add a links list to the site and add links to it that point to your pages inside the document library. You can also use the List View Web Part idea described under "Basic Pages." We will describe how to add the List View Web Part to the home page later in this chapter.

When using Web Part Pages in a meeting workspace, the pages are displayed as tabs on the home page of the workspace so no additional navigational aid should be needed.

There are actually two views of any Web Part Page in a team site. The first is the Shared View, which is available to all users of the site. Users in the Web Designer and Administrator default site groups manage it. For the second view, SharePoint allows you to create a customized view of Web Part Pages called a Personal View. In order to create the Personal View, the user's site groups must allow the Add/Remove Personal Web Parts and Update Personal Web Parts permissions. Using the default site groups, only the Reader site group does not allow users to maintain their own Personal View of a page. You can customize what is displayed on your Personal View using the steps described in the "Managing the Web Part Page" section later in this chapter. Only you can see and manage your Personal View. Using a Personal View allows you to further increase the efficiency with which you use SharePoint by configuring the information displayed to best reflect how you work with it.

Editing Web Part Pages

There is very little you can do to edit a Web Part Page in a team site or portal area. The layout cannot be changed through SharePoint, although the name of the page can be by navigating to the document library where it resides. Once there, edit the properties of the page just like editing properties of other documents in a library. You may be wondering how to change the content of the page. This is accomplished by modifying the web parts displayed on the page, the discussion of which we have separated from our look at the editing of the page and describe under the "Web Parts" section later in this chapter.

Web Part Pages in meeting workspaces provide more editable settings than Web Part Pages in team sites, document workspaces, or portal areas. Renaming, reordering, and deleting can all be done with these pages. All modifications begin using the Modify This Workspace link.

To change the order that pages are displayed on the meeting workspace:

1. Click the Modify This Workspace link near the top-right corner of the screen and click the Manage Pages option.

2. On the Pages pane, as shown in Figure 7-5, click the name of a page you wish to rearrange under the Pages for This Meeting heading.

3. Click the Up or Down button in the Pages pane to change the order of the selected page.

4. Repeat steps 2 and 3 until the pages are listed in the desired order.

5. Click the OK button.

The screen will refresh, displaying the page tabs in the new order specified.
To delete a page in a meeting workspace:

1. Click the Modify This Workspace link near the top-right corner of the screen, and click the Manage Pages option.

2. On the Pages pane, as shown in Figure 7-5, click the Action bar, which initially displays Order. In the Actions menu, select the Delete option.

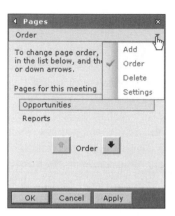

Figure 7-5. *The Pages pane for a meeting workspace*

3. On the Pages pane, click the name of the page you wish to delete in the Pages for This Meeting list.

4. Click the Delete button.

5. When prompted for confirmation, click the OK button.

The screen will refresh, displaying the page tabs except for the deleted page.
To rename a Web Part Page in a meeting workspace:

1. Click the Modify This Workspace link near the top-right corner of the screen, and click the Manage Pages option.

2. On the Pages pane, as shown in Figure 7-5, click the Action bar, which initially displays Order. In the Actions menu, select the Settings option.

3. If the page you want to rename is not the currently displayed page, click the link on the tab for it so that it becomes the currently active page.

4. On the Pages pane, modify the name of the page.

5. Click the OK button.

The screen will refresh, displaying the new name for the Web Part Page on the appropriate tab.

■**Note** You are unable to delete, rename, or reorder the home page of a meeting workspace.

Web Parts

Web parts are an important determining factor for how information is presented to Share-Point users. These reusable components can be placed on Web Part Pages and configured to present SharePoint content in the most beneficial way for your site.

Web parts are not limited to only displaying SharePoint information. They can also provide you with the ability to search and manage data in external databases and file systems. Custom web parts can be developed to provide much of the functionality found in other applications, thereby integrating your SharePoint environment with your other existing systems.

Adding Web Parts to Pages

Once you have either an area or site created, or have added a Web Part Page to an existing site, you will want to customize the display of the page by adding web parts. This is accomplished directly on the page using links provided by SharePoint.

When adding a web part to a portal area, you must first click the Edit Page link in the Actions list in order to gain access to the Modify Shared Page link. Once this is done, all functionality discussed further in this chapter will perform similarly in an area or WSS site.

To add a web part to a page in a team site or document workspace:

1. Determine which view of the page you want to add the web part to by clicking the Modify Shared Page link near the top-right corner of the screen and selecting either the Shared View or Personal View option. If you do not have the ability to modify the Shared View, these options will not be available, and the link will say Modify My Page.

2. Click the Modify Shared Page link near the top-right corner of the screen.

3. On the context menu, hover over the Add Web Parts choice and click the Browse option. The web part galleries, used to organize the available web parts, are described later in this chapter.

4. On the Add Web Parts pane, click the Next or Previous link under the Web Part List until the web part you want to add to the page is listed.

5. Click the name of the web part and, while holding down your mouse button, drag it to a Web Part Zone on the page to the left. A blue line will appear, like in Figure 7-6, showing you where the web part can be placed.

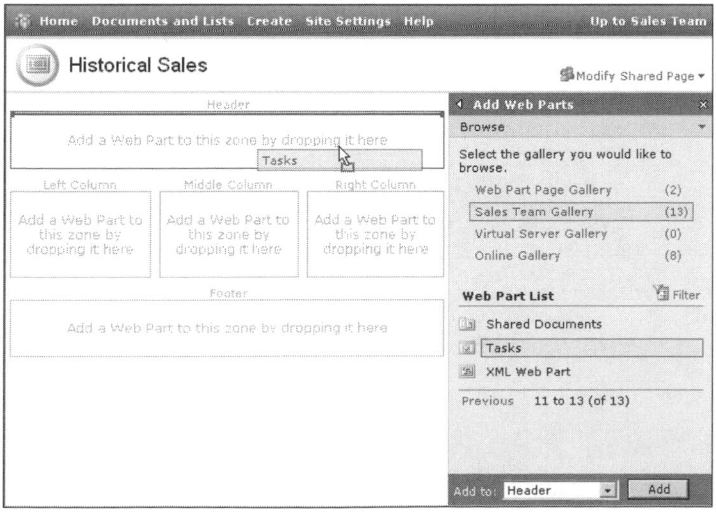

Figure 7-6. *Dragging a web part onto the page*

6. When the line is in the desired zone and in the correct order in that zone, release the mouse button.

7. On the Add Web Parts pane, click the X at the top of the pane to close it.

Adding web parts to a page in a meeting workspace is slightly different from the process used to add them to a page in a site. To do this, perform the following steps:

1. Click the Modify This Workspace link near the top-right corner of the screen.

2. On the context menu, click the Add Web Parts option.

3. On the Add Web Parts pane, click the Action bar, which initially displays Create Lists. In the Actions menu, select the Browse option.

4. On the Add Web Parts pane, click the Next or Previous link under the Web Part List until the web part you want to add to the page is listed.

5. Click the name of the web part and, while holding down your mouse button, drag it to a Web Part Zone on the page to the left. A blue line will appear, like in Figure 7-6, showing you where the web part can be placed.

6. When the line is in the desired zone and in the correct order in that zone, release the mouse button.

7. On the Add Web Parts pane, click the X at the top of the pane to close it.

The page will be refreshed and now show the newly added web part, including any content it displays, in the Web Part Zone.

■**Note** Modifying the web parts on the Shared View of a Web Part Page requires that you be in either the Web Designer or Administrator default site group.

Managing the Web Part Page

After adding web parts to a page, you may need to do many other tasks in order to create a useful Web Part Page. Rearranging, closing, deleting, and connecting web parts are all done after placing the page in Design Mode. Design Mode provides you with the capabilities to modify the presentation of the Web Part Page without needing any programming knowledge.

Shared View vs. Personal View

Your Personal View is managed in the same manner as the Shared View. In order to manage your Personal View of a page, select the Personal View option from the Context Menu of the Modify Shared Page link. If you do not have rights to modify the Shared View, but can still create a Personal View, the Modify Shared Page link will actually say Modify My Page.

Tip If you have modified your Personal View and need to revert all changes back to what is currently displayed on the Shared View, select the Reset Page Content option in the Modify My Page menu.

Rearranging the Page

After placing web parts on the page, you may determine that the page would function better if the web parts were presented in a different order or in different Web Part Zones. SharePoint allows you to easily rearrange the web part on the page once the page is in Design Mode. Design Mode displays the current page, making the management features available to you. To set the page to Design Mode and rearrange web parts:

1. Click the Modify Shared Page link, or Modify This Workspace link when in a meeting workspace, near the top-right corner of the screen.

2. On the context menu, click the Design this Page option. The page will be refreshed and the Web Part Zones will be visible. The page is now in Design Mode.

3. Click the title bar of a web part you want to move and, while holding down the mouse button, drag the web part elsewhere on the page. A blue line will appear showing you where the web part can be placed.

4. When the line is in the desired zone and in the correct order in that zone, release the mouse button.

You may also want to remove web parts that you have determined should no longer appear on the page. There are three ways to keep a web part's content from displaying on the page. The first is to minimize it. Minimizing a web part keeps the title bar displayed but does not display the contents of the web part to the user. To minimize a web part on a page:

1. Place the page in Design Mode as described earlier.

2. On the title bar of the web part you wish to close, click the drop-down arrow on the right.

3. On the web part's context menu, click the Minimize option.

The second method of removing a web part is to close it. Closing the web part keeps it from being displayed, but the web part will still be available in the Web Part Page Gallery discussed later in this chapter. This enables you to quickly add the web part back to the page at a later time. Also, the web part properties that determine behavior or appearance will be retained when the web part is closed and re-added from the Web Part Page Gallery. Modifying web part properties is described later in this chapter. To close a web part on a page, follow the preceding steps for minimizing, but choose the Close option from the web part's context menu.

The last way to remove a web part is to delete it from the page. Deleting the web part keeps it from being displayed in the page and, unlike closing, does not make it available in the Web Part Page Gallery. Once a web part is deleted, adding it again must be done from the gallery where it was initially contained, and any modified properties must be reconfigured. To delete a web part on a page, follow the preceding steps for minimizing but choose the Delete option from the web part's context menu.

Tip Do not be too intimidated to delete a web part from a Web Part Page. You are not deleting the web part from SharePoint, only the specific instance of it on the page you are currently viewing.

Editing Web Part Properties

Each web part has its own collection of settings that determine how it functions and displays information. Editing these properties allows you to make potentially drastic changes in the behavior of the web part, further meeting the needs of your site's users. To edit the properties of a web part:

1. Click the Modify Shared Page link near the top-right corner of the screen.

2. On the context menu, hover over the Modify Shared Web Parts choice and click the name of the web part you want to customize.

3. On the Web Part Properties pane as shown in Figure 7-7, change the properties of the web part.

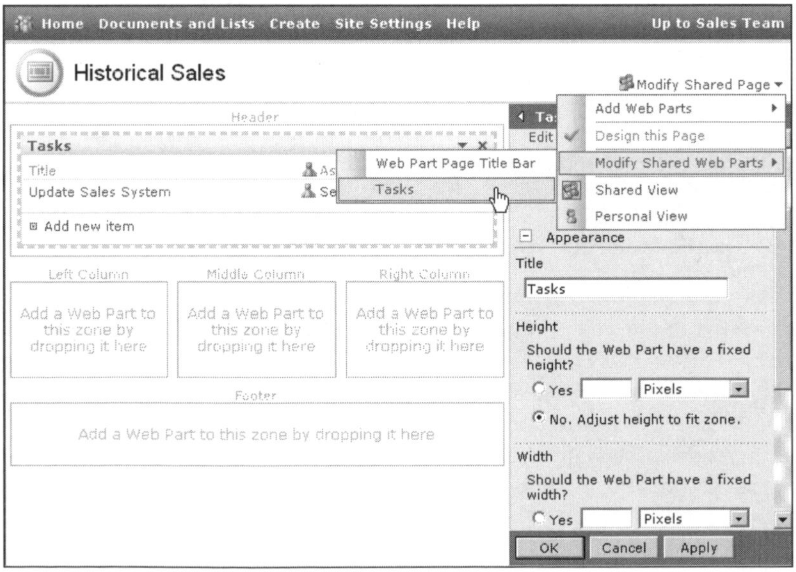

Figure 7-7. *Editing web part properties*

4. Click the OK button.

Different web parts have different settings available for you to use when customizing their behavior. A certain set of properties is used by most web parts, usually under the Appearance, Layout, and Advanced sections of the Web Part Properties pane. These common properties are described in Table 7-1.

Table 7-1. *Common Web Part Properties*

Property	Description
Appearance	
Title	Specifies the text displayed in the title bar.
Height	Specifies a fixed height, or allows the web part to adjust to the zone's height.
Width	Specifies a fixed width, or allows the web part to adjust to the zone's width.
Frame State	Determines whether the web part appears minimized.
Frame Style	Determines whether the title bar and/or a border are displayed with the web part.
Layout	
Visible	Allows you to hide web parts from users while still leaving them on the page. This is useful when making web part connections for which you do not necessarily want the web part displayed.
Direction	Allows you to control the direction that text is displayed in the web part.
Zone	Determines which zone the web part is in.
Part Order	Determines in what order the web part is displayed in the zone with relation to other web parts in that zone.
Advanced	
Allow Minimize/ Close/Zone Change	Determines whether other users are able to rearrange this web part on their Personal Views.
Allow Export Sensitive Properties	Determines whether certain properties are included in a web part export; see "Exporting and Importing Web Parts" later in this chapter.
Detail Link	Causes the title bar to be displayed as a link to this URL.
Description	Displays specified text as a tooltip when the mouse is over the title bar.
Help Link	Indicates the URL that users are taken to if they click the Help option in the web part's context menu.
Icon File	Not currently used.
Missing Assembly Error	Specifies the message to display to users if there is a problem when Share-Point tries to execute the web part.

The previously mentioned List View Web Part, the most commonly used of all of the web parts, contains two additional properties that are very important to its behavior. The Selected View property lets you select which of the list's views will be used to determine how the items are displayed. An Edit the Current View link is available, which allows you to create a custom view specific to the display of the web part.

The other important property specific to a List View Web Part is the Toolbar Type. This property determines what functional links are displayed in the web part. The Full Toolbar option shows the same toolbar you would see on the list screen, while the Summary Toolbar shows only an Add Item/New Document link. The No Toolbar option keeps the web part from displaying any of these links and is useful when the users do not have permission to edit the items in the list or library.

■**Caution** Changes made to a list or library view are not propagated to the List View Web Part. For example, if the filter for a view was changed and you wanted that change to apply to a List View Web Part displaying the list, you would need to edit the web part properties and reselect the view that was modified.

Web Part Connections

One of the more advanced ways in which you can customize the behavior of the web parts on a page is by using connections. Each connection is made between a provider web part and a consumer web part. Web part connections pass information from one web part to another in order to manipulate the contents of the consumer web part. Not all web parts provide connection functionality. The different types of information that can be passed in connections are

- List

- Row

- Cell

- Filter/parameter values

These connections can be created between web parts in order to create various relationships between the information displayed in them. This includes creating parent/child, search/results, and summary/detail relationships. For example, imagine your site has a clients list and a sales list that are both displayed using web parts on the site's home page. You can create a web part connection that provides a row from the clients list to the sales list so that, by selecting a client from the list, the sales list is updated to show only the sales to that specific client. In this example, the connection would cause the clients list web part to display radio buttons next to the rows that you use to select a specific client. This behavior is shown in Figure 7-8.

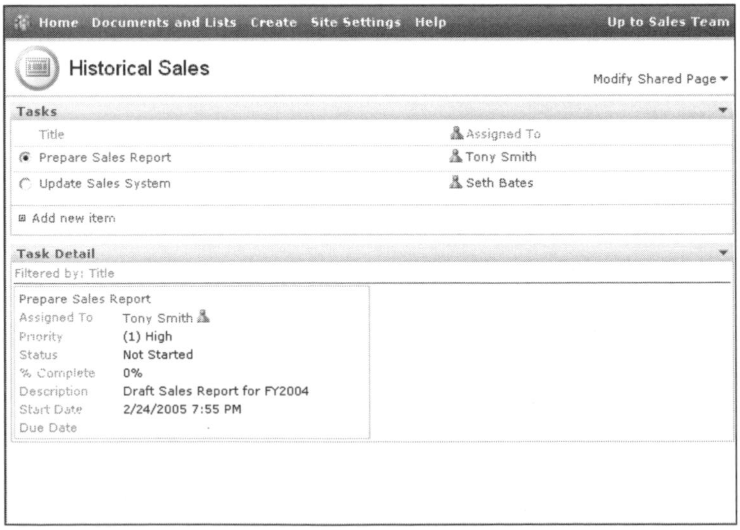

Figure 7-8. *Two task web parts using a connection to display a summary/detail relationship*

To create a web part connection between tasks list web parts, perform the following steps:

1. Place the page in Design Mode as described earlier.

2. On the title bar of the first tasks list web part, click the drop-down arrow on the right.

3. Move the mouse over the Connections option.

4. On the Connection submenu, move the mouse over the appropriate connection type. The available connection types will vary depending on the capabilities of the web part.

5. On the Connection Type submenu that lists the other web parts that can accept this type of connection, click the desired web part.

6. If multiple connection types are available for the target web part, a Choose Connection dialog box will appear. Select the appropriate connection type.

7. If the connection requires further input to know how to associate the two web parts using the connection, the Edit Connection dialog box will appear.

    a. On the Edit Connection dialog box, select the column that should provide the data and click the Next button.

    b. On the Edit Connection dialog box, select the column that should use the provided data and click the Finish button.

The screen will refresh, showing you the newly connected web parts whose content is now impacted by the specified connection.

To remove a connection, perform the following steps:

1. Place the page in Design Mode as described earlier.

2. On the title bar of the web part you wish to close, click the drop-down arrow on the right.

3. Move the mouse over the Connections option.

4. On the Connection submenu, move the mouse over the connection type you want to remove. Currently enabled connections will be marked with a check in the menu.

5. On the Connection Type submenu that lists the other web parts that can accept this type of connection, click the desired web part. Currently enabled connections will be marked with a check in the menu.

6. On the Edit Connection dialog box, click the Remove Connection button.

Exporting and Importing Web Parts

After you have properly configured a web part including both common and unique properties, you may want to reuse the web part with the same settings in other sites or pages. SharePoint provides you with this capability by allowing you to export the web part and then import it into another site. Not all web parts contain this export feature.

Exporting the web part creates an XML file with a .DWP extension that contains the properties of the web part and the information SharePoint needs to execute its functionality. If the Allow Export Sensitive Properties property is disabled, the export will not include certain properties marked as sensitive information. To export a web part, follow these steps:

1. Place the page in Design Mode as described earlier.

2. On the title bar of the web part you wish to export, click the drop-down arrow on the right.

3. On the web part's context menu, click the Export option.

4. On the File Download dialog box, click the Save button.

5. On the Save As dialog box, browse to the directory where you want the DWP file placed and click the Save button.

In order to use this exported web part, or any other DWP provided to you by other users, you must import it into the site as a member of the Administrator site group where you want to use the web part. You can import a web part in one of two ways. The first way to import the DWP file prevents others from using the web part but must be done each time you want to add it to a page. To import a web part using this method, follow these steps:

1. Click the Modify Shared Page link near the top-right corner of the screen.

2. On the context menu, hover over the Add Web Parts choice and click the Import option.

3. On the Add Web Parts pane, click the Browse button.

4. On the Choose File dialog box, browse to the DWP file, select it, and click the Open button.

5. On the Add Web Parts pane, click the Upload button.

6. Under the Uploaded Web Part section, drag the web part onto the page in the same manner used to add web parts described earlier.

The other process used to import a web part file causes the web part to appear in the Site Gallery described later in this chapter. This is beneficial because other users can easily add instances of this imported web part by using the gallery, whereas the previous import method was a one-time-use scenario. To import a web part using this method, follow these steps:

1. On the Site screen, click the Site Settings link on the Site Toolbar.

2. On the Site Settings page, click the Go to Site Administration link under the Administration section.

3. If the Site Administration screen is displayed, click the Go to Top-level Site Administration link under the Site Collection Administration section.

4. On the Top-level Site Administration screen, click the Manage Web Part Gallery link under the Site Collection Galleries section.

5. On the Web Part Gallery screen, click the Upload Web Part link on the toolbar.

6. On the Upload Web Part screen, click the Browse button.

7. On the Choose File dialog box, browse to the DWP file, select it, and click the Open button.

8. On the Upload Web Part screen, click the Save and Close link on the toolbar.

The Web Part Gallery screen will refresh and contain your newly uploaded web part in the list.

Standard Galleries and Web Parts

Both SharePoint Portal Server 2003 and Windows SharePoint Services come with a number of web parts that are available for you to add to your Web Part Pages. These web parts, and any additional web parts added to your SharePoint environment, are organized into galleries.

In a default installation of Windows SharePoint Services or SharePoint Portal Server 2003, there are four galleries, each with their own purpose:

- Web Part Page Gallery

- Site Gallery

- Virtual Server Gallery

- Online Gallery

Web Part Page Gallery

This gallery contains web parts that have been closed on the current Web Part Page. This allows you to add these web parts back onto the page and continue using them. When added to the page, the web parts retain the properties and behavior that they had when they were closed.

Site Gallery

This gallery contains web parts that have been imported into your site along with most of the built-in web parts that come with SharePoint. One of these built-in web parts is the List View Web Part that is used to display the contents of a site's list or library on a Web Part Page. An instance of the List View Web Part will be displayed in the gallery for each list or library that exists on the site. These instances will be displayed using the name of the list or library. Other web parts contained in the Site Gallery are described in the tables that follow.

The Site Gallery provides a different set of web parts when used in an SPS area from what it displays in a WSS site. The web parts available in a SharePoint Portal Server 2003 area are described in Table 7-2. The web parts available via the Site Gallery in a Windows SharePoint Services site are listed in Table 7-3.

Table 7-2. *SPS Site Gallery Web Parts*

Web Part	Description
List View Web Part	An instance of this web part will be displayed in the Site Gallery for each list or library on the site. This web part allows you to display list information on the Web Part Page using one of the list's views specified by the Selected View property of the List View Web Part. You can also create a custom view used only for displaying the list information on the Web Part Page by using the Edit the Current View link on the Web Part Properties pane. Users can be allowed to view, add, or edit list items from the Web Part Page based on the Toolbar Type property of the List View Web Part. This web part was shown previously in Figure 7-8.
Area Contents	Displays the subareas of the current area.
Area Details	Displays the title and current owner of the area.
Content Editor	Allows you to add custom HTML or rich text to a page as shown in Figure 7-9. The Properties pane for this web part provides you with tools to create rich text, enter HTML, or specify an external file to use when generating the contents.
Form Web Part	Allows you to create HTML forms that can then be connected to other web parts to control their content. An example would be to create a simple search that filters the displayed contents of the target web part.
Grouped Listing	Displays the listings for an area. Contains many web part properties to determine exactly how the listings are displayed to the user including the number of columns, size, sorting, and grouping.
Image Web Part	Displays an image on the Web Part Page, allowing you to control alignment and background color.
Links for You	Displays area listings that have been targeted to SharePoint Portal Server Audiences that the user is a member of.
My Alerts Summary	Displays the user's alert results. See the "Alerts" section later in this chapter for more information on alerts.
My Calendar/Inbox/ Mail Folder/Tasks	Connects to Exchange Server 2003 in order to display your calendar, mail inbox, other mail folders, or tasks within the Web Part Page. These web parts are usually used on the portal's My Site.
My Links	Displays a list of personal links. This is intended for use on the portal's My Site.
My Workspace Sites	Displays a list of personal workspace sites. This can only be used on the portal's My Site.
News	Displays listings from the current area. This is intended for use on the News area of the portal.
News Areas	Displays listings from subareas. This is intended for use on the News area of the portal.
News for You	Displays listings that have been targeted to SharePoint Portal Server Audiences that the user is a member of. This is intended for use on the portal's My Site.
Page Viewer Web Part	Allows you to display another web page, file, or folder within your Web Part Page.
Topic Assistant Suggestions	Displays area content suggestions from the SharePoint Portal Server 2003 Topic Assistant. This requires that your technical SharePoint administrator has enabled and configured the Topic Assistant.

Web Part	Description
XML Web Part	Displays an XML document on the Web Part Page. You can optionally specify an XSLT that should be applied to the XML to determine how the XML is rendered. Using this web part requires XML/XSLT development knowledge.
Your Recent Documents	Displays documents that the current user has recently modified. This web part is intended for use on the portal's My Site.

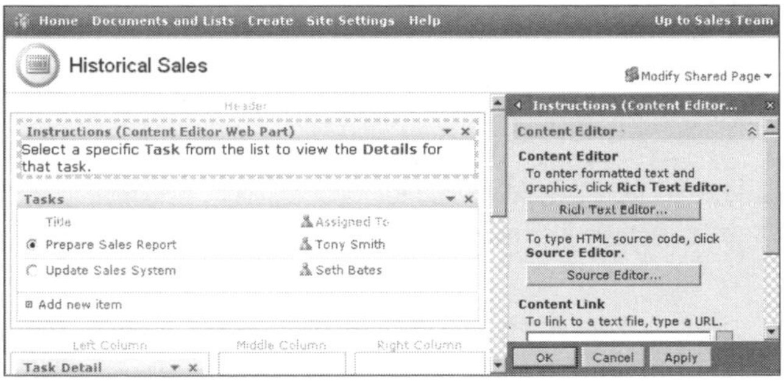

Figure 7-9. *An example of the Content Editor web part*

Table 7-3. *WSS Site Gallery Web Parts*

Web Part	Description
List View Web Part	An instance of this web part will be displayed in the Site Gallery for each list or library on the site. This web part allows you to display list information on the Web Part Page using one of the list's views specified by the Selected View property of the List View Web Part. You can also create a custom view used only for displaying the list information on the Web Part Page by using the Edit the Current View link on the Web Part Properties pane. Users can be allowed to view, add, or edit list items from the Web Part Page based on the Toolbar Type property of the List View Web Part. This web part was shown previously in Figure 7-8.
Content Editor	Allows you to add custom HTML or rich text to a page as shown in Figure 7-9. The Properties pane for this web part provides you with tools to create rich text, enter HTML, or specify an external file to use when generating the contents.
Form Web Part	Allows you to create HTML forms that can then be connected to other web parts to control their content. An example would be to create a simple search that filters the displayed contents of the target web part.
Image Web Part	Displays an image on the Web Part Page, allowing you to control alignment and background color.
Members	Displays a list of the users who have access to the site and allows you to easily view their public profile by clicking their name in the web part.
Page Viewer Web Part	Allows you to display another web page, file, or folder within your Web Part Page.
XML Web Part	Displays an XML document on the Web Part Page. You can optionally specify an XSLT that should be applied to the XML to determine how the XML is rendered. Using this web part requires XML/XSLT development knowledge.

Virtual Server Gallery

This gallery contains web parts that have been installed on the SharePoint server, usually by a technical SharePoint administrator. This is where you will most often find web parts added to your SharePoint environment by your organization.

Online Gallery

The contents of an Online Gallery are retrieved from an external web site. In a standard SharePoint installation, the Online Gallery displays a list of web parts provided by Microsoft. Since the contents are retrieved from an external web site, viewing this gallery requires an available Internet connection.

■**Note** The technical SharePoint administrator has the ability to disable the Online Gallery, resulting in security and performance improvements. If you do not see the Online Gallery in SharePoint, your administrator has disabled it.

As of the time we are writing this chapter, the default Microsoft Online Gallery provides eight web parts for use in SharePoint. These eight web parts are actually instances of the Content Editor web part that have been configured to access information on the MSNBC.com web site. Some of them, like the MSNBC Weather web part, require initial configuration in order to display information appropriate to users of the site.

The available web parts in the Online Gallery are

- *MSNBC Business News*

- *MSNBC Entertainment News*

- *MSNBC News*

- *MSNBC Sports News*

- *MSNBC Stock News*: Requires you to enter a list of symbols for the stocks that you want it to display news for

- *MSNBC Stock Quotes*: Requires you to enter a list of symbols for the stocks that you want it to display quotes for

- *MSNBC Technology News*

- *MSNBC Weather*: Requires you to enter the name of the city or zip code for the location for which you want it to display the weather forecast

Further Customization

You are not limited to using only the web parts that come with SharePoint. Web parts can be developed using Microsoft development tools like Visual Studio .NET 2003. Many software vendors have created custom web parts that can be used with your portal and sites to add new functionality to SharePoint. From navigational displays to enterprise data access and reporting, these web parts can enhance the user experience and productivity when using

SharePoint. Your technical SharePoint administrator and IT staff may be able to provide you with the added functionality you desire for your portal and sites by either writing their own web parts or obtaining them from outside vendors.

Another way to customize your Web Part Pages, although somewhat more advanced than modifying them through SharePoint alone, is by using FrontPage 2003. FrontPage is a web site development and management product that is part of the Office 2003 suite of applications. It includes integration with SharePoint sites that allows you to alter the look and feel of the pages. This includes making numerous changes not available via SharePoint itself.

■**Caution** Editing SharePoint pages using FrontPage 2003 is restricted to users in the Web Designer and Administrator default site groups. In order to successfully use FrontPage to modify SharePoint, some knowledge of web development is important, as it is possible to severely damage the SharePoint site, workspace, or portal area.

You may remember that we stated that once a layout of Web Part Zones is chosen for a Web Part Page, it cannot be modified through SharePoint. One of the features FrontPage 2003 provides is the ability to add or edit the Web Part Zones on a page. Adding HTML, spreadsheets, charts, and the Data View also are enhancements to Web Part Pages provided by FrontPage. To open a Web Part Page for editing in FrontPage 2003:

1. Run the FrontPage 2003 application on your computer.

2. On the File menu, choose Open Site.

3. In the Open Site dialog box, enter the URL to the site, but not a specific page of the site, in the site name box. An example is `http://sharepointserver/sites/Sales`.

4. Click the OK button.

5. When the site opens in FrontPage, the pages are displayed in the Folder List on the left.

6. Double-click the page you want to open for editing, and it will be displayed as shown in Figure 7-10.

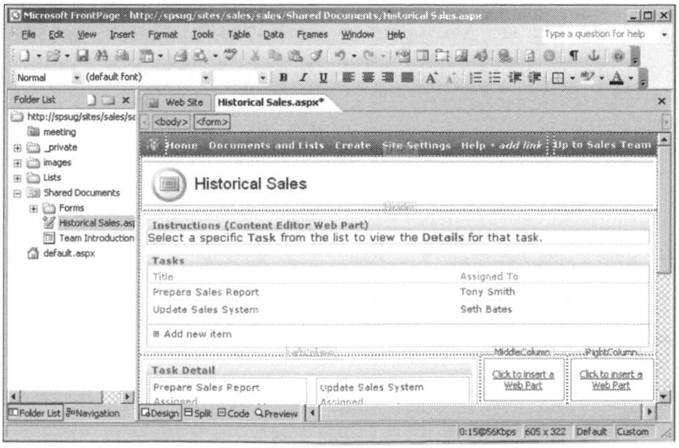

Figure 7-10. *Editing a Web Part Page using FrontPage 2003*

■**Caution** Editing SharePoint pages using FrontPage 2003 causes the pages to become unghosted. This means that they are no longer being displayed based on the underlying SharePoint page templates. When your technical SharePoint administrator applies software upgrades and patches to SharePoint, the unghosted pages may not receive the upgrades appropriately. If this is a concern, refrain from editing pages with FrontPage.

Alerts

After learning about all the ways you can manage and display information in SharePoint, it quickly becomes evident that you cannot possibly be aware of changes to all of the documents and lists in SharePoint that you may want to know about. Having to manually look through SharePoint for new or changed information would be an incredibly inefficient use of time.

When using an information management platform such as SharePoint, the ability to be notified when important documents or data have changed is necessary. Both WSS and SPS provide the ability to receive such alerts when information changes; however, each has a unique set of options and means of managing the alerts.

Alerts in the Portal

The use of alerts in a SharePoint Portal Server portal is limited to users who have been given the Use Personal Features site group permission. All default site groups have this permission except for the Reader site group. If you are in the Reader site group and your SharePoint administrator has not given that group the Use Personal Features permission, you will not be able to perform the steps necessary to receive alerts.

When managing alerts in the portal, there are important settings that specify when and how your alerts notify you of changes in content. The most commonly used setting is the delivery option. The delivery option specifies how a particular alert will notify you of the content changes. The delivery options available by default are

- *My Alerts Summary*: Delivers notifications via a web part usually displayed on the portal's My Site. This web part can also be added to other areas of the portal.

- *E-mail Address*: Delivers notifications via e-mail messages to the e-mail address associated with your SharePoint user profile. The e-mail option also lets you decide how frequently you want the notifications sent. Frequency options are immediate, daily, and weekly.

■**Tip** Alerts set to a frequency of immediate are not generated as soon as a change is made. These notifications are generated on an interval that your technical SharePoint administrator can set. The default setting is 5 minutes.

■**Note** Other delivery options may be available to you in your SharePoint environment, as there are third-party products and custom development that can be done to create new types of delivery options such as using Windows Messenger.

Other options available when managing alerts are deemed advanced options by Microsoft. A valuable advanced option is the Alert Result, which determines the type of content change that you wish to be notified of. Options for the Alert Result are

- *Items are discovered*: Notifies you when new content is found

- *Items are changed*: Notifies you when existing content is modified

The last option, also considered an advanced option, is a filter. The filtering ability is very basic, allowing you to specify that the alert should only notify you of items that either contain, or do not contain, certain keywords.

Subscribing to an Alert in the Portal

If you have been given the Use Personal Features permission for the portal, you will be able to subscribe to many different varieties of alerts.

- *Search*: Notifies you about changes in search results. For example, searching for "Health Insurance" and then subscribing to the search results notifies you of changes to health insurance information within SharePoint.

- *User*: This type of alert has the following unique Alert Result options that you can be notified about:

  - *The user's profile changed*: This occurs when information is updated in the user's SharePoint profile.

  - *The user's personal site changed*: This occurs when the user modifies their My Site.

  - *Items that the user owns are discovered*: This occurs when the user adds content to SharePoint.

  - *Items that the user owns are changed*: This occurs when someone edits content that this user added to SharePoint.

- *Portal Area*: Notifies you about content changes in an entire portal area.

- *List/Library*: Notifies you regarding information in a specific list or library.

- *List/Library Item*: Notifies you when a specific item in a list or library is altered.

Alerts created for a search can notify you when search results have changed. These alerts are created from the Search Results page of the SharePoint portal. User alerts can also be created from the Search Results page as well as from the User Profile page. These alerts are created using the Alert Me link under the appropriate result.

To subscribe to an alert for a search:

1. Navigate to the portal.

2. Enter search criteria in the search box and click the green search button.

3. On the Search Results page, click the Alert Me link in the Actions list on the left.

4. On the Add Search Alert page, modify the name of the alert to something more descriptive.

5. Under the Delivery Options section, choose whether you want to be notified via e-mail, the My Alerts Summary web part, or both.

6. Click the OK button.

Alerts created for a portal area notify you when any items on the portal area have been added or modified. This includes all changes to any list or library within the area.

To subscribe to an alert for a portal area:

1. Navigate to the portal area for which you want to be alerted to content changes.

2. Click the Alert Me link in the Actions list on the left.

3. On the Add Area Alert page, modify the name of the alert to something more descriptive.

4. Under the Delivery Options section, choose whether you want to be notified via e-mail, the My Alerts Summary web part, or both.

5. Click the OK button.

Alerts created for a list or library notify you when any items in that specific list or library have been added or modified. In order to create this type of alert, you must have access to the list or library screen.

To subscribe to an alert for a list or library on a portal area:

1. Navigate to the list or library screen for which you want to be alerted to content changes. This can be done via the Manage Content link in the Actions list, a List View Web Part on the area, or any other link to the list/library.

2. On the List or Library page, click the Alert Me link in the Actions list on the left.

3. On the Add List Alert page, modify the name of the alert to something more descriptive.

4. Under the Delivery Options section shown in Figure 7-11, choose whether you want to be notified via e-mail, the My Alerts Summary web part, or both.

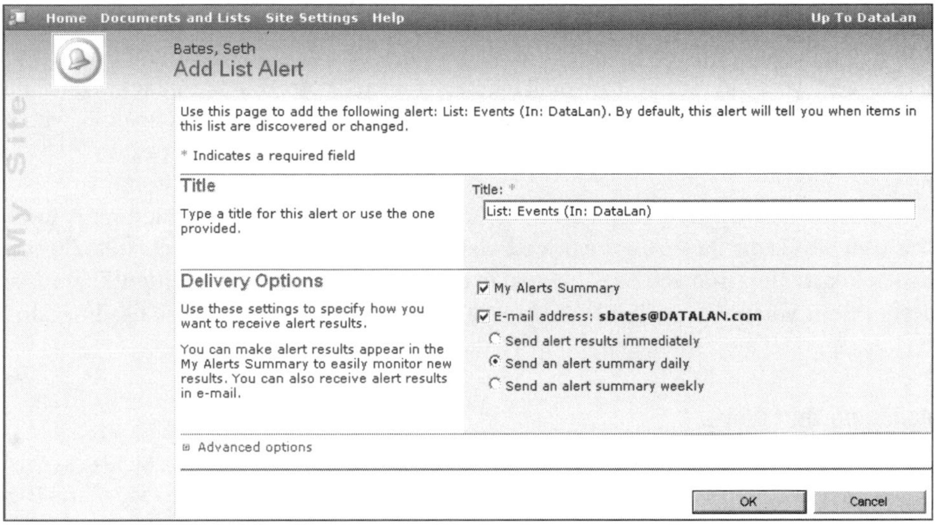

Figure 7-11. *Subscribing to a portal list alert*

5. Click the OK button.

The most granular alert possible is based on a single list item. With access to the list/library screen, you can create an alert for a single list item or document in a portal area.

To subscribe to an alert for a specific list or library item:

1. Navigate to the list or library screen containing the list item or document. This can be done via the Manage Content link in the Actions list, a List View Web Part on the area, or any other link to the list or library.

2. On the List or Library page, display the context menu for the item that you want to be alerted for and choose the Alert Me link.

3. On the Add List Item Alert page, modify the name of the alert to something more descriptive.

4. Under the Delivery Options section, choose whether you want to be notified via e-mail, the My Alerts Summary web part, or both.

5. Click the OK button.

When creating an alert in any of the three preceding scenarios, you have the ability to specify advanced options. To specify advanced options when creating an alert, click the Advanced Options link near the bottom of the Add Area Alert page. You will then be able to specify the type of content change to notify you of under the Alert Result section. Also, under the Filter section you can check the Items Must checkbox, and then choose Contain or Not contain and enter keywords in order to specify the filter condition for identifying the content that you should be notified of. The filter condition looks for the keywords in the item columns as well as the content of documents.

Receiving an Alert

One way to receive an alert is via an e-mail message. Based on the Frequency option selected for the alert, you will receive an e-mail message for each alert that has generated results. The e-mail will contain the text from the content that caused each notification along with links to manage your alerts. These links are similar to the ones described in the next section, "Managing Your Alerts."

The second way to receive alert notifications is using the My Alerts Summary web part. This web part is displayed on the private view of the portal's My Site by default. The web part displays each alert that you have created in the portal along with the content that matches the alert options you have specified. The My Alerts Summary web part is also used to gain access to your personal alert management page, described next.

Managing Your Alerts

Managing your alerts is done from the My Alerts page in the portal. You can access this page via the Manage Alerts link in the Actions list on My Site or from the Go to My Alerts Page link on the My Alerts Summary web part.

The My Alerts page is displayed similarly to how lists and libraries are displayed using different views to display the alerts to the user. The types of views that are available are described in Table 7-4.

Table 7-4. *My Alerts Views*

View	Description
Summary	The default view, it displays the alert name, its active status, the number of current results, and the alert's delivery options.
Document and List Item Alerts	Displays notifications for any list item alerts whose content has been changed. A link to the content is presented along with the user who modified the content, when it was modified, and management links. You must have list item alerts for this view to be accessible.
User	An instance of this view type will be available for each User alert you create. It displays content found based on the unique Alert Results options associated with an alert for a user. A link is available in the Actions list that takes you to the public view of the user's My Site.
Search	An instance of this view type will be available for each Search alert you create. It displays all results of the search that meets the notification criteria of the alert. A link is available in the Actions list that allows you to run the search.
Area	An instance of this view type will be available for each Area alert you create. It displays all content in the area that meets the notification criteria of the alert. Links to the content are presented.
List	An instance of this view type will be available for each List alert you create. Like other instance-based views, it displays all content in the list that meets the alert's notification criteria.

The Summary view is where you can accomplish the management of your alerts. The view, shown in Figure 7-12, contains an Actions list that allows you to perform actions on all alerts in the view. The actions available are Delete, Deactivate, Activate, and Delete All Results. Each alert has a context menu, with the following options, allowing you to work with that specific alert:

- *Edit*: Takes you to a page that allows you to change the alert settings such as delivery options, alert results, and filter

- *Delete*: Removes the alert permanently

- *Activate/Deactivate*: Allows you to temporarily stop the alert from processing and then turn it back on

- *Open*: Takes you to the area, list, or item that the alert is processing

Figure 7-12. *My Alerts Summary view*

The Document and List Item Alerts view allows for the same management features but does not contain context menus for the items. Instead, there are Alert Action links under each alert notification displayed as well as management links in the Actions list of the view.

The other alert views also have similar management links available. Since these other views show the results from a specific alert, their Actions list provides the same functions found on the context menu of the corresponding alert in the Overview view.

Alerts in Sites

Unlike alerts in the portal, anyone with access to a WSS site can subscribe to alerts in that site. You do not need to be in any particular site group or have any specific site group permissions. All notifications from site alerts are generated via e-mail to the address associated with the site user. Since sites are usually the main facilitator of collaboration in SharePoint, alerts play a key role in sites by actively sending notifications to team members alerting them to information that may be crucial to the collaboration effort.

Alerts in sites have different options from alerts in the portal. One option is the Change Type. The Change Type specifies what content changes you should be notified of. This is similar to the Alert Result option found in the portal alerts. Options for the Change Type are

- *All changes*: You are notified of any content change.

- *Added items*: You are notified when new content is added.

- *Changed items*: You are notified when existing content is changed.

- *Deleted items*: You are notified when existing content is deleted.

- *Web discussion updates*: You are notified when comments in web discussions are changed. This only applies to document libraries.

■**Note** Alerts for deleted items do not allow you to undelete them, only to know that they have been deleted.

The other option for managing site alerts is the Alert Frequency. This option determines how often you are sent an e-mail notification. Available frequency options are immediate, daily, and weekly.

■**Tip** Alerts set to a frequency of immediate are not generated as soon as a change is made. These notifications are generated on an interval that your technical SharePoint administrator can set. The default setting is 5 minutes.

Subscribing to an Alert

There are two alert types that you can subscribe to in a WSS site or workspace:

- *List/Library*: Notifies you regarding information in a specific list or library.

- *List/Library Item*: Notifies you when a specific item in a list or library is altered. This alert is especially useful in large lists or libraries to receive notification on a specific item without being notified of changes to other less-important information.

Alerts created for a list/library notify you when any items in that specific list/library have been added or modified. In order to create this type of alert, you must have access to the list or library screen.

To subscribe to an alert for a list or library on a site or workspace:

1. Navigate to the list or library screen for which you want to be alerted to content changes. This can be done via the Quick Launch menu, a List View Web Part on the site, or any other link to the list/library.

2. On the List/Library page, click the Alert Me link in the Actions list on the left.

3. On the New Alert page, shown in Figure 7-13, select the Change Type that you want to be alerted for.

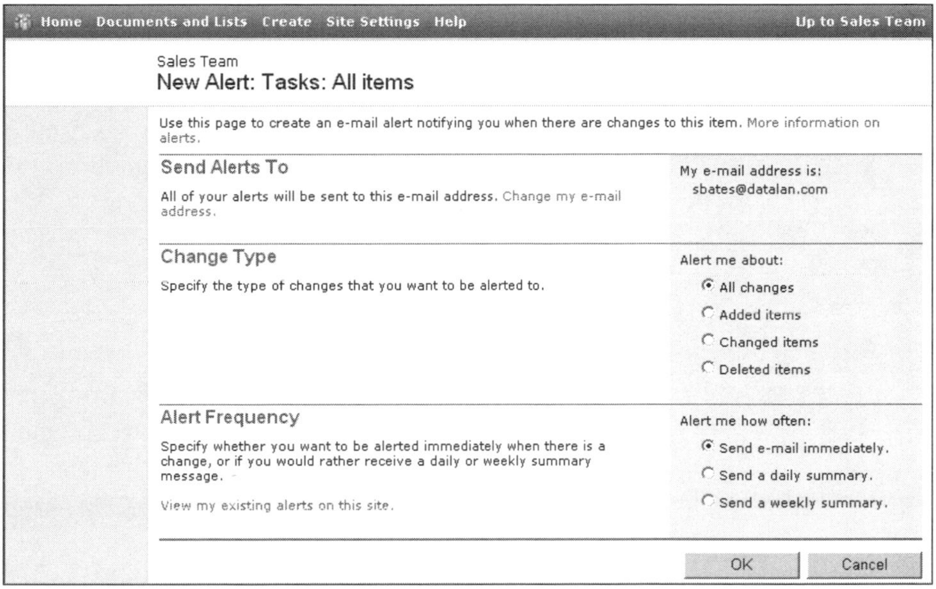

Figure 7-13. *Subscribing to a site list alert*

4. Under the Alert Frequency section, choose how often you wish to receive e-mail notifications.

5. Click the OK button.

You can also create an alert for a single list item in a list or document in a library on the site by performing the following steps:

1. Navigate to the list or library screen containing the list item or document. This can be done via the Quick Launch menu, a List View Web Part on the site, or any other link to the list/library.

2. On the List/Library page, display the context menu for the item that you want to be alerted for and choose the Alert Me link.

3. On the New Alert page, select the Change Type that you want to be alerted for. You will notice that only All changes, Changed items, and Web discussion changes (in document libraries) are available for list/library item alerts.

4. Under the Alert Frequency section, choose how often you wish to receive e-mail notifications.

5. Click the OK button.

Receiving an Alert

Receiving notifications for an alert in a WSS site is done by e-mail. The My Alert Summary web part used in the portal cannot be used with WSS alerts. Just like the alerts created in the portal, notifications are sent based on the frequency option of the alert. An e-mail message is generated for each alert that contains results. Each message contains links to the site, list, and list item that caused the alert to notify you. There is also a link to the My Alerts page where you can manage your alerts, as you see in Figure 7-14.

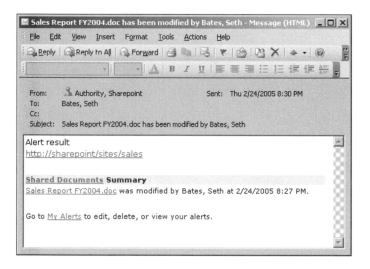

Figure 7-14. *A site alert received via e-mail*

■**Caution** The SharePoint environment must be properly configured with a mail server for e-mails, including alerts, to be sent. If alerts are not being received, have your technical SharePoint administrator verify the SMTP server configuration of your SharePoint environment.

Managing Your Alerts

Alerts are managed on the My Alerts page of a WSS site. Each site contains a separate My Alerts page displaying your alerts for that specific site. SharePoint does not provide the ability for you to view all of your alerts for all WSS sites on a single page. You can get to the My Alerts page from the link in the alert notification e-mail or from the site itself.

To navigate to the My Alerts page shown in Figure 7-15:

1. Navigate to the WSS site that the alert is from.

2. On the site screen, click the Site Settings link in the top menu.

3. On the Site Settings page, click the My Alerts on this Site link in the Manage My Information section.

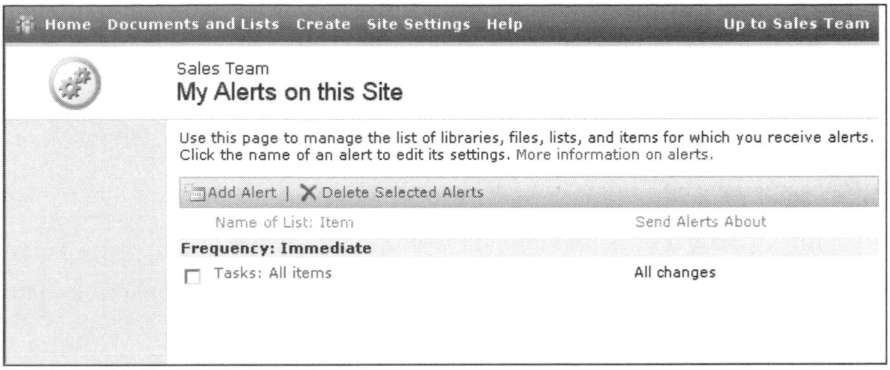

Figure 7-15. *The My Alerts page*

The My Alerts page shows you the name of each alert, the Change Type, and the Alert Frequency in one consolidated view with the alerts grouped by Alert Frequency. You can delete alerts by checking the corresponding checkboxes and clicking the Delete Selected Alerts button on the toolbar. In addition to adding list/library alerts from the specific list or library, you can add them from the My Alerts page by performing the following steps:

1. On the My Alerts on This Site page, click the Add Alert button on the toolbar.

2. On the New Alert page, select the list or library that you want the new alert to notify you for.

3. Click the Next button.

4. On the New Alert page, select the change type that you want to be alerted for.

5. Under the Alert Frequency section, choose how often you wish to receive e-mail notifications.

6. Click the OK button.

To edit an alert from the My Alerts page:

1. On the My Alerts on This Site page, click the name of the alert that you want to edit.

2. On the Edit Alert page, alter the Change Type or Alert Frequency settings.

3. Click the OK button.

Managing Alerts for Other Users

SharePoint does not come with the capabilities for you to perform complete management of alerts for all users of a site. Unfortunately, this means that administrators of a site cannot add alerts for other users to important document libraries or lists in the site. Each user must create their own alerts.

While you cannot add or edit other users' alerts, as a member of the Administrator site group you are able to delete alerts for other users. This is provided especially for the instance when a user's access to the site is revoked. When a user is removed from a site, their Alerts are not automatically deleted. This results in a user without access to the site receiving alerts regarding documents and information they should not see. To delete an alert for other users:

1. Navigate to the WSS site that the alert is from.

2. On the site screen, click the Site Settings link in the top menu.

3. On the Site Settings page, click the Go to Site Administration link in the Administration section.

4. On the Site Administration page, click the Manage User Alerts link in the Management and Statistics section.

5. On the Manage User Alerts page, select a site user from the Display Alerts For drop-down list and click the Update button.

6. After the list of alerts for the selected user is displayed, select each alert you want to delete by selecting the associated checkboxes.

7. Click the Delete Selected Alerts link on the toolbar.

8. On the confirmation dialog box, click the OK button.

Tip Third-party web parts and solutions have been created that can allow an administrator to fully manage all aspects of alerts for other users. In order to leverage this ability, these custom solutions would need to be added to your SharePoint deployment by a technical SharePoint administrator.

■ ■ ■

CHAPTER 8

SharePoint Document Collaboration Solutions

Some of the most common solutions provided through SharePoint are document collaboration solutions. A document collaboration solution facilitates the process through which required materials are created, approved, and distributed. SharePoint Portal Server and Windows SharePoint Services provide many of the tools necessary to create these types of solutions. SharePoint is also integrated with other Microsoft Office System products, such as Word, Excel, and Outlook, that are essential components of many document creation efforts.

In this chapter, we will discuss document collaboration solutions and describe how a SharePoint environment can be configured to support the needs of document collaboration processes. We will discuss a sample document collaboration situation and walk through how a SharePoint-based solution would address the needs of the situation.

Document Collaboration Overview

There are many situations in which individuals work together on an initiative where the end result is the creation of one or more documents. Some examples include the following:

- Annual reports created for distribution to a company's stakeholders

- Client statements created for distribution to clients

- Request for proposals (RFPs) or RFP responses created for distribution to vendors, partners, or customers

- Policy and procedure documents for distribution to an organization's employees

These are just a few examples of collaboration efforts resulting in the creation of documents to be distributed or made available to a defined group of people.

Document collaboration initiatives typically have set deadlines and require the participation of multiple individuals, often from more than one department. The work that these individuals need to complete when creating the document is often interdependent. These dependencies result in a series of tasks that require the participants to monitor the progress of the initiative in order to know when they are able to perform their specific tasks.

Collaboration Teams

The structure of the processes and teams vary between different types of document collaboration efforts. In some cases, the same team of individuals will always work together on collaboration projects, with each person performing a consistent set of tasks for each project. However, more frequently, the individuals needed to participate in a collaboration project will be decided when the project is started.

The team members are often selected based on a combination of factors including their knowledge around the project topic, their skill set, and their availability. The people having the right combination of these factors may be located in different physical locations and, in some cases, work for different organizations. The end result is that organizations need tools that support dynamic and distributed teams, allowing these teams to effectively work together.

Collaboration Resources

There are many resources that are typically brought together when working on a document collaboration effort. The resources required for a collaboration effort can be categorized as follows:

- *Existing information*: Often information that already exists within your organization can be leveraged during the project. This information may be in the form of existing documents, data stored in other applications, information available only in hard copy, knowledge existing in someone's head, or online resources available from third-party sources. These materials may provide details required for reference during a current initiative or may contain information to be directly added to the materials being created. This information must be easy to locate and organize.

- *Collaboration process*: The processes defined within the organization for creating various types of materials can range from simple steps followed to facilitate basic information collection to a structured workflow process that includes defined document development stages and approval steps. Regardless of the complexity, the process must be defined and properly managed.

- *Collaboration tools*: Tools are required that enable the collaboration process. The tools can range from the programs used to create and edit materials to the systems used to facilitate and manage the collaboration effort. These tools must provide the services necessary to support the process regardless of its complexity.

- *Collaboration team*: The individuals participating in the collaboration effort are the most important aspect of the initiative. The people involved need the information necessary to complete their assigned tasks and need the tools that allow them to work as efficiently and accurately as possible.

- *Process management*: Team members participating in the initiative, management staff responsible for the team members, and other individuals having an interest in the materials being generated must all be kept up to date on the overall objectives, deadlines, and progress of the process. Management resources are required that allow the process to be monitored and managed without having a negative impact on deadlines or participants' efficiencies.

Challenges of Document Collaboration

Organizations are becoming increasingly interested in optimizing collaboration efforts. There are many reasons why this has become an increasingly important goal. Your organization may want to reduce the time it takes to generate needed materials, expand the volume of materials being created, or better audit and manage the material creation process to help ensure the quality of materials created.

Microsoft SharePoint includes capabilities designed to address many factors that can negatively impact document collaboration efforts in order to help organizations optimize these processes. Some of these factors include the following:

- *Information that is needed to support the collaboration effort is often spread across many sources*: This information may be in the form of existing materials scattered throughout your organization, Internet-based resources available from third parties, data in applications, documents only available in hard-copy format, or even knowledge stored in someone's head. Very rarely do all the participants know about all of the information that is available and could be leveraged when creating materials. This often results in duplication of effort, since team members will need to re-create information that they are not aware exists. Having information spread across multiple sources and in multiple formats results in the team spending a significant amount of time searching for this relevant information. This searching will often impact other people as well since in many cases the only way to find information is to contact the person who created it or manages it.

- *Multiple versions of the same information exist*: Common methods used to distribute important materials are through e-mail or as hard copy. When previously distributed information is later updated, the updates will also be distributed through e-mail or as hard copy. These distribution approaches result in multiple versions of the same information circulating through the organization. When this occurs, it becomes difficult to identify the most recent and most accurate versions. People will need to request the most up-to-date copy of the items from the owner at the start of the collaboration effort, which impacts their progress and impacts the people from whom they are requesting the information. In some cases, people will simply use the version they feel is the most recent, which can result in outdated materials being used.

- *Staff needing to participate in the process are spread across multiple locations*: In many cases, document collaboration efforts will require the involvement of people having a variety of skills and knowledge. It is not uncommon for the people best suited to participate in a collaborative effort to be based in different locations. When this is the case, information sharing is commonly done through e-mail, making it very difficult to track progress of the process and to manage the materials being shared. This will also result in many of the issues we discussed under the preceding two bullet points. In some situations, it is not possible to share the information through e-mail. This might be due to the size of the documents being worked on or other limiting factors. Also, in some cases it is simply too difficult to coordinate efforts when people are not based out of the same location. This is often due to communications challenges. When information cannot be easily shared or when communications between team members cannot be managed for distributed teams, participants for the process will be selected based on their proximity to each other instead of their knowledge, skills, or availability. This can result in more time being required to complete the effort, and it can negatively impact the quality of the materials created.

- *Managing the effort requires a significant time investment*: Management of document collaboration efforts is often handled through periodically polling participants in order to obtain status information. These efforts often require frequent meetings and discussions to communicate changing goals and deadlines. This results in interruptions of the work being done and can also result in team members having different understandings of goals, responsibilities, and deadlines.

- *Information sharing between team members is inefficient*: In many document collaboration efforts, information is shared via e-mail, printed documents, and word of mouth. As we discussed earlier, this can result in version control issues as these materials are passed around, collected, and assembled into a final document. This can also result in breakdowns in communication. When information is shared in this way, it is difficult maintaining a unified understanding of the goals, deadlines, and responsibilities around the project. It also makes introducing new people into the process after it is under way more difficult, since a significant amount of time would be required to acclimate the new person to the goals, status, location of materials, and overall understanding of the progress to date.

Needs for Document Collaboration

As we discussed earlier, there are many challenges that can negatively impact the effectiveness of the team and the accuracy of the created materials. Any of the challenges we discussed previously can have significant impacts on the effectiveness of document collaboration efforts. Microsoft SharePoint provides capabilities to help address these challenges, which include the following:

- *A single location for all document collaboration resources*: Windows SharePoint Services (WSS) sites are designed to act as a central repository for all collaboration materials. This repository would contain

    - All materials for the effort

    - References to other related internal, external, and third-party information

    - Communications about the project

    - Project and process management information, such as tasks, issues, and status materials

    - Content created during the initiative

This location would also act as the focal point for the management of the process and be available to all team members regardless of location. It would provide a central place where any person can go to get information on the status of the project, review the work done to date, and understand the objectives and goals. Having a central location for all materials also ensures that team members are working on the same and most up-to-date version of these materials.

- *The ability to easily locate available information*: Being able to quickly and easily locate all available information on a specific topic can significantly increase team effectiveness during a document collaboration project. SharePoint Portal Server (SPS) search tools allow you to search across all enterprise information based on keywords or specific criteria. This can save people time when researching a specific topic. It can also significantly reduce duplication of effort, since locating available information will not require any foreknowledge about the existence of the information. Locating information will also be done without the need to invest time in querying people or manually sifting through existing information repositories.

- *The flexibility to support simple and complex collaboration processes*: SharePoint provides basic content approval workflow capabilities, and in conjunction with other Microsoft Office System products can add the process management and advanced workflow capabilities needed to support more complex collaboration processes. These tools are configurable so that overly complex processes or technical requirements do not burden simple document collaboration processes. Conversely, the tools are flexible enough to support complex processes requiring more sophisticated business logic and technical requirements. These tools can be made to support the defined process, instead of your needing to adjust the process to support the requirements and limitations of the tools.

SharePoint Document Collaboration Solutions

The capabilities of SharePoint Portal Server and Windows SharePoint Services that we discussed in Chapters 2 through 7 can be brought together into solutions that can overcome the challenges and address the document collaboration needs discussed previously. These capabilities can be used to create an environment in which teams can work together to create the materials they need.

In order to demonstrate how a SharePoint environment can address document collaboration needs, we will use the RFP response example that we mentioned earlier in this chapter. We will describe the organization of a SharePoint solution that can address the needs of this type of collaborative effort. We will describe the situation in which the solution will be used and then outline the components making up the solution. Finally, we will walk through a typical RFP response workflow to demonstrate how the environment would be used.

■**Note** The solution described in this chapter leverages only those capabilities native to SharePoint. There are many Microsoft and third-party tools that can be added to a SharePoint environment to extend the document collaboration capabilities and provide additional functionality. We will make note of some of the areas that can be enhanced through the use of additional tools as we discuss the RFP response example.

RFP Response Requirements

In our document collaboration example, we will assume our organization frequently responds to requests for proposals (RFPs) to obtain business. We will also assume that our organization has several distributed offices. Our goal will be to provide an RFP response solution that allows our organization to quickly respond to RFP requests and for our response to meet the quality standards of our organization. Additionally, we need to allow distributed RFP response teams to work together as effectively as the teams where all members are based in the same location.

In order to meet the listed goals, we are assuming that our RFP response solution must allow for the following:

- People from any location must be able to participate in the RFP response creation process.

- Team members must be able to easily locate information available within the organization that could be used during the creation of the RFP response.

- Materials and communications related to the RFP response development process must be centrally managed.

- Process management tools such as objectives, task assignments, schedules, and status information must be available to all team members and management staff.

SharePoint Solution Components

Our SharePoint RFP response solution will leverage many of the SharePoint capabilities that we discussed in Chapters 2 through 7. Our sample solution will use the following:

- *Portal areas and listings*: Areas will provide the starting point for navigation through our RFP response solution. Listings within these areas will then provide us with access to the WSS sites that will contain the materials we need while we are creating a response to an RFP. (We discussed portal areas and listings in Chapter 2.)

- *Portal search capabilities*: The portal search capabilities will allow us to locate information we can leverage when developing a response to an RFP. (We discussed portal search capabilities in Chapter 2.)

- *Windows SharePoint Services (WSS) sites*: WSS sites will provide the primary storage and access point for all of the resources that we will be creating and using during the RFP response development process. (We discussed WSS sites in Chapter 3.)

- *Site templates*: We will create site templates to provide the teams of people working on RFP responses with a WSS site structure that includes the components needed to support the RFP response process. (We discussed WSS site templates in Chapter 3.)

- *Lists*: We will use both custom and template lists to track information and manage communication for the development of RFP responses. (We discussed custom lists in Chapter 4 and template lists in Chapter 5.)

- *Libraries*: Documents and images needed during the development of RFP responses will be stored in document and picture libraries. (We discussed libraries in Chapter 6.)

- *Alerts*: Alerts will be used to notify individuals when information within their RFP response sites has changed. (We discussed alerts in Chapter 7.)

- *Web parts*: We will use several of the web parts that come with SharePoint to support our RFP response process. (We discussed web parts in Chapter 7.)

RFP Response Process Definition

The types of components that we discussed earlier will be leveraged in the RFP response solution to support our organization's RFP response process. The following steps outline the high-level flow of events that make up our organization's RFP response process:

1. The team of people responsible for the creation of the RFP response are identified. This team will include the following:

    a. *Sales representative*: Responsible for the overall RFP creation process and for communicating with the company that sent the RFP. The sales representative is the conduit between the company sending the RFP and the individuals responsible for creating the response. The sales representative will be responsible for adding the pricing information to the RFP response based on the products and services outlined by the analyst and designer. This person will also be the one to deliver the RFP response back to the company that sent the RFP.

    b. *Analyst*: Responsible for determining the products and services needed to address the requirements outlined in the RFP. The analyst is also responsible for completing the offerings section of the RFP response.

    c. *Designer*: Responsible for creating estimates for services, detailing licensing requirements, and providing any solution design details required based on the products and services identified by the analyst.

2. The sales representative will initiate the process by creating the site for the RFP response. As part of this step, the sales representative will populate objectives, tasks, timelines, and any relevant documents.

3. The analyst will identify the products and services that are needed to address the requirements listed in the RFP. If any additional information must be requested from the issuer of the RFP to determine these needs, the analyst will work through the sales representative to get this information.

4. The designer will create service estimates and add any design-related information to the products and services listed by the analyst. The designer will request additional information of the analyst if any clarification is needed on the product and services information created by the analyst.

5. The analyst will write the offering's description in the RFP Response document based on the information compiled by the designer.

6. The sales representative will review the information added by the analyst and add the necessary product cost information. The sales representative will also add any additional references or background information required.

7. The sales representative will perform a final review of the RFP response and then deliver the response to the issuer of the RFP. The sales representative will then be responsible for closing out the RFP response process and updating the status as the deal progresses.

SharePoint Environment Layout

We will need to configure several components in our SharePoint environment to address the needs of our RFP response process. In order to help determine the configuration of these components, we need to make certain assumptions about our SharePoint environment. The assumptions that we will be making include the following:

- We have a SharePoint environment that includes both SharePoint Portal Server and Windows SharePoint Services.

- Portal searching and indexing has been configured for our environment. For the purposes of this sample, there will not need to be any specific content included in the search results. However, to deploy a similar solution into a production environment, you would need searching and indexing configured so that all relevant materials within SharePoint and in other repositories within your organization could be searched using the SharePoint portal search. A technical administrator of the SharePoint environment would need to configure this.

- A technical administrator has deployed a subsite viewer web part for use within the SharePoint environment. This web part will list the subsites located under the site where the web part is placed. This will be the only web part that we will refer to which is not provided in a default SharePoint deployment. While it is not required to have this web part in order to navigate through a WSS site hierarchy, having it provides a significant usability enhancement to SharePoint. There are several subsite viewer web parts available and freely downloadable. If you are unsure where to go to obtain a subsite viewer web part, you can refer to the book web site (`http://www.sharepointextras.com`) for more information.

The layout of the components that we will be using in our RFP response process sample includes the following:

- *Resources area*: This area is provided by default under the Topics area in a new Share-Point portal. We will use the Resources area to refer to general resources that are being made available to the organization. These resources may include phone directories, access to enterprise applications, references to enterprise materials, and so on. For our RFP response environment, we will use the Resources area to reference a Presentation Materials site that contains graphics, logos, and other resources approved by the organization for use when creating new materials, such as RFP responses.

- *Divisions area*: This area is also provided by default under the Topics area in a new SharePoint portal. This area is used to group resources for specific divisions or departments within the organization. For our RFP response environment, this area will include a reference to the Sales area, which will contain references to sales-related resources.

- *Sales area*: This area is provided by default under the Divisions area in a new SharePoint portal. This area is used to group all resources that are relevant to the company's sales group. This would include all reference to sites, external content, materials, and so on that sales personnel would find valuable. For our RFP response environment, this area will include a reference to an RFP Responses site that contains the individual document collaboration sites for RFP response projects.

- *Presentation Materials site*: Referenced from the Resources area, this site contains resources provided by the organization for use when creating new materials. This can include graphics, logos, company description information, templates, general references, and the like. For the purpose of our example, we will be using the Presentation Materials site to manage graphics, such as company logos and charts, and standard text items, such as a company description and product descriptions. In our example, this site will contain the following components:

  - *Presentation Materials*: This document library will be used to store and organize standard materials for use when creating new documents. This will include company details, product descriptions, references, testimonials, templates, and so on.

  - *Presentation Graphics*: This picture library will be used to store and organize standard company graphics. This will include company logos, charts, and other graphics.

  - *Contacts*: This contacts list references the individuals responsible for the materials stored in this site. This information makes it easy for people to identify and contact the owners of presentation materials when they have a question about an item or notice errors in available materials.

- *How To*: This custom list will be used to store basic instructions on how to incorporate the presentation materials or presentation graphics into documents and how to perform other tasks related to using these materials.

- *Links*: This links list is used to reference any external resources that are considered standard materials but that are stored in other locations. This would include any third-party materials available through the web.

- *RFP Responses site*: Referenced from the Sales area, this site contains all RFP responses created by the company. It will also contain the document workspaces that were used to facilitate the creation of these RFP responses. In our example, this site will contain the following components:

  - *Document workspaces*: Created as part of the RFP response process, these workspaces are based on the Document Workspace template we discussed in Chapter 3.

  - *RFP Responses*: This document library contains the documents created in response to the specific RFP requests received.

- *Document Workspace template*: This template will be used to create workspaces that will be located within the RFP Responses site. These workspaces will be used to manage the resources needed to support the creation of specific RFP responses. In our example, this site will contain the following resources:

  - *Shared Documents*: This document library will contain materials being collected or created for an RFP response. For our example this library will include estimate sheets, presentations, the original RFP, and the RFP response being created.

  - *Announcements*: This announcements list will contain any news around the RFP response of which the RFP response team should be aware. This may include announcements around extensions to deadlines, updates to available resources, or notifications of team assignment changes.

  - *Contacts*: This contacts list will contain relevant contact information related to the RFP response. This would include the RFP issuer's information as well as any additional contacts provided by the issuer. It would also include contact information for the members of the RFP response team.

  - *Events*: This events list will contain information about any events related to the RFP response. This would include any meetings being held to review RFP content, the RFP due date, meetings to present the RFP response to the customer, and so on.

  - *Links*: This links list will contain references to any web sites related to the RFP response. This list would include references to the RFP issuer's Internet site and references to any third-party Internet resources relevant to the response creation process.

  - *Tasks*: This tasks list will contain all the task assignments for the creation of the RFP response.

  - *General Discussion*: This discussion board will be used to manage communications between the team members concerning the RFP response.

Figure 8-1 depicts the layout of these resources.

Figure 8-1. *RFP response resource layout*

In order for you to walk through the RFP response process as we describe it, these resources must be configured within your SharePoint environment. The following steps outline how to configure these resources. For details around the specifics of how to perform any of the described configuration tasks, you can refer to the chapter that discusses the specific item.

Configuring the Divisions Area

As we described earlier, the Divisions area will contain references to the various divisions within the organization. We need to update the Divisions area to support the needs of our RFP response process. Figure 8-2 depicts the desired layout of the Divisions area.

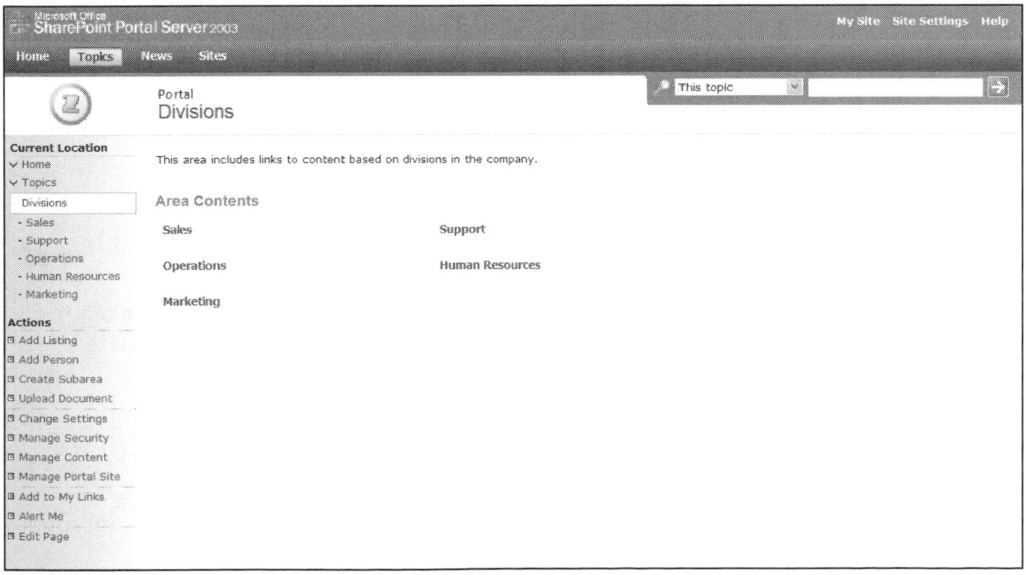

Figure 8-2. *Divisions area*

The following steps describe how to update the Divisions area for our RFP example:

1. Remove the Grouped Listings web part from the Middle Left Zone of the Divisions area page.

2. Add the Area Contents web part to the Middle Left Zone of the Divisions area page.

Configure the Sales Area

The Sales area will reference sales-related resources and, for our example, is the entry point used to access the RFP Responses site that will contain all RFP response resources. The default layout of the Sales area will support our RFP example. Figure 8-3 depicts the desired layout of the Sales area.

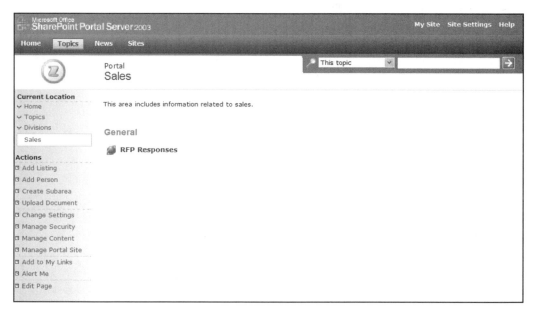

Figure 8-3. *Sales area*

Configuring the Resources Area

The Resources area will contain general company materials used by people across the organization. For our example, this area will reference the Presentation Materials site that contains graphics and documents to be used when creating corporate materials, such as presentations or client documentation. The default layout of the Resources area will support our RFP example. Figure 8-4 depicts the desired layout of the Resources area.

Creating and Configuring the Presentation Materials Site

The Presentation Materials site will contain all standard documents and graphics for use when creating new corporate materials. Figure 8-5 depicts the desired layout of the Presentation Materials site.

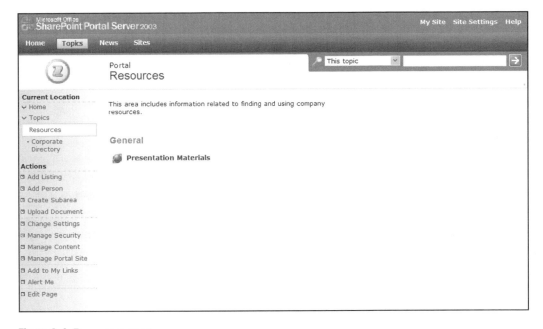

Figure 8-4. *Resources area*

Figure 8-5. *Presentation Materials site*

The following steps describe how to create and configure the Presentation Materials site:

1. Create the Presentation Materials site.

   a. Create a listing for the site in the Resources area.

   b. Base the site on the Blank Site template.

2. Create the Presentation Materials document library.

   a. Base the Presentation Materials document library on the document library type.

   b. Select to display the library in the Quick Launch list.

3. Configure the Presentation Materials document library.

   a. Create a column called Item Type that is a Choice type and make it required. The choices for Item Type should be set to Company Details, Product Descriptions, General Inserts, and References and Testimonials. This column should be saved with no default value.

   b. Create a column called Owner that is a Single line of text type and make it required. The Owner column should allow for a maximum of 30 characters to be entered.

   c. Update the All Documents view by placing the Item Type column in Position 3 and placing the Owner column in Position 4.

   d. Create a new view called By Item Type, make it the default view, and include the following columns: Type, Name (linked to document), Owner, Modified, and Modified By. Sort by Name (linked to document) and group by Item Type.

   e. Create a new view called By Item Type Collapsed and include the following columns: Type, Name (linked to document), Owner, and Modified. Sort by Name (linked to document). Group by Item Type with the group collapsed.

4. Create the Presentation Graphics picture library.

   a. Base the Presentation Graphics library on the picture library type.

   b. Select to display the library in the Quick Launch list.

5. Configure the Presentation Graphics picture library.

   a. Create a column called Item Type that is a Choice type and make it required. The choices for Item Type should be set to Company Details, Product Descriptions, General Inserts, and References and Testimonials. This column should be saved with no default value.

   b. Create a column called Owner that is a Single line of text type and make it required. The Owner column should allow for a maximum of 30 characters to be entered.

   c. Update the All Pictures view by placing the Item Type column in Position 4 and placing the Owner column in Position 5.

   d. Create a new view called By Item Type, make it the default view, and include the following columns: Selection Checkbox (select a picture), Type, Name (linked to display items), Owner, Picture Size, File Size, and (must be selected for picture library details view) Sort by Name (linked to display items) and group by Item Type.

    e. Create a new view called By Item Type Collapsed and include the following columns: Selection Checkbox (select a picture), Type, Name (linked to display item), Owner, Picture Size, and (must be selected for picture library details view) Sort by Name (linked to display items). Group by Item Type with the group collapsed.

6. Create the Contacts list.

    a. Base the Contacts list on the Contacts list template.

    b. Select to display the list in the Quick Launch list.

7. Create the How To list.

    a. Base the How To list on the Custom list template.

    b. Select to display the list in the Quick Launch list.

8. Configure the How To list.

    a. Create a column called Details that is a Multiple lines of text type and make it required. This column should allow rich HTML text.

    b. Update the All Items view so that it displays Attachments, Title (linked to item), and Details. Select to sort by Title (linked to item).

    c. Create a new view called Titles Only and include Attachments and Title (linked to item). Sort by Title (linked to item).

9. Create the Links list.

    a. Base the Links list on the Links list template.

    b. Select to display the list in the Quick Launch list.

10. Update the Presentation Materials site page.

    a. Place the Presentation Materials library web part in the Left Zone, and choose to display the By Item Type Collapsed view and use the Summary Toolbar.

    b. Place the Presentation Graphics library web part in the Left Zone below the Presentation Materials library web part, and choose to display the By Item Type Collapsed view and use the Summary Toolbar.

    c. Place the How To list web part in the Right Zone, and choose to display the Titles Only view and use the Summary Toolbar.

    d. Place the Links list web part in the Right Zone below the How To list web part.

    e. Place the Contacts list web part in the Right Zone below the Links list web part.

11. Add the following content to the Presentation Materials Library. This content will be used in the RFP response process walk-through that follows.

    a. *A company background Word document named Company Background*: Set the Item Type to Company Details.

    b. *A company value-add proposition Word document named Company Value-Add*: Set the Item Type to Company Details.

    c. *One or more reference Word and Excel documents*: Set the Item Type to References and Testimonials.

12. Add the following content to the Presentation Graphics library. This content will be used in the RFP response process walk-through that follows.

    a. A company offerings JPG or GIF image named Offerings

    b. A company logo JPG or GIF image named Company Logo

13. Add any additional relevant documents, pictures, contact information, how-to instructions, and links to the site libraries and lists.

Creating and Configuring the RFP Responses Site

The RFP Responses site will contain all sites created to manage specific RFP responses. This site will also contain documentation related to RFP response policies and procedures. Figure 8-6 depicts the desired layout of the RFP Responses site.

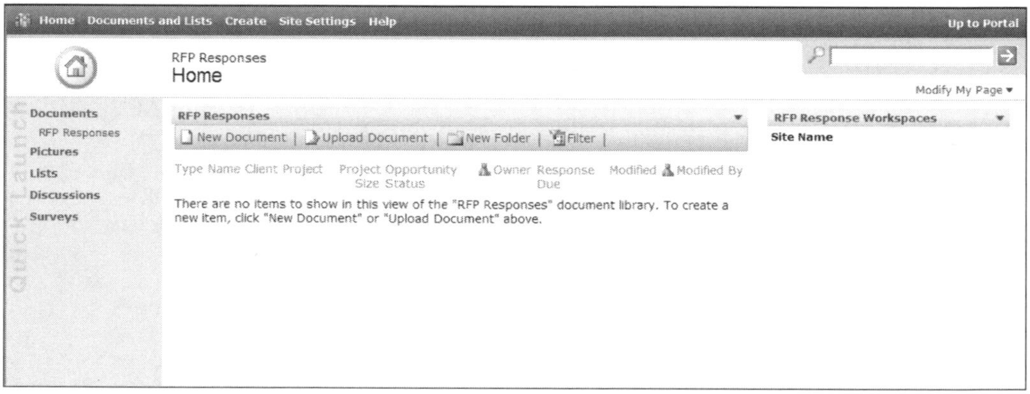

Figure 8-6. *RFP Responses site*

The following steps describe how to create and configure the RFP Responses site:

1. Create the RFP Responses site.

    a. Create a listing for the site in the Sales area.

    b. Base the site on the Blank Site template.

2. Create the RFP Responses document library.

    a. Base the RFP Responses library on the document library type.

    b. Select to display the library in the Quick Launch list.

3. Configure the RFP Responses document library.

    a. Create a column called Client that is a Single line of text type and make it required.

    b. Create a column called Project that is a Single line of text type and make it required.

    c. Create a column called Project Size that is a Currency type and make it required.

d. Create a column called Owner that is a Lookup type and make it required. Leave the Get Information From value as User Information and the In This Column value as Display Name. Leave the Include Presence Information and the Add to Default View options checked.

e. Create a column called Response Due that is a Date and Time type and make it required. This column should be set to Date Only.

f. Create a column called Opportunity Status that is a Choice type and make it required. The choices for Opportunity Status should be set to In Development, Submitted, Won, and Lost. This column should be saved with a default value of In Development.

g. Update the All Documents view so that it displays Type (icon linked to document), Name (linked to document with edit menu), Client, Project, Project Size, Opportunity Status, Owner, Response Due, Modified, and Modified By. Select to sort by Client and Project.

h. Create a new view called By Client and include the following columns: Project, Project Size, Opportunity Status, Owner Response Due, Modified, and Modified By. Select to sort by Project and group by Company.

i. Create a new view called By Opportunity Status and include the following columns: Client, Project, Project Size, Owner Response Due, Modified, and Modified By. Select to sort by Client and Project and group by Opportunity Status.

j. Edit the library template. The template is a Word document. It should be edited so that it represents a document template for a new RFP response. This template should include the sections that make up an RFP response and use the layout of a standard response. It should also include any standard text that should be part of any RFP response.

4. Update the RFP Responses site page.

a. Place the RPF Responses library web part in the Left Zone, and choose to display the All Documents view and use the Full Toolbar.

b. Place the Subsite viewer web part in the Right Zone and make the title read RFP Response Workspaces.

■**Note** This assumes that a SharePoint technical administrator has added a subsite viewer web part to the SharePoint environment. As we mentioned earlier, there are several subsite viewer web parts available that can be freely downloaded.

The resources needed for the RFP response process are now configured.

RFP Response Process Walk-Through

Now that we have configured the resources needed for the RFP response process, we can discuss the steps that will be followed when creating a new RFP response. During this discussion, we will describe how each of the areas and sites that you configured previously are used during the RFP response process. We will describe how people in each of the roles listed earlier (sales representative, analyst, and designer) will work together to create the RFP response.

When we walk through the RFP response process, we will assume the following:

- An RFP response has been received from a client or potential client. For the purposes of our example, we will call this company DataLan Corporation.

- The team of people that will be involved in the process have been identified.

- The entire organization is authorized to view the materials in an RFP response site, but only the individuals defined as the response creation team can edit information within the site.

The following steps describe the process that we will walk you through to develop the response for the RFP received from DataLan Corporation.

1. Assuming the role of sales representative, create a new RFP Response document for the received RFP.

    a. Create a new document in the RFP Responses document library of the RFP Responses site called DataLan 2005 using the New Document option in the library's menu.

    b. Add general information to the document, such as client name, headers, and any necessary details.

    c. Save the new document and during the save, add appropriate values to the document properties presented. Table 8-1 shows the values to set for each of the listed properties.

    Table 8-1. *RFP Summary List Values*

Column	Value
Client	DataLan Corporation
Project	2005 RFP
Project Size	$200,000
Owner	Sales representative (this would be the name of the sales representative)
Response Due	12/01/2005
Opportunity Status	In Development

2. The sales representative creates a new workspace to facilitate the creation of the RFP response. The new workspace will be created using the Create Document Workspace option from the DataLan 2005 document context menu.

3. The sales representative will add all initial information to the DataLan 2005 site.

   a. Grant the analyst and designer Contributor-level access within the site using the Members web part. When adding these individuals, select to send them an e-mail about the new site and in the e-mail body describe that they have been selected to be part of the team for creating the DataLan 2005 RFP response. The team members will then go to the site to review the information about the received RFP.

   b. Grant Domain Users Reader-level access within the site using the Members web part.

   c. Add the received RFP from DataLan Corporation to the site.

   d. Add a link to the Links list that references the Presentation Materials site. If you do not know the URL for the Presentation Materials site, you can navigate to the site and copy the URL from the web browser's address bar.

   e. Add a link to the Links list that references the issuer's web site, http://www.datalan.com, and call this link DataLan Internet Site.

   f. Add the tasks that must be done to create the RFP response to the Tasks list. Table 8-2 lists the tasks that should be created.

Table 8-2. *Task List Values*

Title	Assigned To	Start Date	Due Date
Add company background, value proposition information, and references.	Sales representative	12/01/2005	12/02/2005
Determine products and services needed to address RFP needs.	Analyst	12/03/2005	12/05/2005
Compile service time estimates and product licensing requirements needed to support the defined products and services.	Designer	12/06/2005	12/08/2005
Enter product and services detailed descriptions into the RFP response including diagrams required.	Analyst	12/09/2005	12/11/2005
Add costs for products and services.	Sales representative	12/12/2005	12/12/2005
Response review.	Sales representative	12/15/2005	12/15/2005
Submit response to client.	Sales representative	12/16/2005	12/16/2005

■**Note** Third-party products are available that will consolidate all tasks assigned to a person across all SharePoint task lists to provide them with a consolidated list of assigned tasks. This would allow people to go to a single location in the portal to view all tasks that they have been assigned.

4. The sales representative will check out the RFP Response document and add the background, value proposition information, and references.

    a. Click the Presentation Materials link to go to the Presentation Materials site and insert any necessary text from company background, value proposition, and references into the RFP response.

    b. Add any other information you require to the introduction of the RFP Response document.

    c. Once done, check the document back in.

5. All team members will set up alerts to monitor important changes to information within the site.

    a. Create an alert that notifies you of all changes on the Tasks list and select to be notified immediately.

    b. Create an alert that notifies you when items are added to the General Discussion discussion board and select to be notified immediately.

    c. Each team member should set up these two alerts for themselves.

Note Third-party products are available that allow select individuals to set up alerts for others within a site. This would allow the sales representative to set up the alerts for all the team members when the site is initially created.

---

6. The sales representative updates the Percent Complete column to 100% for the "Add company background, value proposition information, and references" task.

7. The analyst will receive a notification that the Tasks list has changed and go to the site to define the products and services that are needed to respond to the RFP. As part of this process, the analyst will have to request additional information needed to complete the product and service needs definition.

    a. The analyst will add a new discussion to the General Discussion board with a subject of "Additional Information Needed" and a body listing several pieces of information required to determine the product and service requirements.

    b. The sales representative will get a notification about the change to the General Discussion board and will review the discussion details added by the analyst. The sales representative will then obtain the required information from the client and post a response containing this information to the "Additional Information Needed" discussion.

    c. The analyst will get a notification about the change to the General Discussion board and will review the information provided in the response from the sales representative. This discussion is held using a SharePoint discussion board instead of through e-mail so that the information is available to the entire team and so that it is saved for future reference.

■**Note** There are third-party products that allow e-mail communication to be directed to a library, which would allow for discussion had via e-mail and the e-mail messages to be stored in the RFP Responses site.

8. Now, acting as the analyst role, create a document that lists the products and services to be included in the RFP response.

   a. Create a new document called Products and Services and place this document in the Shared Documents library on the DataLan 2005 RFP response workspace.

   b. Check out the Products and Services document and update it so that it contains the products and services needed to respond to the RFP request.

   c. Once all updates have been made to the Products and Services document, check it back into the library.

9. The analyst updates the percent complete column to 100% for the "Determine products and services needed to address RFP needs" task.

10. The designer will receive a notification that the Tasks list has changed and go to the site to review the products and services information created by the analyst. The designer will determine the service time estimates and the product licensing necessary to support this information.

    a. The designer will check out the Products and Services document and add service time estimates and product license details.

    b. Once done, the designer will check the document back in. We check the document out and then back in instead of just editing it so that everyone will know who is currently working on the document and to make sure that no one else uses the document while the designer is making edits. With the document checked out, the designer can save and close the document while still keeping it checked out so that others cannot make changes.

11. The designer updates the percent complete column to 100% for the "Compile service time estimates and product licensing requirements needed to support the defined products and services" task.

12. The analyst will receive a notification that the Tasks list has changed and go to the site to update the RFP Response document with information from the Product and Services document.

    a. Check out and update the RFP Response document, adding information that was created as part of the Product and Services document. Organize this information to fit within the RFP response structure.

    b. Insert the Offerings images into the RFP response from the Presentation Graphics library in the Presentation Materials site by having the DataLan 2005 RFP Response document open, selecting the Offerings image from the Presentation Graphics library, and using the Send To option.

    c. Once done making edits, check the RFP Response document back in.

13. The analyst updates the percent complete column to 100% for the "Enter product and services detailed descriptions into the RFP response including needed diagrams" task.

14. The sales representative will receive a notification that the Tasks list has changed. The sales representative will open the RFP Response document and add the product and services costs.

15. The sales representative updates the percent complete column to 100% for the "Add costs for products and services" task.

■**Note** Real-time communication capabilities can be incorporated into the SharePoint environment by configuring Microsoft Live Communications Server. This would enable the team to ask questions and discuss the process through real-time communication, or chat, using MSN Messenger. This would also add team member presence information to the environment, allowing team members to see the availability of other team members.

---

16. The sales representative will review the completed RFP response. The sales representative will open the RFP Response document and make any necessary final update.

17. The sales representative updates the percent complete column to 100% for the "Response review" task.

18. The sales representative will then send the RFP response to the client and update the "Submit response to client" task.

19. The sales representative will publish the final DataLan 2005 document to the RFP Responses library in the RFP Responses site using the Publish to Source Location option from the DataLan 2005 document context menu in the DataLan 2005 document workspace.

20. The sales representative will update the Opportunity Status value of the DataLan 2005 document in the RFP Responses site to Submitted.

21. After the business is won or lost, the sales representative will update the Opportunity Status value of the DataLan 2005 document in the RFP Responses site to Won or Lost.

■**Note** Workflow capabilities can be added to the SharePoint environment through the use of available third-party products. These products allow for specific individuals to be notified when they are required to perform an action, reminders to be sent when tasks go past due, and the ability to look at the workflow process to identify the current status of the overall process. The site containing the RFP response materials could also be automatically archived or deleted at the end of the process.

Figure 8-7 shows the final RFP Responses site after the RFP response has been created.

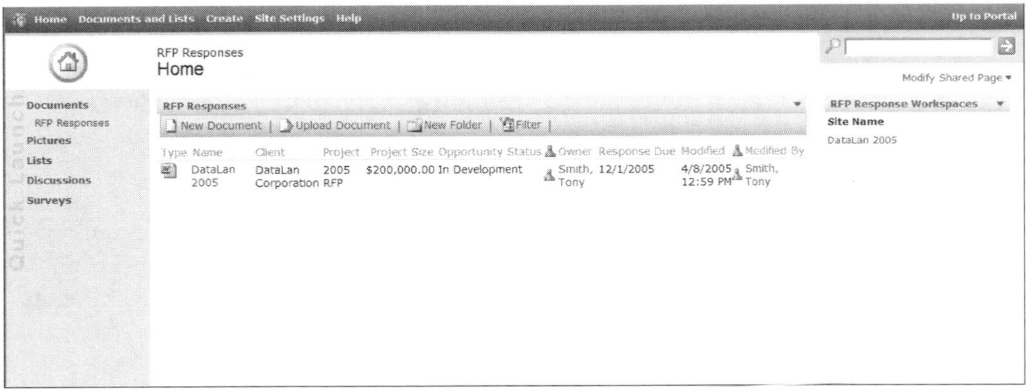

Figure 8-7. *Final RFP Responses site*

Figure 8-8 shows the final DataLan Corporation RFP response site.

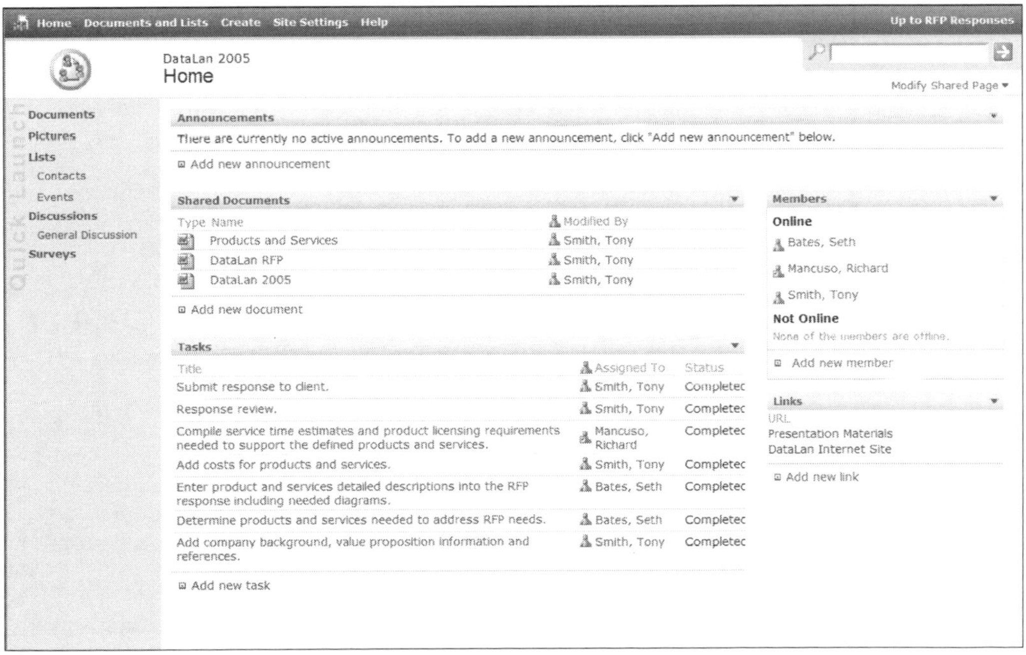

Figure 8-8. *DataLan 2005 RFP response site*

Benefits of SharePoint Document Collaboration Solutions

There are several benefits that your organization can gain by using a SharePoint environment to support document collaboration processes. These benefits range from time savings and staff efficiency to providing more accurate materials and giving all stakeholders, managers, and team members exposure into the process and materials.

The benefits that your organization will receive from using your SharePoint environment for document collaboration solutions will depend on how well the document collaboration capabilities you include map to the business needs. As with any solution, document collaboration capabilities must map to the business processes that they support, and these solutions must provide value to the people who are expected to use them. Our RFP response process example describes a simple process. The configuration of an RFP response process within your organization would need to leverage the tools necessary to support your specific collaboration requirements.

The following are some of the most common benefits organizations receive from providing document collaboration solutions through their SharePoint environment:

- *Reduction of document creation life cycle*: This is accomplished through the increased effectiveness of the team. Team members are given the following:

  - A structure in which work can be consolidated. All materials related to a project, regardless of type (documents, images, tasks, links, and so on), can be stored in this location.

  - Tools that allow members to be notified of events that occur around the project, enabling people to be kept aware of information changes and project status.

  - The ability to review and manage the tasks that they are assigned.

  - With the use of the portal searching capabilities, the ability to quickly locate materials that can be leveraged as part of their document collaboration initiative.

- *Improvement of individuals' effectiveness*: This is provided through the following:

  - Document collaboration solutions allow individuals to easily participate in collaboration efforts at any point in the process.

  - These solutions reduce the need for frequent meetings on document collaboration initiatives, which optimizes the use of individuals' time.

  - Since these solutions are web-based, individuals participating in the process may be selected based on their skill sets and availability instead of their physical proximity to the other team members.

  - Having all materials centrally located allows for much easier information management and retrieval.

- *Inclusion of external individuals in the process*: Managing your collaboration efforts through your SharePoint environment

  - Not only allows you to include distributed individuals within your company in the process, but also allows you to include individuals who are external to your organization, such as third-party partners, consultants, and staff at subsidiaries. These individuals can directly participate in the process, leveraging the same tools as those used by internal staff.

  - Allows for all participants to share a common experience when working on a collaboration project.

- *Track and manage the process*: Team members and managers in the organization can go to the SharePoint site being used to manage a collaborative effort to review the current status and all current materials related to the effort. This reduces the need to make telephone calls or send e-mails requesting status information to the various team members. Managers and team members can view the current status of the effort without negatively impacting its progress.

Tips for Creating Effective Document Collaboration Solutions

When building any solution, it is important to make sure that it meets the business needs and provides value to both the people using it and the company overall. When deploying document collaboration solutions within your SharePoint environment, there are several points to keep in mind that can help ensure the document collaboration solution meets the desired requirements:

- *Leverage the integration points with Microsoft Office 2003*: This will allow people to work with the materials located in the SharePoint environment through the tools that they are familiar with, like Word and Excel.

- *Automate tasks where possible*: Automating tasks makes the process easier for people to use and allows you to provide a higher degree of process efficiencies. This is done by using features such as creating document workspaces through a document in a document library, which we discussed in our walk-through. This allows for information to be automatically moved to appropriate storage locations so that the people using the process do not need to perform these types of tasks manually.

- *Create a portal and site structure that maps to the way people use the information*: It is important to make the navigation structure as intuitive as possible in order to help facilitate the use of the environment.

- *Create templates that provide a consistent structure*: These templates should be used across initiatives and include all of the key components needed to support the process. It is important to keep these templates up to date as needs change and as better ways of supporting the initiatives are identified.

- *Include all of the resources necessary to support the process*: As we noted in our example walk-through, there are several third-party products available that can enhance the usability of the document collaboration solutions and of the overall SharePoint environment. It is important to make the processes as easy to use as possible to ensure that these processes are not perceived by users as being too complicated or as unnecessary burdens.

- *Make sure the process provides value to all the people involved*: The solution should provide value to the team members as well as the overall company. This value needs to be understood by everyone involved.

- *Train individuals on the use of the solution and on the overall process*: It should not be assumed that all people involved will know how to use the tools or that they have a full understanding of the collaboration process. Regardless of the length of time the process has been in place, it is important to provide training on the process and on how the tools support this process. Materials should also be provided that people can use as reference after the training. This will help ensure that everyone involved has the same understanding of the process and the tools that support the process. Plans should also be put in place to handle the training of new staff that join the company.

- *Monitor the solution's effectiveness and make incremental changes where appropriate*: It is rarely the case that a newly deployed process will take into account all potential scenarios that the process will end up supporting. It is important to monitor the process and the use of the tools in order to make any optimizations necessary to address challenges that will be identified after the solution is deployed.

■ ■ ■

CHAPTER 9

SharePoint Project Collaboration Solutions

Many information workers spend a significant amount of time working on projects. These projects range from small teams being tasked with completing a specific job, such as creating a simple presentation or updating some standard company materials, to multiple individuals working on a complex long-term project, like introducing a new product line into the company or creating a five-year corporate plan. SharePoint Portal Server and Windows SharePoint Services provide many capabilities that help facilitate and manage team-based projects.

In this chapter, we will discuss project collaboration solutions and describe how you can use SharePoint to support the needs of team-based projects. We will describe a sample project collaboration scenario and step through how a SharePoint-based solution can address the needs of our scenario.

Project Collaboration Overview

It is often very challenging to successfully complete a project so that it meets all desired business objectives, is completed within the desired timeframe, and meets its budget expectations. Projects require the coordination of many types of resources, including people, processes, and information, to be successful. Information workers spend a significant amount of time performing project-based work, and as a result, the efficient management, organization, and execution of projects is vital to a company's success.

Many factors can impact the overall success of a project. SharePoint provides capabilities that enhance the project collaboration process to help overcome these issues. These capabilities are designed to help support all aspects of a project including the following:

- Project planning
  - Define business justification and objectives.
  - Define measures of success.
  - Organize the team.
  - Assign tasks.
  - Create schedules and milestones.
  - Provide cost estimates.
  - Define deliverables.

- Project execution

    - Collaboratively create project materials, including deliverables and reference materials.

    - Manage issues and risks.

    - Manage tasks.

    - Manage scope.

    - Manage procurement and vendors.

    - Communicate project-related decisions, status, and key metrics.

    - Release final deliverables.

- Project closeout

    - Archive project materials for future reference.

    - Evaluate project successes and failures.

From a regulatory compliance assessment to a new product development introduction process, most projects include these steps. However, the degree to which they are addressed and the formality around each step will vary based on the needs of the project and the project management approach used by the organization.

Challenges of Project Collaboration

When a significant amount of employees' time is spent working on projects, strong project collaboration and management is needed to ensure the success of active initiatives. Participants must be able to contribute to the project as efficiently as possible.

There are many challenges SharePoint can help address during a single project, some of which are listed here:

- *Difficulty managing project-related information*: Project-related information may be scattered throughout an organization, with each participant having their own copy of the project documents to work from. Other documentation is stored in shared locations, such as network drives. E-mail is then often used as the method of disseminating information. All of this leads to challenges when people need to find materials for the project, resulting in a significant amount of time being spent looking for information. There can be negative impacts on other individuals' time as well, since assistance is often required from other team members to locate items.

- *Lack of communication*: Projects can suffer from a lack of communication between participants. Whether it is the fault of the participants or the system in place to facilitate the project, communication breakdowns lead to unproductive time and additional risk. Participants may not know what responsibilities they have. Decisions made, scope changes identified, and updates to objectives are not broadcast to the people who are impacted. This lack of communication can lead to redundant work, missed deadlines, and frustrated employees. Also, managers and stakeholders may not have the necessary exposure into the project, which can result in management frustrations.

- *Collaboration for geographically dispersed teams*: Ideally, everyone involved in a project would be in close contact with each other. However, more frequently this is becoming the exception rather than the rule. Project teams are increasingly composed of participants in different locations. Organizations want to create project teams based on individuals' skill sets and availability instead of their geographic location. Time zone differences become an issue when people in different locations need to work on the same project. Also, all project materials need to be accessible by all team members regardless of their location.

- *Lack of visibility into the project*: Project sponsors, managers, stakeholders, and team members all need the ability to review project materials, understand project status, and be made aware of changes to the scope and objectives. Key metrics, however, are often not readily available. Instead, the project manager must compile this information on demand, impacting their time and often impacting the time of others when status information needs to be collected.

- *Managing changing resources*: Ideally, projects would contain a complete and consistent set of participants who are all available from the start of the project and contribute through to the end. However, many projects, especially longer term initiatives, often have teams that are more dynamic, changing over time based on people's availability and the skills needed at each point of the project. New participants must be educated on project goals and notified of previous project decisions, and responsibilities must be reassigned to them. Members leaving the project will often take the knowledge they have gained with them, which in some cases is not documented, so it is lost to the rest of the team. They also may be removed in the middle of their tasks, which then need to be reallocated to other team members. Knowledge transfer during changes in project teams is critical in order to avoid the negative impacts these changes can have on the projects.

Needs for Project Collaboration

Due to the large amount of time spent by employees on projects, the efficiency with which these projects are run can have a significant impact on your entire organization. The challenges discussed previously can have detrimental effects on the success of such projects and the overall productivity of the organization.

SharePoint provides many capabilities that can be used during project collaboration efforts to help mitigate the affects of the challenges discussed earlier. These include the following:

- *Providing a central repository of all project materials*: Rather than having project information scattered throughout an organization, SharePoint provides you with a central storage area for all documents, data, and project management–related information. Storing project resources in a central repository also provides participants access to tasks, objectives, decisions, and deadlines and any changes to these items. This will allow for easier education of new members, reduce the time it takes for participants to find information, and allow for easier management of the project by the project manager.

- *Allowing repository access from any location*: The project repository can be available to all involved individuals regardless of their location. This allows project members who are in different locations, including those who are traveling, to effectively participate in the project.

- *Providing notification of changes in information to participants*: Project members need to be made aware of changes to relevant information. This includes changes to their responsibilities, documents, deadlines, objectives, or scope. SharePoint allows team members to select the items they want to be notified about.

- *Providing project exposure to managers and stakeholders*: When managers and stakeholders have a great deal of interest in the outcome of a project, providing them with access to project materials, including project metrics, can help manage their expectations as the project progresses. These individuals need access to these items when they need them without having to request them from the project manager, potentially negatively impacting the progress of the project. SharePoint capabilities allow for the introduction of a process that provides these metrics to stakeholders with little or no work from the project manager. This can reduce extra demands on the team while ensuring that stakeholders are kept well informed.

SharePoint Project Collaboration Solutions

SharePoint Portal Server 2003 and Windows SharePoint Services provide many benefits to the organization, management, and collaboration of projects. The components that we have discussed in Chapters 2 through 7 can be combined to enhance the productivity and efficiency of projects in your organization.

In this chapter, we will walk you through the creation of a sample project using the tools available in SharePoint. The focus will be on addressing the challenges described earlier in an effort to allow for easier project collaboration and management. This will include the creation and customization of a team site used to facilitate the project. We will then walk through typical usage of the solution for participants in the various project roles.

■**Note** The solution described in this chapter leverages only those capabilities native to SharePoint. There are many Microsoft and third-party tools that can be added to a SharePoint environment to extend the project collaboration capabilities. We will make note of some of the places where additional solutions can be introduced to enhance the project collaboration process.

Service Plan Project Requirements

In our project collaboration example, we will use SharePoint features to facilitate the management of a new project within our organization. This project will be focused around introducing a service plan offering for one of our organization's existing product lines. The project team is performing all of the tasks necessary to design the makeup of this offering, introduce it into the offerings list, and prepare to market the offering.

In our example, we will assume that our organization has several offices and that the project team members are located across these offices. Our goal is to provide a solution that will allow us to increase the productivity of the project members to help ensure that the project is successfully completed on time and on budget. To meet this goal, we must allow for the following:

- People from any location must have access to the project information and be able to contribute to the project.

- All project resources must be stored in a single repository to ease the burden of searching for needed materials and to help with project team member transitions.

- Project members must have the ability to receive notifications when important documents are modified or added to the project repository. A place for important announcements to be broadcast to the project team must also be provided and allow team members to subscribe to these announcements.

- All managers and stakeholders must have access to project materials including key metrics that allow them to understand the health of the project.

- The project manager must be able to control security around sensitive financial documents.

Service Plan Project Process Definition

Our project collaboration sample solution will leverage many of the SharePoint capabilities that we discussed in Chapters 2 through 7.

The following steps describe the high-level flow of events that will make up our project collaboration process:

1. The need to organize a project based on a request from a business sponsor is identified.

2. The project participants are identified. The participants include the following:

    a. *Business sponsor or executive stakeholders*: The individual or group who has championed the project in the organization. These people may be ultimately responsible for determining the success or failure of the project. They may also be in charge of budgetary and other business decisions within the organization.

    b. *Project manager*: The individual responsible for the day-to-day management of the project. This person tracks resources, tasks, and budget in an effort to drive the project towards a successful completion.

    c. *Project team members*: The participants of the project responsible for performing the majority of the tasks making up the project.

3. The project manager will initiate the project process by creating the project site.

4. The project manager will customize the project site to include the SharePoint lists, libraries, and web parts that will help to facilitate the project.

5. The project manager will grant permissions to the site to the other participants of the project. These participants will receive e-mail notifications about the SharePoint site that will serve as a repository for project collaboration.

6. Team members will visit the site and collaborate around the introduction of the service plan. This includes the creation and management of tasks, schedule, documents, contacts, and project metrics. They can also subscribe to SharePoint alerts that will allow them to be notified of changes to information that concerns them.

7. The site will be used to facilitate the collection of data and information important to the organization's decision-making process. Projected costs, expected revenue, and nonmonetary benefits will all be incorporated into the project's decisions.

8. Business sponsors and other stakeholders will be able to access the site and have access to project metrics including project costs and hours spent.

9. Deliverables will be finalized and approved. In this example, the deliverable is the completed service plan.

10. After project completion, the project site will remain available for historical purposes. This will allow future projects to reuse any materials created during this project.

SharePoint Environment Layout

There are several SharePoint components we will configure to allow our environment to support the needs of our service plan creation process.

The layout of the components that we will be using in our project collaboration process example includes the following:

- *Projects area*: This area is provided as part of a default SharePoint portal under the Topics Area. This area is used to group project sites. For our project collaboration example, this area will include a reference to the site for our service plan creation project.

- *Genesis Service Plan Introduction site*: Referenced from the Projects area, this site contains the information being used to manage the project around introducing a new service plan offering for the Genesis line of products our organization sells. It will contain the following components used to facilitate the collaborative efforts of project members as they create the service plan:

  - *Shared Documents*: This document library will be used to store and organize most documents collected and created during the project. This includes both deliverable documents that are ultimately sent to executive stakeholders as well as intermediary documents created during the project to facilitate collaboration.

- *Financial Documents*: This document library will be used to store and organize documents containing sensitive financial information that should only be viewable by project managers and business sponsors. Only the project manager and business sponsors will have access to this library.

- *Announcements*: This announcements list is used to convey important messages to the project team.

- *Contacts*: This contacts list is used to maintain a list of all important project contacts and their contact information. In addition to project team members, this list may include vendors, consultants, and customer contacts.

- *Events*: This events list is used to manage deadlines and milestones for the project.

- *Issues*: This issues list is used to monitor and mitigate issues or potential risks to the successful completion of the project. These issues must be dealt with by the project manager or other individuals to ensure the project progresses on schedule.

- *Links*: This links list will contain references to any related web sites that contain information relevant to the project.

- *Project Metrics*: This custom list contains key metrics for the project, allowing business sponsors an easy way to monitor the progress of the project.

- *Project Details*: This custom list allows project participants to quickly see an overview of the project status and whom to contact for more information.

- *Tasks*: This tasks list will be used to maintain the work items needed to complete the project. This may initially include high-level tasks and grow as the project progresses and additional work is determined. This list will allow users to easily see their tasks as well as letting the project manager monitor the completion of the workload.

- *General Discussion*: This discussion board will be used to facilitate communications among the project team.

Figure 9-1 depicts the layout of these resources.

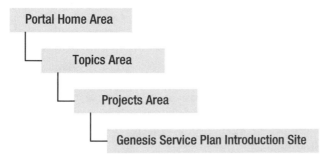

Figure 9-1. *Genesis Service Plan Introduction project collaboration layout*

In order for us to step through the use of our project collaboration site, we must configure the resources described previously within our SharePoint environment. The following steps outline how to configure these resources. For details of the specifics of how to perform any of the described tasks, you can refer to the earlier chapter that discusses the specific component.

Configuring the Projects Area

The Projects area will reference the sites created to manage specific projects. The default layout of the Projects area will support our project collaboration example. Figure 9-2 depicts the desired layout of the Projects area.

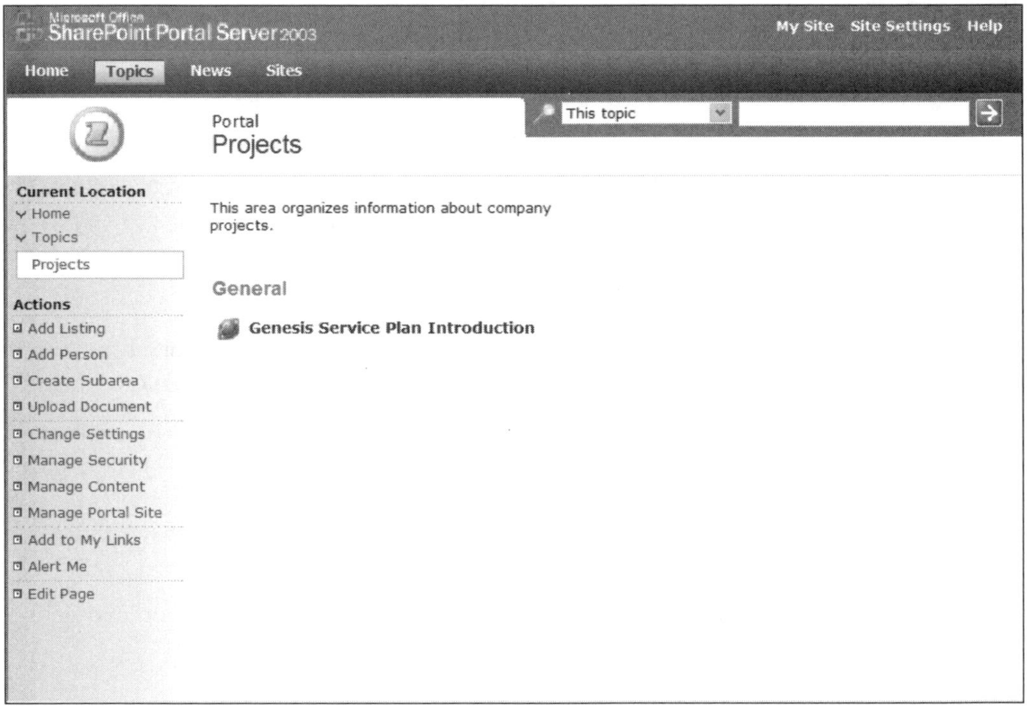

Figure 9-2. *Projects area*

Creating and Configuring the Genesis Service Plan Introduction Site

The Genesis Service Plan Introduction site will contain all resources related to the management and collaboration of the Genesis Service Plan Introduction project. Since the Team Site template available from Windows SharePoint Services provides many of the lists and libraries that will be beneficial for our project site, we will start our site creation by using this template. Figure 9-3 depicts the layout of the Genesis Service Plan Introduction site after we have fully configured the template-based site using the steps in this section.

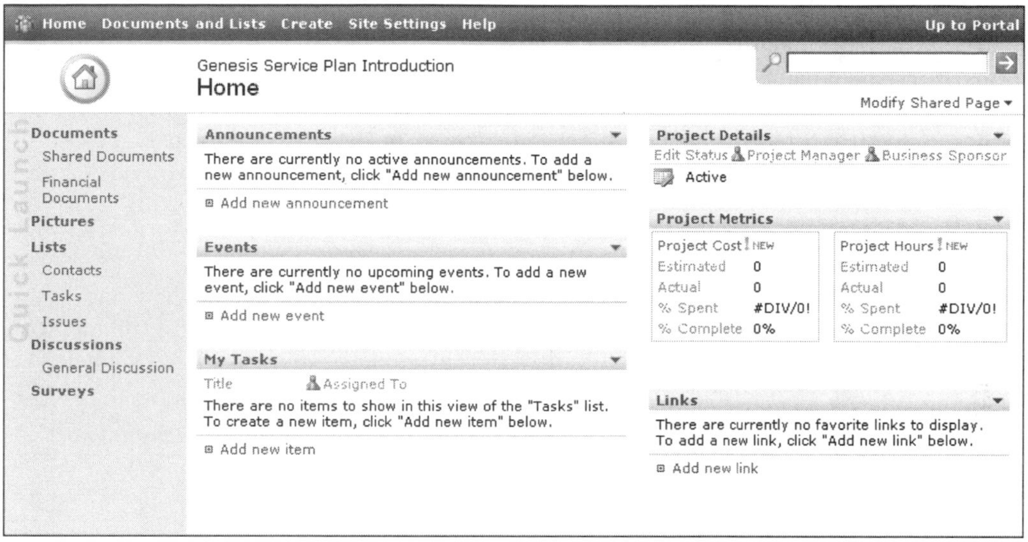

Figure 9-3. *Configured Genesis Service Plan Introduction site*

■**Tip** Saving this site layout as a template, and then having your technical SharePoint administrator install it as a top-level site template, can allow you to quickly create a new project site based on this configuration for every project in the organization.

The following steps describe how to create and configure the Genesis Service Plan Intro-duction site:

1. Create the Genesis Service Plan Introduction site.

   a. Create a listing for the site in the Projects area.

   b. Base the site on the Team Site template in order to provide the project with the fol-lowing lists and libraries:

      • Shared Documents

      • Announcements

      • Contacts

      • Events

      • Links

      • Tasks

      • General Discussion

2. Configure the Shared Documents library.

   a. Enable versioning.

   b. Create a column called Category that is a Choice type and make it required. The choices for the Category column should be set to Deliverable, Project Management, Reference, and Status Report. This column should be saved with no default value.

   c. Update the All Documents view by placing the Category column in Position 3.

   d. Create a new standard view called By Category, make it the default view, and include the following columns: Type, Name (linked to document with edit menu), Modified, Modified By, and Checked Out To. Sort by Name (linked to document with edit menu) and group by Category.

3. Create the Financial Documents library based on the Document Library template. Allow this library to be displayed in the Quick Launch bar.

4. Configure the Financial Documents library.

   a. Enable versioning.

   b. Change the security so that the Administrator site group is the only group with access to the library by removing all other site groups.

   c. Create a column called Category that is a Choice type and make it required. The choices for the Category column should be set to Invoices, Purchase Orders, Financial Reports, and Expense Reports. This column should be saved with no default value. Add this column to the default view.

   d. Update the All Documents view by placing the Category column in Position 3.

5. Create the Issues list based on the Issues list template. Allow this list to be displayed in the Quick Launch bar.

6. Configure the Issues list.

   a. Change the choices for the Category column to Requirements Change, Business Decision, Project Risk. Allow fill-in choices and set the default choice to Other.

   b. Create a column called Resolution that is a Multiple lines of text type. Set the Allow Rich HTML Text option to No.

   c. Create a column called Type that is a Choice type and make it required. The choices for the Type column should be set to Schedule, Financial, Quality, Functionality, and Customer Satisfaction. This column should be saved with no default value. Add this column to the default view.

7. Create the Project Metrics list based on the Custom List template. Do not display the Project Metrics list in the Quick Launch bar.

8. Configure the Project Metrics list.

   a. Rename the Title column to Type.

   b. Create a column called Estimated that is a Number type with a default of 0.

    c. Create a column called Actual that is a Number type with a default of 0.

    d. Create a column called % Spent that is a Calculated type. Specify a formula of =Actual/Estimated and set the return type to Number. Specify 0 decimal places and to show the column as a percentage.

    e. Create a column called % Complete that is a Number type with a default of 0. Specify 0 decimal places and to show the column as a percentage.

    f. Create a new standard view called Boxed, make it the default view, and include the following columns: Type (linked to item with edit menu), Estimated, Actual, % Spent, % Complete. Set the Style to the Boxed option.

9. Enter initial data in the Project Metrics list.

Create two items in the list with the values shown in Table 9-1. These metrics are examples of data that may be relevant for stakeholder visibility. The actual metrics used during a project will depend on the important project information that most interest the business sponsors.

Table 9-1. *Initial Project Metrics Values*

Column	First Item Value	Second Item Value
Type	Project Cost	Project Hours
Estimated	0	0
Actual	0	0
% Complete	0	0

10. Create the Project Details list based on the Custom List template. Do not display the Project Details list in the Quick Launch bar.

11. Configure the Project Details list.

    a. Change the Title column so that it is not required.

    b. Create a column called Status that is a Choice type and make it required. The choices for the Status column should be Active, Completed, Cancelled, and On Hold with a default of Active. Add this column to the default view.

    c. Create a column called Project Manager that is a Lookup type. This column should retrieve options from the User Information list using the Display Name column. Add this column to the default view.

    d. Create a column called Business Sponsor that is a Lookup type. This column should retrieve options from the User Information list using the Display Name column. Add this column to the default view.

    e. Change the order of the list columns so that Title is last.

    f. Remove the Title and Attachments columns from the All Items view. Add the Edit (link to edit item) column as the first column in the All Items view.

12. Enter initial data in the Project Details list.

Create a list item with the values shown in Table 9-2.

Table 9-2. *Initial Project Details Values*

Column	Value
Status	Active
Project Manager	(None)
Business Sponsor	(None)

13. Update the Genesis Service Plan Introduction site page. The goal of the home page should be to communicate project summary and status information to executive sponsors and team members, display content that team members would be accessing most often, and provide important project-related communications.

    a. Remove the Site Image web part.

    b. Place the Project Details list view web part in the Right Zone at the top. Set Toolbar Type to No Toolbar and Selected View to All Items.

    c. Place the Project Metrics list view web part in the Right Zone under the Project Details web part. Set Toolbar Type to No Toolbar and Selected View to Boxed.

    d. Place the Tasks list view web part in the Left Zone under the Events web part. Change the title to My Tasks and set the selected view to the My Tasks view.

    e. Delete the default list item from the Announcements list.

Service Plan Project Process Walk-Through

After creating and configuring the SharePoint environment described previously, we will now describe the project flow that would be followed to create the Product Service Plan. We will discuss how each of the SharePoint components previously mentioned can assist you during the project collaboration process. Each role on the project (Project Manager, Project Team Member, and Business Sponsor) will use the project site differently but combine their efforts to ultimately deliver the service plan to the organization.

Our walk-through of the project collaboration process will include the following preconditions:

- Our organization is a product-based company whose catalog of products includes a line called Genesis.

- At the current time we do not offer a service plan for our Genesis product line, and it has been decided that we should pursue this offering as both a complementary revenue stream and a means of increasing customer satisfaction.

- The executive team has designated one of their members as the business sponsor and primary contact for this initiative. The project manager and project team members have also been identified.

- Project managers and business sponsors have defined the initial schedule and budget for the project.

These steps describe the process followed to develop the Genesis Product Service Plan based on the preceding preconditions:

1. The project manager creates the Genesis Service Plan Introduction site described earlier in this chapter to facilitate the project.

2. The project manager then adds all initial information to the project site.

   a. Add information to the Project Metrics and Project Details lists as described in Tables 9-3 and 9-4. This information must be kept current throughout the project's life cycle to ensure that all stakeholders are effectively aware of the project's state.

   Table 9-3. *Project Metrics Values*

Column	First Item Value	Second Item Value
Type	Project Cost	Project Hours
Estimated	10,000	160
Actual	0	0
% Complete	0	0

   Table 9-4. *Project Details Values*

Column	Value
Status	Active
Project Manager	Rob Jersey
Business Sponsor	Aaron Bates

   b. Add the Project Plan document that was created along with the business sponsor into the Shared Documents library. Specify the Category as Project Management.

   c. Add a link to the Links list that references the corporate web site page containing information on the Genesis product.

3. The project manager next sets the security for the Genesis Service Plan Introduction site and chooses to send the e-mail notification to each user. The project manager then configures the desired access levels for all individuals needing access to this project site including

   a. *Project manager*: Administrator site group

   b. *Project team members*: Contributor site group

   c. *Business sponsor and executive stakeholders*: Reader or Contributor site group depending on their desired involvement. You should also provide these users with access to the Financial Documents library by adding them to the library's security with appropriate permissions.

4. All team members will receive an e-mail notification with a link that they will use to visit the project site. Since external access was configured for the SharePoint environment, team members are able to access the Genesis Service Plan Introduction site from any location that has Internet connectivity.

5. All team members will set up alerts to monitor important changes to information within the site.

   a. Create an alert that notifies you of all changes on the Tasks list and select to be notified immediately.

   b. Create an alert that notifies you of all changes on the Shared Documents library and select to be notified in a daily summary.

   c. Create an alert that notifies when items are added to the Announcements list and select to be notified immediately.

■**Note** There are third-party products available that allow select individuals to set up alerts for others within a site. This would allow the project manager to set up the alerts for all the team members when the site is initially created.

---

6. The project manager, along with contributors, adds tasks to the Tasks list as defined in Table 9-5.

Table 9-5. *Genesis Service Plan Tasks List Values*

Title	Assigned To	Start Date	Due Date
Create initial service plan document.	Project manager	11/01/2005	11/02/2005
Determine services needed to address a service plan for the Genesis product.	Team member	11/03/2005	11/05/2005
Create estimates for number of service plans sold for each of the next 5 years at 3 different price points.	Team member	11/05/2005	11/07/2005
Estimate service plan startup costs and yearly costs for the next 5 years.	Team member	11/05/2005	11/07/2005
Add cost and revenue estimates to the service plan document.	Team member	11/08/2005	11/11/2005
Add soft benefits to service plan document.	Team member	11/10/2005	11/12/2005
Organize Plan review.	Project manager	11/13/2005	11/13/2005
Submit Genesis Service Plan to board.	Business sponsor	11/16/2005	11/16/2005

7. Team members receive notifications that tasks have been added and go to the site to view the new tasks. These team members can be located in separate offices throughout the organization, or even access the site remotely, and still contribute to the same central project repository used by others on the project.

8. The process of creating the Genesis Service Plan will proceed as each participant on the project accomplishes their tasks and collaborates with other individuals.

    a. As tasks are worked on, the user whom the task is assigned to will use the Shared Documents library to store draft documents. This includes a draft document outlining the services and products needed to support the service plan. These documents are categorized using the custom columns created earlier to allow users to more easily find and manage the documents.

■**Note** Real-time communication capabilities can be incorporated into the SharePoint environment by configuring Microsoft Live Communication Server. This would enable the team to ask questions and discuss the process through real-time communication, or chat, using MSN Messenger. This would also add team member presence information to the environment, allowing team members to see the availability of other team members.

---

    b. When tasks are completed, their Status and % Complete information is updated, thereby notifying other participants through the SharePoint alerts.

    c. The project manager will add announcements and events to the appropriate lists during the course of the project, as well as keep the Project Metrics list current to reflect the progress of the project team.

    d. All team members will contribute to the Contacts list in an effort to ensure that all project-related information is maintained in a single repository. Team members will also contribute to the Issues list so that the entire team is able to collaborate on resolutions to potential problems with the project.

    e. During this process, the business sponsor is able to access the site to view the progress of the project via the Project Metrics list on the site's home page. The business sponsor is also able to see the progress of the team by reviewing the draft Genesis Service Plan document.

9. When all estimates have been created and added to the Genesis Service Plan document in the Shared Documents library, the project manager will organize a Plan Review meeting. The result of this meeting will be a finalized version of the plan document. See Chapter 10 for more information on using SharePoint as part of a meeting management solution.

10. The business sponsor then accesses the project site to retrieve and print copies of the Genesis Service Plan document for use in the presentation to the board. During the presentation, the business sponsor could also access the document in the SharePoint site in an effort to show it to the board.

11. Once the board approves the plan, the project manager will update the Status column of the list item in the Project Details list to Completed. The SharePoint site will remain in existence as a repository of information used to create the plan. If similar information is needed for future projects, the site can be easily accessed to reuse existing documents or data.

■**Note** This example uses standard SharePoint components for project collaboration and management. For more enhanced project management capabilities, you can leverage Microsoft Project Server 2003. Project Server 2003 integrates with Windows SharePoint Services in order to provide more advanced enterprise project management capabilities.

Figure 9-4 shows the project site as it would appear during the collaboration process described previously.

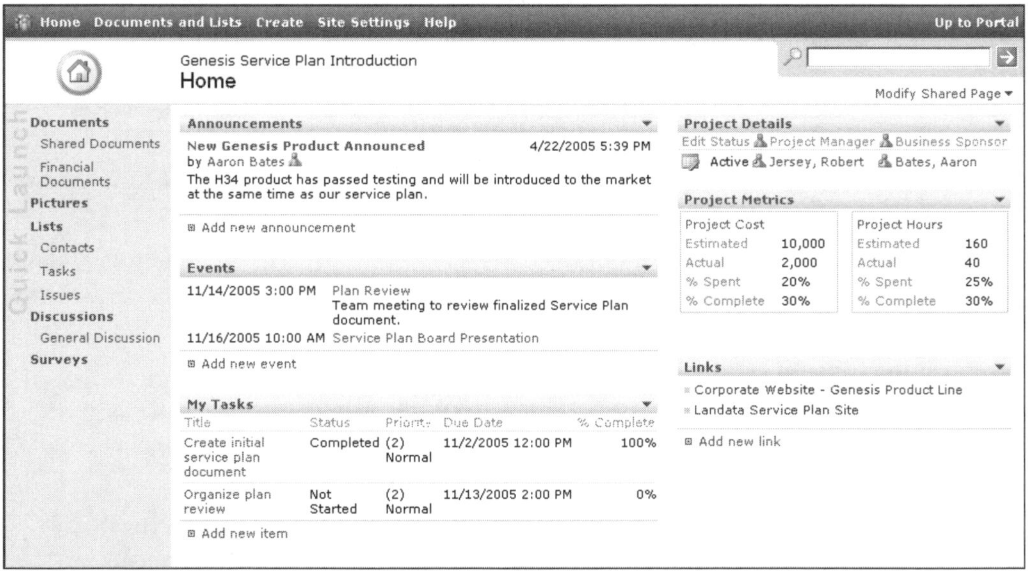

Figure 9-4. *Genesis Service Plan Introduction site*

Benefits of SharePoint Project Collaboration Solutions

There are many benefits that can be gained from introducing SharePoint-based project collaboration solutions into an organization. The benefits that an organization will receive will be dependent on the process and solution introduced.

The following are some of the most common benefits organizations receive from introducing SharePoint project collaboration solutions:

- *Increase collaboration efficiency and information reliability*: Centrally storing project-related materials reduces the amount of time team members spend looking for project information and ensures they are all working with the same documents and data. New team members have a single point of reference for most of their project questions and can more quickly acclimate themselves to an active project. The team members leaving the project do not take all of their knowledge with them, since this information is maintained in the central SharePoint repository. Visibility into projects also allows managers and stakeholders to better gauge the status and overall health of a project. Access to this information via SharePoint sites alleviates the need for project managers to compile and disperse project metrics to business sponsors and executives, freeing up their time to focus on the management of the project effort.

- *Provide project notifications*: As project members are working on a project, it is important to keep these individuals informed of changes that could impact their work. Having the ability for individuals to be notified of key project information changes is important and allows all participants to be kept aware of changes in project status.

- *Allow remote individuals to participate more actively*: In addition to the increased efficiencies a SharePoint project collaboration solution provides to the internal project team, it can provide value by including external individuals like vendors or consultants in the process. Allowing partners or customers to access the project repository and contribute to the information helps to ensure the success of the project for all parties involved. When partners or customers can participate in project collaboration, you reduce potential miscommunications or transition delays and allow these individuals to participate in the project at the same level as those within the organization.

Note External access to your SharePoint site must be configured and managed by your technical SharePoint administrator and network administrator.

- *Improve communication*: Keeping team members informed of decisions, changes, and project status reduces the chances of inefficiencies in the project. The chances of redundant or extraneous effort are diminished when this information is continually available to all interested parties.
- *Use existing productivity tools*: If you already use Microsoft Office to create documents and perform personal productivity tasks, SharePoint technologies allow you to continue to use these tools while expanding their capabilities to include the project and team collaboration capabilities described in this chapter.

Tips for Creating Effective Project Collaboration Solutions

When creating project collaboration solutions, it is important that the solution maps to the project management process and facilitates the successful completion of the project. The following are several points that should be kept in mind when creating project collaboration solutions:

- *Incorporate change management*: New solutions intended to improve processes within an organization require change management in order to succeed. When people are comfortable performing their tasks the current way, they may feel uncomfortable or challenged by a new project collaboration solution. In order to prove successful, a change management plan should be incorporated by providing training and assistance for everyone involved. This process should also include promoting the value of the new approach and identifying how it will benefit those who will be using it. If the change management around a new solution is not properly managed, those involved are likely to resist adopting it, thereby not receiving the potential benefits.

- *Provide managers and stakeholders visibility into the project*: It is extremely important that everyone involved in the project, from the business sponsor to the team members, have access to the information they need when they need it. Allowing executives to access the project materials and be able to review project status information and other key metrics allows these individuals to keep informed. It also ensures that everyone has a shared vision of project objectives, timelines, issues, and status.

- *Ensure remote access is available*: Allowing project team members to contribute to the project regardless of location can reduce the duration of tasks and allow project members to continually be involved in the collaboration processes. In addition to providing access to remote team members, partners or customers can be allowed to participate in the project by directly accessing the project materials.

■ ■ ■

CHAPTER 10

SharePoint Meeting Management Solutions

Another type of solution commonly created using SharePoint is the meeting management solution. Meeting management solutions are used to manage meeting life cycles. A meeting life cycle includes all tasks followed before, during, and after a meeting. The tasks can be grouped into the following categories:

- *Planning for the meeting*: Includes tasks such as setting the meeting time and place, inviting attendees, tracking attendee responses, defining the agenda, and collecting materials that will be used during the meeting.

- *Facilitating the meeting*: Includes tasks such as following the agenda, presenting materials, recording decisions that are made, and tracking action items that are identified.

- *Post-meeting follow-up*: Includes tasks such as managing action items and publishing post-meeting materials, such as meeting minutes.

SharePoint Portal Server and Windows SharePoint Services provide the tools necessary to manage the complete life cycle of a meeting. SharePoint also integrates with other Microsoft Office System products, like Outlook and Live Communications Server, which provide additional meeting management capabilities and are frequently used to support several aspects of the meeting life cycle. While we will not be discussing these other products in detail, we will note areas where they would provide value to the meeting management process.

In this chapter, we will discuss the meeting life cycle and describe how your SharePoint environment can be configured to help manage meetings. We will discuss a sample meeting scenario and step through how a SharePoint-based solution would be configured and used to manage these meetings.

Meeting Management Overview

Meetings occur every day in most organizations. For some meetings attendees sit in the same room, while for others attendees are in different locations and participate via conference call. In many cases, meetings are a combination of these two situations. Some people will be sitting together within the same room, while others are connected from remote locations and participate via conference call.

SharePoint provides capabilities necessary to support all of these types of meetings, allowing for the coordination and management of meetings regardless of attendee locations or schedule types. SharePoint can be used to manage the entire life cycle of a meeting. The meeting life cycle includes the following:

- Planning the meeting

    - Setting the meeting time and place

    - Identifying and notifying attendees

    - Defining the meeting objectives and agenda

    - Creating and collecting materials to be presented and distributed at the meeting

- During the meeting

    - Facilitating the meeting with the goal of following the defined agenda

    - Distributing and discussing materials

    - Making and documenting decisions

    - Identifying and recording action items

    - Confirming identified objectives are met

- After the meeting

    - Distributing follow-up materials

    - Managing the completion of action items

SharePoint capabilities can be used to help manage all of these aspects of a meeting.

Challenges of Meeting Management

Many people spend a significant amount of time in meetings during a normal workweek. The more time people spend in meetings, the less time they have to perform their primary job functions. This can have several negative impacts:

- Staff productivity can be reduced when a significant amount of time is spent in meetings.

- Additional staff may be needed to offset productivity reductions due to meetings.

- Staff may be required to spend more hours at work to handle their primary workload and to attend necessary meetings.

As a result of these concerns, SharePoint provides capabilities necessary to create meeting management solutions that help to optimize the effectiveness of meetings. This can reduce the time meetings require and reduce the number of meetings needed.

Through the deployment of SharePoint document collaboration and project management solutions like those discussed in Chapters 8 and 9, the number of meetings needed for related projects can often be reduced. However, when meetings cannot be avoided, it is important to try to make them as efficient and effective as possible. This will allow for meetings to be as short as possible while confirming they meet all defined objectives. This can also help reduce the number of future meetings required on the same topic.

Many factors can negatively impact the effectiveness and efficiency of meetings. Share-Point meeting management solutions can help address many of these factors including the following:

- *Insufficient meeting preparation*: It is not uncommon for meetings to be held with little to no preparation prior to the meeting. This is frequently the case when meeting objectives and agendas are not documented and distributed to attendees prior to a meeting. The lack of communication of the details around a meeting, specifically the agenda and objectives, results in people going into a meeting unprepared. Without giving attendees time prior to the meeting to review agendas, objectives, and materials and to perform any necessary research on the meeting topics, meetings run significantly longer than necessary. These meetings will also frequently not meet all the identified objectives, which can result in the need for follow-up meetings on the same topic.

- *Insufficient attendee management*: It is often the case that there are some number of key attendees needed in a meeting for the defined meeting objectives to be reached. These might be managers who would make final decisions on the topic or individuals who would be responsible for carrying out a specific task. If these key individuals are unable to attend the meeting due to travel or some other scheduling conflict, the meeting is either rescheduled or multiple meetings are held on the topic. There are also instances where attendance is not monitored, so it is not known prior to the meeting if one or more key people will not be attending. When needed individuals do not attend, time spent by other attendees is wasted.

- *Meeting not remaining focused on the objectives*: When meetings digress onto other topics, meeting time can be unnecessarily spent on discussions that do not relate to the objective of the meeting. Often these discussions are held with people in attendance who do not have involvement in these other topics, wasting their time and impacting the effectiveness of the meeting. The topics to which the meetings digress also often need to be revisited, since all people required for the discussion may not be in the meeting.

- *Attendees not having the same understanding of decisions made*: Even when individuals feel a meeting was effective, it is common for attendees to come away with different understandings of the decisions made. This will result in confusion and can negatively impact work related to these decisions. Also, people not in attendance at the meeting often are only updated on meeting decisions through word of mouth, which can cause additional confusion around decisions made.

- *Follow-up actions are not completed*: Many meetings result in follow-up actions that have to be completed to meet the overall meeting's objectives. When follow-up actions are not properly managed, they will often go undone or will not get completed in the necessary timeframe. Many times follow-up actions are only loosely or informally assigned. Due to this, priorities are not set and due dates are not defined.

Needs for Meeting Management

There are several capabilities that can be introduced using SharePoint to help maximize meeting effectiveness and address the meeting challenges we discussed previously:

- *Coordinating meeting planning*: SharePoint includes tools that will allow meeting planners to define meeting objectives, coordinate the creation of meeting objectives and agendas, collect meeting materials, and track meeting attendance. These tools provide a consistent method of performing these tasks and allow all appropriate individuals to contribute to the development of these resources.

- *Allowing information to be easily disseminated prior to the meeting:* The meeting coordinator is given the ability to easily distribute information to attendees, allowing these attendees to better prepare for the meeting. This can reduce the amount of time spent during the meeting reviewing the materials and allows attendees to more effectively contribute during the meeting.

- *Allowing for easy facilitation of the meeting:* Meeting objectives, agenda, and presentation materials are organized and easily accessible for the meeting. These materials are also accessible to individuals who are participating remotely, allowing all participants regardless of location to have the same level of access to meeting resources. Also, during the meeting, identified action items and decisions that are made can be documented and tracked.

- *Allowing post-meeting materials to be easily distributed*: After a meeting, any documents, such as meeting minutes, created as a result of the meeting can be distributed. Also, any action items identified during the meeting can be managed to ensure that they are completed within the required timeframe.

SharePoint Meeting Management Solutions

We can leverage the SharePoint Portal Server and Windows SharePoint Services capabilities that we discussed in Chapters 2 through 7 to create effective meeting management solutions that support the entire meeting life cycle.

We will create and demonstrate a meeting management solution. In our example, we will be creating a meeting workspace that will be used to facilitate quarterly business review meetings. We will assume these review meetings are held quarterly and our organization has a goal to reduce the time these meetings require.

In our example, we will describe the setup and structure of the meeting management solution that supports our situation. We will then step through the typical use of the solution to manage a sample quarterly business review meeting.

■Note The solution described in this chapter leverages only those capabilities native to SharePoint. There are many Microsoft and third-party tools that can be added to a SharePoint environment to extend the meeting management capabilities provided. We will make note of some of the places where additional solutions can be introduced to enhance the meeting management process.

Quarterly Business Review Meeting Requirements

In our meeting management example, we will assume that there is a team of people who meet quarterly to review the company's key initiatives and financial status information. These meetings are also used to set and discuss overall organizational goals and to make strategic corporate decisions.

We will also assume that our organization has several offices around the world and that the meeting attendees are located across these offices. Our goal is to provide a solution that will allow us to increase the efficiency of these meetings in order to reduce their length and to help ensure all meeting objectives are met.

To meet these goals, we must allow for the following:

- People from any location must be able to participate in the meetings and have access to the information presented at the meetings.

- Meeting facilitators must be able to collect and organize meeting objectives, agendas, and materials to be presented and allow the participants to review these materials prior to the meeting.

- During a meeting, attendees must have access to all materials presented regardless of their location, and meeting facilitators must be able to track decisions reached and action items identified.

- After a meeting, assigned action items must be managed and post-meeting materials must be distributed.

Quarterly Business Review Meeting Process Definition

Our meeting management sample solution will leverage many of the SharePoint capabilities that we discussed in Chapters 2 through 7. The following steps describe the high-level flow of events that will make up our meeting management process:

1. The time comes to begin planning for the next quarterly business review meeting.

2. The meeting participants are identified and include the following:

    a. *Meeting coordinator*: The person responsible for booking the meeting.

    b. *Meeting facilitators*: Individuals who will define meeting objectives and agendas and create needed meeting materials. They will also be running the meeting and presenting during the meeting.

    c. *Meeting attendees*: All individuals who will be attending the meeting. These individuals may be attending locally or from remote locations.

3. The meeting coordinator will initiate the meeting planning process by creating the meeting workspace and populating initial details, such as the time, the location, and the attendee list.

4. The meeting facilitators will collect the meeting agenda, objectives, and materials to be distributed and presented during the meeting.

5. The meeting facilitators will inform attendees of the availability of meeting materials with sufficient time for the attendees to review these materials and prepare for the meeting.

6. After all information has been posted to the meeting workspace, attendees will review this information to prepare for the meeting. This preparation may include the creation of discussions related to the meeting topics and research around the meeting topics.

7. At the start of the meeting, attendees who are local to the meeting location will go to this location. Attendees at remote locations will dial into a conference number to verbally participate and will access the meeting workspace to view items being presented.

8. During the meeting, the facilitators will present the items available in the meeting workspace, keeping the meeting focused on the defined objectives and agenda. Individuals participating in the meeting from remote locations will access these same materials.

9. As decisions are made and action items are identified during the meeting, the facilitators will track these items in the meeting workspace.

10. After the meeting, the coordinator will facilitate the collection of any post-meeting materials, such as the meeting minutes.

11. The meeting coordinator will manage the completion of the action items that were identified during the meeting. The progress of these action items will be tracked within the meeting workspace.

SharePoint Environment Layout

There are several SharePoint components we will configure to allow our environment to support the needs of our meeting management process. In order to help define the configuration of these components, we will be making the following assumptions about the SharePoint environment:

- You have a SharePoint environment that includes both SharePoint Portal Server and Windows SharePoint Services.

- A technical administrator has deployed a subsite viewer web part for use within your SharePoint environment. This will be the only web part we will refer to that is not provided in a default SharePoint deployment. While it is not required to have this web part to navigate through a WSS site hierarchy, having it provides a significant usability enhancement to SharePoint. Several subsite viewer web parts are available and freely downloadable. If you are unsure where to go to obtain a subsite viewer web part, you can refer to this book's web site (http://www.sharepointextras.com) for more information.

The layout of the components that we will be using in our meeting management process example includes the following:

- *Management area*: This area is located under the Topics area and will reference resources used by the company's senior management team. For our example, this area will include a reference to the Business Planning site.

- *Business Planning site*: Referenced from the Management area, this site contains resources needed by the business planning team to track and manage corporate objectives. Examples of information contained here would be corporate objective statistics and high-level corporate analytics.

- *Quarterly Business Review Meeting Template workspace*: Located within the Business Planning site, this workspace will act as the template from which all project status meeting workspaces will be created. This workspace will contain all resources necessary to support our quarterly business planning process. In our example, this site will contain the following components:

  - *Document Library*: This document library is used to store and organize materials being collected for the meeting. It will also contain any materials that would be distributed after the meeting.

  - *Action Items*: This task list is used to track action items identified during the meeting. It is also used after the meeting to track the progress of these actions to confirm that they are completed within the necessary timeframe.

  - *Agenda*: This agenda list contains all of the agenda items that will be discussed during the meeting.

  - *Attendees*: This attendees list contains the list of individuals who were invited to the meeting and their attendance status.

  - *Decisions*: This decisions list contains a record of the decisions that were made at the meeting.

  - *General Details*: This custom list includes the basic information about the meeting.

  - *Links*: This links list will contain references to any web sites needed for reference during the meeting or in preparation for the meeting.

  - *Objectives*: This objectives list contains the goals or desired outcomes of the meeting.

  - *General Discussion*: This discussion board will be used to manage communications between meeting attendees prior to the meeting.

Figure 10-1 depicts the layout of these resources.

Figure 10-1. *Quarterly Business Review Meeting Management layout*

In order for us to step through the use of our meeting workspace, we must configure the listed resources within our SharePoint environment. The steps in the upcoming text outline how to configure these resources. For details around the specifics of how to perform any of the described tasks, you can refer to the chapter that discusses the specific component.

Creating and Configuring the Management Area

The Management area will reference the resources available to support the organization's senior management team. Figure 10-2 depicts the desired layout of the Management area.

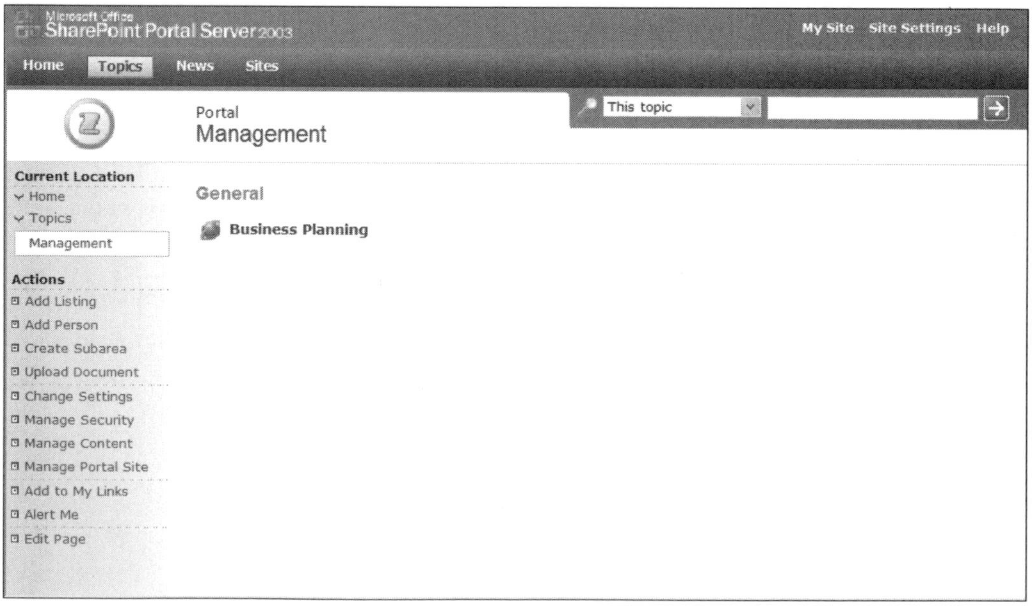

Figure 10-2. *Management area*

The following steps define how to create and configure the Management area:

1. Create the Management area, placing it under the Topics area.

2. Update the Management area by removing the Area Detail web part.

Creating and Configuring the Business Planning Site

The Business Planning site will contain all resources related to supporting senior business planning. For the purposes of our meeting management example, we will only discuss creating the resources necessary for managing the quarterly business review meetings. We will not discuss the creation of other resources that would be located in this site, such as strategic business goals or corporate analytics. Figure 10-3 depicts the layout of the Business Planning site.

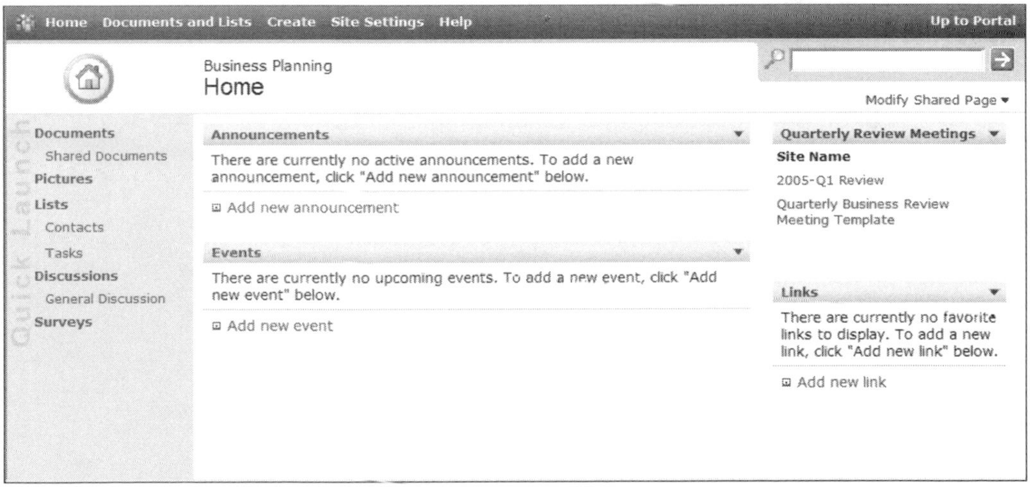

Figure 10-3. *Business Planning site*

The following steps describe how to create and configure the Business Planning site:

1. Create the Business Planning site.

   a. Create a listing for the site in the Management area.

   b. Base the site on the Team Site template.

2. Set the security for the Business Planning site. Configure the desired access levels for all individuals needing access to this site and the meeting workspace sites below it.

3. Update the Business Planning site page.

   a. Delete the Site Image web part.

   b. Place the subsite viewer web part in the Right Zone above the Links web part and make the title read Quarterly Review Meetings.

■Note This assumes that a SharePoint technical administrator has added a subsite viewer web part to the SharePoint environment. As we mentioned earlier, several subsite viewer web parts are available that can be freely downloaded.

Creating and Configuring the Quarterly Business Review Meeting Template Workspace

The Quarterly Business Review Meeting Template workspace will be used as the template for creating business review meeting workspaces. Figure 10-4 depicts the desired layout of the Home page of the Quarterly Business Review Meeting Template workspace.

Figure 10-4. *Home page of the Quarterly Business Review Meeting Template workspace*

Figure 10-5 depicts the desired layout of the Action Items page of the Quarterly Business Review Meeting Template workspace.

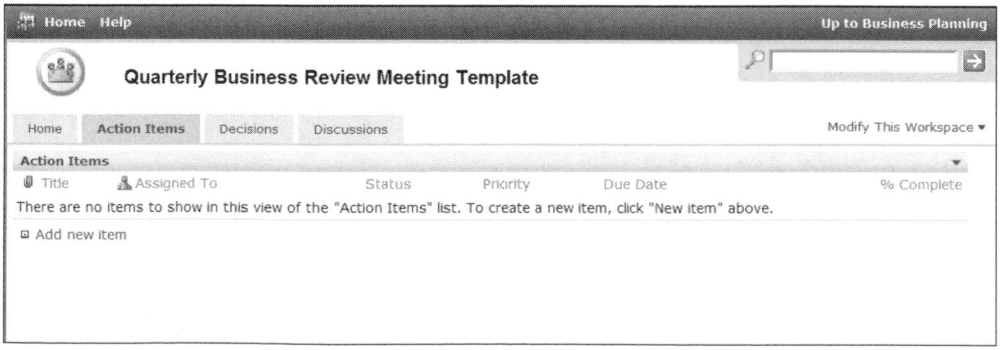

Figure 10-5. *Action Items page of the Quarterly Business Review Meeting Template workspace*

Figure 10-6 depicts the desired layout of the Decisions page of the Quarterly Business Review Meeting Template workspace.

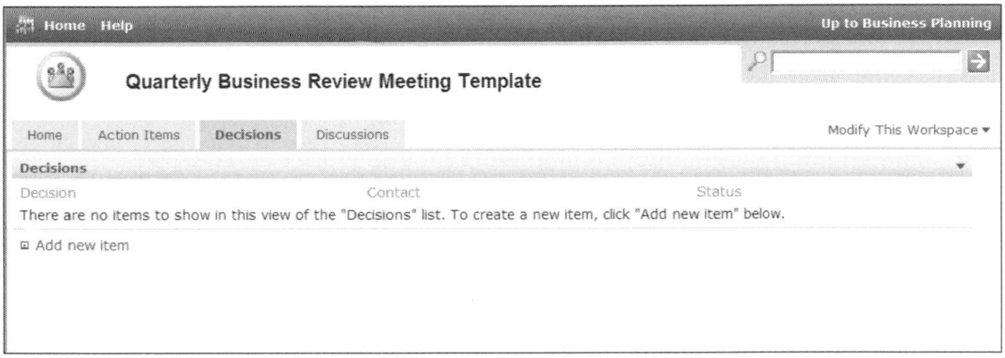

Figure 10-6. *Decisions page of the Quarterly Business Review Meeting Template workspace*

Figure 10-7 depicts the desired layout of the Discussions page of the Quarterly Business Review Meeting Template workspace.

Figure 10-7. *Discussions page of the Quarterly Business Review Meeting Template workspace*

The following steps describe how to create and configure the Quarterly Business Review Meeting Template workspace:

1. Create the Quarterly Business Review Meeting Template workspace.

    a. Create the workspace under the Business Planning site.

    b. Base the site on the Multipage Meeting Workspace template.

2. While on the Home page, create the Document Library based on the Document Library template.

3. Configure the Document Library.

    a. Create a column called Category that is a Choice type and make it required. The choices for the Category column should be set to Handouts, Meeting Minutes, Presentations, and References. This column should be saved with no default value.

    b. Update the All Documents view by placing the Category column in Position 3.

    c. Create a new view called By Category, make it the default view, and include the following columns: Type, Name (linked to document with edit menu), Modified, Modified By, and Checked Out To. Sort by Name (linked to document with edit menu) and group by Category.

4. While on the Home page, create the Links list based on the Links list template.

5. While on the Home page, create the General Details list based on the Custom list template.

6. Configure the General Details list.

    a. Rename the Title column to Coordinator.

    b. Create a column called Facilitators that is a Multiple lines of text type. Set the Allow Rich HTML Text option to No.

    c. Create a column called Dial-In Number that is a Single line of text type.

    d. Update the All Items view so that it displays Edit (link to edit item), Coordinator, Facilitators, and Dial-In Number. Select to sort by Title.

7. Organize the items on the Home page.

    a. Place the General Details list web part in the Left Zone above the Objectives web part. Choose to display the All Items view and use the No Toolbar option.

    b. Place the Document Library web part in the Right Zone below the Agenda web part. Choose to display the By Category view and use the Full Toolbar.

    c. Place the Links list web part in the Right Zone below the Document Library web part.

8. Rename Page 1 to Action Items.

9. While on the Action Items page, create the Action Items list based on the Task list type.

10. Place the Action Items list web part in the Left Zone on the Action Items page. Choose to display the All Tasks view.

11. Rename Page 2 to Decisions.

12. While on the Decisions page, create the Decisions list based on the Decisions list type.

13. Place the Decisions list web part in the Left Zone on the Decisions page.

14. Create a new page called Discussions.

15. While on the Discussions page, create the General Discussion discussion board based on the General Discussion type.

16. Place the General Discussion web part in the Left Zone on the Discussions page. Update the web part properties so that the Threaded view is displayed.

17. Save the Quarterly Business Review Meeting Template workspace as a site template.

    a. Set the file name to QuarterlyReviewMeetingTemplate.

    b. Set the template title to Quarterly Business Review Meeting Workspace Template.

The resources needed for the Meeting Management example are now configured.

Quarterly Business Review Meeting Walk-Through

Now that we have configured the meeting management resources, we can discuss the steps that will be followed to manage a quarterly business review meeting. During this discussion, we will describe how the resources that you configured are used to support our meeting management process.

When we walk through the quarterly business review meeting process, we will assume that we have a business review meeting every quarter and a goal is to reduce the time that this meeting requires while confirming all meeting objectives are met.

The following steps describe the process that we will follow to manage the quarterly business review meeting:

1. The meeting coordinator creates a new workspace for the meeting.

    a. Create a new workspace called 2005-Q1 Review under the Business Planning site. This can be done using Microsoft Outlook 2003 by creating a new Outlook meeting request and leveraging the Outlook workspace creation options discussed in Chapter 3. It could also be done through the normal site creation process from within the Business Planning site.

    b. Base the new workspace on the Quarterly Business Review Meeting Workspace template that we created earlier in this chapter.

■**Note** We name the site based on the date of the meeting to make the meetings easy to identify and locate. We use the year—quarter format since most subsite viewer components list sites in alphabetical order. This will list the meeting sites in the appropriate date order, making them easier to locate.

---

2. The meeting coordinator will add all initial information to the 2005-Q1 meeting workspace.

    a. Create a new entry in the General Details list that includes the information for the meeting. Table 10-1 shows the values to set for each column in the General Details list.

    Table 10-1. *General Details List Values*

Column	Value
Coordinator	Cherry Tun-Smith
Facilitators	Seth Bates and Tony Smith
Dial-In Number	800-555-1212

    b. Add meeting objectives to the Objectives list. Table 10-2 lists the objectives to add to the Objectives list.

Table 10-2. *Objectives List*

Objective
Financial review of quarter.
Review effectiveness of current product marketing approach.
Evaluate proposed partnership with Kurbel Corporation.

3. The coordinator and facilitators will configure alerts to monitor important changes to information within the site.

    a. Create an alert that notifies you of all changes to the Objectives list and select to be notified daily.

    b. Create an alert that notifies you of all changes to the Agenda list and select to be notified daily.

    c. Create an alert that notifies you of all changes to Document Library items and select to be notified daily.

    d. Create an alert that notifies you of all items added to the General Discussions list and select to be notified daily.

    e. Each team member should configure these four alerts for themselves.

■**Note** There are third-party products available that allow identified individuals to configure alerts for others within a site. This would allow the coordinator to set up the alerts for the facilitators.

---

4. Meeting facilitators will add agenda items to the meeting workspace. Table 10-3 lists the agenda items that should be added.

Table 10-3. *Agenda List*

Subject	Owner	Time
Review Q1 2005 Financials.	Tony Smith	15 minutes
Review Effectiveness of Current Product Marketing.	Tony Smith	15 minutes
Review Kurbel Partnership Objectives and Proposed Plan.	Seth Bates	15 minutes
Determine if Kurbel Partnership should be approved.	Seth Bates	30 minutes

5. The facilitators add documents to the workspace that will be used during the meeting. Table 10-4 lists the documents that should be added.

Table 10-4. *Documents to Be Added*

Document Name	Document Type	Category Value
Q1 2005 Financials	Microsoft Excel	Presentations
Product Marketing Review	Microsoft PowerPoint	Presentations
Kurbel Partnership Plan	Microsoft Word	Reference
Kurbel Partnership Financial Projections	Microsoft Excel	Reference

6. A facilitator will review agenda items added by another facilitator and then create a discussion in the General Discussion list on the Discussion tab with a subject of "Proposed Meeting Topic." The body of the discussion should state that the facilitator would like to propose the addition of a meeting topic to discuss the impact of the recent bankruptcy of our distribution partner.

7. The other facilitator will receive a notification of the new discussion and respond indicating agreement to the addition to the agenda. The facilitator will then update the agenda items to reflect the new item. The item will be added to the bottom of agenda and have a subject of Discuss Distribution Partner Bankruptcy Impact with an owner of Tony Smith and a time of 30 minutes.

8. The meeting organizer will send out a notice to meeting attendees stating that the meeting materials are available.

9. Meeting attendees will visit the meeting workspace prior to the meeting to review the materials available for the upcoming meeting.

10. On the day of the meeting, facilitators will present the information in the meeting workspace to the attendees.

11. Remote attendees will connect to the dial-in number for the meeting and connect to the meeting workspace to access the materials being discussed.

■**Note** Conferencing solutions are available that would allow the remote attendees to connect to the facilitator's session so that they can access the exact instances of items that the facilitators are working with.

Live Communications Server can be used during the meeting to allow for sidebar discussions to occur during the meeting that do not disrupt the meeting. This chat capability allows for the sidebars to be held between any two attendees, regardless of location.

---

12. As decisions are made during the meeting, they will be noted in the Decisions list. Also as action items are identified, they will be noted in the Action Items list. Table 10-5 lists the decisions to add to the Decisions list. Table 10-6 lists the action items to add to the Action Items list.

Table 10-5. *Decisions to Be Added*

Decision	Contact	Status
Reevaluate marketing approach in 6 months.	Tony Smith	Final
Accept the Kurbel partnership assuming contract is acceptable to legal.	Seth Bates	Pending Approval
Current distribution partnership will be ended and a new partner must be identified.	Tony Smith	Final

Table 10-6. *Action Items to Be Added*

Title	Priority	Assigned To	Description	Due Date
Review and finalize Kurbel partnership agreement.	Normal	Seth Bates	Review agreement and determine if acceptable. Make any necessary updates.	5/20/2005
Locate new partner replace current to distribution partner.	Normal	Tony Smith	Identify new partner that can replace our current distribution partner.	6/10/2005
Create Meeting Minutes	Normal	Cherry Tun-Smith	Create Meeting Minutes for this meeting and post on site.	4/16/2005

13. After the meeting, the coordinator will add the meeting minutes to the workspace.

   a. Add a document to Document Library called Meeting Minutes and set the category to Meeting Minutes.

   b. Set the Create Meeting Minutes action item status to Completed.

14. As the action items are completed, the status of the associated action item will be updated by the owner of the task.

Figure 10-8 shows the final 2005-Q1 Review meeting workspace Home page.

Figure 10-8. *2005-Q1 Review meeting workspace Home page*

Figure 10-9 shows the final 2005-Q1 Review meeting workspace Action Items page.

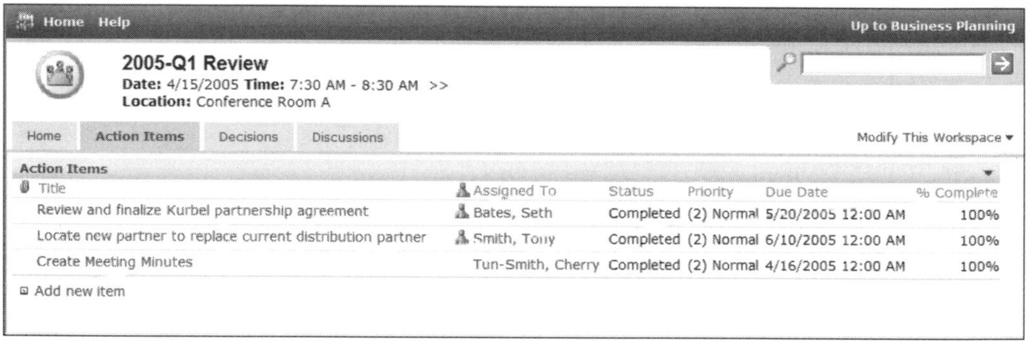

Figure 10-9. *2005-Q1 Review meeting workspace Action Items page*

Figure 10-10 shows the final 2005-Q1 Review meeting workspace Decisions page.

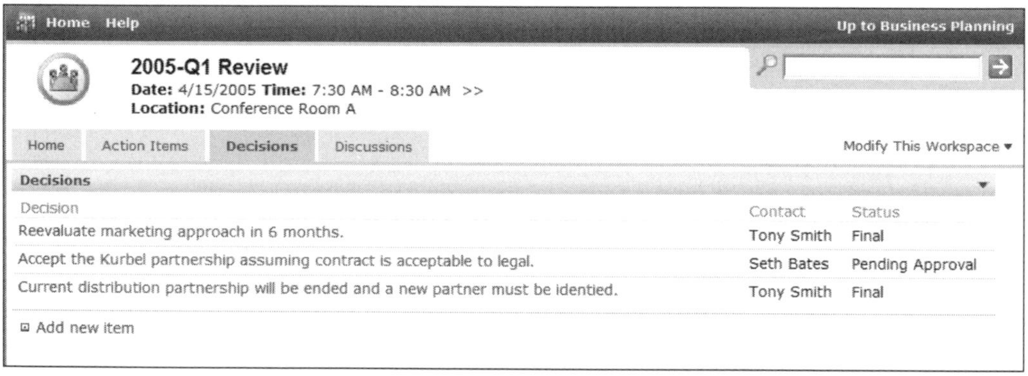

Figure 10-10. *2005-Q1 Review meeting workspace Decisions page*

Figure 10-11 shows the final 2005-Q1 Review meeting workspace Discussions page.

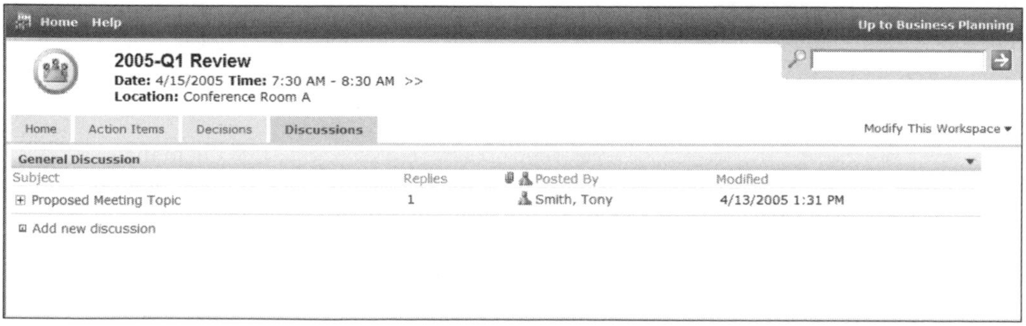

Figure 10-11. *2005-Q1 Review meeting workspace Discussions page*

Benefits of SharePoint Meeting Management Solutions

There are many benefits that can be realized by creating SharePoint-based meeting management solutions. The specific benefits that your organization will receive will vary based on the goals of the meeting workspaces created and how well these workspaces integrate into the process they are supporting.

The following are some of the most common benefits organizations receive from creating SharePoint meeting management solutions:

- *Make meetings more effective*: Using a SharePoint meeting management workspace that integrates with the company's meeting processes allows for better organization of information. All attendees can visit the workspace prior to the meeting to review materials and prepare for the meeting. This allows them to make sure that they have all the information and materials necessary to effectively participate in the meeting. Also, during a meeting, the workspace is used to track progress against the agenda and objectives and is used to track action items and decisions made during the meeting. This allows the facilitators to more easily keep the meeting focused on the appropriate topics and make sure that the meeting satisfies the identified objectives.

- *Reduce the number of meetings*: Reducing the number of meetings needed on a topic is done by making meetings more effective, as we discussed in the previous paragraph. This allows for more to be accomplished in a shorter period of time, which reduces the need for additional meetings on the same topic. Also, by more easily allowing remote individuals to participate in meetings, meetings can be held that include attendees participating regardless of location.

- *Manage action items after a meeting*: Using the SharePoint meeting workspace can allow for action items identified during the meeting to be easily documented as they are identified. Also, after the meeting, these action items can then be tracked and managed through the workspace to make sure they are completed within the allotted time.

Tips for Creating Effective Meeting Management Solutions

When creating meeting management solutions, as with any other solution, it is important that the solution meets the business needs and provides a significant perceived value to the process it is supporting. The following are several points that should be kept in mind when creating meeting management solutions:

- *Manage the introductions of the solutions*: The introduction of meeting management solutions requires change management. These solutions introduce a change to the way people work together. This change must be properly managed for it to be successful, since the methods for managing meetings are often engrained into the culture of an organization. Given this, introducing meeting management solutions requires that this culture change. If the change management aspects are not managed, it is very likely people will not adopt the new meeting management process. The end result would be that no benefits would be realized within the organization.

- *Include all of the necessary resources to properly manage the meeting:* The meeting management solution must include elements that address all aspects of the meeting management process. This includes all processes needed to manage pre-meeting tasks, the resources needed during the meeting, and resources needed to track action items and post-meeting materials. This will help with the adoption of the new meeting management process and ensure that the process meets its full potential.

- *Verify remote attendees have an adequate level of access:* One of the best ways to increase the efficiency of meetings is to provide remote attendees the same level of participation in the meeting as people participating locally. This requires verifying remote participation is properly designed and configured.

■ ■ ■

CHAPTER 11

SharePoint Information Center Solutions

Another common type of solution provided through SharePoint is the Information Center solution. Information Centers are places where resources are organized and made available to other groups. Traditional intranets and extranets are examples of Information Centers. Share-Point provides many features that can make managing Information Centers and the materials contained in them much easier than using traditional intranet or extranet approaches.

In this chapter, we discuss Information Centers and describe how a SharePoint environment can be configured to create effective Information Center solutions. Figure 10-5 depicts the desired layout of the Action Items page of the Quarterly Business Review Meeting Template workspace.

a sample Information Center solution and describe the steps to follow to configure, manage, and access materials in the Information Center.

Information Center Overview

There are many situations in which a group of people manages materials for use by other groups. These information managers will be responsible for the creation and management of materials and making these materials available to the information consumers who need them. Some examples of this type of information sharing include the following:

- Human resources intranet sites, in which a company's HR group needs to provide information such as forms, benefit details, and policy and procedure information to employees of the organization.

- Customer portals, in which an organization makes information available to their clients. This information may include client statements, client forms, and general reference or marketing materials.

- Sales portals, in which resources needed by sales representatives will be made available. Information placed here may include proposal templates, available reference stories, and sales toolkits.

- Corporate news centers, in which an organization will place information about key events that occur within the company or external events that impact the company. Some examples of corporate news are major industry events, the acquisition of new customers, the introduction of new product lines, and announcements about employee birthdays or childbirths.

These are just a few examples of Information Center solutions. Many different methods are used to manage these information-sharing needs, including the following:

- Publishing materials in a web-based platform such as a company intranet or extranet

- Placing materials in common file shares such as shared network drives or Exchange public folders

- Pushing out materials via e-mail as they are made available

Each of these methods presents its own set of benefits and drawbacks. Publishing the materials to a web site makes these items much more accessible from remote locations, but it often requires assistance from the IT group to publish the items, and notification of changes to information are typically handled manually. Placing the materials in a common file share can be done without the need of IT assistance, but these shares are not always available remotely and lack the polished presentation you can have with a web-based solution. Pushing out materials via e-mail does address the notification issue, but results in the management of the materials being owned by the information consumers instead of information managers. This can result in version confusion and misplaced information needing to be re-sent based on individual requests.

Challenges of Information Centers

Organizations that provide solutions through which information is shared between various departments and groups can face several challenges that make these solutions ineffective. Some of the common challenges that creating Information Center solutions through Share-Point can address include the following:

- *Reliance on IT to publish information*: Many organizations have adopted the use of web-based solutions, like intranets and extranets, to publish information out to the organization. One common example of this is human resources sites. These sites focus on providing benefits information, forms, and policy details to employees. These web-based solutions often require the IT department to publish the materials to the intranet or extranet. As a result, IT resources spend a significant portion of time managing the publishing process of materials owned by other groups. In this situation, instead of the priority for publishing items being based on the needs of the information owner, the priority must be set based on its relative priority to other information being published by the IT group and other IT responsibilities. The result is that information is not made available as quickly as it could be, and materials are not always published within the desired timeframe of the information owner.

- *Keeping information current*: Many organizations find it difficult to keep published information current. In many cases, a significant effort is taken to initially build an information-sharing solution. However, once the initial setup is complete and focus is shifted to other initiatives, materials are not properly managed and quickly become outdated. As a result, people will not rely on this information and will instead contact the information owners directly to get materials in order to ensure that they have the most current information. This negatively impacts the time of the information owner since that person needs to service all of these individual information requests, and it will negatively impact the time of the information consumer since requesting the information will take longer than if the person could gain access to the materials on their own.

- *Servicing requests for information*: Organizations that do not have solutions to publish materials or that have ineffective solutions have to rely on information owners to manually distribute information as information consumers request it. Servicing individual information requests can require a significant time investment. It will also often result in delays before information consumers receive the materials that they need.

- *Finding information*: As a growing number of groups within an organization make information available, it becomes increasingly difficult for information consumers to locate all materials related to a specific topic or requirement. This will result in a significant amount of time being spent by information consumers trying to locate needed materials. It also often results in information being overlooked, causing delays or redundant efforts.

- *Unwanted notifications*: In many situations, information owners want to notify consumers when new information is made available or existing materials are updated. The challenge they have is knowing which consumers are interested in the information. In order to make sure all interested consumers are notified, the information owners often send an e-mail notification to all consumers. This can result in individuals receiving a large number of these types of notifications, many of which are not important to them. The result is an internal "spam" situation where time is spent sifting through unwanted information and where it is easy to miss a notification that is important to the individual among all the others that are not.

Needs for Information Centers

The primary goal of Information Centers is to make information easily available to information consumers. There are several common needs that SharePoint Information Centers can fulfill to help address the preceding challenges and meet this goal:

- *Allow information owners to publish and update their own information*: The groups that own information are given the ability to manage the publishing of their materials. This reduces their reliance on the IT group to update the information and allows information owners to set their own priorities, schedules, and processes for managing and publishing materials. The tools for publishing the information are easy to use, requiring only a minimal amount of training without a significant amount of technical expertise.

- *Provide subscription-based notifications:* Information consumers are given the ability to identify the types of materials that are important to them and are able to configure subscriptions that allow them to be notified of changes to these materials.

- *Allow for simple information retrieval:* Information consumers are able to easily locate needed materials. Navigating through information is intuitive and can be mapped to the way people work. Also, searching capabilities are needed that allow people to easily find information related to specific topics or needs.

- *Allow for the introduction of new resources based on expanding needs*: When Information Center solutions are successful, they will continue to grow over time to support new information-sharing needs. Also, as organizations grow and the way people work with the information changes, the structure of these resources need to change to meet the updated needs.

SharePoint Information Center Solutions

We can leverage the components discussed in Chapters 2 through 7 to create Information Center solutions. These solutions allow information owners to manage and publish materials that will be used by information consumers who need these materials. We will create an Information Center to manage human resources materials, and we will discuss how individuals throughout an organization would access these resources.

HR Information Center Requirements

In our HR Information Center, we will be publishing materials the human resources group makes available to employees of the company. These materials will include required forms; information about company benefits, policy, and procedure resources; and new hire orientation materials.

We will assume that the information being provided is accessible by all employees within the organization. In making this information available, our organization wishes to meet the following goals:

- The Human Resources department must be able to manage their own resources.

- People within the organization need the ability to subscribe to specific information, allowing them to be notified of changes to this information.

- The resources in the HR Information Center must be available to all employees regardless of their location.

- Materials in the HR Information Center must be easy to locate. This includes being available through the organization's enterprise-searching capabilities and being easily browsed.

HR Information Center Environment Layout

There are several SharePoint components we will configure for our Information Center example. The layout of the components in our HR Information Center includes the following:

- *Teams area*: This area will be located under the Topics area. It will be used to group our team-based resources. This includes the Information Centers for departments and other teams within the organization, such as committees or other cross-functional groups. For the purpose of our example, this area will contain a reference to our HR Information Center site.

- *Human Resources site*: Referenced from the Teams area, this site is the entry point into our HR Information Center. This site will contain all of the materials, services, and subsites needed to support Human Resource's information-sharing needs. In our example, the Human Resources site will contain the following components:

- *Announcements*: This announcements list will contain any human resources announcements related to materials in the HR Information Center. This would include announcements about updated information or other noteworthy changes to the site.

- *Events*: This events list will contain information about upcoming human resources events such as hosted seminars or form entry deadlines.

- *Links*: This links list is used to reference external human resources–related sites such as retirement plan provider and medical insurance provider sites.

- *Service Provider Contacts*: This contacts list provides the contact details for human resources–related services such as medical insurance or retirement planning management contacts.

- *Benefits site*: This subsite of the Human Resources site will contain resources related to employee benefits. In our example, this site will contain the following components:

  - *Content Editor web part*: The Content Editor web part will be used to create HTML content that provides a summary of benefit information and any corporate disclaimers around this information.

  - *Benefits*: This document library contains documents detailing company benefit information.

- *Forms site*: Located under the Human Resources site, this subsite will contain all forms that the employees need. This would include medical forms, dental forms, vacation request forms, and so on. In our example, this site will contain a Forms document library that contains these materials.

- *New Hire Orientation site*: Located under the Human Resources site, this subsite will contain resources needed by new employees. In our example, this site will contain the following components:

  - *Shared Documents*: This document library will contain orientation materials for new hires such as general overview presentations, instructions on how to set up the telephone greetings, and retirement plan initial setup details.

  - *Links*: This links list will contain references to resources, forms, policies, and benefits information located in other sites that are important for new employees to review.

- *Policies and Procedures site*: Located under the Human Resources site, this subsite will contain information related to corporate policies and procedures. In our example, this site will contain the following components:

  - *Content Editor web part*: This web part will be used to provide HTML content containing the general corporate policy and procedure statement.

  - *Policies and Procedures*: This document library will contain the organization's policies and procedures.

Figure 11-1 depicts the layout of the HR Information Center resources.

Figure 11-1. *HR Information Center resources layout*

The following steps define how to configure the listed resources. For additional details on configuring specific types of components, you can refer to the chapter that discusses the component.

Creating and Configuring the Teams Area

The Teams area will contain references to Information Centers for the various departments and groups within an organization. Figure 11-2 depicts the desired layout of the Teams area.

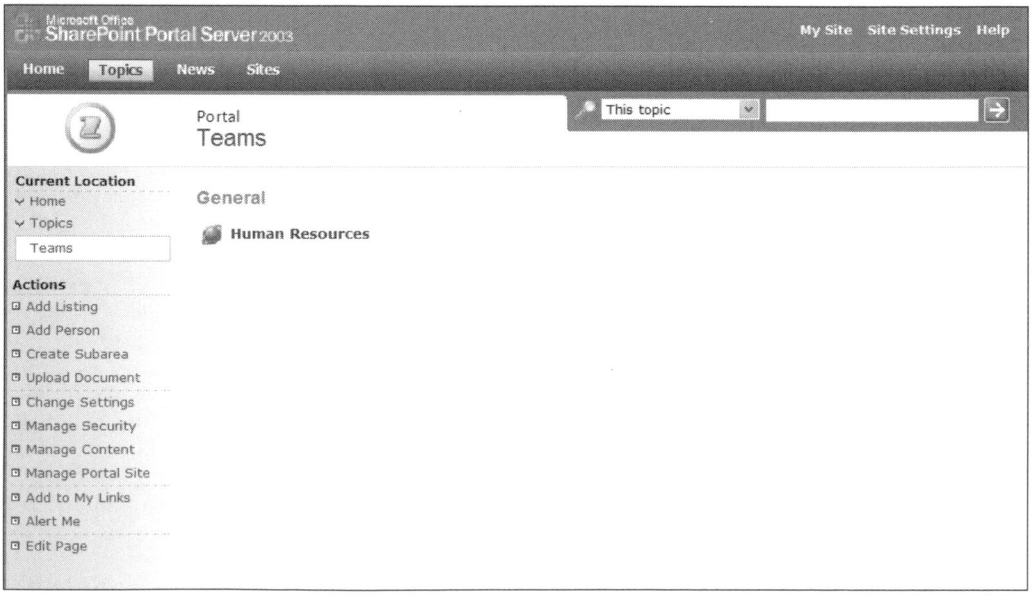

Figure 11-2. *Teams area*

The following steps describe how to create and configure the Teams area:

1. Create the Teams area.

   a. Place the area under the Topics area.

   b. Leave the Expiration Date field blank.

2. Organize items in the Teams area by removing the Area Details web part from the Top Zone.

Creating and Configuring the Human Resources Site

The Human Resources site will contain all HR Information Center resources. Figure 11-3 depicts the layout of the Human Resources site.

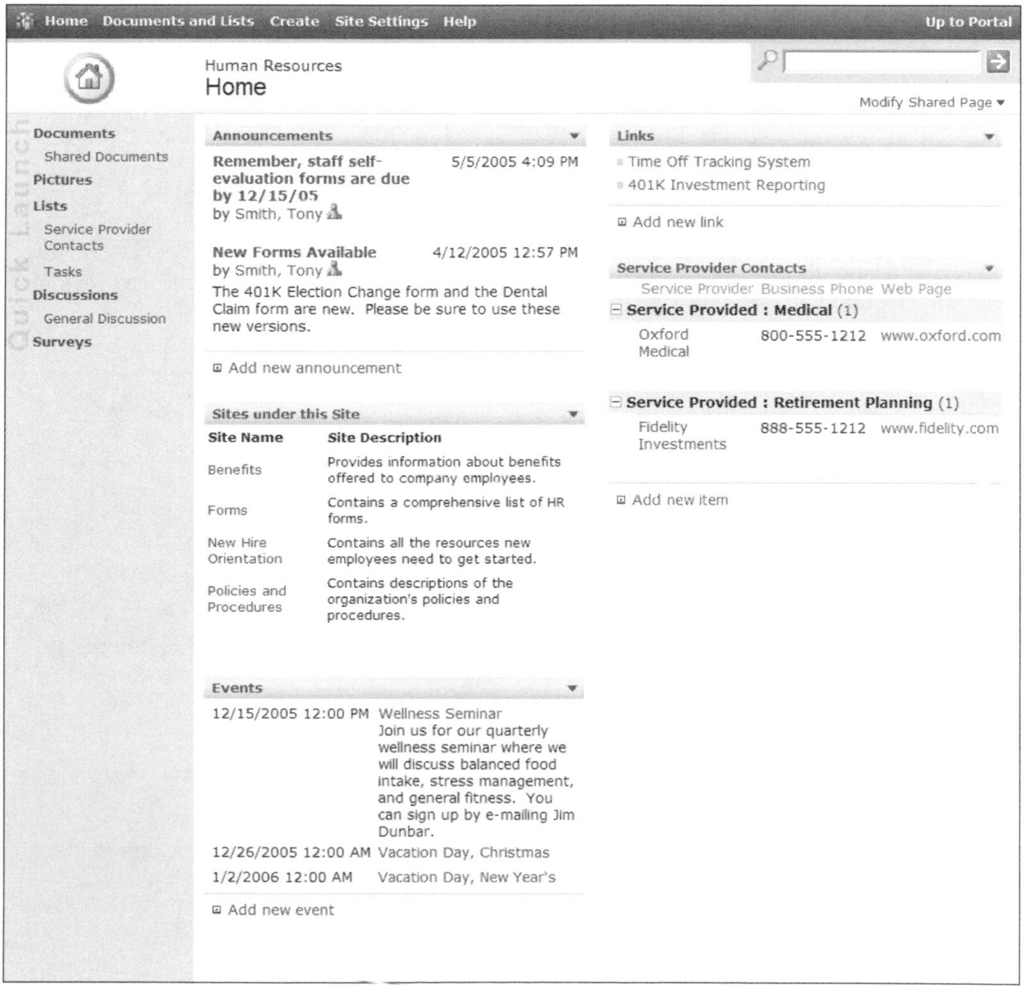

Figure 11-3. *Human Resources site*

The following steps describe how to create and configure the Human Resources site:

1. Create the Human Resources site.

   a. Create a listing for the Teams area.

   b. Base the site on the Team Site template.

2. Set the security of the Human Resources site so that HR staff has Contributor access and all other employees have Reader access.

3. Configure the Contacts list.

   a. Rename the list to Service Provider Contacts and remove the description.

   b. Rename the Last Name column to Service Provider.

   c. Rename the First Name column to Contact Person.

   d. Rename the Job Title column to Service Provided.

   e. Update the All Contacts view so it displays Service Provider (linked to item with edit menu), Service Provided, Business Phone, Web Page, Fax Number, Contact Person, and E-mail Address. Select to Sort by Service Provided and Service Provider.

   f. Create a new view called By Service Provided and select to display Service Provider (linked to item), Business Phone, and Web Page. Select to sort by Service Provider and group by Service Provided.

■**Note** We customize the Contacts list instead of creating a custom list so that the list information can be viewed in Outlook as a contacts list, as discussed in Chapter 5.

---

4. Organize the items on the Human Resources site page.

   a. Remove the Site Image web part from the Right Zone.

   b. Place a Subsite Viewer web part in the Left Zone under the Announcements list web part. Rename the Title field to Areas.

■**Note** This assumes that a SharePoint technical administrator has added a subsite viewer web part to the SharePoint environment. There are several third-party subsite viewers available for use.

---

   c. Place the Service Provider Contacts list web part in the Right Zone under the Links list web part and select to display the Initial View.

5. Populate the Human Resources site elements.

    a. Add the items in Table 11-1 to the Announcements list.

Table 11-1. *Announcements List Details*

Title	Body	Expiration
Remember, staff self-evaluation forms are due by 12/15/05.		12/16/05
New forms available.	The 401K Election Change form and the Dental Claim form are new. Please be sure to use these new versions.	1/15/06

    b. Add the items in Table 11-2 to the Events list.

Table 11-2. *Events List Details*

Title	Begin	End	Description
Wellness Seminar	12/15/05 12:00 PM	12/15/05 2:00 PM	Join us for our quarterly wellness seminar where we will discuss balanced food intake, stress management, and general fitness. You can sign up by e-mailing Jim Dunbar.
Vacation Day, Christmas	12/26/05		
Vacation Day, New Year's	1/2/06		

    c. Add the items in Table 11-3 to the Links list.

Table 11-3. *Links List Details*

URL Address	URL Description	Notes
http://TimeOff/default.htm	Time Off Tracking System	Location where vacation and personal time should be recorded
http://InvestorSummary/default.htm	401K Investments Reporting	Retirement benefit reporting system

    d. Add the items in Table 11-4 to the Service Provider Contact list.

Table 11-4. *Service Provider Contact List Details*

Service Provider	Service Provided	Business Phone	Web Site	Fax Number	Contact Person	E-mail Address
Fidelity Investments	Retirement Planning	888-555-1212	http://www.fidelity.com	888-555-1111	Jim Dunbar	jdunbar@company.com
Oxford Medical	Medical	800-555-1212	http://www.oxford.com	800-555-1111	Ellen Swift	eswift@company.com

Creating and Configuring the Benefits Site

The Benefits site is located under the Human Resources site. This site will contain information related to the benefits provided to employees of the organization. Figure 11-4 depicts the Benefits site layout.

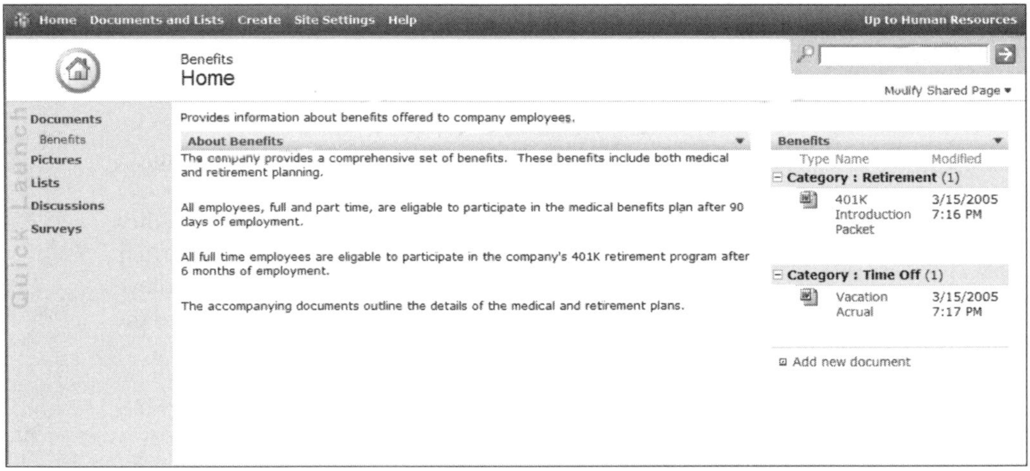

Figure 11-4. *Benefits site*

The following steps describe how to create and configure the Benefits site:

1. Create the Benefits site.

   a. Create the site under the Human Resources site.

   b. Set the description to "Provides information about benefits offered to company employees."

   c. Select to inherit security from the parent site.

   d. Base the site on the Blank Site template.

2. Create the Benefits library.

   a. Base the library on the Document Library template.

   b. Select to display the library in the Quick Launch menu.

3. Configure the Benefits library.

   a. Create a column called Category that is a Choice type and make it required. The choices for the Category column should be Medical, Retirement, and Time Off. This column should be saved with no default value.

    b. Update the All Documents view by placing the Category column in Position 3.

    c. Create a new view called By Category, make it the default view, and include the following columns: Type, Name (linked to document), and Modified. Sort by Name (linked to document) and group by Category.

4. Organize the items on the Benefits site page.

    a. Remove the Site Image web part from the Right Zone.

    b. Place the Content Editor web part in the Left Zone.

    c. Rename the title of the Content Editor web part to "About Benefits" and add the following text to the Content Editor web part: "The company provides a comprehensive set of benefits to employees. These benefits include both medical and retirement plans. All employees, full and part time, are eligible to participate in medical benefit plans after 90 days of employment. All full-time employees are eligible to participate in the company's 401K retirement program after 6 months of employment."

    d. Place the Benefits library web part in the Right Zone. Choose to display the By Category view.

5. Populate the Benefits library with the documents listed in Table 11-5.

Table 11-5. *Benefits Library Details*

Name	Type	Category
401K Introduction Packet	Word	Retirement
Vacation Accrual	Word	Time Off

Note The information made available in the Information Center can come from a number of sources such as other enterprise locations, third parties, or other SharePoint areas. For example, if the human resources group was planning to switch to a new health care provider, they could create a project site only the human resources group has access to that would contain all of the resources related to selecting and then migrating to the new health care provider. This area would also contain any materials that would be made available once the health care provider transition was complete. The Information Center would list the documents related to the current medical provider until the migration to the new provider is complete. At that point, the documents related to the new provider collected in the project site can be moved to the Information Center to replace those related to the old provider.

Creating and Configuring the Forms Site

The Forms site is located under the Human Resources site and contains all HR-related forms. Figure 11-5 depicts the desired layout of the Forms site.

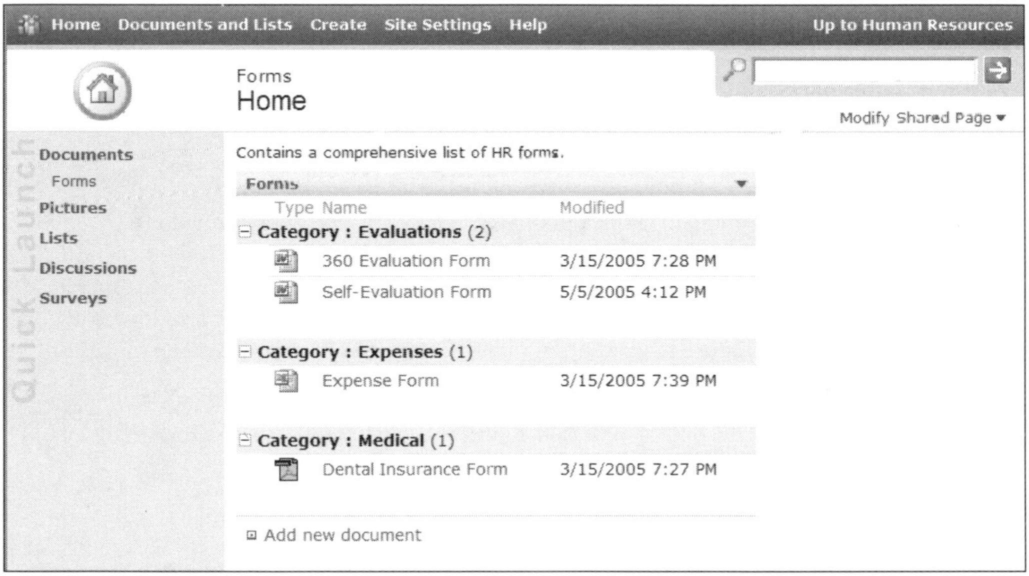

Figure 11-5. *Forms site*

The following steps describe how to create and configure the Forms site:

1. Create the Forms site.

   a. Create the site under the Human Resources site.

   b. Set the description to "Contains a comprehensive list of HR forms."

   c. Select to inherit security from the parent site.

   d. Base the site on the Blank Site template.

2. Create the Forms library.

   a. Base the Forms library on the Document Library template.

   b. Select to display the library in the Quick Launch menu.

3. Configure the Forms library.

   a. Create a column called Category that is a Choice type and make it required. The choices for the Category column should be 401K, Evaluations, Expenses, Medical, New Hire, and Time Off. This column should be saved with no default value.

   b. Update the All Documents view by placing the Category column in Position 3.

   c. Create a new view called By Category, make it the default view, and include the following columns: Type, Name (linked to document), and Modified. Sort by Name (linked to document) and group by Category.

4. Organize the items on the Forms site page.

   a. Remove the Site Image web part from the Right Zone.

   b. Place the Forms library web part in the Left Zone. Choose to display the By Category view.

5. Populate the Forms library with the documents listed in Table 11-6.

Table 11-6. *Forms Library Details*

Name	Type	Category
Dental Insurance Form	PDF	Medical
Expense Form	Excel	Expense
360 Evaluation Form	Word	Evaluations
Self-Evaluation Form	Word	Evaluations

Creating and Configuring the New Hire Orientation Site

The New Hire Orientation subsite is located under the Human Resources site and contains materials that are important to new employees. Figure 11-6 depicts the desired layout of the New Hire Orientation site.

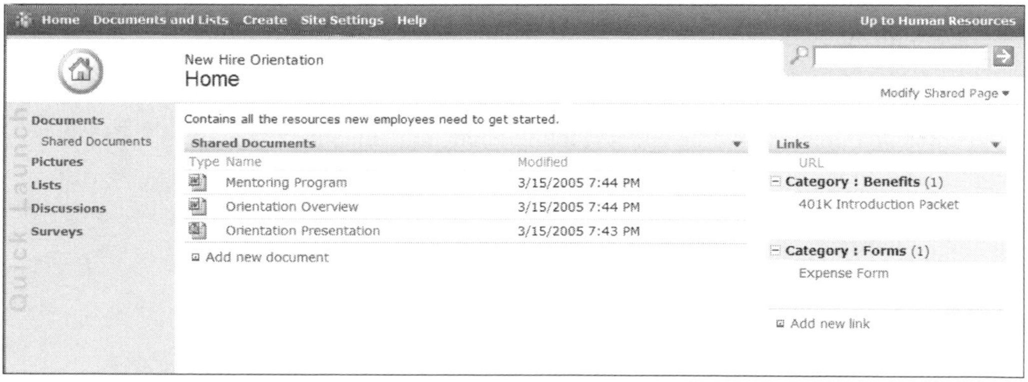

Figure 11-6. *New Hire Orientation site*

The following steps describe how to create and configure the New Hire Orientation site:

1. Create the New Hire Orientation site.

   a. Create the site under the Human Resources site.

   b. Set the description to "Contains all the resources new employees need to get started."

   c. Select to inherit security from the parent site.

   d. Base the site on the Blank Site template.

2. Create the Links list.

   a. Base the Links list on the Links list template.

   b. Select to not display the list in the Quick Launch menu.

3. Configure the Links list.

   a. Create a column called Category that is a Choice type and make it required. The choices for the Category column should be Benefits, Forms, Procedures, and Resources.

   b. Create a new view called By Category, make it the default view, and include the URL column. Sort by URL and group by Category.

4. Create the Shared Documents library.

   a. Base the library on the Document Library template.

   b. Select to display the library in the Quick Launch menu.

5. Configure the Shared Documents library by creating a new view called Initial View that includes the following columns: Type, Name (linked to document), and Modified. Sort by Name (linked to document).

6. Organize the items on the New Hire Orientation site page.

   a. Remove the Site Image web part from the Right Zone.

   b. Place the Shared Documents library web part in the Left Zone. Choose to display the Initial View.

   c. Place the Links list web part in the Right Zone. Choose to display the By Category view.

7. Populate the New Hire Orientation site elements.

   a. Add the items in Table 11-7 to the Links list.

Table 11-7. *Links List Details*

URL Address	URL Description	Category
Expense Form you added to the Forms site	Expense Form	Forms
401K Introduction Packet you added to the Benefits site	401K Introduction Packet	Benefits
HR Policies and Procedures site you created	Company Policies and Procedures	Procedures
`http://intranet/default.htm`	Company Intranet	Resources

b. Add the documents in Table 11-8 to the Shared Documents library.

Table 11-8. *Shared Documents Library Details*

Name	Type
Orientation Presentation	PowerPoint
Mentoring Program	Word
Orientation Overview	Word

Creating and Configuring the Policies and Procedures Site

The Policies and Procedures site is located under the Human Resources site. This site will contain corporate policy and procedure information. Figure 11-7 depicts the desired layout of the Policies and Procedures site.

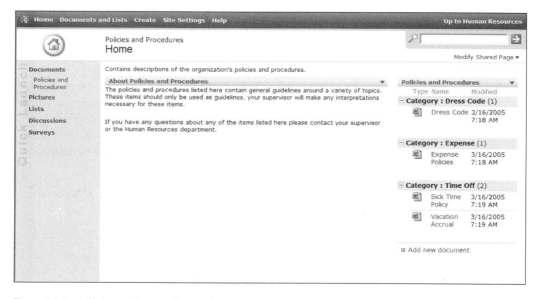

Figure 11-7. *Policies and Procedures site*

The following steps describe how to create and configure the Policies and Procedures site:

1. Create the Policies and Procedures site.

    a. Place the site under the Human Resources site.

    b. Set the description to "Contains descriptions of the organization's policies and procedures."

    c. Select to inherit security from the parent site.

    d. Base the site on the Blank Site template.

2. Create the Policies and Procedures library.

    a. Base the library on the Document Library template.

    b. Select to display the library in the Quick Launch menu.

3. Configure the Policies and Procedures library.

    a. Create a column called Category that is a Choice type and make it required. The choices for the Category column should be Dress Code, Expense, Time Off, and Travel.

    b. Update the All Documents view by placing the Category column in Position 3.

    c. Create a new view called By Category, make it the default view, and include the following columns: Type, Name (linked to document), and Modified. Sort by Name (linked to document) and group by Category.

4. Organize the items on the Policies and Procedures site page.

    a. Remove the Site Image web part from the Right Zone.

    b. Place the Content Editor web part in the Left Zone.

    c. Change the title of the Content Editor web part to "About Policies and Procedures" and add the following content to the Content Editor: "The policies and procedures listed here contain general guidelines around a variety of topics. These items should only be used as guidelines. Your supervisor will make any interpretations necessary for these items. If you have any questions about any of the items listed here, please contact your supervisor or the Human Resources department."

    d. Place the Policies and Procedures library web part in the Right Zone. Choose to display the By Category view.

5. Populate the Policies and Procedures library with the documents listed in Table 11-9.

Table 11-9. *Policies and Procedures Library Details*

Name	Type	Category
Dress Code	Word	Dress Code
Expense Policies	Word	Expense
Sick Time Policy	Word	Time Off
Vacation Accrual	Word	Time Off

The resources needed for the HR Information Center are now configured.

HR Information Center Walk-Through

Unlike the other scenarios we have discussed, many of the steps we followed during the setup of the Information Centers are done on an ongoing basis. Adding materials to the site and updating existing materials will occur regularly. Also, resources provided through the site will change over time as new needs are identified. When updating information in the Information Center, it is important to keep the following in mind:

- Announcements can be used to highlight changes made to information in the site. By creating announcements that highlight changes made, you are making it easier for users to be kept aware of recent updates that may impact them.

- Announcements should be used to highlight the introduction of new types of content and to provide details around how to leverage this content.

- Resources in the Information Center should be kept current. This will promote repeat usage and will help ensure users that the information in the center is reliable.

We will not step through the ongoing maintenance of the Information Center, as many of the steps to perform this maintenance are subsets of the steps we discussed earlier in this chapter. Instead we will discuss how individuals will consume the information in the HR Information Center. To support this, we will make the following assumptions about our Information Center:

- All company staff have access to the materials in the HR Information Center.

- Searching and indexing have been properly configured in the SharePoint environment by the technical administrator, and the Human Resources site is configured to be included in searching and indexing.

People needing access to materials in the HR Information Center will typically access these materials using one of two methods, browsing to information or searching for information.

■**Note** Anyone wanting to be made aware of when changes are made to the content in the Information Center can create alerts so that they are notified when changes to relevant information is made. For more information on configuring alerts, please refer to Chapter 7.

Browsing to Information

Individuals browse to the information they need by navigating through the site hierarchy to locate materials. It is very important to organize the site structure in a way that is intuitive to information consumers and so that it maps to the way they would typically use the information.

In our example, individuals browsing to information will click through the portal Topics and Teams areas to access the Human Resources site. From the Human Resources site, people will click the desired subsite and materials that they need.

Searching for Information

When individuals search for information, they are typically selecting to locate all materials related to a specific topic. In a SharePoint environment, there are two ways to do this. The best method is to use the portal search, discussed in Chapter 2, to perform a basic or advanced search across all portal content. The second method is to use the Windows Share-Point Services search tools, discussed in Chapter 3, to find relevant information within a specific site.

If we wanted to perform an advanced portal search to locate information, we would follow these steps:

1. Navigate to the advanced search screen by clicking the magnifying glass icon on the Search Tools section of a portal area.

2. On the Advanced Search page, select the search parameters and values to locate. For our example, we will search for documents where the following are true:

   a. Search by Type value is set to Documents.

   b. Title contains Travel.

The preceding search will return the travel materials from the HR Information Center along with travel information from any other location in the portal. For example, if a Sales Information Center existed and contained sales travel planning procedures, these materials would also be returned.

If the Category attribute of elements has been configured to be included in the Advanced Search by a SharePoint technical administrator, we could also search for materials where the Category field is Time Off. This would return all materials where the Category column is set to this value. This can be a powerful tool, especially when common attribute names are used consistently across all sites. This would allow very specific searches to be done. For example, if you consistently use a Customer column to attribute materials to a specific customer, you can perform searches to locate all information that exists for a specific customer.

If we want to locate materials only within a specific site, such as the Forms site under the Human Resources site, we can use the Windows SharePoint Services search capabilities. The following steps describe how to do this:

1. Navigate to the Forms site within the HR Information Center.

2. In the Search Tools section of the page, enter the word "Expense" into the search box and click the green arrow.

All documents containing the word "Expense," which will include the Expense Form document, will be returned. The WSS search tools only search within the current site. Also, no advanced search capabilities are available.

Benefits of SharePoint Information Centers

Creating SharePoint Information Centers can result in several benefits to an organization. While the benefits received will vary based on the purpose and composition of the Information Center, the following are some of the most common benefits organizations will receive from introducing Information Centers:

- *Information owners can own the management of their information*: By deploying Share-Point Information Center solutions, organizations allow information owners to own the management and distribution of their materials. SharePoint enables information owners to publish materials without the need for technical people to get involved. This allows the owners to set their own priorities, schedules, and processes for managing information.

- *Information consumer self-service*: Information Centers provide a central location where various resources can be stored. This information can be organized based on how consumers would need to retrieve it. Consumers are also provided with alerting capabilities, allowing them to be kept informed of changes to information important to them. Providing these self-service solutions allows consumers to have access to the materials that they need when they need them. This also significantly reduces the number of requests for materials information owners will need to service.

- *Easy location of relevant information*: The SharePoint search capabilities allow individuals to easily find information on a topic of interest. Materials across all information sources can be located. With proper organization and categorization of materials in Information Centers, these searches can be made very specific. This ensures all pertinent materials are located and fewer unnecessary items are returned in search results.

Tips for Creating Information Centers

When creating Information Centers, there are several points that should be kept in mind so that these solutions are effective:

- *Have defined owners for all materials*: It is important that owners be defined for all posted materials. These individuals need to understand their responsibilities concerning managing the information, and they need to be provided with sufficient time to properly perform the defined management tasks.

- *Use consistent attribute names and values for materials*: When SharePoint is used to manage resources for multiple groups, it is important to plan for searching and retrieval of the information. An important part of this planning is identifying a common set of metadata, or attributes, for use in the organization. This will enable more robust searching and ensure that all appropriate materials are returned.

- *Keep information current*: It is not uncommon for Information Centers to be deployed and then not regularly maintained. When this occurs, individuals will stop visiting the site and will not use the materials in it. By keeping information current and continually improving the resources available, the Information Center will become a valuable corporate resource.

Index

A

Actions section
  Add Listing link, 18
  Add News link, 29
  Add Person link, 20
  Advanced Search Link, 41
  Change Location link, 19
  Change Settings link, 13
  Create Subarea link, 13
  Edit Page link, 21–24, 31–33
  Manage Groups link, 26
  Manage Portal Site link, 16, 19
  Manage Security Link, 15
  Manage Sites option, 34, 36
  options, 7
  Show More link, 40
  Sites area, 34
Active Directory group
  adding to site groups, 10
Activity Information
  site collection usage statistics, 86
Add a Listing by Entering Text option
  Add Listings page, 18–19
Add a Site Group page
  creating new site groups, 75
Add Area Alert page
  Alert Result section, 235
  Delivery Options section, 234
Add Column page 103
  Name and Type section, 38
  Optional Settings for Column section, 38
Add Link to Site option
  Actions section, Sites area, 34, 35
Add Link to Site page
  creating a site listing for an existing site, 35
  creating top-level WSS site, 64
Add List Alert page
  Delivery Options section, 234
Add List Item Alert page
  Delivery Options section, 235
Add Listings option
  Actions section, 7
Add Listings page
  adding listings to area, 18
  Change Location link, 121
Add New User to Area page
  adding new area security, 15

Add News Listing by Entering Text option
  Add News page, 30
Add News page
  adding news to News area, 29
Add Person option
  Actions section, 7
Add Person page
  adding a person listing, 20
Add Search Alert page
  Delivery Options section, 234
Add to My Links option
  Actions section, 8
  options for search results, 40
Add Users page, 70
  adding users to site groups, 10
  security for custom lists, 101
Administrators site group, 10, 69
  updating site themes, 78–79
Advanced Edit Rights on Area page
  editing existing area security, 15
Advanced Search page, 39
Agenda list
  changing list item order, 150
  introduction, 149
Alert Frequency section
  New Alert page, 239
Alert Me link
  Actions section, 8
  List or Library page, 234–235
  options for search results, 40
  Search Results page, 234
Alert Result section
  Add Area Alert page, 235
  options, 233
alerts
  alerts in sites, 237–238
    managing alerts, 240–241
    managing alerts for other users,
      241–242
    receiving alerts, 240
    subscribing to, 238–239
  alerts in the portal, 232–233
    managing alerts, 236–237
    receiving alerts, 236
    subscribing to, 233–235
  introduction, 232
All Documents view
  document libraries, 165

All Forms views
  form library, 183
All Sources option
  Advanced Search page, 39
Allow Export Sensitive Properties property
  Web Parts, 226
And option
  Advanced Search page, 39
Announcements template, 131
Apply Theme to Web Site page
  updating site themes, 79
Areas
  creating an area, 13
  alerts, 233–234
  Create Subarea option
    Actions section, 7
  creating, 13
  editing properties, 13–14
  introduction, 6–9
  managing, 12
    through portal site map, 16–17
  navigating, 9
  security, 14
    adding new area security, 15
    deleting existing information, 15
    editing existing information, 15
  special areas, 27
    Home area, 27–28
    News area, 29–33
    Sites area, 33–38
    Topics area, 28
Area Contents Web Part
  web parts available in SPS Site Gallery, 228
Area Details Web Part
  web parts available in SPS Site Gallery, 228
Area Listings Bar, 6
  navigating through areas, 9
  Sites link, 64
Area view
  My Alerts page, 236
Areas section
  Add Link to Site page, 36, 64
arithmetic operators, 111
Attendees list template, 153
  managing, 153–154

■B
Basic Meeting Workspace template, 55
Basic Pages, 212
  creating, 212–213
  viewing and editing, 213–214
Benefits site
  creating and configuring for HR
    Information Center, 316–317
  environment layout for HR Information
    Center, 311

Blank Meeting Workspace template, 56
Blank Site template, 52
Browse Sites By section
  Sites area, 34
Browser Access Statistics
  usage statistics, 84
Business Planning site
  creating and configuring for meeting
    management process example, 295
  environment layout for meeting
    management process example, 293
By Area view
  organizing search results, 40
By Author view
  organizing search results, 40
By Date view
  organizing search results, 40
By Site view
  organizing search results, 40

■C
Calculated type
  managing columns for custom lists,
    111–112
Calendar view
  calendar type, 113
  managing views for custom lists, 118
Change Column page 103
  Delete button, 103
  Optional Settings for Column section, 37
Change Cross-Site Group Settings page, 77
Change Field Order screen
  changing position of columns, 104
Change General Settings screen
  form library, 186
  options for customizing settings, 98
Change Group Order page
  deleting existing groupings, 26
  editing existing groupings, 26
Change Location link
  Add News page, 30
  Add Person page, 20
Change Location window, 30
  adding listings to area, 19
Change Permissions screen, 102
  Add Users link, 101
Change Settings option
  Actions section, 8
Change Settings page
  accessing through Portal Site Map, 17
  editing a person listing, 23
  editing listings, 21
  editing news items, 31
  editing properties of area, 14
Change Site Title and Description page, 78

Change Type option
   New Alert page, 239
   options, 238
Choice type
   managing columns for custom lists, 105
comparison operators, 111
concatenation operator, 111–112
Contacts list template
   exporting contacts, 133
   importing contacts, 134
   introduction, 132–133
   linking with Outlook, 135–136
content approval
   document library, 177
Content Editor Web Part
   web parts available in SPS Site Gallery, 228
   web parts available in WSS Site Gallery,
      229
Content Managers site group, 10
Content section, 9
   meeting workspaces, 55
   Modify This Workspace link, 62
   subsite viewer web part, 62
   team sites and document workspaces, 49
Contributors site group, 10, 69
Corporate news centers
   as Information Centers, 307
Create Area page
   accessing through Portal Site Map, 17
   creating an area, 13
Create button
   New Cross-Site Group page, 76
   New SharePoint Site page, 65
Create Document Workspace page
   Creating for a document in a document
      library, 171
   creating from document in site, 69
Create page
   Custom List link, 91
   Document Library link, 164
   Form Library link, 182
   Picture Library link, 189
Create Page page
   Web Pages section, Sites and Workspaces
      link, 65
Create Site Group button
   Add a Site Group page, 75
Create Site option
   Actions section, Sites area, 34–35, 64
Create Subarea option
   Actions section, 7
   Portal Site Map, 17
Create View screen
   Calendar View link, 118
   Standard View link, 117
cross-site groups

changing membership, 77
creating, 76
deleting, 77
editing, 76
managing, 75
New Cross-Site Group page, 76-78
New SharePoint Site page, 65
Currency type
   managing columns for custom lists, 107
Current Area Navigation, 7
   navigating through areas, 9
Custom List template
   creating and configuring Project Details
      list, 279
   creating and configuring Project Metrics
      list, 278–279
   creating How To list, 257
custom lists, 91
   adding a listing to the portal, 121
   adding items, 92
   attachments, 94
   content approval, 98–99
   creating, 91–92
   creating a list template, 119–120
   creating with Excel, 125–127
   data manipulation with the Datasheet
      view, 96
   deleting items, 93
   deleting lists, 120
   editing items, 93
   filtering and sorting, 94–95
   introduction, 91
   managing, 97
   managing columns, 102–104
      Calculated type, 111–112
      Choice type, 105
      Currency type, 107
      Date and Time type, 108
      Hyperlink or Picture type, 109
      Lookup type, 108–109
      Multiple lines of text type, 105
      Number type, 106
      Single line of text type, 104
      Yes/No type, 109
   managing views, 113
      Calendar view, 118
      Standard and Datasheet views, 113–117
   security, 100–102
   settings, 98
   using views, 96
   working with, 92
Customize List option
   Actions section, Sites area, 34, 37
Customize List screen
   Change General Settings link, 98
   Columns section, 103

Customize List screen *(continued)*
  Add New Column link, 103
  Change the Order of the Fields link, 104
  General Settings section, 97
    Change Permissions for this List link, 101–102
    Delete this List link, 121
    Select a Portal Area for this List link, 121
  Views section
    Add a New View link, 117–118
Customize Sites page
  Columns section, Add a New Column link, 37

■D

datasheet type, 113
  using Datasheet views, 113
Datasheet view
  advanced features, 127
  advanced features for working with libraries, 209
  data manipulation for custom lists, 96
  data manipulation in document libraries, 174
  integrating lists into Office, 161
  managing views for custom lists, 113–116
Decision Meeting Workspace template, 56
Decisions list template, 150
Delete option
  Portal Site Map, 17
Delete Web Site page, 79–80
deleting lists, 120
deleting site templates, 82
deleting sites, 79
Delivery Options section
  Add Area Alert page, 234
  Add List Alert page, 234
  Add List Item Alert page, 235
  Add Search Alert page, 234
Details view
  picture library, 191
discussion boards
  as component of WSS sites, 45
Discussion Boards list template, 155
  using, 156
Display Alerts For drop-down list
  Manage User Alerts page, 242
Display tab
  Change Settings page, 14, 22–23, 32
Divisions Area
  configuring for RFP response, 253–254
  environment layout for RFP response, 251
Document and List Item Alerts view
  My Alerts page, 236
document collaboration, 3, 243
  challenges, 245–246

needs, 246–247
overview, 243
  resources, 244
  teams, 244
SharePoint environment layout, 250–252
  configuring Divisions area, 253
  configuring Presentation Materials site, 254, 256–257
  configuring Resources area, 254
  configuring Sales area, 254
  creating and configuring RFP responses site, 258–259
  RFP responses process walk through, 260–266
SharePoint solutions, 247
  benefits, 266–267
  components, 248–249
  RFP response process definition, 249–250
  RFP response requirements, 248
  tips for creating effective solutions, 267
document library, 163
  adding a listing to the portal, 180
  adding documents, 167–168
  content approval, 177
  creating, 164–165
  creating a library template, 179–180
  data manipulation using Datasheet, 174
  deleting the library, 180
  differences between portal document libraries and site document libraries, 181
  document template, 176–177
  document workspaces, 171
  editing documents, 169
    check-out and check-in, 169–170
    edting document properties, 171
  filtering and sorting documents, 166
  folders, 166–167
  General Settings screen, 175
  managing, 175
  managing columns, 178
  managing views, 178–179
  New Document link, 167–168
  security, 178
  Upload Multiple Files link, 169
  using views, 165–166
  versions, 173–174
Document Library link
  Create page, 164
Document Library screen
  New Folder link, 166
document template
  document library, 176
  options, 176

Document Template section
  New Document Library page, 164
Document Versions section
  New Document Library page, 164
Document Workspace template, 52
  environment layout for RFP response, 252
document workspaces 48–51
  category of site, 46
  components, 46–47
  creating for document, 171
  creating from document in site, 68
  creating subsites, 65
  creating with Office 2003, 67–68
  Document Workspace template, 52
  navigating through, 60–61
  Publish to Source Location page, 172
Documents and Lists page
  Sites, Document Workspaces, or Meeting
    Workspaces link, 61
Download Pictures screen
  picture library, 197

■E

Edit Folder page
  document libraries, 167
Edit Item page
  Attach File link, 94
  editing items in custom lists, 93
Edit option
  Portal Site Map, 17
Edit Page option
  Actions section, 8
Edit Properties page
  edting document properties, 171
  editing picture properties, 195
Edit Site Group Membership page, 11, 71
Edit Site Group page
  changing permissions, 74
Edit Site Listing page
  editing an existing site listing, 36
Edit View option
  Actions section, Sites area, 34
Events list template
  exporting events, 139
  integrating into meeting workspaces, 141
  introduction, 136
  linking with Outlook, 139–140
  recurrence, 137–139
Excel
  creating custom lists, 125–127
  exporting library metadata to, 208–209
  exporting lists to, 160
  exporting SharePoint lists to, 123
Excel list, 124–125, 160–161
Existing Listing option
  Add Listings page, 18

Explorer View
  document libraries, 165
  form library, 183

■F

File Name section
  Save Site as Template page, 81
Filmstrip view
  picture library, 191
form library, 182
  adding forms, 184–185
  Change General Settings screen, 186
  creating, 182
  creating with InfoPath Publishing Wizard,
    207
  editing form properties, 185
  editing forms, 185
  folders and versions, 186
  form templates, 187–188
  managing, 186
  managing columns and views, 188
  merge forms, 185
  other library management, 189
  relink forms, 188
  using views, 183
  working with, 183
Form Library link
  Create page, 182
Form Template section
  New Form Library page, 182
Form Versions section
  New Form Library page, 182
Form Web Part
  web parts available in SPS Site Gallery, 228
  web parts available in WSS Site Gallery,
    229
Forms site
  creating and configuring for HR
    Information Center, 318–319
  environment layout for HR Information
    Center, 311
Front Page 2003
  Web Part Pages, 231

■G

General Settings screen
  custom lists, 98
  picture library, 200
  SharePoint document libraries, 175
General tab
  Change Settings page, 14, 21, 23, 31
Genesis Service Plan Introduction site
  creating and configuring, 276–280
  environment layout for project
    collaboration, 274

Go to Site Administration link
  Site Settings page, 242
group sites. *See* cross-site groups
Grouped Listing Web Part
  web parts available in SPS Site Gallery, 228
grouping
  editing existing groupings, 26
Grouping and Ordering page
  adding new groupings, 25
  managing grouping and ordering of
    listings, 24
Grouping Management options
  deleting existing groupings, 26
  Rename option, 26

■H

Help link
  Portal Toolbar, 7
Home area, 12
  introduction, 27–28
HR Information Center
  environment layout, 310–312
    Benefits site, 316–317
    Forms site, 318–319
    Human Resources site, 313–315
    New Hire Orientation site, 319–321
    Policies and Procedures site, 321–322
    Teams area, 312–313
  introduction, 310
  walk through, 323
    browsing to information, 323
    searching for information, 324
Human Resources site
  creating and configuring for HR
    Information Center, 313–315
  environment layout for HR Information
    Center, 310
  intranets as Information Centers, 307
Hyperlink or Picture type
  managing columns for custom lists, 109

■I

IF() function, 112
Image Web Part
  web parts available in SPS Site Gallery, 228
  web parts available in WSS Site Gallery,
    229
Include Content section
  Save Site as Template page, 81
InfoPath Publishing Wizard
  creating form libraries, 207
Information Centers, 3, 307
  benefits of SharePoint solutions, 325
  challenges, 308–309
  environment layout for HR Information
    Center, 310–312

Benefits site, 316–317
  Forms site, 318–319
  Human Resources site, 313–315
  New Hire Orientation site, 319–321
  Policies and Procedures site, 321–322
  Teams area, 312–313
  HR Information Center, 310
  needs, 309–310
  overview, 307–308
  role of, 309
  solutions, 310
  tips for creating, 325
information management
  accessing for document collaboration, 247
  dissemination prior to meeting, 290
  document collaboration, 244–245
  inefficiency of sharing information in
    document collaboration, 246
  information spread across many sources
    in document collaboration, 245
  multiple versions of information in
    document collaboration, 245
  project collaboration and, 270–273
information retrieval
  role of information centers, 309
Information Worker solutions
  sum of products and services of Office
    System, 1
Issues list template
  current issues, 146
  introduction, 145
  related issues, 146
  reports, 147
Item Details option
  options for search results, 40

■L

libraries, 163
  advanced integration with Office 2003,
    202
    Open and Save, 202–204
    Shared Workspace Task Pane, 204–206
  as component of WSS sites, 45
  document library, 163
    creating, 164
    managing, 175–181
    working with, 165–174
  exporting metadata to Excel, 208–209
  form library, 182
    creating, 182
    managing, 186–189
    working with, 183–186
  picture library, 189
    creating, 189
    managing, 200–202
    working with, 190–200

Link to Existing Content option
  Add News page, 30
Links for You Web Part
  web parts available in SPS Site Gallery, 228
Links list template
  changing list item order, 131
  introduction, 130
list data
  editing with Datasheet view, 127
List or Library page
  Alert Me link, 234–235
List view
  My Alerts page, 236
List View Web Part, 214
  web parts available in SPS Site Gallery, 228
  web parts available in WSS Site Gallery, 229
listing management
  Move Listing page, 22, 32
List/Library alert, 233
  subscribing to in a portal area, 234
  subscribing to in WSS site or workspace, 238
List/Library Item alert, 233
  subscribing to in a portal area, 235
  subscribing to in WSS site or workspace, 238
Listing Management options
  changing approval status of listing, 22
  Delete option, 24
  drop-down list, 21–22
  Edit option, 21, 23
  Move option, 22
Lists
  Customize List screen
    accessing , 34, 37
    Change General Settings link, 98
    Columns section, 103-104
    General Settings section, 97, 101-102, 121
    Views section 117-118
  Existing Listing option
    Add Listings page, 18
  exporting to Excel, 123–125
  lists as component of WSS sites, 45
Live Communications Server
  contained in Office System, 1
Lookup type
  managing columns for custom lists, 108–109

■**M**

Manage Content option
  Actions section, 8
Manage Permission Inheritance page
  permissions options, 72

Manage Portal Site option
  Actions section, 8
Manage Security option
  Actions section, 8
  Portal Site Map, 17
Manage Security Settings page
  accessing through Portal Site Map, 17
  editing existing area security, 15
  New User option, 15
  Remove Permissions option, 16
Manage Site Groups page
  Add a Site Group option, 75
  changing permissions, 74
  Delete Selected Site Groups option, 75
Manage Sites and Workspaces page, 61
Manage Sites option
  Actions section, Sites area, 34, 36
Manage User Alerts link
  Site Administration page, 242
Manage User Alerts page
  Display Alerts For drop-down list, 242
Manage Users page
  Add Users option, 10, 70
  Edit Site Groups of Selected Users option, 11
  Remove Selected Users option, 11, 72
Management area
  creating and configuring for meeting management process example, 294
  environment layout for meeting management process example, 293
meeting management, 3, 287
  benefits of SharePoint solutions, 305
  challenges, 288–289
  environment layout for quarterly business review meeting, 292–294
    Business Planning site, 295
    Management area, 294
    Quarterly Business Review Meeting Template workspace, 296–299
  needs, 290
  overview, 287–288
  quarterly business review meeting, process definition and requirements, 291–292
  solutions, 290
  tasks, 287
  tips for creating effective solutions, 305
  walk through for quarterly business review meeting, 299–302, 304
meeting workspace lists
  introduction, 148
  lists for meetings in series, 149
Meeting Workspace task pane
  Outlook 2003, 66

meeting workspaces
    Basic Meeting Workspace template, 55
    Blank Meeting Workspace template, 56
    category of site, 46
    components, 46–47
    creating a Web Part Page, 216
        changing order that pages are displayed
        in, 217
    creating subsites, 65
    creating through Outlook 2003, 66–67
    Decision Meeting Workspace template, 56
    integrating events list into, 141–142
    introduction, 54–55
    Multipage Meeting Workspace template,
        58
    navigating through, 61
        subsites, 62
    Recurring Meeting Workspace template,
        59–60
    Social Meeting Workspace template, 57
Members Of page
    Change Cross–Site Group Settings option,
        77
    updating cross-site groups, 77
Members site group, 10
Members Web Part
    web parts available in WSS Site Gallery,
        229
Merge Forms View
    form library, 183
Modify Shared Page link
    accessing, 219
Move Listing page
    Change Location option, 22, 32
Multipage Meeting Workspace template, 58
Multiple lines of text type
    managing columns for custom lists, 105
My Alerts on this Site link
    Site Settings page, 240
My Alerts page
    managing alerts, 240–241
    views available, 236
My Alerts Summary Web Part
    web parts available in SPS Site Gallery, 228
My Calendar/Inbox/Mail Folder/Tasks Web
        Part
    web parts available in SPS Site Gallery, 228
My Cross-Site Groups page
    Delete Selected Cross-Site Groups option,
        78
    editing cross-site groups, 77
    New Cross-Site Group menu option, 76
    updating cross-site groups, 77
My Forms View
    form library, 183
My Links Web Part
    web parts available in SPS Site Gallery, 228

My Site
    introduction, 41
    private view, 42
    public view, 44
    Targeted links section, 19–20, 30
My Site link
    Portal Toolbar, 6
My Workspace Sites Web Part
    web parts available in SPS Site Gallery, 228

▪N
Name and Description section
    New Cross-Site Group page, 76
navigating through WSS sites, 60
    meeting workspaces, 61
        subsites, 62
    team sites and document workspaces, 60
        subsites, 61
New Alert page
    Alert Frequency section, 239
    Change Type option, 239
New Cross-Site Group page
    creating new cross-site group, 76
New Document Library page
    Document Template section, 164
    Document Versions section, 164
New Document link
    document library, 167–168
New Folder link
    Document Library screen, 166
New Form Library page
    creating form library, 182
    Form Template section, 182
    Form Versions section, 182
New Hire Orientation site
    creating and configuring for HR
        Information Center, 319–321
    environment layout for HR Information
        Center, 311
New Item page
    adding items to custom lists, 92
New List page
    creating custom lists, 91
New Meeting form
    Outlook 2003, 66
New Meeting Request
    Outlook 2003, 66
New Picture Library page
    Picture Versions section, 190
New Recurring Meeting
    Outlook 2003, 66
New SharePoint Site page
    creating subsites, 65
    creating top-level WSS site, 64
Newest Sites list
    Sites area, 35

News area, 12
    adding news items, 29–30
    deleting news items, 33
    editing news items, 30–32
    introduction, 29
News Areas Web Part
    web parts available in SPS Site Gallery, 228
News for You Web Part
    web parts available in SPS Site Gallery, 228
News in the Area Listings Bar
    navigating to the News area, 30, 32–33
News Management options
    changing approval status of news item, 32
    Delete option, 33
    Edit option, 31
    editing news items, 32
    Move option, 32
News Web Part
    web parts available in SPS Site Gallery, 228
Number of Hits per Page
    usage statistics, 84
Number type
    managing columns for custom lists, 106

■O

Objectives list template, 151
Office 2003
    advanced datasheet features, 161
    advanced integration with libraries,
        202–209
    creating custom lists with Excel, 125–127
    creating new document workspaces,
        67–68
    exporting lists to Excel, 160–161
    exporting SharePoint lists to Excel,
        123–125
    intergrating lists, 159
Office System
    products and services, 1
Online Gallery, 230
Operating System Access Statistics
    usage statistics, 84
Operation Completed Successfully page
    creating templates, 81
operator types, 111
operators 111-112
Or option
    Advanced Search page, 39
Outlook
    creating meeting workspaces, 66–67
    linking with Contacts list, 135–136
    linking with Events list, 139–140
Owners section
    New Cross-Site Group page, 76

■P

Page List
    meeting workspaces, 55
Page tab
    Change Settings page, 14
Page Viewer Web Part
    web parts available in SPS Site Gallery, 228
    web parts available in WSS Site Gallery,
        229
Pages, 211
    Basic Pages, 212
        creating, 212–213
        viewing and editing, 213–214
    Create Page page, 65
    Edit Page option, 8
    Web Part Pages, 214
        creating, 214–216
        editing, 217–218
        viewing, 216
Pages pane
    meeting workspaces, 218
permissions
    changing site group permissions, 74
    setting site creation permissions, 73
Permissions section
    New SharePoint Site page, 65
picture library, 189
    adding pictures, 193
    check-out and check-in, 195
    creating, 189–190
    download, 196–197
    editing picture properties, 195
    editing pictures, 194
    filtering and sorting pictures, 192
    folders, 192
    General Settings screen, 200
    managing, 200
    managing columns, 200
    managing views, 201
    other library management, 202
    send to feature, 198–199
    slide show feature, 199
    using views, 190–191
    Version History screen, 196
    versions, 196
    working with, 190
Picture Library link
    Create page, 189
Picture Versions section
    New Picture Library page, 190
Policies and Procedures site
    creating and configuring for HR
        Information Center, 321–322
    environment layout for HR Information
        Center, 311

portal
adding a document library listing, 180
adding a listing to, 121
alerts, 232–233
subscribing to, 233
introduction to using, 5
My Site, 41
private view, 42–43
public view, 44
site groups, 9
adding users, 10
changing existing assignment, 11
deleting existing assignment, 11
portal areas. *See* Areas.
portal document libraries
compared to site document libraries, 181
portal listings
adding listings, 18–19
adding person listing, 20
compared to site lists, 122
deleting listings, 24
editing listings, 21–22
editing person listing, 23–24
introduction, 17
managing grouping and ordering of
listings, 24
adding new groupings, 25
deleting existing groupings, 26
editing existing groupings, 26
portal search, 38
advanced search, 38, 40
simple search, 38
working with search results, 40–41
Portal Site Map
Add Listing option, 19
drop-down options, 16
managing areas, 16
Manage Security option, 17
Portal Toolbar, 6
My Site link, 41, 43
Presentation Materials site
cofiguring for RFP response, 254, 256
environment layout for RFP response, 251
updating for RFP response, 257
processes
document collaboration, 244
flexibility for document collaboration, 247
project collaboration, 3, 269
benefits of SharePoint solutions, 284–285
challenges, 270–271
needs, 271–272
overview, 269–270
service plan project process definition,
274
service plan project process walk through,
280–283

service plan project requirements,
272–273
SharePoint environment layout, 274–276
configuring the projects area, 276
Genesis Service Plan Introduction site,
276–280
solutions, 272
tips for effective solutions, 286
Project Server
contained in Office System, 1
Projects area
configuring, 276
environment layout for project
collaboration, 274
publish and update information
role of Information Centers, 309
Publish to Source Location page
creating document workspaces, 172
Publishing tab
Change Settings page, 14, 21, 23, 31

Q
quarterly business review meeting
environment layout, 292–294
Business Planning site, 295
Management area, 294
Quarterly Business Review Meeting
Template workspace, 296–299
process definition, 291–292
process walk through, 299–302, 304
requirements, 291
Quarterly Business Review Meeting Template
workspace
creating and configuring for meeting
management process example,
296–297, 307
environment layout for meeting
management process example, 293
Quick Launch list
team sites and document workspaces, 49

R
Readers site group, 10, 69
Recurring Meeting Workspace template,
59–60
Referrer URL Statistics
usage statistics, 84
Relink Forms screen
form library, 188
Rename Group page
editing existing groupings, 26
repository
accessing for project collaboration, 271
centralizing for project collaboration, 271
resources
document collaboration, 244

introducing new resources, 310
project collaboration and, 271–273
single location for document
    collaboration, 246
Resources area
    configuring for RFP response, 254
    environment layout for RFP response, 251
RFP Response Site
    components for document collaboration
        solutions, 248
    components and referencing on
        environment layout for RFP
        response, 252
    configuring Divions area, 253–254
    configuring Resources area, 254
    configuring Sales area, 254
    creating and configuring Presentation
        Materials site, 254, 256–258
    creating and configuring site, 258–259
    environment layout, 250–253
    process definition, 249–250
    process definition for document
        collaboration, 249–250
    process walk through, 260–266
    requirements, 248
    requirements for document collaboration
        solutions, 248
    SharePoint solution components, 248–249
Rich Text Editor
    features, 212
Rights section
    Add a Site Group page, 75

■**S**

Sales area
    cofiguring for RFP response, 254
    environment layout for RFP response, 251
Sales portals
    as information centers, 307
Save Site as Template page
    creating templates, 81
Search alert, 233
    subscribing to, 234
Search by Date values
    Advanced Search page, 40
Search by Properties information
    Advanced Search page, 39
Search by Type value
    Advanced Search page, 39
Search for Sites section
    Sites area, 34
search results
    changing grouping, 41
    changing sorting, 41
    organizing into views, 40
Search Results page
    Alert Me link, 234

Search Results section
    Add Link to Site page, 35, 64
Search tab
    Change Settings page, 14, 22, 24, 32
Search Toolbar
    WSS site searches, 83
Search Tools, 7
    team sites and document workspaces, 49
Search view
    My Alerts page, 236
security
    document library, 178
    options for custom links, 100–102
    project collaboration requirements, 273
    Manage Security Settings page
        accessing through Portal Site Map, 17
        editing existing area security, 15
        New User option, 15
        Remove Permissions option, 16
Security Site Group
    actions available, 8
Selected Account Name list
    Add Person page, 20
Selected View property
    List View Web Part, 229
Send To application options
    picture library, 198
service plan project
    process walk through, 280–284
    requirements for project collaboration,
        272
shared page
    Modify Shared Page link, accessing, 219
Shared Workspace task pane
    creating document workspaces with
        Office 2003, 67
    library integration with Office 2003,
        204–206
SharePoint lists
    exporting to Excel, 123–125
SharePoint Portal Server
    as part of SharePoint technologies, 2
    contained in Office System, 1
    description, 2
    portal as entry point to SharePoint
        environment, 5
    portal searches, 38–41
    tools, 4
    value of, 2
SharePoint technologies
    introduction, 1–2
Simple Edit Rights on Area page
    editing existing area security, 15
Simple List view
    organizing search results, 40
Single line of text type
    managing columns for custom lists, 104

Site Administration page
  Manage User Alerts link, 242
  Management and Statistics section
    Delete This Site link, 79
    Save Site as Template link, 81
    View Site Usage Data link, 85
  Users and Permissions section
    Manage Cross-Site Groups option,
      76–77
    Manage Permission Inheritance link, 72
    Manage Site Groups link, 74–75
Site Collection Usage Summary screen, 87
site document libraries
  compared to portal document libraries, 181
Site Gallery, 227
  web parts available in SharePoint Portal
    Server 2003 area, 227–229
  web parts available in Windows
    SharePoint Services site, 229
Site Group Name and Description section
  Add a Site Group page, 75
site groups
  adding users, 70
  changing existing assignments, 71
  changing permissions, 73–75
  Contributors site group, 10, 69
  creating, 74–75
  deleting, 75
  deleting existing assignments, 71
  Edit Site Group Membership page, 11, 71
  Members site group, 10
  Readers site group, 10, 69
  Security Site Group, actions available, 8
site layouts, 48
  meeting workspaces, 53–60
  team sites and document workspaces,
    48–53
Site Link section
  Add Link to Site page, 35, 64
Site Listing Management options
  Edit Item option, 36
Site Listings Management options
  Delete Item option, 36
site lists
  compared to portal lists, 122
Site Settings link
  Portal Toolbar, 7
Site Settings page
  adding users to site groups, 70
  Administration section
    Configure Site and Workspace Creation
      link, 73
    Go to Site Administration link, 72, 74, 75,
      76, 77, 79, 81, 83, 85, 87, 89, 120, 242
    Manage Users link, 70, 72
  changing existing site group assignments,
    71

Customization section
  Apply Theme to Site link, 79
  Change Site Title and Description link, 78
Manage Sites and Workspaces link, 62
My Alerts on this Site link, 240
Site Collection Administration section
  Go to Top-level Site Administration link,
    120
site statistics, 83
  site collection usage statistics, 86–87
  site hierarchy, 87
  storage space allocation, 88–89
  usage statistics, 84–85
Site Template Gallery page
  Edit icon, 82–83
site templates
  creating, 80–81
  deleting, 82
  editing, 82
Site Toolbar
  Documents and Lists link, 61
  meeting workspaces, 54
  Site Settings link, 61, 70, 71, 73, 74, 76, 77,
    78, 79, 82
  team sites and document workspaces,
    48–49
Site Usage Report page
  Select Report drop-down list, 85
sites
  categories, 46–47
  changing general site details, 78–80
  components, 45
  Create Site option
    Actions section, Sites area, 34–35, 64
  creating subsites, 66
  creating top-level WSS site, 65
  creation, 63–69
  introduction, 45
  managing cross-site groups, 75–78
  managing site security
    changing site group permissions, 73–75
  managing site security, 69–73
  Save Site as Template page, 81
  searches, 83
Sites and Workspaces page, 62
  deleting sites, 79
  Select a View
    All option, 61
Sites area, 12
  introduction, 33
  site listings, 35
    creating site listing for existing site, 35
    deleting an existing site listing, 36
    editing an existing site listing, 36
    managing attributes for site listings,
      37–38
  tools, 34

Sites I Have Created list
  Sites area, 35
Sites in the Area Listings Bar
  navigating to Sites area, 35–37
slide show feature
  picture library, 199
Social Meeting Workspace template, 57
Sort By value option
  sorting search results, 41
special lists, 155
Spotlight Sites section
  Sites area, 34
standard lists
  introduction, 129–130
standard type, 113
Standard views
  creating, 117
  managing views for custom lists, 113–116
Storage Information
  site collection usage statistics, 86
Storage Space Allocation page
  viewing site storage allocation, 89
subscription-based notifications
  role of information centers, 309
subsites
  changing permission inheritance for
    subsites, 72
  creating, 65
SUM() function, 112
Summary view
  My Alerts page, 236
Survey list template, 157
  rating scale, 158
  responding to survey, 159
surveys
  as component of WSS sites, 45

■**T**

Tasks list template
  introduction, 143–144
Team Site template, 51
  links list created and displayed by default,
    213
team sites, 48–51
  Blank Site template, 52
  category of site, 46
  components, 46–47
  creating subsites, 65
  navigating through, 60
    subsites, 61
  Team Site template, 51
Teams area
  creating and configuring for HR
    Information Center, 312
  environment layout for HR Information
    Center, 310

template lists, 129
  meeting workspace lists, 148–149
    Agenda list, 149–150
    Attendees list, 153–154
    Decisions list, 150–151
    Objectives list, 151
    Text Box list, 151–152
    Things to Bring list, 152–153
  special lists, 155
    Discussion Boards, 155–157
    Survey list, 157–159
  standard lists, 129–130
    Announcements list, 131–132
    Contacts list, 132–136
    Events list, 136–142
    Issues list, 145–148
    Links list, 130–131
    Tasks list, 143–144
Template Selection page
  creating subsites, 66
  creating top-level WSS site, 65
templates
  Operation Completed Successfully page,
    81
  Save Site as Template page, 81
Text Box list template, 151–152
TEXT() function, 112
themes, updating for sites, 78–79
Things to Bring list template
  introduction, 152–153
Thumbnails view
  picture library, 191
time investment
  geographical dispersion of in document
    collaboration, 246
Title and Description section
  New SharePoint Site page, 64–65
  Save Site as Template page, 81
Toolbar Type property
  List View Web Part, 229
Top-Level Site Administration page
  Site Collection Administration section
    View Site Collection Usage Summary
      link, 87
    View Site Hierarchy link, 88
    View Storage Space Allocation link, 89
  Site Collection Galleries section
    Manage Site Template Gallery link,
      82–83, 120
top-level WSS sites
  creating, 63
Topic Assistant Suggestions Web Part
  web parts available in SPS Site Gallery, 228
Topics area, 12
  default layout, 6
  introduction, 28

■U

Upload Document option
    Actions section, 8
Upload Multiple Files link
    document library, 169
Use Personal Features permission
    portal, 233
User Access Statistics
    usage statistics, 84
User alert, 233
User Information
    site collection usage statistics, 86
User view
    My Alerts page, 236

■V

Version History screen
    picture library, 196
Versions Saved page
    document library, 173
View Properties screen
    check-out and check-in, 195
Views
    Create View screen
        Calendar View link, 118
    Edit View option
        Actions section, Sites area, 34
    Selected View property
        List View Web Part, 229
    Standard View link, 117
Virtual Server Gallery, 230

■W

Web Designers site group, 10, 69
    updating site themes, 78–79
Web Part Page Gallery, 227
Web Part Pages, 214
    creating, 214–216
    editing, 217–218
    viewing, 216
Web Part Zones, 214
Web Parts, 218
    adding to Pages, 219–220
    as component of WSS sites, 46
    common properties, 223
    exporting and importing web parts,
        225–227
    further customization, 230–231
    managing the Web Part Page, 220
        editing web part properties, 222–223
        rearranging the Page, 221–222
        Shared View vs. Personal View, 220
        web part connections, 224–225
    standard galleries, 227
        Online Gallery, 230
        Site Gallery, 227–229

        Virtual Server Gallery, 230
        Web Part Page Gallery, 227
Web Site Address section
    New SharePoint Site page, 64–65
Windows Server 2003
    Windows SharePoint Services as add-on, 2
Windows SharePoint Services
    as part of SharePoint technologies, 2
    contained in Office System, 1
    tools, 4
    value of, 2

■X

XML Web Part
    web parts available in SPS Site Gallery, 229
    web parts available in WSS Site Gallery,
        229

■Y

Yes/No type
    managing columns for custom lists, 109
Your Recent Documents Web Part
    web parts available in SPS Site Gallery, 229

forums.apress.com

FOR PROFESSIONALS BY PROFESSIONALS™

JOIN THE APRESS FORUMS AND BE PART OF OUR COMMUNITY. You'll find discussions that cover topics of interest to IT professionals, programmers, and enthusiasts just like you. If you post a query to one of our forums, you can expect that some of the best minds in the business—especially Apress authors, who all write with *The Expert's Voice*™—will chime in to help you. Why not aim to become one of our most valuable participants (MVPs) and win cool stuff? Here's a sampling of what you'll find:

DATABASES

Data drives everything.

Share information, exchange ideas, and discuss any database programming or administration issues.

INTERNET TECHNOLOGIES AND NETWORKING

Try living without plumbing (and eventually IPv6).

Talk about networking topics including protocols, design, administration, wireless, wired, storage, backup, certifications, trends, and new technologies.

JAVA

We've come a long way from the old Oak tree.

Hang out and discuss Java in whatever flavor you choose: J2SE, J2EE, J2ME, Jakarta, and so on.

MAC OS X

All about the Zen of OS X.

OS X is both the present and the future for Mac apps. Make suggestions, offer up ideas, or boast about your new hardware.

OPEN SOURCE

Source code is good; understanding (open) source is better.

Discuss open source technologies and related topics such as PHP, MySQL, Linux, Perl, Apache, Python, and more.

PROGRAMMING/BUSINESS

Unfortunately, it is.

Talk about the Apress line of books that cover software methodology, best practices, and how programmers interact with the "suits."

WEB DEVELOPMENT/DESIGN

Ugly doesn't cut it anymore, and CGI is absurd.

Help is in sight for your site. Find design solutions for your projects and get ideas for building an interactive Web site.

SECURITY

Lots of bad guys out there—the good guys need help.

Discuss computer and network security issues here. Just don't let anyone else know the answers!

TECHNOLOGY IN ACTION

Cool things. Fun things.

It's after hours. It's time to play. Whether you're into LEGO® MINDSTORMS™ or turning an old PC into a DVR, this is where technology turns into fun.

WINDOWS

No defenestration here.

Ask questions about all aspects of Windows programming, get help on Microsoft technologies covered in Apress books, or provide feedback on any Apress Windows book.

HOW TO PARTICIPATE:

Go to the Apress Forums site at **http://forums.apress.com/**.
Click the New User link.